S.O.S.

'SAVING OUR STATE'

The Integrity Ireland Guide to dealing with Corruption, Cronyism and Criminality in the Irish Justice System

Version 1 - 2015

AN ROINN DLÍ AGUS CIRT AGUS COMHIONANNAIS
DEPARTMENT OF JUSTICE AND EQUALITY

(Alternatively)

'State of Shame'

Dealing with Tricksters, Thugs, Tyrants & Thieves
in the Irish Justice System

Law Society of Ireland

An tSeirbhís Chúirteanna
Courts Service
IRELAND

THE INTEGRITY IRELAND 'S.O.S.' GUIDE

Version 1 - 2015

ISBN: 978-1-906628-72-7

Published by CheckPoint Press, Ireland

www.checkpointpress.com

CheckPoint
Press

This guidebook belongs to:

Tel:

DISCLAIMER, ACKNOWLEDGEMENTS & COPYRIGHTS

Disclaimer: This rudimentary 'S.O.S.' manual has been produced by Members of Integrity Ireland as a service to, and for the benefit of other Integrity Ireland Members and supporters in strict accordance with the declared Rules & Guidelines of the Integrity Ireland Community. It does not purport to be 'legal advice' other than in context of assisting untrained or misinformed litigants in their dealings with agents or agencies of the State (and/or with affiliates thereof) who are engaged in the misuse or abuse of authority and position - most notably those who operate under the remit of the Irish Justice System, particularly within the Government, An Garda Síochána, the legal profession and in the Irish Courts.

Whilst all due care has been taken in compiling this Guide to ensure it is accurate at the time of publication, it remains the sole responsibility of the reader-user to ensure the accuracy and/or applicability of the information herein, and that the same is used or applied lawfully and appropriately. Neither Integrity Ireland nor any of its members (other than the individual end user) may be held responsible for the use, misuse, misunderstanding or inaccuracy of the information herein, and it is under this specific condition that this Guide is made publicly available.

Acknowledgements & Copyrights: The materials herein have been collated from a variety of sources under the 'fair use' public copyright doctrine including Irish and EU Statutes; other publicly-accessible articles and records including the Citizens Information, Wikipedia and various State agency websites; and from quotes and articles in Irish newspapers. Other information has been supplied by insiders, whistleblowers and retirees in State agencies, and from the personal experiences of Integrity Ireland members & supporters. Gratitude is extended to all of those sources for their contributions. Thanks also to Village Magazine; The Journal.ie; Dr Finbarr Markey and Barrister Gary Fitzgerald for permission to quote their articles, as well as to The National Land League; Peoples Internet Radio; Open Your Mind Radio; Reality Ireland; Indymedia; Tir na Saor; the Water Protest Movement; The Hub Ireland; Eviction Free Country; Right 2 Homes; Irish Media Alliance; independent TD's Clare Daly, Mick Wallace, Joan Collins and MEP Luke Flanagan, and many, many courageous others who are involved in the citizens rights movement, for their support and encouragement in compiling this Guide. Thanks also to columnist Shane Ross TD and reporters Susan Mitchell of the Sunday Business Post and to Justine McCarthy of the Sunday Times for their insightful and courageous reporting on the chronic failings in our justice system, as well as to those news columnists, reporters and social media activists of integrity who are willing to acknowledge, and speak the truth.

As the various laws, rules and regulations are changed or amended, or as more contributions are submitted for incorporation into this Guide, it is anticipated that successive Volumes will be updated and republished. Readers are respectfully invited to send suggestions, amendments, corrections or any other contributions by email to: 'sos@integrityireland.ie'. Thank you.

(With special thanks to Peter, James & John, to all our friends & supporters, and to the rest of the I-I gang)

INTEGRITY

"If you don't stand for something you will fall for anything."
Gordon A. Eadie

"If not us, then who? If not now, then when?"
John E. Lewis

"A few people of integrity can go a long way."
Bill Kauth

This Guide is dedicated to those who would see a better world for our children.

Table of Contents

THE INTEGRITY IRELAND MISSION STATEMENT

"Encouraging openness, transparency and justice in the institutions of the Irish State, and serving as a support network for wronged citizens."

(Long form)

1. To encourage openness, transparency and justice in the institutions of the Irish State, through the accurate and objective reporting of issues and events that run contrary to the principles of natural justice; that breach the Articles of the Irish Constitution; and/or violate the fundamental human rights of the citizen.

2. To serve as a moral and practical support network for wronged citizens, incorporating access to the combined knowledge of the membership, and to the facilities on the website.

integrity ireland

www.integrityireland.ie   www.integrityireland.ie

Citizens for Justice, Transparency and Accountability

..challenging corruption, cronyism, and criminal cover-ups..

Integrity Ireland is a citizens-driven network and support group set up to tackle corruption and malfeasance in this State, particularly within the legal profession and law enforcement – and their respective oversight bodies; the Law Society, the Garda Ombudsman and the Courts.

We deserve better than this Ireland!

One by one - together - we CAN make a difference!

Please check out the benefits of I-I membership online.

INTRODUCTION

It should be clear by now to everyone involved in the *Integrity Ireland* project that by-and-large, Irish State Institutions are wholly unfit for purpose.. unless of course, one accepts that 'the purpose' is to protect the establishment at the expense of the rest of us.

It is perhaps stating the obvious when we note that these institutions—albeit being utterly unfit to serve their mandates to the public—are actually quite efficient at frustrating any efforts in holding rogue authority figures to account. Those who head up these institutions have all the resources of the State at their disposal as well as the services of multiple layers of obedient bureaucrats who are well-versed in the practices of evasiveness, non-accountability, media spin, and protecting the powers that be at all costs. In this manner today's generation has inherited a Civil and Public Service which reflects the morality of the current leadership. When that leadership comprises politicians and administrators of the lowest moral character who will not hesitate to lie, cheat or finagle their way to the top—regardless of the damage it is doing to the country—then clearly, these institutions are NOT to be trusted.

Anyone who has had a serious problem with institutions of the State; such as the much-maligned HSE, the Department of Education or An Garda Síochána (for example) quickly runs into a wall of obstructionism, denials and endless deferments designed to frustrate any efforts to get to the truth. We need only look at the decades-long Morris, Moriarty and Mahon Tribunals which cost the Irish taxpayer hundreds of millions in *unvouched* costs and expenses; the shocking Residential Institutions, Magdalene Laundries and symphysiotomy scandals; the systematic denial of justice, and the State-sponsored intimidation of individual abuse survivors; the targeting of Garda whistleblowers; the ongoing suppression by the Ministry of Justice of hundreds of legitimate complaints of serious Garda wrongdoing; and the farcical banking inquiries – to see how efficiently 'the powers that be' are, when protecting themselves in circumstances that are morally indefensible. This is an alarming situation which should be absolutely unacceptable in a so-called democratic republic, and it remains a matter of bewilderment to many outside professionals that the Irish people continue to put up with this, especially after so much sacrifice in the historical quest for sovereignty and freedom from oppression.

This endemic problem cannot be solved 'from the bottom up' because the problem is NOT in the lower ranks. Most people who enter State institutions are decent, hardworking and sincere at the time they begin their careers – but a system that is controlled by corrupt or compromised authorities cannot but reflect *their* particular skewed 'values' – which in turn demands compliance from subordinates if they are to prosper in that environment. Indeed, trying to maintain one's moral integrity in these compromised conditions only ensures that there will be no meteoric rise to the top for any such earnest souls. *That* overprized experience is reserved for those who understand the dynamics of cronyism, and whose consciences have been dulled by the promise of promotion.

In such a manner, nepotism, bias and clandestine 'favours' done and received have greatly undermined the efficacy and purpose of an overblown public sector whose misguided concept of 'service' is rooted in an abject deference, as demanded by venal superiors. Rooted in a conscience-numbing 'jobs-for-life' culture where 'professional standards' are alarmingly inconsistent and where bonus payments are dished out gratuitously, it is little wonder that even the most junior of officials soon develops an inappropriate sense of cosy entitlement, and comes to see 'service to the public' as a nuisance and a distraction from their *real* day-to-day duties; which is to gratuitously serve and protect their superiors and thus protect their own wages, prospects and pensions. After decades of creeping disregard and contempt for the public, these are the so-called 'values' which underlie practically all of our State institutions. This includes our so-called 'statutory oversight bodies'—the various regulators, ombudsmen, tribunals and 'special review panels'—whose Board members and adjudicators have been cherry-picked from a disturbingly shallow pool of well-connected operators who absolutely *know* which side their bread is buttered. Solemn proclamations by State agencies that these appointments are being made only after a *'robust, impartial and transparent interview process'* are simply not credible. The same creeping malaise infests An Garda Síochána where senior management do not 'rise through the ranks' on merit, but instead, gain promotion based upon their political and social affiliations. This causes considerable dismay amongst dedicated ranking Gardaí as well as fuelling public disquiet that our so-called *'Guardians of the Peace'* might occasionally struggle to distinguish who it is they are actually being paid to serve; the people, or a corrupt political establishment? Unfortunately, the same is also generally true of our judicial appointments system which is anything but 'truly independent' or 'transparent', functioning in effect as a gilt-edged platform of reward for compliant legal professionals who are already well-embedded in prevailing political circles. When it comes to positions of trust, power or authority it seems, it's just more of the same old cronyism and nepotism at work—with all of the same old expected outcomes—and the higher we go of course, the greater the perceived risk of ethical and moral contamination.

CORRUPTION, CRONYISM & CRIMINAL COVER-UPS

Nobody is suggesting that corruption doesn't exist in some form or another in every country on earth. However, what makes Ireland somewhat unique when it comes to domestic corruption in the 21st Century, is the breadth and depth of that corruption in such a young and supposedly 'modern' democracy, where so many agencies of the State prioritise (as an undeclared objective) the exploitation and deception of the public; the cover-up of systemic white-collar and political crime; and the protection of well-connected wrongdoers who profit abundantly, and repeatedly, at our collective expense. But this endemic duplicity didn't become an established—even accepted—part of the socio-political culture overnight. It is the product of the coming-together of a number of elements which, although they may to some extent explain how our 'land of saints and scholars' has fallen so far, does not in any moral sense excuse the behaviour of those involved, nor release us from our collective moral duty to challenge, expose and confront those responsible.

Some of the elements which have contributed to this 'perfect storm' scenario are:

- Ireland's tribal past and the ingrained urge to 'look after' one's friends, relatives and supporters; an understandable, even admirable ethos - until, being done at others' expense.

- The 700 years of British rule which set a colonial-style model of oppressive governance which is now being aped - to a certain extent - by those in positions of power.

- The inheritance of a fully-fledged State infrastructure from the British which was adopted more-or-less wholesale by the fledgling Irish State, but *without* the requisite expertise, experience or checks-and-balances required to function efficiently or truly democratically.

- The evolution of a massively-overblown and wasteful Public Service upon whose good will and support each successive Government depends; the culture of routine pay increases and lifelong entitlement that prevails amongst Civil & Public Service managers in particular; and the prevailing ethos of 'protect the Minister and the establishment at all costs' - regardless of how they are performing for the public.

- The historical deference of the State and its employees to other institutions or perceived 'authorities' (most notably the Catholic Church, and more recently the bankers, the senior bond holders, international corporations, the Troika et al) at the expense of the rights of ordinary citizens.

- The fact that most of the so-called 'statutory oversight bodies' / ombudsmen / tribunals of investigation / review panels or 'official enquiries' in operation today are staffed by 'connected' insiders who have a vested interest in protecting the status quo.

The resulting moral and systemic failures in Irish State institutions has been greatly compounded by the greed, arrogance and ruthless ambition of certain political leaders of the recent past and the attitudes of selfish entitlement of their supporters and cronies - many of whom have found themselves being casually promoted to lofty positions of prestige and power for which they were neither technically, nor morally qualified. Arguably, this is what lies at the heart of the problem in the Irish justice system today; too many compromised cronies, and not enough persons of courage, character and conviction who are willing and able for the task.

This is why *Integrity Ireland* was set up to tackle corruption 'from the top down' especially within An Garda Síochána, the legal profession and the Courts. Because if you *do* have a serious problem with another State institution, agency or individual, you will invariably find yourself dealing with the Gardaí, with lawyers and/or ultimately with the Courts. And if these particular institutions cannot be trusted then we are in a very serious predicament indeed. Because if our law*makers* become the law*breakers* – then arguably, there is no real 'law' anymore, and certainly no real justice for ordinary citizens. For those of us seeking legitimate relief in 21st Century Ireland, the so-called 'Irish justice system' has become a disturbing oxymoron – a hugely disappointing contradiction-in-terms which exists it seems, only to serve the interests of the favoured few at the great personal expense of the many. It is in effect one great big lie being foisted on a largely-unaware Irish public by well-connected, professional elites whose unworthy interests and ambitions remain dependent upon our ignorance, and upon the longstanding pretence that our legal system and our Courts are in fact something more than the contrived instruments of a so-called 'legal profession'—sponsored chiefly by vested interests—that deals largely in exploitation and profiteering; the collective product of a deceptive propaganda, couched in deliberately obscure language, and wrapped in an oppressive medieval pageantry. Sadly, it has been no great surprise to discover that some of the worst examples of corruption, fraud and malfeasance occur amongst the higher ranks of An Garda Síochána, by State-sponsored 'legal professionals' and by the administrators and adjudicators in our Courts – in close competition of course with some of the more prominent representatives of the established political parties acting in collaboration with the so-called 'privileged elites'.

The *Integrity Ireland* project is not the first attempt to do something about corruption in the Irish justice system, but it is probably fair to say that our recent combined anti-corruption campaigns have done more to unsettle errant authority figures than any previous efforts by ordinary citizens. Certain strengths and weaknesses in our campaigns are becoming evident as we try out various tactics, and we need to be alert as to what is effective, and what is not. For example, the recent submission of hundreds of serious complaints of Garda wrongdoing was reluctantly received by the Minister for Justice with a solemn public promise that 'something' would definitely be done about it. That 'something' now appears to be the typical Government response – that of endless denials, delays and deferments (in the guise of a so-called 'Independent Review Mechanism') which is clearly designed to exhaust complainants' resolve. But now that we are organised as a group and are communicating freely with each other, the usual State tactics of sending out contrived generic 'personal letters' along with convoluted and dismissive referrals to other agencies is simply not cutting the mustard - at least, not any more. No doubt, urgent discussions are afoot in Ministerial Offices as to how to kick this particular can of worms down the road – at least until the next election – when it will of course become someone else's embarrassing problem. After months of hollow excuses, prevarications and delays, it is clear that those who have so very reluctantly 'assumed responsibility' for this mess have absolutely no intention of dealing with matters in an open, honest and forthright manner – not unless they are forced or embarrassed into doing so. And even then, any such 'official response' will no-doubt consist of some last-minute frantic attempt at 'damage control' where the *real* truth will again become the very first casualty. Meanwhile, as per usual in this wayward State of ours, justice for the ordinary citizen goes a-begging.

For compromised State agencies so heavily invested in suppressing evidence of their own wrongdoing the only remaining option is to string us along using all the resources at their disposal hoping that we will eventually tire of the chase. Firstly, they deny any wrongdoing and give us the proverbial run-around. Then, if we persist, they refer us to some other agency or State Department or, more disturbingly, use other indirect 'solutions' such as Garda harassment or intimidation to remind us of our 'proper place'. Finally, if we continue, undeterred, to insist on some *proper* response, they simply go silent – leaving us wondering why our legitimate questions and complaints are being systematically suppressed and ignored? The key it seems is to keep us waiting, indefinitely, heaping delay upon frustrating delay as we vainly hope that 'someone in authority' will actually do the honourable thing. But then we return to the original question; why on earth would they do *that*!? For certainly there is no profit in it – at least not for them. After years and years of fruitless attempts trying to secure openness, transparency and accountability; and after so many ordinary citizens' lives have been ruined by this systemic corruption, craven hypocrisy and lack of any proper accountability – surely we can all agree that it's now time to try something different.

TACKLING ISSUES – BY TACKLING THE INDIVIDUAL TRANSGRESSORS
A man commits a crime. He gets caught. He is prosecuted and sentenced to jail. Everyone understands that he has done wrong. Even he understands that his actions were wrong and he has to pay a penalty. *The bad action needs to have a consequence for the person who acts wrongly.* And that's why civilised societies have justice systems that penalise wrongdoing – otherwise we would have chaos, anarchy and injustice everywhere.

The problem we are facing in Ireland is that many of our authority figures, most noticeably senior Gardaí, lawyers and civil servants are engaging in routine criminal activity and are doing so with apparent impunity. It is a shocking 'Catch 22' situation when the custodians of our justice system are operating in effect as if they were a criminal organisation preying on ordinary citizens and abusing all of their statutory responsibilities. After a lifetime of mundane abuses of the law and the Constitution many of these individuals believe they are above the law – and who can blame them? Whether it be Garda Management, the Office of the DPP, or barristers and solicitors raking in unvouched fees hand-over-first on State projects; or any other number of consultants, State Board appointees or the favoured friends and relatives of senior politicians benefiting from 'insider' deals and appointments; the plain fact of the matter is that the public are getting very poor value indeed from Irish State institutions – and that is putting it mildly.

Unqualified Ministers-of-State and senior civil servants mask their incompetence by hiring expensive self-styled 'consultants' (at the taxpayers' expense of course) whose main area of expertise seems to be finding new ways to fleece an unsuspecting public. Amidst stifled giggles, foreign experts struggle to find the words to describe the rampant incompetence and stupidity on display – not to mention the incoherent arrogance of State agents whose misplaced attitudes of privileged entitlement belong back in the dark ages. The recent voting machines; toll booths; water charges and Eircode fiascos all spring to mind. With all due respect to those who sincerely do their best in difficult circumstances; one wonders indeed what it costs the country to support legions of inept, arrogant and compromised State employees – who are not only NOT doing their jobs properly in the first place, but who are in many cases doing the very opposite of what they have been paid to do; namely, to serve and protect the Irish public and uphold the the law and the Constitution – and NOT to abjectly promote the corrupt agendas of amoral elites.

As for justice and the administration of justice? Well, there is a relatively simple premise which governs our Irish judicial system. The Constitution *'Bunreacht nah Eireann'* (literally, *'the Basic Law of Ireland'*) is the prevailing legal document that sets out citizens' fundamental rights and how Ireland *should* be governed. The law (as interpreted and applied by the Government and the Courts) is supposed to be a literal, case-specific interpretation of the Constitution. Likewise, judges are supposedly, *'independent in their functions, subject only to the law and the Constitution.'* But what happens when judges for example do NOT abide by the law or the Constitution? What happens when they act in capricious and prejudiced ways? Can they be sacked for incompetence – for making unconstitutional or clearly unjust decisions? The sad answer is no—not at present—not unless two-thirds of the Oireachtas agrees to impeach them; something that hasn't yet happened in modern Ireland despite all the evidence of incompetence, corruption and even criminal activity by certain members of the judiciary.

With all due respect to the *best* of our judges it matters little apparently, that manifestly unjust decisions are being made on a routine basis in our Courts – in direct contravention of our Constitution and of all the principles of natural justice. A recent example was when one of our members *proved* in Court that Gardaí had conspired with the Office of the DPP to falsely arrest and detain him. Having spent many months and several thousand euros defending himself, this individual was rightfully astonished when the judge refused him any compensation whatsoever— not even his travelling expenses—and no-one from the State-sponsored opposition got even a token slap on the wrist.

Other routine examples include Court Hearings being held (illegally) in the absence of Plaintiffs; of Court files being improperly interfered with; of routine fraud and perjury going unpunished; of irascible judges barking orders at bewildered lay litigants; of litigants being forcibly removed for simply asserting their right to speak; and of Gardaí blocking the public's entry to supposedly 'public' Courtrooms. To add insult to injury, we then have certain judges overruling each other's legitimate Orders, publicly contradicting each other and sometimes even contradicting their *own* previous rulings and decisions – and all of this is being paid for by us, the gullible taxpayer! In short; there is very little to inspire confidence in our legal system as it stands. It is in the main unpredictable, inconsistent, chaotic and largely unmanageable – at least for ordinary citizens – who are justifiably losing faith in a so-called 'justice system' where certain judges operate *outside* of their jurisdiction and remit—often personally conflicted—and sometimes even in contravention of the Constitution itself. In this manner inept, errant or wayward judges can undermine and even subvert the Constitution at will – safe in the knowledge that they cannot be sacked, and safe in the knowledge that ultimately 'the system' will protect its own. This unsettling reality was recently demonstrated in the response of the current Minister for Justice upon receipt of a petition containing thousands of signatures requesting the impeachment of a District Court Judge. The petition was contemptuously returned by the Minister with the absurd and nonsensical declaration; *"I have no role to play in this matter."*

So what happened to judges being 'subject to the law and the Constitution' then, and where are the checks and balances in this so-called 'justice system' – a system where 5 out of 6 judges are members of the ruling political party when appointed to the bench – by the Government - and where JAAB (*the Judicial Appointments Advisory Board*) has not held even ONE single judicial interview in over 11 years!? We really have to ask ourselves again; who is being taken for fools here folks? Our judges are supposed to be the very *best* of us. They are supposed to be wise, judicious, fair and independent. They are there to protect us from abuses of the law and the Constitution - *not* to facilitate them. Unfortunately—and with all due respect to those few notable exceptions to this rule—this is exactly what is happening on a daily basis in many of our Courts, and you or I—or any other unsuspecting citizen—could be the next unwitting victim. But there IS something that we can do about this.

TAKING DIRECT ACTION

As we said before, it is pointless trying to tackle this problem from the bottom up, where you face layer after layer of frustrating bureaucracy and will likely never ever get to the real source of the problem. We need to go straight to the top – or at least, go straight to the source. And the source of any given problem is usually someone in authority who is abusing their power and position. The type of 'someone' who *could* effect positive change in the system if they really wanted to. Somehow, we have to convey the message to these people on a very *personal* level that it simply isn't worth the trouble of NOT doing their jobs correctly – and it certainly isn't going to be a pleasant or profitable experience for them if they continue to actively conspire to visit knowing injustices on ordinary, trusting citizens! You see, the main reason they act like this in the first place is because they profit from it either *directly* (via legal fees / bribes / 'favours' / brown envelopes etc), or *indirectly* through enhanced promotion prospects for example, because it is abundantly clear that the way to the top in compromised institutions is to be ruthlessly efficient at promoting that institution's agenda - which in this case, is to reward the deception, abuse and exploitation of the public, and to punish any efforts at decency and truth (think of the treatment of the Garda whistleblowers). In this manner a whole cabal of career sociopaths have emerged at the top positions in Irish society and governance - and you can bet your bottom dollar that they are NOT going to give up those coveted positions out of any personal sense of shame. Sociopaths and psychopaths simply don't 'do' guilt. They do greed, selfishness and exploitation of others, and can do so untroubled by any real sense of empathy for those they are exploiting.

Clearly, passively following *their* rules in submitting official complaints or taking legal action against the State isn't working, and hundreds of I-I Members will testify painfully to that. Whether it be the Garda Ombudsman (GSOC); the complaints department at the Law Society; or trying to take a civil action for damages in the Courts, the experience of most I-I Members is that it is an exercise in pure futility and frustration. Even in those rare cases where a legitimate complainant manages to get an erring State body into Court and is ready to prove culpability in some serious wrongdoing, the State will fight the claim tooth-and-nail to the bitter end, regardless of the facts. Then, at the very last moment, and having dragged the complainants through years of unnecessary and often-painful litigation (at the taxpayer's expense) State agencies enter into secret settlements with the complainants (again, at OUR expense) under the strict condition that those complainants do NOT disclose any of the details - thus ensuring that nobody in authority is ever held properly to account. It is an utterly disgraceful and even perverse scenario when errant authority figures can basically fund their own repeated misconduct at the taxpayers' expense, knowing they will never personally be held to account for the awful damage and distress they are causing. In this manner, authority figures who have committed some appalling acts of negligence and malfeasance (whilst being paid by us) find themselves in this perennial 'win-win' situation, arrogantly defending their own wrongdoing using all of the resources of the State (at OUR expense again); and then, in the ultimate gesture of contempt, coercing everyone involved into silence by dipping again, into the public purse.

Clearly, expecting 'the system' to hold its own erring administrators properly to account is, quite frankly, a fool's game and a colossal waste of our time and resources. What is needed is a direct and uncompromising approach that targets individual transgressors in some *effective* way that will seriously get their attention and encourage them to reform at the very least; something that will counteract a dysfunctional system populated in the main by compromised State agents who have scant respect for the public and who cannot be trusted to fulfil their mandates in an open, honest and transparent manner. The fact is that ALL citizens – including lawyers, Gardaí and Judges – are subject to the law. This leads us to an obvious question: If a Garda were to order another person to commit a crime – is that person obliged to obey that Garda? No, of course not! In fact, not only are we legally required to abide by the law of the land, but according to the *Reporting Obligations* of the *Criminal Justice Act 2011* we are obliged (under pain of serious penalty) to report offences where, *"there is prima facie evidence of the commission of a relevant offence."* In other words, if we know that a particular crime has been committed then technically speaking, we *should* immediately report that crime. All the more so perhaps when those committing the offence are the very people entrusted with the administration of justice. It might seem a bit odd at first to be reporting solicitors, senior civil servants and erring Gardaí <u>to</u> the Gardaí, but in circumstances where the respective 'statutory authorities' (the Law Society, the Garda Ombudsman and the Ministry for Justice for example) are actively complicit in covering up serious wrongdoing – and where the Irish Courts simply cannot be trusted to protect our rights in any consistent way – then the law-abiding citizen really has no other choice but to report matters to the Gardaí and have those complaints officially lodged on the Garda PULSE system. At least that way, there is some 'official record' of what is going on that can't (or at least shouldn't) mysteriously 'disappear' and, whether or not there is any subsequent proper investigation by Gardaí or the DPP, at least WE can make reference to these criminal reports when lodging information on the I-I HAFTA Database or on public forums, or, when taking any other actions in defence of our fundamental rights.

The recent use of private prosecutions in the District Court by members of the public is also proving to be an effective deterrent against abuses by rogue authorities, and is a facility enshrined in Common Law which should not be underestimated. In the abject failure of the Gardaí and the DPP in prosecuting blatant criminality amongst authority figures, it is refreshing to know that we can take the initiative - at no financial cost to ourselves - to initiate a criminal prosecution in the Courts. It is a very new concept for many of these repeat offenders in positions of power and authority; to hear they have been summoned to a public Court to answer for their sins and may even face a criminal conviction - despite their connections in high places! Likewise, the simple premise of absolutely refusing to be a party to any activities being engaged in by authority figures which appear to be unlawful or unconstitutional, places us back in the moral and constitutional position of authority over rogue agents of the State. So, each and every time you are wronged by an authority figure, you take direct action. You don't just sit and moan about the situation – you take action! You lodge a formal complaint with the <u>head</u> of their institution (not their line manager); you also lodge a criminal complaint with An Garda Síochána and send a copy to the Garda Commissioner; you also take action in the District Court and, if appropriate, you also bill the individual for wasting *YOUR* precious time. We can't guarantee that you will get full satisfaction every time, but we *can* guarantee that you will get their immediate attention – and that in itself is a big step forwards.

This has become a key strategy in our battle against endemic corruption, criminality and cover-ups by State agents; to tackle <u>each and every instance of injustice</u> visited upon our members, and target the individual transgressors with the full weight of the law, with the Articles of the Constitution and with the rules and regulations of the institution where they are employed. Exposure on social media is another tool that should not be underestimated, because it builds another public record. Whatever their rank or position, and whatever their own perceived sense of importance, the fact of the matter is that ALL Irish citizens are subject to the law and the Constitution – and clearly, some of these individuals need to be reminded of this quite urgently. No-one likes hearing that a public, criminal complaint has been lodged against them – especially those with an inflated sense of their own importance and perceived immunity from accountability – and maybe, just maybe, the knowledge that we are ready and willing to challenge and expose serious wrongdoing by senior authority figures, will help to draw their attention to their own solemnly-sworn obligations and responsibilities, and perhaps encourage them to be a touch more diligent and conscientious in their approach to their work? Alternatively, erring authorities face the prospect of public exposure and embarrassment as we publish the various complaints that have been lodged against them, and pursue with a relentless determination, our absolute fundamental right to justice.

There are seven main ways we intend to achieve this:

- By gathering information for the HAFTA Database so that individual I-I Members will be better informed as to the histories of erring authority figures.

- By putting I-I Members in personal contact with the victims of rogue authorities for the purposes of direct moral support and to provide first-hand witnesses in any subsequent legal actions or formal complaints.

- To lodge formal written criminal complaints with Garda HQ and the respective authorities 'for the record'; and by publicly naming-and-shaming those authority figures who seriously breach the law or the Constitution, or who routinely abuse their positions in contravention of their respective Oaths of Office.

- By initiating criminal proceedings in our own names in the District Court, thus sidestepping the need to engage with ineffective State agencies and supposed 'statutory oversight bodies' and raising the prospect of criminal convictions being delivered on rogue authorities.

- By refusing, absolutely, to knowingly comply with - or be a party to - unlawful, criminal or unconstitutional activity - especially when instigated by the authorities.

- By billing rogue authority figures for the time, costs and stresses visited upon us.

- By maintaining our own unity, integrity and determination - thereby counteracting the unjust imbalances within 'the system' and promoting a genuine cultural change in the attitudes, morals and ethics of the public sector.

In addition to other anti-corruption tactics, such as attendance at Court Hearings, making citizens' arrests, and the daring use of social media; this is how we hope to ensure more openness, transparency and accountability in Irish institutions and less routine injustice – by working together in *personally* confronting corruption, cronyism and criminal cover-ups in direct and courageous ways, and by ensuring that those responsible cannot continue to act with impunity and contempt for the public, for the law, and for our hard-won Constitution. A solemn Constitution to which they are each duty-bound, under oath, to protect, uphold and respect.

This modest Guide, and the *Integrity Ireland* movement, does NOT comprise, *"..a wholesale, collateral attack on the establishment..."* as has been stated in the mainstream media. Nor are we criticising the sincere efforts of those within the establishment who endeavour to maintain their personal integrity in morally-challenging circumstances. No, this Guide is just our first modest attempt to empower ordinary citizens to stand up against abuse and oppression - especially when that oppression is clearly unjust, immoral and even illegal.

It *IS* absolutely true to say however, that the *Integrity Ireland* movement is a direct and definitive 'attack' (per se) on the rampant *corruption* that exists within the Irish establishment today - and we will be making absolutely no apologies for that. Indeed, if any particular individual, agency or institution named in this Guide feels that they have been unjustly maligned or defamed in this publication (and notwithstanding our sincere undertakings to correct any factual errors herein), then that party should of course immediately issue proceedings 'in the overall interests of truth, justice and transparency' and we will gladly and willingly respond by producing the evidence and witnesses in support of our position in the open forum of OUR public Courts.

If you want to hear more about how we can help you, and how you can help others, please consider joining us at www.integrityireland.ie because..

"One by one – together – we CAN make a difference!"

Using this Guide

This Guide is our first attempt to produce information and guidelines that will help you to negotiate an often convoluted and confusing 'justice system' with some level of understanding. It is a work in progress that was born out of the experiences of other *Integrity Ireland* members who, in some cases, have experienced decades of frustration, abuse and exploitation at the hands of corrupt authority figures and errant legal professionals, and who want to ensure that others do not suffer the same experience. This principle lies at the heart of the *Integrity Ireland* ethos; that in helping others, that ultimately, we also help ourselves.

For legal reasons it needs to be emphasised that we do not claim to be offering 'legal advice' nor are we qualified to do so - other than as a result of the combined experiences of *Integrity Ireland* members who have freely offered to share their experiences and insights with others. What we *do* claim to be offering here is some intelligible method whereby lay litigants in particular can *begin* to understand the basics of dealing with law enforcement, lawyers and the Irish Courts - especially in adverse situations - so that you are not overly disadvantaged or subject to unfair exploitation by those who might capitalise on your lack of knowledge or understanding.

As we learn more about 'the system' and how it operates we will update this Guide and publish new versions - doing our best to ensure that only 'key' information is included and thereby keeping the Guide to a practical length. In the same vein however, we realise that this Guide is limited in its current form particularly when it comes to progressing lay-litigant's cases through the Irish Courts. Such are the bewildering intricacies and perplexities of the various Courts processes (which are each different from each other) it would be impossible - in a Guide of this nature - to cover all the options and possibilities with some measure of coherence and clarity. Therefore we would always advise - if you can afford it - to seek out a trusted legal advisor who will undoubtedly be able to provide a far more comprehensive overview of the convolutions of our archaic Courts system, than the modest offerings contained in this Guide.

This Guide is produced in A4 format for ease of photocopying the various forms that are used by *Integrity Ireland* members as displayed in Appendixes II & III. These forms are free to use and can be copied and shared with others at will, and we would strongly advocate that these forms are put to immediate use, because the more of us that engage in the tactics of direct action - the sooner the authorities will realise that they cannot continue abusing their mandates to serve the people - at least, not without *some* consequences. We would ask however, that if you are *not* a fully signed-up active member of *Integrity Ireland* who has agreed to abide by our Terms & Guidelines, that you please remove the logo before using those forms. Better still, sign up with us using the application forms provided, and gain all of the advantages of full membership.

The remainder of the Guide is copyrighted to *CheckPoint Press* and we would ask that if you require further copies that you purchase new copies directly from us so that any modest profits generated can be recycled back into *Integrity Ireland* projects and support. Bulk or wholesale orders can be sourced at 30% discount by emailing 'bookstore@checkpointpress.com'. Alternatively, you can purchase this Guide online from all the major retailers worldwide or by quoting the ISBN and title to your local bookstore: *978-1-906628-72-7: The Integrity Ireland S.O.S. Guide, Version 1, 2015.* Discounted copies will also be made available to I-I Facilitators and Members, and to those who attend I-I meetings.

Finally, as you read through this Guide, please feel free to alert us as to any apparent errors or mistakes, or, feel free to suggest additional materials which can be incorporated into subsequent versions by emailing 'sos@integrityireland.ie'. All original materials submitted to us will of course be credited to the respective author(s) upon request.

STM October 2015

PART
1

THE CONSTITUTION

CRIMES & CULPABILITY

CONSTITUTION IS...

A constitution means a collection
of basic principles of governance
enacted through one or more
documents. In addition to these,
there are numerous laws and
amendments concerning the basic
document and a large number of
constitutional conventions,
customs and judicial verdicts.

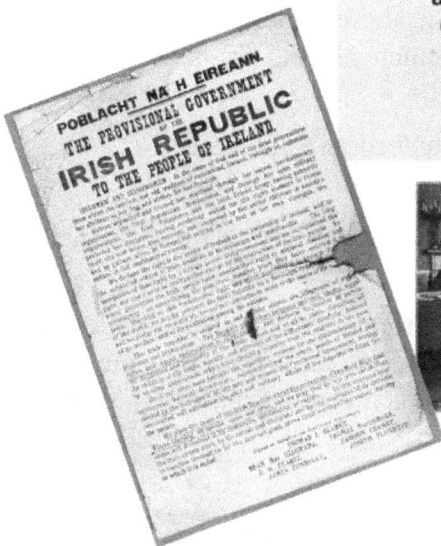

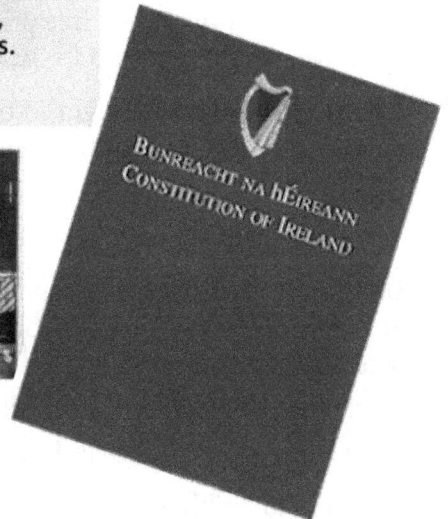

The Constitution - A Brief Summary

The Constitution of Ireland is the basic law of the State. It was adopted by plebiscite in 1937. It is the successor of the Constitution of Dáil Éireann (1919) and the Constitution of the Irish Free State (1922). The Constitution states that all legislative, executive and judicial powers of Government derive from the people. It sets out the form of government and defines the powers of the President, the two Houses of the Oireachtas and the Government. It also defines the structure and powers of the courts, sets out the fundamental rights of citizens and contains a number of directive principles of social policy for the general guidance of the Oireachtas. The Constitution may be amended only by referendum.

The Constitution outlines what are considered the fundamental rights of the citizen. The definition of rights in the Constitution covers five broad headings: personal rights, the family, education, private property and religion.

Personal Rights: the Constitution declares that all citizens are equal before the law; it guarantees to defend and vindicate the personal rights of citizens in its laws: it provides that there will be no deprivation of personal liberty except in accordance with law; it provides for the right to 'habeas corpus'; it guarantees the inviolability of citizens' dwellings except in accordance with law; and it guarantees, subject to public order and morality, liberty to express freely one's convictions and opinions, the right to assemble peaceably and without arms, and the right to form associations and unions.

The Family: the State recognises the family as a moral institution possessing inalienable and imprescriptible rights, and guarantees to protect it and the institution of marriage.

Education: the State recognises the primacy of the family in the education of children and undertakes to provide for free primary education and to supplement and aid private educational initiative, with due regard to the rights of the parents.

Private Property: the right to own private property is guaranteed and its exercise is subject only to the exigencies of the common good.

Religion: the Constitution guarantees freedom of conscience and the free profession and practice of religion, subject only to public order and morality.

Unenumerated Rights: In addition to the foregoing personal rights specifically provided for in the words of the Constitution, the Courts have held in a series of cases that there are other personal rights whose existence "result(s) from the Christian and democratic nature of the State", and which are implicitly guaranteed by the Constitution.

The Courts have ruled that these unenumerated personal rights include:

The right to bodily integrity, **the right not to have one's health endangered by the State**, the (qualified) right to work and to earn a livelihood, the right to marital privacy, **the right of access to the courts**, the right of the citizen to sue the State in court, **the right to justice and fair procedures**, the right to travel within and without the State, the right to marry, the rights of the unmarried mother in regard to her child.

This list is not exhaustive and it is also likely that the Courts will identify more, as yet unenumerated, personal rights in future.

Citizens, and in certain cases non-citizens, have the right to apply to the courts to protect from infringement their rights under the Constitution or to have a judgement pronounced as to whether legislation is compatible with the Constitution, provided the legislation affects, or is likely to affect, the person challenging it. Moreover, the President may before signing a Bill refer it to the Supreme Court for a decision on its compatibility with the Constitution. These procedures have been employed on a number of occasions.

SELECTED ARTICLES OF THE IRISH CONSTITUTION

The Constitution is the fundamental law of Ireland which guarantees certain inalienable rights. These Articles are listed here in context of the main problems reported by I-I members when dealing with statutory authorities. It may be useful to have these quotes to hand when facing apparent abuses of your Constitutional rights - after all, what's the point of having a Constitution if we don't abide by it - and if we don't insist that the statutory authorities abide by it as well? Please remember that any clear or deliberate breach of the Constitution by any authority figure renders that particular action—or that person's position—illegitimate and/or illegal.

BUNREACHT NA hÉIREANN

[Constitution of Ireland]

In the Name of the Most Holy Trinity, from Whom is all authority and to Whom, as our final end, all actions both of men and States must be referred,

We, the people of Éire, Humbly acknowledging all our obligations to our Divine Lord, Jesus Christ, Who sustained our fathers through centuries of trial, Gratefully remembering their heroic and unremitting struggle to regain the rightful independence of our Nation,

And seeking to promote the common good, with due observance of Prudence, Justice and Charity, so that the dignity and freedom of the individual may be assured, true social order attained, the unity of our country restored, and concord established with other nations,

Do hereby adopt, enact, and give to ourselves this Constitution.

ARTICLE 6: THE STATE
1. All powers of government, legislative, executive and judicial, derive, under God, from the people, whose right it is to designate the rulers of the State and, in final appeal, to decide all questions of national policy, according to the requirements of the common good.

2. These powers of government are exercisable only by or on the authority of the organs of State established by this Constitution.

ARTICLE 9:THE STATE
3. Fidelity to the nation and loyalty to the State are fundamental political duties of all citizens.

ARTICLE 11: THE STATE
All revenues of the State from whatever source arising shall, subject to such exception as may be provided by law, form one fund, and shall be appropriated for the purposes and in the manner and subject to the charges and liabilities determined and imposed by law.

ARTICLE 12: THE PRESIDENT
1. There shall be a President of Ireland (Uachtarán na hÉireann), hereinafter called the President, who shall take precedence over all other persons in the State and who shall exercise and perform the powers and functions conferred on the President by this Constitution and by

law.

8. The President shall enter upon his office by taking and subscribing publicly, in the presence of members of both Houses of the Oireachtas, of Judges of the Supreme Court and of the High Court, and other public personages, the following declaration:

"In the presence of Almighty God I , do solemnly and sincerely promise and declare that I will maintain the Constitution of Ireland and uphold its laws, that I will fulfil my duties faithfully and conscientiously in accordance with the Constitution and the law, and that I will dedicate my abilities to the service and welfare of the people of Ireland. May God direct and sustain me."

ARTICLE 15: THE NATIONAL PARLIAMENT
4.1° The Oireachtas shall not enact any law which is in any respect repugnant to this Constitution or any provision thereof.

4.2° Every law enacted by the Oireachtas which is in any respect repugnant to this Constitution or to any provision thereof, shall, but to the extent only of such repugnancy, be invalid.

5.1° The Oireachtas shall not declare acts to be infringements of the law which were not so at the date of their commission.

ARTICLE 17: Dáil Éireann
2. Dáil Éireann shall not pass any vote or resolution, and no law shall be enacted, for the appropriation of revenue or other public moneys unless the purpose of the appropriation shall have been recommended to Dáil Éireann by a message from the Government signed by the Taoiseach.

ARTICLE 20: LEGISLATION
2.1° A Bill other than a Money Bill may be initiated in Seanad Éireann, and if passed by Seanad Éireann, shall be introduced in Dáil Éireann.

3. A Bill passed by either House and accepted by the other House shall be deemed to have been passed by both Houses.

ARTICLE 24:LEGISLATION
1. If and whenever on the passage by Dáil Éireann of any Bill, other than a Bill expressed to be a Bill containing a proposal to amend the Constitution, the Taoiseach certifies by messages in writing addressed to the President and to the Chairman of each House of the Oireachtas that, in the opinion of the Government, the Bill is urgent and immediately necessary for the preservation of the public peace and security, or by reason of the existence of a public emergency, whether domestic or international, the time for the consideration of such Bill by Seanad Éireann shall, if Dáil Éireann so resolves and if the President, after consultation with the Council of State, concurs, be abridged to such period as shall be specified in the resolution.

ARTICLE 27: Reference of Bills to the People
1. A majority of the members of Seanad Éireann and not less than one-third of the members of Dáil Éireann may by a joint petition addressed to the President by them under this Article request the President to decline to sign and promulgate as a law any Bill to which this article applies on the ground that the Bill contains a proposal of such national importance that the will of the people thereon ought to be ascertained.

ARTICLE 29: INTERNATIONAL RELATIONS
1. Ireland affirms its devotion to the ideal of peace and friendly co-operation amongst nations founded on international justice and morality.

4.4° Ireland affirms its commitment to the European Union within which the member states of that Union work together to promote peace, shared values and the well-being of their peoples.

5.2° The State shall not be bound by any international agreement involving a charge upon public funds unless the terms of the agreement shall have been approved by Dáil Éireann.

ARTICLE 34: THE COURTS

1. Justice shall be administered in courts established by law by judges appointed in the manner provided by this Constitution, and, save in such special and limited cases as may be prescribed by law, shall be administered in public.

5.1° Every person appointed a judge under this Constitution shall make and subscribe the following declaration:

"In the presence of Almighty God I do solemnly and sincerely promise and declare that I will duly and faithfully and to the best of my knowledge and power execute the office of Chief Justice (or as the case may be) without fear or favour, affection or ill-will towards any man, and that I will uphold the Constitution and the laws. May God direct and sustain me."

ARTICLE 35: THE COURTS

1. The judges of the Supreme Court, the High Court and all other Courts established in pursuance of Article 34 hereof shall be appointed by the President.

2. All judges shall be independent in the exercise of their judicial functions and subject only to this Constitution and the law.

3. No judge shall be eligible to be a member of either House of the Oireachtas or to hold any other office or position of emolument.

4. 1° A judge of the Supreme Court or the High Court [or any other judge apparently] shall not be removed from office except for stated misbehaviour or incapacity, and then only upon resolutions passed by Dáil Éireann and by Seanad Éireann calling for his removal.

ARTICLE 37: THE COURTS

1. Nothing in this Constitution shall operate to invalidate the exercise of limited functions and powers of a judicial nature, in matters other than criminal matters, by any person or body of persons duly authorised by law to exercise such functions and powers, notwithstanding that such person or such body of persons is not a judge or a court appointed or established as such under this Constitution.

2. No adoption of a person taking effect or expressed to take effect at any time after the coming into operation of this Constitution under laws enacted by the Oireachtas and being an adoption pursuant to an order made or an authorisation given by any person or body of persons designated by those laws to exercise such functions and powers was or shall be invalid by reason only of the fact that such person or body of persons was not a judge or a court appointed or established as such under this Constitution.

ARTICLE 38: TRIAL OF OFFENCES

1. No person shall be tried on any criminal charge save in due course of law.

2. Minor offences may be tried by courts of summary jurisdiction.

3. 1° Special courts may be established by law for the trial of offences in cases where it may be determined in accordance with such law that the ordinary courts are inadequate to secure the effective administration of justice, and the preservation of public peace and order.

5. Save in the case of the trial of offences under section 2, section 3 or section 4 of this Article no person shall be tried on any criminal charge without a jury.

ARTICLE 39: TRIAL OF OFFENCES
Treason shall consist only in levying war against the State, or assisting any State or person or inciting or conspiring with any person to levy war against the State, or attempting by force of arms or other violent means to overthrow the organs of government established by this Constitution, or taking part or being concerned in or inciting or conspiring with any person to make or to take part or be concerned in any such attempt.

ARTICLE 40: FUNDAMENTAL RIGHTS
1. All citizens shall, as human persons, be held equal before the law.

3.1° The State guarantees in its laws to respect, and, as far as practicable, by its laws to defend and vindicate the personal rights of the citizen.

3.2° The State shall, in particular, by its laws protect as best it may from unjust attack and, in the case of injustice done, vindicate the life, person, good name, and property rights of every citizen.

4.1° No citizen shall be deprived of his personal liberty save in accordance with law.

4.2° Upon complaint being made by or on behalf of any person to the High Court or any judge thereof alleging that such person is being unlawfully detained, the High Court and any and every judge thereof to whom such complaint is made shall forthwith enquire into the said complaint and may order the person in whose custody such person is detained to produce the body of such person before the High Court on a named day and to certify in writing the grounds of his detention, and the High Court shall, upon the body of such person being produced before that Court and after giving the person in whose custody he is detained an opportunity of justifying the detention, order the release of such person from such detention unless satisfied that he is being detained in accordance with the law.

5. The dwelling of every citizen is inviolable and shall not be forcibly entered save in accordance with law.

6.1° The State guarantees liberty for the exercise of the following rights, subject to public order and morality: –
    i The right of the citizens to express freely their convictions and opinions.

    The education of public opinion being, however, a matter of such grave import to the common good, the State shall endeavour to ensure that organs of public opinion, such as the radio, the press, the cinema, while preserving their rightful liberty of expression, including criticism of Government policy, shall not be used to undermine public order or morality or the authority of the State. The publication or utterance of blasphemous, seditious, or indecent matter is an offence which shall be punishable in accordance with law.

    ii The right of the citizens to assemble peaceably and without arms. Provision may be made by law to prevent or control meetings which are determined in accordance with law to be calculated to cause a breach of the peace or to be a danger or nuisance to the general public and to prevent or control meetings in the vicinity of either House of the Oireachtas.

    iii The right of the citizens to form associations and unions. Laws, however, may be enacted for the regulation and control in the public interest of the exercise of the foregoing right.

6.2° Laws regulating the manner in which the right of forming associations and unions and the right of free assembly may be exercised shall contain no political, religious or class discrimination.

ARTICLE 41: THE FAMILY
1.1° The State recognises the Family as the natural primary and fundamental unit group of Society, and as a moral institution possessing inalienable and imprescriptible rights, antecedent and superior to all positive law.

1.2° The State, therefore, guarantees to protect the Family in its constitution and authority, as the necessary basis of social order and as indispensable to the welfare of the Nation and the State.

ARTICLE 45: DIRECTIVE PRINCIPLES OF SOCIAL POLICY
1 The State shall strive to promote the welfare of the whole people by securing and protecting as effectively as it may a social order in which justice and charity shall inform all the institutions of the national life.

2 The State shall, in particular, direct its policy towards securing:–

i That the citizens (all of whom, men and women equally, have the right to an adequate means of livelihood) may through their occupations find the means of making reasonable provision for their domestic needs.

ii That the ownership and control of the material resources of the community may be so distributed amongst private individuals and the various classes as best to subserve the common good.

iii That, especially, the operation of free competition shall not be allowed so to develop as to result in the concentration of the ownership or control of essential commodities in a few individuals to the common detriment.

iv That in what pertains to the control of credit the constant and predominant aim shall be the welfare of the people as a whole.

3.2° The State shall endeavour to secure that private enterprise shall be so conducted as to ensure reasonable efficiency in the production and distribution of goods and as to protect the public against unjust exploitation.

4.1° The State pledges itself to safeguard with especial care the economic interests of the weaker sections of the community, and, where necessary, to contribute to the support of the infirm, the widow, the orphan, and the aged.

*   *   *

Pertinent Amendments:
12ᵗʰ December 1996: Sixteenth Amendment of the Constitution Act, 1996 [Provided for the refusal of bail by a court to a person charged with a serious offence where it is reasonably considered necessary to prevent the commission of a serious offence by that person.]

14ᵗʰ November, 1997: Seventeenth Amendment of the Constitution Act, 1997 [Provided that the confidentiality of discussions at meetings of the Government would be respected save only where the High Court, in certain specified circumstances, determined that disclosure should be made.]

27ᵗʰ March, 2002: There is no Twenty-second Amendment. The Twenty-second Amendment of the Constitution Bill, 2001 [relating to the removal of a judge from office and providing for a body to be established by law to investigate or cause to be investigated conduct constituting misbehaviour by a judge or affected by incapacity of a judge] was not passed by the Houses of the Oireachtas.

Civil Offence or Criminal Offence - What's the Difference?

It would be impossible to explain in detail, in any coherent manner, the complexities of the legal system in Ireland - without producing a whole new 10,000-page legal manual. But there are a few basics which we need to understand so that we don't get inadvertently tangled in complicated and confusing situations which will no doubt play into the hands of the opposition.

The first thing to understand is the difference between *civil* offences and *criminal* offences, and the easiest way to explain this in context of the *Integrity Ireland* project is to assume that the offence (whatever it may be) is being committed against us. Basically, if someone commits a civil offence against you (such as defamation, or if you have a personal injury claim) your only real option is to take them to Court because the Gardaí have no direct responsibility to investigate civil matters. If you win your case in Court, then the only 'punishment' for the opposition is that they pay you a sum of money in compensation, and (hopefully) also your legal costs.

On the other hand, criminal offences are *supposed* to be prosecuted by the State, as displayed in the list on the following pages. So for example, if someone steals your wallet, then that person can be prosecuted by the State for *'Theft From Person 08b'*. The thief would also face a Court hearing, but the punishment if he is found guilty would be a fine (payable to the State) or a prison term. You, the victim of the theft, do not receive any compensation (unless it is offered voluntarily) and may not even be involved in the prosecution at all, unless called as a witness.

So the main difference is that in the case of a *civil* offence, the onus is on YOU (as the person alleging injury) to initiate a claim through the civil Courts. YOU control the process either as a lay-litigant or through your legal team. In the case of *criminal* offences, it is *usually* the responsibility of the State (via the Gardaí or the Office of the DPP) to prosecute wrongdoers. Both types of claims are heard before judges (or before judges *and* juries for serious criminal offences) in whatever Court is appropriate (see pp.163-164). However, what most of us didn't know is that there IS an option for ordinary citizens to prosecute in their own names, i.e. without going via the Gardaí and/or the DPP. This is where the *Common Informer* legislation comes in (see Part 2). But before you can prosecute someone directly, you need to identify which particular crime they have committed. This is why we have drawn up the list and tables on the following pages, so that you can clearly identify when a crime is being committed against you by persons ostensibly employed by us to 'protect and serve' or otherwise administer justice. So, don't be shy. Let them know that the abuse, deceptions, criminality and cover-ups stops now!

* * *

The list of crimes on the following pages is taken from the Central Statistics Office. It is reproduced here as a quick-reference for you to be able to identify, without too much confusion or preamble, which particular offence may have been committed against you. The tables on the following pages are self-explanatory and are there to help non-legally trained persons match abusive or illicit behaviour by authority figures with the *Irish Crime Classification System*.

The main advantage of having this list is to facilitate private prosecutions by ordinary citizens using the *Common Informer 1861* legislation - for those times when authority figures overstep their mandates and visit crimes on the public. It is absolutely vital that we start holding erring authority figures to account, because, quite frankly, no-one in our justice system seems remotely interested in doing so. Indeed, it is now a matter of public record that those charged with maintaining and administering justice in Ireland are absolutely failing in their Constitutional responsibilities - if not on a case-by-case individual level, then most certainly as a collective.

If you can add to our list or identify other scenarios where these crimes relate to improper conduct by the authorities - then please feel free to email us at sos@integrityireland.ie. Thank you.

Types of Criminal Offences - Summary, Indictable & Hybrid

Keeping the legal jargon to a minimum, there are basically only two types of criminal offence in Ireland, because 'hybrid' offences (as the word suggests) are offences which could be classified under either of the other two categories - depending on a range of legal criteria.

From our layperson's perspective, it is probably enough to understand that the terms 'summary' and 'indictable' basically mean 'minor' and 'major' offences respectively. It is important that we understand the difference though, because if we initiate a private criminal prosecution in our own names, then we can only maintain control (or 'jurisdiction') over the prosecution of that case as long as it remains a summary (or minor) offence. Generally speaking, summary offences will attract a prison term of less than 12 months, or a fine (depending on the class of offence) as follows. Class A (up to) €5,000; B, €4,500; C, €2,500; D, €1,000 & E, €500. These cases are dealt with by one judge sitting *without* a jury in the District Court. Indictable (major) offences on the other hand have to be dealt with in a higher Court usually before a judge and jury. There are some exceptions to these generalities which fall into the 'hybrid' category, but for the purposes of a basic understanding of how the criminal prosecution system works, this should help explain the situation.

You see, any citizen can *initiate* a criminal prosecution in the District Court by using the *Common Informer* legislation based on the Petty Sessions (Ireland) Act 1851. But if the Court decides that the offence is NOT a summary offence, but must be tried on indictment, then the case has to be heard in a higher Court before a judge and jury. If this happens, then jurisdiction for the continuation and prosecution of the case is passed to the Office of the DPP (the Director of Public Prosecutions) and they take over the case. Now this would be all well and good if the Office of the DPP was staffed by genuinely 'independent' and diligent professionals who prosecuted crimes in the name of the people according to the principles of natural justice. But again, there appears to be a major problem in the way that the Office of the DPP does business, with an abject failure to prosecute 'connected' or white-collar criminals, and compounded by a reckless enthusiasm in targeting motorists, minor offenders and public protestors for example.

It is a very handy 'get out of jail free' card for rogue authority figures - knowing that they can only be prosecuted privately by ordinary citizens at the *summary* (minor offence) level where they face only *one* judge and very limited consequences - and if things get too serious then the matter will be passed to the DPP who can then decide - without explaining the decision to *anyone* believe it or not - whether or not to continue the prosecution at the *indictable* (major offence) level. This is why is is important that we understand the difference between summary and indictable offences, because if we really do want to have our day in Court - safe from interference from the State - then we have to present our case, and maintain the case, at the summary level in the District Court. Alternatively, we can initiate proceedings in the District Court for indictable (more serious) offences, but we will then have to accept that jurisdiction will be passed to the State, along with the high likelihood that the wagons will be circled - as per usual. But all is not lost, because European legislation is coming into effect in November 2015 which will oblige the DPP to give *some* explanation for her often unfathomable decisions. And if you or I are the party that initiates the criminal complaint in the District Court, then at least we will have a direct personal interest in the case, and can lobby the DPP about any developments.

Finally, although there is a statutory time limit of 6 months within which a summary offence has to be prosecuted, Section 7.4 of the Criminal Justice Act 1951 exempts indictable offences from any such time limits. In other words, if you have evidence of serious wrongdoing then there is NO time limit for taking private prosecutions. So, let's form an orderly queue, shall we?

'HYBRID OFFENCES' i.e. Indictable Offences

Which May be Dealt With Summarily by the District Court

(From the Irish Statute Book: Criminal Justice Act, 1951)

This list of selected 'hybrid' offences should assist you when deciding which category of offence you are going to prosecute. Remember, even though these offences are defined as 'indictable' (i.e. more serious offences that *should* normally be dealt with in the higher Courts before a judge and jury) these *can* be assigned to one judge in the District Court - under certain conditions. The full list of offences can be sourced online under the criminal Justice Act 1951.

> 53.—(1) The District Court may try summarily a person charged with an indictable offence under this Act if—
>
> (a) the Court is of opinion that the facts proved or alleged constitute a minor offence fit to be tried summarily,
>
> (b) the accused, on being informed by the Court of his or her right to be tried with a jury, does not object to being tried summarily, and
>
> (c) the Director of Public Prosecutions consents to the accused being tried summarily for the offence.
>
> (2) On conviction by the District Court for an indictable offence tried summarily under subsection (1) the accused shall be liable to a fine not exceeding £1,500 or imprisonment for a term not exceeding 12 months or both such fine and imprisonment.

The entries **in bold** below indicate offences that *could* be levied against authority figures who are criminally abusing their positions and powers. We have to remind ourselves that just because they are wearing a uniform, cloak or wig, that they are still bound by the law and the Constitution - arguably, even more so. So we need to rethink our mental conditioning and realise (for example) that if we have made a legitimate citizen's arrest on an authority figure and the Gardaí fail or refuse to accept jurisdiction (which they are repeatedly doing), then technically, they are guilty of offences against No's 2 and 9 below, because technically, if WE are making the citizen's arrest, then WE (and not the passive Gardaí) are engaged in the 'lawful apprehension' of the subject - right? Likewise, any official who attempts to obstruct, delay, obfuscate or prevent our access to justice is, technically 'obstructing the administration of justice' as per No 2 below.

Offence

1. An offence in the nature of a public mischief.
   1516 Public mischief-annoying phone calls, wasting police time
   1534 Public mischief, pervert course of justice, conceal offence

2. An indictable offence consisting of any form of obstruction of the administration of justice or the enforcement of the law.

3. Perjury.

4. Riot or unlawful assembly, where the Court is of opinion that the act constituting the offence was not done in furtherance of an organised conspiracy or, if so done, that the conspiracy is at an end. *(Is it riot or unlawful assembly when Gardaí are deployed illegally to quash our Constitutional rights?)*

5. Assault occasioning actual bodily harm.

9. An offence under section 38 of the Offences against the Person Act, 1861.

Assault with intent to commit felony, or on peace officers, &c.

38. Whosoever shall assault any person with intent to commit felony, or shall assault, resist, or wilfully obstruct any peace officer in the due execution of his duty, or any person acting in aid of such officer, **or shall assault any person with intent to resist or prevent the lawful apprehension or detainer of himself or of any other person for any offence,** shall be guilty of a misdemeanor, and being convicted thereof shall be liable, at the discretion of the court, to be imprisoned for any term not exceeding two years, with or without hard labour.

13. An offence under the Forgery Act, 1913.

(2) A person shall be treated for the purposes of this Part as making a false instrument if he or she **alters an instrument so as to make it false in any respect** (whether or not it is false in some other respect apart from that alteration). *(This may apply to inaccurate Court records or Orders; falsified Garda statements etc)*

21. An attempt to commit an offence which the District Court has, by virtue of any enactment (including this Act), jurisdiction to try summarily.

Criminal Justice Act, 1951, Section 10: Obtaining by false pretences.

10.—A person who by any **false pretence, with intent to defraud,** obtains anything capable of being stolen or causes it to be delivered to himself or to any other person for the use or benefit or on account of himself or any other person, shall be guilty of a misdemeanour and on conviction shall be liable to penal servitude for a term not exceeding five years or to imprisonment for a term not exceeding two years.

Amendment of section 42 of the Offences against the Person Act, 1861.

11.—(1) In this section references to **common assault and battery** are to offences under section 42 of the Offences against the Person Act, 1861.

(2) A person convicted of common assault or battery shall be liable to a fine not exceeding fifty pounds or, at the discretion of the Court, imprisonment for a term not exceeding six months.

(3) Common assault and battery may be summarily prosecuted on complaint made by or on behalf of the aggrieved person or otherwise.

(4) The adjudication of a complaint as to common assault or battery shall not affect any civil remedy that the complainant may have against the defendant in respect of the subject matter of the complaint.

* * *

Just a Thought: It might be an interesting tactic to deploy - especially in more serious cases - to initiate *indictable* proceedings in the District Court (via the Common Informer process), which then has to be continued (or not) by the DPP. If the DPP (for whatever undisclosed reason) fails to prosecute, then you could issue *summary* proceedings for some lesser offence against the same perpetrator - and process the case to conclusion yourself, playing the role of prosecutor. This would <u>not</u> fall under the double-jeopardy rule (where a person cannot be tried twice for the same crime) because technically, they are two different offences. The only thing you would have to watch out for though, is the 6-month time limit for initiating summary proceedings.

Irish Crime Classification System – Condensed (ICCSc)

IRISH CRIME CLASSIFICATION SYSTEM-CONDENSED (ICCSc)	ICCS Four Digit Code
01 HOMICIDE OFFENCES	
01A MURDER/MANSLAUGHTER/INFANTICIDE	0111-0113
01B DANGEROUS DRIVING LEADING TO DEATH	0121-0122
02 SEXUAL OFFENCES	
02A RAPE OF A MALE OR FEMALE	0211
02B DEFILEMENT OF A BOY OR GIRL LESS THAN 17 YEARS OLD	0212 02C
SEXUAL OFFENCE INVOLVING MENTALLY IMPAIRED PERSON	0213 02D
AGGRAVATED SEXUAL ASSAULT	0214
02E SEXUAL ASSAULT (NOT AGGRAVATED)	0215
02F OTHER SEXUAL OFFENCES	0221-0224
03 ATTEMPTS/THREATS TO MURDER, ASSAULTS, HARASSMENTS AND RELATED OFFENCES	
03A MURDER-ATTEMPT	0311
03B MURDER-THREAT	0312
03C ASSAULT CAUSING HARM, POISONING	0321-0322
03D OTHER ASSAULT	0323-0324
03E HARASSMENT AND RELATED OFFENCES	0331-0335
04 DANGEROUS OR NEGLIGENT ACTS	
04A DANGEROUS DRIVING CAUSING SERIOUS BODILY HARM	0411
04B DRIVING/IN CHARGE OF A VEHICLE WHILE OVER LEGAL ALCOHOL LIMIT	0412 04C
DRIVING/IN CHARGE OF A VEHICLE UNDER THE INFLUENCE OF DRUGS	0413 04D
DANGEROUS/CARELESS DRIVING AND MOTORWAY OFFENCES	0414
04E SPEEDING	0415
04F ENDANGERMENT WITH POTENTIAL FOR SERIOUS HARM/DEATH	0421 04G
ABANDONING A CHILD, CHILD NEGLECT AND CRUELTY	0422 04H
DANGEROUS USE OF VESSEL (AIR, SEA) OR FACILITIES	0423-0424
04I ENDANGERING (ROAD) TRAFFIC	0425
05 KIDNAPPING AND RELATED OFFENCES	
05A FALSE IMPRISONMENT	0511
05B ABDUCTION OF PERSON UNDER 16 YEARS OF AGE	0522
06 ROBBERY, EXTORTION AND HIGHJACKING OFFENCES	
06A ROBBERY OF AN ESTABLISHMENT OR INSTITUTION	0611
06B ROBBERY OF CASH OR GOODS IN TRANSIT	0612
06C ROBBERY FROM THE PERSON	0613
06D BLACKMAIL OR EXTORTION	0621
06E CARJACKING, HIGHJACKING/UNLAWFUL SEIZURE OF OF AIRCRAFT/VESSEL	0631
07 BURGLARY AND RELATED OFFENCES	
07A AGGRAVATED BURGLARY	0711
07B BURGLARY (NOT AGGRAVATED)	0712
07C POSSESSION OF AN ARTICLE (WITH INTENT TO BURGLE, STEAL, DEMAND)	0713
08 THEFT AND RELATED OFFENCES	
08A THEFT/TAKING OF VEHICLE AND RELATED OFFENCES	0811-0812
08B THEFT FROM PERSON	0821
08C THEFT FROM SHOP	0822
08D OTHER THEFTS, HANDLING STOLEN PROPERTY	0823-0826,0831
09 FRAUD, DECEPTION AND RELATED OFFENCES	
09A FRAUD, DECEPTION AND RELATED OFFENCES	0911-0917, 0921-0924, 0931, 0941
10 CONTROLLED DRUG OFFENCES	
10A IMPORTATION OF DRUGS	1011

IRISH CRIME CLASSIFICATION SYSTEM-CONDENSED (ICCSc)	ICCS Four Digit Code
10B CULTIVATION OR MANUFACTURE OF DRUGS	1012 10C
POSSESSION OF DRUGS FOR SALE OR SUPPLY	1021 10D
POSSESSION OF DRUGS FOR PERSONAL USE	1022
10E OTHER DRUG OFFENCES	1031-1032
11 WEAPONS AND EXPLOSIVES OFFENCES	
11A EXPLOSIVES, CHEMICAL WEAPONS OFFENCES	1111-1114
11B FIREARMS OFFENCES	1121-1122
11C OFFENSIVE WEAPONS OFFENCES (NEC)	1131
11D FIREWORKS OFFENCES	1141
12 DAMAGE TO PROPERTY AND TO THE ENVIRONMENT	
12A ARSON	1211
12B CRIMINAL DAMAGE (NOT ARSON)	1212
12C LITTER OFFENCES	1221
13 PUBLIC ORDER AND OTHER SOCIAL CODE OFFENCES	
13A DISORDERLY CONDUCT	1311-1314
13B TRESPASS OFFENCES	1321-1322
13C LIQUOR LICENSING OFFENCES	1331-1333
13D PROSTITUTION OFFENCES	1341-1343
13E REGULATED BETTING/MONEY, COLLECTION/TRADING OFFENCES	1351-1354
13F OTHER SOCIAL CODE OFFENCES (NEC)	1361-1365
14 ROAD AND TRAFFIC OFFENCES (NEC)	
141 DRIVING LICENCE/INSURANCE OFFENCES	1411-1412
142 VEHICLE TAX/REGISTRATION OFFENCES	1421-1422
143 ROADWORTHINESS/REGULATORY OFFENCES	1431-1433
144 ROAD TRANSPORT/PUBLIC SERVICE VEHICLE OFFENCES	1441-1443
15 OFFENCES AGAINST GOVERNMENT, JUSTICE PROCEDURES AND ORGANISATION OF CRIME	
15A OFFENCES AGAINST GOVERNMENT AND ITS AGENTS (NEC)	1511-1518
15B ORGANISATION OF CRIME AND CONSPIRACY TO COMMIT CRIME	1521-1522
15C PERVERTING THE COURSE OF JUSTICE	1531-1534
15D OFFENCES WHILE IN CUSTODY, BREACH OF COURT ORDERS	1541-1542,1551-1556
16 OFFENCES NOT ELSEWHERE CLASSIFIED (NEC)	
161 IMPORTATION/CONTROL/WELFARE OF ANIMALS OFFENCES	1611-1614
162 FISHERIES/MARITIME OFFENCES	1621-1622
163 USE OF DATA, ELECTRONIC COUNTERFEIT AND BROADCASTING OFFENCES	1631-1633
164 MISCELLANEOUS OFFENCES	1641-1648

Offences listed in the Irish Crime Classification System (ICCS) which can possibly be attributed to authority figures abusing their offices or authority.

Listed Offence	Examples of when authority figures may be guilty
0111 Murder	If a person dies during an arrest or while in custody at the direct hands of the authorities
0112 Manslaughter	If a person dies during an arrest or in custody, or as an indirect result of the wrongdoing or negligence of those responsible for the person's safety
0113 Infanticide	
0121 Manslaughter (traffic fatality)	If a person dies as a result of a traffic incident involving an authority figure
0122 Dangerous driving causing death	If a person dies as a result of a traffic incident involving an authority figure, including high-speed chases
0211 Rape of a male or female	
0212 Defilement of a boy or girl less than 17 years old	
0213 Sexual offence involving mentally impaired person	
0214 Aggravated sexual assault	If manhandled in a sexual way that causes injury
0215 Sexual assault (not aggravated)	If manhandled, and private parts are touched
0221 Incest	
0222 Child pornography offences	
0223 Child pornography - obstruction of warrant	
0224 Gross indecency	
0311 Murder-attempt	Any serious physical assault or attempted assault whereby death could ensue
0312 Murder-threat	Spoken, written or gestured indicators that one's life is in danger
0321 Assault causing harm	Any physical assault where injury is caused, including

	psychological and emotional injury
0322 Poisoning	
0323 Assault or obstruction of Garda/official, resisting arrest	When a lay-person (member of the public) initiates a citizen's arrest, that person becomes the 'official' listed here. Therefore, if someone (even a Garda) obstructs your attempts to arrest another person (including authority figures) then this offence applies.
0324 Minor assault	When manhandled without due cause
0331 Harassment, stalking, threats	When 'targeted' by Gardaí in particular; for example, being followed, stopped or arrested without due cause, or having your home or office 'watched'
0333 Menacing phone calls	This could be used against banks, solicitors, or debt-collection agencies who threaten 'consequences' for non-payment of debts, fines, bills etc
0334 Incitement to hatred offences	
0335 Demanding payment of debt causing alarm	This could be used against banks, solicitors, or debt-collection agencies who threaten 'consequences' for non-payment of debts, fines, bills etc
0411 Dangerous driving causing serious bodily harm	In the event of a traffic collision or hit-and-run incident
0412 Driving/In charge of a vehicle while over legal alcohol limit	
0413 Driving / In charge of a vehicle under the influence of drugs	
0414 Dangerous/careless driving and motorway offences	
0415 Speeding	
0421 Endangerment with potential for serious harm/death	Any scenario involving the authorities which has the potential for serious harm or death, such as a violent arrest or attempted arrest without due cause
0422 Abandoning a child, child neglect and cruelty	When the authorities conspire to separate children from their parents
0423 Unseaworthy/Dangerous use of boat or ship	When marine authorities raid a fishing vessel (for example) for blocking the Shell pipelayer?

0424 False alarm/Interference with aircraft or air transport facilities	
0425 Endangering traffic offences	Any dangerous acts or activities involving vehicles such as placing 'official' obstacles on the road, or advancing vehicles towards legitimate demonstrators or protestors
0511 False Imprisonment	Any act (including false arrest) which restrains or detains someone in a place against their will
0512 Abduction of person under 16 years of age	Whenever a child is removed from their home by 'the authorities' (Gardai / TUSLA / HSE etc)
0611 Robbery of an establishment or institution	This charge could be levied against so-called white collar criminals such as bankers and civil servants who have in effect 'stolen' their wages and pensions from us – i.e. the institutions of the Irish State and its affiliates such as AIB
0612 Robbery of cash or goods in transit	
0613 Robbery from the person	The issuing of illegitimate fines, or when items are unlawfully seized in an arrest or a search of premises
0621 Blackmail, extortion	'Extortion' is defined as, "The practice of obtaining something, especially money, through force or threats"
0631 Carjacking, highjacking/unlawful seizure of aircraft/vessel	When a vehicle is seized by the authorities without proper cause or in illegitimate or suspicious circumstances
0711 Aggravated burglary	When one's home (or office) is raided and harm is caused to the occupier (incl. emotional / psychological harm)
0712 Burglary (not aggravated)	When one's residence / office is raided and items seized
0713 Possession of an article (with intent to burgle, steal, demand)	This could be used against solicitors and barristers who misuse their license to practice; or rogue Gardai using their 'equipment' (vehicles, batons, dodgy warrants etc)..
0811 Theft/Unauthorised taking of vehicle	When a vehicle is seized by the authorities without proper cause or in illegitimate or suspicious circumstances
0812 Interfering with vehicle (with intent to steal item or vehicle)	When property 'goes missing' after a stop or seizure of a vehicle
0821 Theft from person	The issuing of illegitimate fines, or when items are unlawfully seized in an arrest or a search of premises

0822 Theft from shop	
0823 Theft from vehicle	When property 'goes missing' after a stop or seizure of a vehicle
0824 Theft / Unauthorised taking of a pedal cycle	
0825 Theft of, or interference with, mail	Any provable instances where one's post is being interfered with by the authorities - or others
0826 Theft of other property	As stated
0831 Handling or possession of stolen property	As stated
0911 Fraud, deception, false pretence offences	This one applies mainly to solicitors and barristers who lie in Court documents or send you questionable 'bills'. Also applies to any agent of the State who is engaged in fraud, deception or 'pretending' to do a particular job
0912 Forging an instrument to defraud	Rewriting, backdating or stating deliberate untruths in official letters. Or any affidavit or document submitted to the Gardaí or the Courts which is deceptive
0913 Possession of an article for use in fraud, deception or extortion	Any 'instrument' used by the authorities (paperwork, vehicles, uniforms) whilst committing crime
0914 Falsification of accounts	
0915 Offences under the Companies Act	This one is interesting given the fact that certain State agencies (such as the Courts Service) are actually registered as private companies
0916 Offences under the Investment Intermediaries Act	
0917 Offences under the Stock Exchange Act	
0921 Money laundering	
0922 Embezzlement	Converting public funds for private use
0923 Fraud against the European Union	
0924 Importation/Sale/Supply of tobacco	
0931 Counterfeiting notes and coins	
0941 Corruption (involving public office holder)	Any time that any 'official' does something improper for

	personal gain or to improve their circumstances – such as taking bribes or covering-up crimes by colleagues
1011 Importation of drugs	
1012 Cultivation or manufacture of drugs	
1021 Possession of drugs for sale or supply	
1022 Possession of drugs for personal use	
1031 Forged or altered prescription offences	
1032 Obstruction under the Drugs Act	
1111 Causing an explosion	
1112 Making of explosives	
1113 Possession of explosives	
1114 Chemical weapons offences	
1121 Discharging a firearm	
1122 Possession of a firearm	The *inappropriate* display of a firearm by a Garda - in a public Courthouse for example?
1131 Possession of offensive weapons (not firearms)	
1141 Fireworks Offences (for sale, IGNITING etc.)	
1211 Arson	
1212 Criminal damage (not arson)	If damage is caused to one's property due to improper actions such as breaking down a door etc
1221 Litter offences	
1311 Affray/Riot/Violent disorder	When Gardaí in particular misuse their authority in crowd-control situations, or when their actions provoke, instigate or cause violence or disorder
1312 Public order offences	
1313 Drunkenness offences	

1314 Air rage-disruptive or drunken behaviour on aircraft	
1321 Forcible entry and occupation (not burglary)	If damage is caused to one's home or property during an arrest or repossession
1322 Trespass on lands or enclosed areas	As above
1331 Liquor licensing offences	
1332 Registered clubs offences	
1333 Special restaurant offences	
1341 Brothel keeping	
1342 Organisation of prostitution	
1343 Prostitution, including soliciting etc.	
1351 Offences under the Betting Acts	
1352 Collecting money without permit, unauthorised collection	This may apply to the issuing of fines by certain 'official bodies' or orders from judges to 'donate to the poor box'
1353 Offences under Gaming and Lotteries Acts	
1354 Permit/License offences for casual/street trading	
1361 Bestiality	
1362 Indecency	
1363 Allowing a child (under 16 years) to beg	
1364 Bigamy	
1365 Begging	
1411 Driving licence-failure to have, produce, etc.	
1412 Insurance-failure to have, produce, display, etc.	
1421 No tax, non-display of tax, unregistered vehicle etc.	

1422 Misuse of Trade Licence	
1431 Misuse of trailers, weight and other offences	
1432 Obstruction under Road Traffic Acts	When a person is stopped by a Garda in circumstances which might be dangerous to other road users
1433 Other road offences	
1441 Road Transport - carriage of goods offences	
1442 Public Service Vehicle offences	
1443 Light rail offences (Luas)	
1511 Treason	Defined as: *"A violation of allegiance to one's State. The betrayal of a trust or confidence; breach of faith; treachery."*
1514 Impersonating member of An Garda Síochána	Are members of An Garda Síochána guilty of this if they are NOT doing their jobs properly and are in breach of their solemn Garda Oath?
1515 Electoral offences including personation	
1516 Public mischief-annoying phone calls, wasting police time	Any Garda who is NOT doing their job properly is arguably wasting police time. Likewise with false allegations or reports *by* Gardaí to other agencies
1517 Criminal Assets Bureau offences	
1518 Non compliance with Garda direction	Does this also apply to non-compliance with a legitimate citizen's arrest – by a citizen?
1521 Criminal organisation offences (organised crime)	If State agencies are engaged in systematic wrongdoing, does this render them a criminal organisation?
1522 Conspiracy to commit a crime	Any official or agent of the State who is knowingly involved in the preparations for, and/or the commission of a crime
1531 Perjury	Perjury is the intentional act of lying under oath or swearing a false oath (written or spoken) in any official proceeding (such as tribunal or a Court)
1532 Interfering with a jury (embracery)	This could apply to judges who engineer the submissions

	in a jury trial to secure a predetermined result
1533 Assisting offenders	Rogue authority figures helping other rogue authority figures commit or cover-up their crimes?
1534 Public mischief, pervert course of justice, conceal offence	'Public mischief' is making false accusations. Any authority figure who does ANYTHING to interfere with, obstruct or pervert justice is guilty of this offence
1541 Escape or help to escape from custody	Authority figures who try to assist colleagues from being held accountable may be guilty of this offence
1542 Prison offences	
1551 Breach of Domestic Violence Order (protection, safety, barring)	
1552 Breach of bail	
1553 Failure to comply under Sex Offenders Act	
1554 Breach of order under Family Law Act	
1556 Other failure to comply with court order, jury summons, warrant etc.	This offence applies to any occasion when 'they' fail to respect a summons or a court order
1611 Illegal importation of animals	
1612 Control of horses offences	
1613 Dog ownership offences (licence, control etc.)	
1614 Offences against animals	
1621 Breaches of EU fishing quota/related EU regulation	
1622 Merchant shipping/Maritime safety offences	
1631 Unauthorised accessing of data	When 'official bodies' (such as Gardaí) listen in to phone calls, intercept emails or post without a warrant
1632 Recording, possession, distribution of counterfeit material	

1633 Unauthorised broadcasting and illegal signal reception	When 'official bodies' (such as Gardaí) listen in to phone calls and/or intercept emails without a warrant
1641 Abortion	
1642 Procuring or assisting in abortion	
1643 Concealment of birth	
1644 Destroying/Disposing of a dead body	If authority figures are alerted as to the whereabouts of a dead body and do NOT investigate, then they may be guilty of conspiracy under this charge
1645 Pawnbroking offences	
1646 Offences in connection with rail travel	
1647 Employment permit offences (relating to non-Irish national)	
1648 Immigration offences/carrier liability	

Please remember that this list is only an aid to help you determine what *criminal* offences may have been committed against you, so that when you lodge a complaint or issue a private prosecution, you prevent any attempt by the authorities to fog the issue and claim for example that 'this is an issue for the Civil Courts'. This excuse has been used many times by the Gardaí when presented with formal *criminal* complaints of fraud, perjury, and other deliberate attempts to interfere with the administration of justice for example - where the usual response is to try to convince the would-be complainant that 'this is a civil matter'. But as can be clearly seen in the text of the letter on p.130 it IS the responsibility of An Garda Síochána to deal with instances of fraud and perjury. But unfortunately, they seem to keep forgetting this. What is genuinely unsettling is the fact that we had to press so hard, for so long, to just get a simple acknowledgement that fraud and perjury in the Courts was a an actual crime - to be dealt with by Gardaí! But now that this is an established fact, then WE are the fools if we let unscrupulous solicitors and barristers - and even judges - get away with this any more. So, if the Gardaí don't act, then let's issue proceedings in our own names.

Another major area of concern are the routine frauds and deceptions being carried out by public officials and elected representatives when expense claims are overstated for instance; when forged invoices are submitted; when public funds are squandered recklessly; and when contracts and tenders are used to garnish 'favours' (for HSE Managers for example). The Gardaí and the DPP are *supposed* to be chasing up these crimes - and are *supposed* to be prosecuting these offences in our names - but for some mysterious reason, they don't appear to be too interested in going near anyone 'connected'. So, let's not forget the fact that every single tax-payer in this country (and that means everyone who has to buy a pint of milk or a loaf of bread) - that we ALL have a direct 'interest' in these crimes, because it is OUR money that is being squandered, stolen and embezzled. This opens the door for ANY citizen to prosecute these offenders, as covered in Part 2 of this Guide.

PART 2

THE COMMON INFORMER LEGISLATION

The PETTY SESSIONS (Ireland) ACT, 1851

AN IRISH PETTY SESSIONS.—(SEE NEXT PAGE.)

Prosecuting by Common Informer - An Overview

(Abridged, from various sources as indicated)

Any member of the public, acting as a **'common informer'** can go directly to the Court to take a prosecution. The **common informer** acting as a prosecutor must present evidence which is admissible, legally obtained and not hearsay. Tribunal proceedings or reports are not admissible in any prosecutions. A summary offence is a minor offence, triable in the District Court with the judge acting as judge and jury and a maximum penalty of two years in jail or a €1,5000 fine. A summary offence may be prosecuted by a **common informer** provided there is no statutory provision to the contrary. They may of course also be prosecuted by the Garda, aided by the DPP. **The DPP has no power to intervene in summary proceedings to force the withdrawal of a prosecution brought by a common informer.** An indictable offence is a more serious offence, triable in the Circuit or Central Criminal Court with a jury and no limit on penalty. An indictable offence may only be prosecuted by the DPP. **A common informer** can pursue indictable proceedings in the early stages up to the order for return for trial but the DPP alone can pursue it from then to a verdict. *(Village Magazine, Feb 2013)*

* * *

At common law, any private individual capable of giving information about the commission of an offence, such as the victim of that offence, could prosecute as a **'common informer'**. This right to pursue a private prosecution remains, but **common informer**s are no longer competent to prosecute charges on indictment.* In practice, few victims mount private prosecutions through the District Courts despite their entitlement to do so.

* Section 9(1) of the Criminal Justice (Administration) Act 1924 abolished the right of **common informers** to prosecute cases on indictment. See further Walsh (2002) at pp.592-4. *(Trinity College Law School, 2007)*

* * *

No single body or person has a monopoly in the prosecution of criminal offences in Ireland. At common law any person (known as a **common informer**) is competent to initiate and conduct a criminal prosecution. This broad competence is now confined to minor offences which are tried summarily (Criminal Justice (Administration) Act, 1924, Sect. 9). For offences which will be tried by judge and jury (more serious offences) the **common informer** can still initiate the prosecution and maintain it up to the point where the defendant is sent for trial by judge and jury (State (Ennis) v Farrell, 1966, IR 107). At this point the prosecution will either be taken over by the public prosecutor or it will fall. Prosecutorial powers also vest in several statutory bodies… Like the **common informer** these bodies are confined to summary prosecutions. Where a statutory body fails to take a prosecution in any case which is within its remit the public prosecutor can step in and initiate the prosecution (Attorney General v Healy, 1928, IR 460). *(From a Report by Rita Cahill)*

* * *

The common law recognises the right of the **common informer** to prosecute summary offences. A **common informer** is a member of the public and cannot be a body corporate (GAA v Windle Unreported, Supreme Court June 22, 1993). A **common informer** can, however, be a person who is not an eye-witness. In McCormack v Carroll (1910) 45 ILTR 7, Pallas LCB held that a fishery inspector who was not an eye-witness could act as a **common informer**. In a modern context, there are many statutory bodies (such as local authorities, the HSE and the ODCE) which are given a specific right to prosecute certain offences summarily by the legislature. Previously a garda prosecuting a summary offence without the fiat of the DPP would do so as a **common informer** (see DPP v Roddy [1977] IR 177). This would appear to have been brought to an end by section 8 of the Garda Síochána Act 2005. *(James B Dwyer B.L., 2007)*

The Common Informer Procedure

The discovery of a process enshrined in Common Law whereby an ordinary citizen can apply directly to the District Court for a summons in order to hold another citizen to account for alleged wrongs, has been a most welcome discovery. However, despite this process being robustly defended by no less a figure than Justice Gerald Hogan in 2013, and despite all the quotes in our Constitution about 'justice for all' - it seems that the establishment - or at least those elements of the establishment who would prefer to remain unaccountable for their errant actions - are determined to obstruct or forestall any attempts by the public to avail of this legislation. Here's hoping that the information on the following pages will help ordinary citizens avail of justice without the necessity of having to rely on 'the authorities' or on costly legal teams to secure *some* accountability on the part of those who believe they are above the law.

The following pages detail the Court Rules and the respective legislation involved. As usual, the legal verbiage is obtuse, complicated and difficult to wade through, and you can be absolutely sure that if you make even the slightest error in 'procedure' the establishment will leap at that chance to prevent your prosecution going forwards. This has already been demonstrated in Castlebar Courthouse in 2015 where some of the most outrageous incidents of overt bias, injustice, collusion between State agencies, assaults and intimidation by Gardaí, and repeated breaches of due process have been deployed against lay litigants who have attempted to enforce this legislation. But don't be disheartened, because with each and every illegitimate attempt by the authorities to prevent or forestall these legitimate prosecutions brings thousands more eyes to bear on what is *really* going on in our Courts and in the corridors of power today.

The Procedure

1. First of all, make sure you have an absolutely solid case to present, with clear and unequivocal evidence of a wrong being committed against you. You will also have to be able to demonstrate to the judge that you are an 'interested party'.

2. Identify the crime(s) that have been committed from the lists provided at Part 1 of this Guide. If you can also identify whichever Acts, Laws or Statutes have been breached (see Part 3), that will help reinforce your claim - and prevent any improper attempts to dismiss the allegations.

3. Decide which District Court you need to approach. You may have to seek clarity from the Courts Service on this point depending on where the offence was committed; by whom; and whether or not you can use a Court in your own jurisdiction, or, in the offender's jurisdiction.

4. According to the official 1851 rules you now have a choice to either; (a) walk straight into a District Court Hearing and *verbally* address the Judge and make your allegations; or (b) you fill out the appropriate forms and present a sworn statement to the Court. Having not yet tried the purely verbal approach, we will continue here with the paper process - which we would recommend. (But if anyone wants to try the verbal route, please let us know how you get on).

5. Print out forms **15.1 Summons** and **15.3 Information** (see Appendix II) or, go to your local District Court Office and *try* to get copies. (Reports coming in indicate that the Courts Service has not been very forthcoming of late). There is NO charge for these forms, and NO duty to be paid. Alternatively, search the www.courts.ie website for the originals, but you should find that the ones produced in this Guide are probably more practical to use).

6. Fill out the information form (15.3) in clear language, making sure all of the required details are included.

7. Fill out the summons form (15.1) likewise, and make sufficient copies of both forms to be lodged with the Court, served on the other party, and to keep for yourself.

8. Take the forms into the next sitting of the District Court and present them to the Clerk, Registrar or Judge. (Note: The Courts Service have advised us that for practical reasons they would *prefer* if we notified them in advance of any intention to request a summons from a Judge, but apparently this is NOT required by the rules. You will have to weigh up the advantages and disadvantages of extending a courtesy that might work against your interests if the Court Service has advance notice of your intentions.)

9. If all is in order, then the Judge should sign the summons. However, in order to forestall any last-ditch efforts by the opposition to block your prosecution going forwards after-the-fact (such as taking judicial review proceedings based on the District Court Judge *not* doing his job properly) please make sure that you question the judge 'on the record' as to whether all procedures and protocols have been properly followed.

10. Next, you 'serve' the summons on the accused either in person or by pre-paid registered post. Make sure you are absolutely clear on what the service requirements are, or else this will afford the opposition another opportunity to obstruct the progress of the case.

11. Turn up in Court on the appointed day to assume the role of prosecutor. Make sure you are well prepared with a clear and progressive list of questions, and that you have all of your evidence and witnesses to hand. Do *not* think that you can simply 'wing it' and rely on verbal arguments and common sense, because you can be sure that the opposition *will* be well prepared.

12. Naturally, you should ensure you are accompanied by other I-I Members and that contemporaneous notes are taken during the Hearing using the Court Report Forms in Appendix II. Follow all the usual I-I procedures for attending Court (including wearing your I-I badges).

- Open with a Constitutional affirmation (see Appendix II).

- Ask all officials present to identify themselves and affirm their oaths of office.

- Make sure that things progress at YOUR pace and with YOUR full understanding.

- Make sure someone fills out a Court Hearing Report form for your records (p.290)

- Do not allow yourself to be intimidated, rushed, bamboozled, diverted or otherwise distracted from the matter at hand. Stay on script, politely but firmly.

- If the opposition does not abide by the rules, point this out 'for the record'.

- If the Judge does not abide by the rules - point this out 'for the record'- reminding the Court that you are 'standing by the Constitution' and you are requiring him/her to do the same.

- If there is any blatant disregard for the law, for Court Rules or for the Constitution, then have the courage to denounce the proceedings (politely but firmly) and read out your 'Constitutional Declaration of Non-Cooperation' (on p.282 & p.283) and exit the Courtroom.

- Then, <u>without delay,</u> lodge further Common Informer proceedings *and* criminal complaints with the Gardaí as against any and all who participated in the illegalities, including any Officers of the Court (clerks ' registrars / solicitors / barristers) and/or members of the judiciary. Send each a Formal Notification of a Criminal Complaint (Appendix II) - and send a copy to *Integrity Ireland* for our records, and for publication.

The District Court Forms required for the Common Informer procedure can be found in Appendix II on pages 278 - 280.

This is the original legislation. It is still in force today. Given that this legislation was introduced during British rule, any references to Britain or its other colonies; to out-of-date currency; or any other irrelevant reference, can of course be ignored. A full I-I breakdown of this important legislation continues on the following pages, and it is crucial that you are completely familiar with all aspects if you are to lodge a successful action against an errant authority figure.

PETTY SESSIONS (Ireland) ACT, 1851

Informations and Complaints.

10. Whenever information shall be given to any justice that any person has committed or is suspected to have committed any treason, felony, misdemeanor, or other offence, within the limits of the jurisdiction of such justice, for which such person shall be punishable either by indictment or upon a summary conviction; or that any person has committed or is suspected to have committed any such crime or offence elsewhere out of the jurisdiction of such justice, either in Great Britain or Ireland, or in the Isles of Man, Jersey, Guernsey, Alderney, or Sark, and such person is residing or being, or is suspected to reside or be, within the limits of the jurisdiction of such justice; or that any person has committed or is suspected to have committed any crime or offence whatsoever on the high seas, or in any creek, harbour, haven, or other place in which the Admiralty of England or Ireland have or claim to have jurisdiction, or on land beyond the seas, for which an indictment can be legally preferred in any place in the United Kingdom of England and Ireland, and such person is residing or being, or is suspected to reside or be, within the limits of the jurisdiction of such justice; or whenever a complaint shall be made to any justice as to any other matter arising within the limits of his jurisdiction, upon which he shall have power to make a summary order, it shall be lawful for such justice to receive such information or complaint, and to proceed in respect to the same, subject to the following provisions:

1. Whenever it is intended that a summons only shall issue to require the attendance of any person, the information or complaint may be made either with or without oath, and either in writing or not, according as the justice shall see fit:

2. But whenever it is intended that a warrant shall issue for the arrest or committal of any person, the information or complaint shall be in writing, and on the oath of the complainant or of some person or persons, on his behalf:

3. Whenever any such information shall have been taken on oath and in writing that any person has committed or is suspected to have committed any indictable crime or offence (or any offence for which such person shall be punishable upon summary conviction, and for whose arrest the justice shall issue a warrant), it shall be lawful for the justice, if he shall see fit, to bind the informant or complainant by recognizance (A a.*) or (C.) to appear at the court or place where the defendant is to be tried or the complaint is to be heard to prosecute or give evidence, as the case may be, against such person:

4. In all cases of summary jurisdiction the complaint shall be made, when it shall relate to the nonpayment of any poor rate, county rate, or other public tax, at any time after the date of the warrant authorizing the collection of the same, and, when it shall relate to the nonpayment of money for wages, hire, or tuition, within one year from the termination of the term or period in respect of which it shall be payable, and, when it shall relate to any trespass, within two months from the time when the trespass shall have occurred, and in any other case within six months from the time when the cause of complaint shall have arisen, but not otherwise:

And in all cases of summary jurisdiction any person against whom any such information or complaint shall have been made in writing shall, upon being amenable or appearing in person or by counsel or attorney, be entitled to receive from the clerk of petty sessions a copy of such information or complaint, on payment of the sum of sixpence to such clerk; and such clerk shall in no case allow the original information or complaint to be taken out of his possession.

Process to enforce appearance.

11. The manner in which persons against whom any such informations or complaints as aforesaid shall have been received by any justice shall be made to appear to answer to the same shall be subject to the following provisions:

> 1. In all cases of indictable crimes and offences (where an information that any person has committed the same shall have been taken in writing and on oath) the justice shall issue a warrant (B b.) to arrest and bring such person before him, or some other justice of the same county, to answer to the complaint made in the information (and which warrant may be issued or executed on a Sunday as well as on any other day); or if he shall think that the ends of justice would be thereby sufficiently answered, it shall be lawful for him, instead of issuing such warrant, to issue a summons in the first instance to such person, requiring him to appear and answer to the said complaint; but nothing herein contained shall prevent any justice from issuing a warrant for the arrest of such person at any time before or after the time mentioned in such summons for his appearance; and whenever such person shall afterwards appear or be brought before any such justice, he shall proceed according to the provisions herein-after contained as to taking the evidence against such person, and committing such person for trial:

> 2. In all cases of summary jurisdiction the justice may issue his summons (B a.) directed to such person, requiring him to appear and answer to the complaint; and it shall not be necessary that such justice shall be the justice or one of the justices by whom the complaint shall be afterwards heard and determined; and in all cases of offences where such person shall not appear at the required time and place, and it shall be proved on oath either that he was personally served with such summons or that he is keeping out of the way of such service, (the complaint being in writing and on oath,) the justice may issue a warrant to arrest and bring such person before him or some other justice of the same county, to answer to the said complaint; and when such person shall afterwards be arrested under such warrant, the justice before whom he shall be brought may either by warrant (E b.) commit him to gaol, until the hearing of the complaint, or may discharge him upon his entering into a recognizance (C), with or without sureties, at the discretion of the justice, conditioned for his appearance at such hearing:

And each summons or warrant shall be signed by the justice or one of the justices issuing the same, and it shall state shortly the cause of complaint, and no summons or warrant shall be signed in blank; and in every case where the offence shall have occurred or the cause of complaint shall have arisen within the petty sessions district for which the justice issuing any such summons or warrant shall act, but the party or witness to whom such summons shall be directed or against whom such warrant shall be issued shall reside in an adjoining county, it shall be lawful for such justice to compel the appearance of such party or witness at the hearing of the charge or complaint within such district, in like manner as if such party or witness resided in such district, although such justice may not be a justice of such adjoining county.

Service of summonses. *(Abridged)*

3. Every summons shall be served upon the person to whom it is directed by delivering to him a copy of such summons, or, if he cannot be conveniently met with, by leaving such copy for him at his last or most usual place of abode, or at his office, warehouse, counting-house, shop, factory, or place of business, with some inmate of the house not being under sixteen years of

age, a reasonable time before the hearing of the complaint; and such last-mentioned service shall be deemed sufficient service of such summons in every case except where personal service shall be specially required by this Act; and in every case the person who shall serve such summons shall endorse on the same the time and place where it was served, and shall attend with the same at the hearing of the complaint to depose., if necessary, to such service:

Powers to enforce attendance of witnesses.
13. Whenever it shall be made to appear to any justice that any person within the jurisdiction of such justice is able to give material evidence for the prosecution in cases of indictable offences, or for the complainant or defendant in cases of summary jurisdiction, and will not voluntarily appear for the purpose of being examined as a witness, such justice may proceed as follows:

1. He may issue a summons (B a.) to such person, requiring him to appear at a time and place mentioned in such summons, to testify what he may know concerning the matter of the information or complaint, and (if the justice shall see fit) to bring with him and produce for examination such accounts, papers, or other documents, as shall be in his possession or power, and as shall be deemed necessary by such justice; but in any case of an indictable crime or offence, whenever the justice shall be satisfied by proof upon oath that it is probable that such person will not attend to give evidence without being compelled so to do, then, (the information or complaint being in writing and on oath,) instead of issuing such summons as aforesaid, he may issue a warrant (B b.) in the first instance for the arrest of such person:

2. And in any case, when any person to whom a summons shall be issued in the first instance shall neglect or refuse to appear at the time and place appointed by such summons, and no just excuse shall be offered for such neglect or refusal, then, (the information or complaint being in writing and on oath,) after proof upon oath that such summons was personally served upon such person, or that such person is keeping out of the way of such service, and that he is able to give material evidence in the case, the justice before whom such person should have appeared may issue a warrant (B b.) to arrest such person, and to bring him at the time and place appointed for the hearing of the case, to testify and to produce such accounts, papers, and documents as may be required as aforesaid:

3. In all cases of prosecutions for offences the evidence of the informer or party aggrieved shall be admissible in proof of the offence; and in all cases of complaints on which a justice can make an order for the payment of money, or otherwise, the evidence of the complainant shall be admissible in proof of his complaint; and in cases of wages, hire, or tuition the evidence of the master or employer may, in the discretion of the justices, be admitted in proof against the complaint:

4. All witnesses shall be examined upon oath; and any justice before whom any such witness shall appear for the purpose of being so examined shall have full authority to administer to every such witness the usual oath.

5. Whenever any person shall appear as a witness, either in obedience to a summons or by virtue of a warrant, (or shall be present, and shall be verbally required by the justice or justices to give evidence,) and he shall refuse to be examined upon oath concerning the matter of the information or complaint, or shall refuse to take such oath, or having taken such oath shall refuse to answer such questions concerning the said matter as shall then be put to him, or shall refuse or neglect to produce any such accounts, papers, or documents as aforesaid, (without, offering any just excuse for such refusal,) the justice or justices then present may adjourn the proceedings for any period not exceeding eight clear days, and may in the meantime by warrant (E b.) commit the said witness to gaol, unless he shall sooner consent to be sworn or to testify as aforesaid, or to produce such accounts, papers,

or documents, as the case may be; and if such witness, upon being brought up upon such adjourned hearing, shall again refuse to be sworn, or to testify as aforesaid, or to produce such accounts, papers, or documents, as the case may be, the said justices, If they shall see fit, may again adjourn the proceedings, and commit the witness for the like period, and so again from time to time until he shall consent to be sworn or to testify as aforesaid, or to produce such accounts, papers, or documents, as the case may be (provided that no such imprisonment shall in any case of summary jurisdiction exceed one month in the whole); but nothing herein contained shall be deemed to prevent the justice or justices from sending any such case for trial, or otherwise disposing of the same in the meantime, according to any other sufficient evidence which shall have been received by him or them:

6. Whenever in cases of indictable offences the justice or justices shall see fit, they may bind the witnesses by recognizance (A b.*) or (C.) to appear at the trial of the offender and give evidence against him; and whenever any witness shall refuse to be so bound it shall be lawful for the justice or justices by warrant (E b.) to commit him to the gaol of the county or place in which the person accused is to be tried, there to be imprisoned until the trial of the person accused, unless in the meantime such witness shall duly enter into recognizance (C.) before some justice of the county in which such gaol shall be situated; but if afterwards, from want of sufficient evidence or other cause, the justice or justices before whom the person accused shall have been brought shall not commit him or hold him to bail, it shall be lawful for such justice or justices or any other justice of the county by warrant (E d.) to order the keeper of the gaol to discharge such witness:

7. In all cases of summary jurisdiction it shall be lawful for the justices by whom any order for payment of money, not being in the nature of a penalty for an offence, shall be made, to order the party at whose instance any witness shall have been summoned to pay to such witness such sum, not exceeding two shillings and sixpence, as to such justices shall seem fit, for his expenses or loss of time for each day of attending to give evidence, and, in default of payment thereof at such time as such justice shall appoint, then to issue a, warrant to levy the amount thereof by distress of the goods of such party:

And no person who shall be summoned to attend before any court of petty sessions, or before any justice out of petty sessions, as a witness, shall be liable to arrest for debt whilst at such court, or at the place where such justice shall sit, or whilst proceeding to or returning from the same, provided he shall proceed and return by the most direct road without unnecessary delay; and it shall be lawful for the court out of which the writ or process shall have issued to order the discharge of any person who shall be so arrested.

Courts Rules Pertaining to the Common Informer Procedure

1. (1). Where in the first instance a summons is sought pursuant to section 10 of the Petty Sessions (Ireland) Act 1851 to require the attendance before the Court of a person against whom a complaint is made, the complaint shall be made to a Judge and may be made with or without oath as the Judge shall direct.

(2). Where the complaint is made on oath it shall be made by sworn information (Form 15.3 Schedule B).

(3). Having received such complaint, the Judge may issue a summons (Form 15.1 Schedule B) in any case in which that Judge has jurisdiction in the district to which he or she is assigned.

Application to and issue of summons by Court Office.
2. (1). When, upon application made to an appropriate office (within the meaning of section 1(14) of the Courts (No. 3) Act 1986 as amended) pursuant to section 1(3) of the Courts (No. 3) Act 1986 as amended, for the issue of a summons in relation to an offence, a summons is issued, such summons shall be in the Form 15.2 Schedule B.

Contents of summons and Court to which returnable.
3. (1). A summons shall state shortly and in ordinary language particulars of the cause of complaint or offence alleged, and shall state the name of the person against whom the complaint has been made or who is alleged to have committed the offence and the address (if known) at which he or she ordinarily resides.

(2). A summons issued by an appropriate office and to which rule 2(1) of this Order relates shall also notify such person that he or she will be accused of that offence at a sitting of the District Court to be specified in the summons. Such summons shall also contain the particulars specified in section 1(6) of the Courts (No. 3) Act 1986 as amended.

(3). Every summons shall require the appearance of the person to whom it is directed at a sitting of the Court having jurisdiction to deal with the complaint or the offence alleged, provided that the court at which such person is required to appear shall -

(a) Where the summons is issued by a Judge, be a court within the area of jurisdiction, of that Judge, or

(b) Where the summons is issued by an appropriate office be a court within the district in which a judge has jurisdiction in relation to the offence to which the summons relates.

4. Two or more complaints or offences may be alleged in the one summons.

O.15, r.5 Signing of summonses
5. (1). A summons issued by a Judge shall be signed by the Judge who issues it and no summons shall be signed in blank.

(2). A summons against a person who is a member of the Garda Síochána shall be signed by a Judge.

(3). (a) Where a summons is signed by a Judge such summons shall not be avoided by reason of the death of that Judge or by reason of his or her ceasing to hold office

(b) Where a summons is issued by an appropriate office such summons shall not be avoided by reason of the death of the appropriate District Court Clerk whose name is specified on the summons or by reason of his or her ceasing to hold office.

Copies for service

6. In the case of every summons issued otherwise than by transmitting it by electronic means to the person who applied for it or a person acting on his or her behalf, there shall be issued with such summons a copy thereof for service upon each person to whom the summons is directed. Where a summons is issued by transmitting it by electronic means to the person who applied for it or a person acting on his or her behalf, a true copy of such summons shall be served upon each person to whom the summons is directed by electronic means.

May be served in any part of the State.

7. A summons may be served in any part of the State and upon service being effected in a manner prescribed by these Rules, the person against whom the complaint is made or the offence is alleged shall be as effectively bound by the proceedings as if he or she resided within the area of jurisdiction of the Judge issuing it or (if issued out of an appropriate office) within the limits of the court area or areas to which the appropriate Clerk whose name is specified on the summons has been assigned.

8. Where an enactment constituting an offence states the offence to be the doing or the omission to do any one of a number of different acts in the alternative, or states any part of the offence in the alternative, the acts, omissions or other matters stated in the alternative in the enactment may be stated either in the alternative or in the conjunctive in the summons alleging such offence.

9. In alleging an offence contrary to any statute or statutes it shall be sufficient to state the substance of the offence in ordinary language with such particulars of the offence as may be necessary for giving reasonable information as to the nature of the complaint, and it shall not be necessary to negative any exception or exemption from or qualification to the operation of a statute creating such offence.

Summons in lieu of a warrant

10. Where under Order 16, rule 1(1) of these Rules a warrant is sought for the arrest of a person charging that person with having committed an indictable offence a Judge may, if he or she thinks fit, instead of issuing a warrant issue a summons requiring the appearance of that person, notwithstanding that the complaint had been made by information on oath and in writing. A Judge who has issued such summons may at any time (the complaint having been made by information) issue a warrant for the arrest of that person.

(Sketches courtesy of www.maggieblanck.com)

* Provisions relating to the issue of summonses in matters other than criminal matters are contained in Order 99 of these Rules. (See following page)

District Court Rules, Order: 99

Issue of summonses by a clerk in matters other than criminal matters *

[Summons — application for]

1.   Whenever it is intended to commence proceedings (not being proceedings to which the Courts (No. 3) Act, 1986 relates) in the District Court against a person, and the issue of a summons is sought requiring the appearance of that person before the Court, on a matter or issue which the Court has jurisdiction to hear and determine, application to sign and issue such summons may, unless otherwise provided, be made to the Clerk for the court area wherein that person ordinarily resides or carries on any profession, business or occupation.

[— Form of, signing and issue of]

2.   The applicant for the issue of such summons shall lodge with such Clerk a duly completed summons in the Form 99.1, Schedule C (or such modification thereof as may be appropriate), together with a copy or copies for service. The Clerk shall unless otherwise provided by statute or by rules of court, list the matter or issue for hearing at a sitting of the Court, record the place, date and time of hearing on each document and, having signed and dated the same, shall issue them to the applicant for service.

[— Court to which returnable]

3.   Every summons issued under this Order shall require the appearance of each person to whom it is directed at a sitting of the Court having jurisdiction to deal with the matter or issue set out in the summons, provided that such sitting shall be a sitting of the Court for the court area to which such Clerk is assigned and shall be within the district in which a Judge of the District Court has jurisdiction in relation to the matter or issue aforesaid.

[— Service of lodgment of]

4.   Save where otherwise provided, the provisions of Order 10 (Service of Documents) of these Rules shall mutatis mutandis apply to summonses signed and issued in proceedings to which this Order relates.

[— Order 15 (in part) to apply to]

5.   The provisions of rules 4, 5, 6, 7, 8 and 9 (with any necessary modifications) of Order 15 of these Rules shall apply to summonses signed and issued in proceedings to which this Order relates.

Just a Thought: It might be an interesting tactic to deploy - especially in more serious cases - to initiate *indictable* proceedings in the District Court (via the Common Informer process), which then has to be continued (or not) by the DPP. If the DPP (for whatever undisclosed reason) fails to prosecute, then you could issue *summary* proceedings for some lesser offence against the same perpetrator - and process the case to conclusion yourself, playing the role of prosecutor. This would not fall under the double-jeopardy rule (where a person cannot be tried twice for the same crime) because technically, they are two different offences. The only thing you would have to watch out for though, is the 6-month time limit for initiating summary proceedings.

---

*Provisions relating to the issue of summonses in respect of offences are contained in Order 15 of these Rules. (See previous pages)

"Prosecute a Banker" (A DIY guide for Village readers)

The following article was written for Village Magazine in January, 2011 by Barrister Gary Fitzgerald kindly reproduced here with the advisory that its contents may not be precisely pertinent in Ireland's 2015 legal system, noting that 'the establishment' is, apparently, actively seeking ways to 'water down' the legislation precisely because of the potential to hold errant establishment figures to account. So, no great surprises there either! So, lets make use of this valuable piece of legislation while we still can.

Since the beginning of the banking crisis in September 2008, the government's strategy has been to protect the banks at all costs. With the IMF/EU deal announced recently, it is now clear that the government intends that the taxpayer will pay for bank losses irrespective of the impact on public services and on the wider economy. The final cost of this policy is not yet known, and it may never be known. We have lost track of the billions of euro already spent and the billions more promised. The government's decisions may lead to national bankruptcy. The voters will get a chance to express their opinion on this policy in the upcoming general election.

It is also clear that there will not be any criminal prosecution of senior bankers under this government. More than two years have passed since this crisis began and apart from a little grandstanding by the Gardaí in March 2010 (with the arrest of Sean FitzPatrick) and the occasional public statement by the Gardaí, nothing appears to have happened. In a previous article I wrote about how some of these criminal offences were not very complex. Two in particular carry jail terms of up to 5 years and a number of board members from both Anglo Irish Bank and Irish Life and Permanent could be prosecuted and face jail terms of up to 35 years. Voters may take direct action against politicians on polling day, but is there any direct action they may take to prosecute white-collar criminals?

The general rule in criminal law is that the State prosecutes the defendant on behalf of the people. For serious cases the Director of Public Prosecutions (DPP) initiates the prosecution and for minor offences it is the responsibility of the individual Garda who is in charge of the case to initiate a prosecution. But audit is not the only possible source of criminality that could ground an action; and the Financial Regulator is, for example, investigating allegations that banks provided "false and misleading information" to NAMA about the value of their toxic property loans.

But there is a little-used process whereby any individual may initiate a criminal prosecution. This is known as the right of Common Informer. Over recent years the rights of the Common Informer have been limited by Acts of the Oireachtas, but the basic right still exists. The rest of this article will set out the process involved in taking a criminal case by way of Common Informer. But first, it is necessary to explain some principles of sentencing in criminal law.

Sentencing Offenders

A summary offence is a minor offence, triable in the District Court, with the judge acting as both judge and jury. The maximum penalty is two years in jail or a fine of up to €5,000. An indictable offence is a serious offence, triable in the Circuit Criminal Court or the Central Criminal Court. The case is heard by a judge and jury and there is no limit on jail term or fine. The punishment available for any individual offence is set out in the relevant statute. For many crimes the statute sets out a punishment if the case is tried in the District Court and a heavier punishment if the case is heard in the Circuit Criminal Court. The choice of court is, in general, determined by the prosecuting authority (such as the DPP).

For example, S197 of the Companies Act 1990 makes it an offence for an officer of a company to give a false statement to the company's auditors. S240 (as amended) sets the punishment for that offence as follows:

Summary offence a fine of €1,900 and/or up to 1 year in jail

Indictable offence a fine of €12,600 and/or up to 5 years in jail

Should more than one false statement be given to auditors, for example, were a false statement made in each of 7 different years, the defendant could be charged with 7 instances of the same offence. Were the prosecution to be successful, it would be up to the judge to determine if the sentences should be served concurrently or consecutively. Were the former chosen then the defendant would serve a 5 year jail term, while in the latter case he would serve a 35 year jail term (5 years x 7 offences). The normal procedure is for concurrent sentences to be handed down but if the offences are serious enough then the judge may impose a consecutive sentence, or a combination of both.

The Common Informer procedure
Any private individual may initiate a criminal prosecution as a Common Informer. The process begins with the making of a complaint under S10 of the Petty Sessions Act 1851. That act states that a complaint is made to a judge of the District Court. If the judge is satisfied that there is a prima facia case then he must issue a summons for the defendant to appear in court to answer the complaint. The judge must ensure that there is substance to the complaint and may refuse to issue a summons. But the evidential threshold that the Common Informer must reach at this stage is low. There is no time-limit on the making of the complaint by the Common Informer for offences that may be tried either in the District Court or the Circuit Criminal Court.

Right at the outset the Common Informer has an important decision to make. He may seek a prosecution for summary offences only. In this case the Common Informer has full control of the prosecution and the DPP cannot interfere with the prosecution. Or the Common Informer may seek to try the offences as indictable offences. Here the Common Informer has control of the early stage of the proceedings but thereafter the DPP is obliged to take over. The DPP may either continue with the prosecution or decide to stop it.

This decision is a difficult one. On the one hand, in the District Court, the Common Informer has full control and there is no room for political interference. But on the other hand the possible punishment for the very serious crimes that have been committed is low. It may be that no one will ever spend time in jail for these banking offences due to inaction by the authorities. In this case, it would be a success if a 1 year jail term were handed down. Also the Common Informer must produce evidence to prove each element of the offence, a point which is discussed further below.

The solution here might be to initially seek to have the offences tried in the Circuit Criminal Court. If the DPP does not continue with the prosecution, then the case may be taken again, this time in the District Court. This should not fall foul of the long standing legal principle of double jeopardy. This states that it is not possible for a defendant to be tried for the same crime twice. It was developed as a vital protection of citizens from an abuse of the power of prosecution by the State. But according to S4A(4) of the Criminal Justice Act 1967 that does not arise in these circumstances. If the DPP does not continue with the prosecution, another case may be taken at a later time. It is not clear if this section would withstand the inevitable constitutional challenge by any proposed defendants.

The Evidence
The most difficult part of any private criminal prosecution will be the gathering of evidence. The State has wide resources such as powers of arrest, search and seizure. It may detain suspects for questioning and ask the court to issue warrants for the searching of offices and private homes. The Common Informer has none of these resources, but the burden of proof is the same. In order for a prosecution to succeed, the Common Informer must be able to prove all the elements of

the offence beyond a reasonable doubt. Attempting a prosecution without this evidence is, at best, counterproductive. Some of the white-collar crimes are complex, but others are relatively simple. But even for simple offences the evidence must be sufficient to meet the burden of proof. The offence of giving a misleading statement to an auditor contains the following elements:

- The statement must be false, misleading or deceptive;

- It must relate to a material fact;

- It must be made by an officer of the company;

- It must be made to the auditors of a company; and

- The defendant must have known the statement was false, or have made the statement recklessly.

The key evidence here would be the testimony of the auditors. The precise date and time of the making of the statement would need to be proven. Co-operation of the auditors would be desirable but not essential. Expert evidence must be tendered that proves that the misleading statement was material to the audit. Failure on any of those elements and the prosecution will also fail. But auditors are not the only possible crimes that could ground a and the Financial Regulator are investigating allegations that banks provided "false and misleading information" to NAMA about the value of their toxic property loans.

Conclusion
Following recent complaints from Michael McGrath TD, the Gardaí and the Financial Regulator are investigating allegations that banks provided "false and misleading information" to NAMA about the value of their toxic property loans. It is possible that complaints could also be made about possible inaccurate information provided by the banks some time before that – immediately before the bank guarantee. But both of these possible wrongdoings could also be prosecuted by Common Informers.

The right of a Common Informer is limited, but still very powerful. It has never been used in this way. Normally it is used as a procedural device to allow an individual Garda to initiate a prosecution. There is no reason why a properly researched, funded and proven case would not work. Any case would need to have access to legal advice from criminal lawyers, financial advice from accountants and auditors and sufficient resources to deal with the legal challenges that the powerful defendants would inevitably raise. But if the DPP and the incoming government fail to take action against Ireland's corporate criminals, ordinary citizens should use this residual power. It is vital for the future of our democracy that the rich and powerful are treated by the law on equal terms as the poor and weak.

Gary Fitzgerald is a practising barrister and recently resigned as chairman of the Greens National Executive Council.

Village Magazine, January 2011

*   *   *

So, no excuses any more folks - and no more winging and moaning about what the bad guys have been up to.. because here's your golden opportunity to take the initiative. Stop being a soft target for tricksters, thugs, tyrants and thieves in the corridors of power. This is OUR country and OUR children's futures they are messing with. 100 years since the Rising - and nearly 70 years of supposed independence - and we are *still* being taken for fools and amadans by a corrupt, arrogant, governing elite. 700 years of sweat, tears and bloodshed in order to throw off the yoke of oppression and injustice - and yet here we are all over again…?

PART
3

ACTS, LAWS & STATUTES

Law of the Republic of Ireland
(From Wikipedia, the free encyclopaedia)

The law of Ireland consists of; (i) constitutional law, (ii) statute law and (iii) common law. The highest law in the State is the Constitution of Ireland, from which all other law derives its authority. The Republic has a common-law legal system with a written constitution that provides for a parliamentary democracy based on the British parliamentary system, albeit with a popularly elected president, a separation of powers, a developed system of constitutional rights and judicial review of primary legislation.

The sources of Irish law reflect Irish history and the various parliaments whose law affected the country down through the ages. Notable omissions from the list include laws passed by the first and second Dáil, and the Brehon Laws which were traditional Celtic laws, the practice of which was only finally wiped out during the Cromwellian conquest of Ireland. These latter laws are void of legal significance and are of historical interest only.

(I) Constitutional Law: The Irish Constitution was enacted by a popular plebiscite held on 1 July 1937, and came into force on 29 December of the same year. The Constitution is the cornerstone of the Irish legal system and is held to be the source of power exercised by the legislative, judicial and executive branches of government. The Irish Supreme Court and High Court exercise judicial review over all legislation and may strike down laws if they are inconsistent with the constitution.

The Constitution can only be amended by referendum. A proposal to amend the Constitution is introduced into Dáil Éireann (the lower house of parliament) as a bill and if passed by the Dáil, and passed or deemed to have been passed by the Senate (the upper house), is put to the people. Only Irish citizens resident in the state may vote. There is no threshold for such referendums and a simple majority of voters is sufficient for a proposal to be passed. Once passed by the people the President signs the referendum bill into law. As of November 2011, there have been 33 such referendums: 23 of which were approved by the people and 10 of which were rejected. The constitution was also amended twice during an initial transitional period of three years following the election of the first President of Ireland, when amendments could be made without recourse to the people.

(II) Statute Law: Modern-day statute law is made by the bicameral National Parliament — more commonly know by its Irish name, the Oireachtas. Acts of the Oireachtas are split into sequentially numbered sections and may be cited by using a short title which gives the act a title roughly based on its subject matter and the year in which it was enacted. While the Oireachtas is bicameral, the upper house, the Senate, has little power which at most allows the Senate to delay rather than veto legislation, something that has only happened a small handful of times.

Article 50 of the Constitution of Ireland carried over all laws that had been in force in the Irish Free State prior to its coming into force on 29 December 1937. A similar function had been fulfilled by Article 73 of the Constitution of the Irish Free State, which carried over all legislation that had been in force in Southern Ireland. As a result, while the Irish state has been in existence for less than one hundred years, the statute book stretches back in excess of 800 years. By virtue of the Statute Law Revision Act 2007, the oldest Act currently in force in Ireland is the Fairs Act 1204. The statute law of Ireland includes law passed by the following:

Pre-union Irish Statutes:
- the King of England as a lawgiver for Ireland, and the Parliament of Ireland (1169–1800)

- English and British statutes, which applied to Ireland in their original enactment or were subsequently applied to Ireland

- the King of England (1066–1241)
- the Parliament of England (1241–1706)
- the Parliament of Great Britain (1707–1800)
- Statutes of the United Kingdom of Great Britain and Ireland
- the Parliament of the United Kingdom, which applied to Ireland in their original enactment or were subsequently applied to Ireland (1 January 1801 to 5 December 1922)
- Statutes of independent Ireland
- the Oireachtas of the Irish Free State (6 December 1922 to 28 December 1937)
- the present Oireachtas (from 29 December 1937 to date)

Secondary Legislation: Notwithstanding the declaration in the 1937 constitution that the Oireachtas is to be "the sole and exclusive" legislature, it has long been held that it is permissible for the Oireachtas to delegate its law-making power(s) to other bodies as long as such delegated legislation does not exceed the "principles and policies" set out in the relevant authorising statute.

All instances of delegated legislation in the Republic are known as statutory instruments, although only a small sub-set of these are numbered as statutory instruments and published by the Stationery Office. This latter subset is composed of statutory instruments which are required to be laid before the Oireachtas or which are of general application.

In addition, a body of charters, statutory rules and orders and other secondary legislation made prior to independence in 1922 continues to be in force in Ireland insofar as such legislation has not been revoked or otherwise ceased to be in force.

(III) Common Law: Ireland was the subject of the first extension of England's common law legal system outside England. While in England the creation of the common law was largely the result of the assimilation of existing customary law, in Ireland the common law was imported from England supplanting the customary law of the Irish. This, however, was a gradual process which went hand-in-hand with English (then British) influence in Ireland.

As with any common-law system, the Irish courts are bound by the doctrine of *stare decisis* ['let the decision stand'] to apply clear precedents set by higher courts and courts of co-ordinate jurisdiction. The main exception to this rule being that the Supreme Court has declared itself not to be bound by its own previous decisions.

While the doctrine clearly means that the present High Court is bound by decision of the present Supreme Court, it is not altogether clear whether the decisions of courts which previously performed the function of courts of last final appeal in Ireland – such as the British House of Lords – bind the present High Court. In Irish Shell v. Elm Motors, Mr. Justice McCarthy doubted that decisions of pre-independence courts bound the courts of the state, stating that "in no sense are our Courts a continuation of, or successors to, the British courts." However the other two judges on the panel hearing the case declined to express an opinion on the matter as it had not been argued at the hearing of appeal. Post-independence judgments of the British courts, and all judgments of the American and Commonwealth courts are of persuasive value only and do not bind the Irish courts.

European Union law: The European Communities Act 1972, as amended, provides that treaties of the European Union are part of Irish law, along with directly effective measures adopted under those treaties. It also provides that government ministers may adopt statutory instruments to implement European Union law and that as an exception to the general rule such statutory instruments have effect as if they were primary legislation.

International Law: Ireland is a dualist state and treaties are not part of Irish domestic law unless incorporated by the Oireachtas. An exception to this rule might well be the provision in the constitution which says that "Ireland accepts the generally recognised principles of international law as its rule of conduct in its relations with other States." However while this provision has been held to assimilate the doctrine of sovereign immunity into domestic law, the Supreme Court have held that the provision is not capable of conferring rights on individuals.

The dualist approach in international law contained in the Irish Constitution allows the state to sign and ratify treaties without incorporating them into domestic law. Thus while Ireland was one of the first states in Europe to ratify the European Convention on Human Rights it was one of the last to incorporate the Convention into domestic law. And when done it was not directly incorporated into Irish law but given indirect, sub-constitutional, interpretative incorporation.

In Crotty v. An Taoiseach, the Irish Supreme Court asserted a power to review the constitutionality of treaties signed by the state, such that the government could be prevented from signing up to international agreements which would be contrary to the constitution. A ruling which has resulted in ad hoc amendments to the constitution to permit the state to ratify treaties that might otherwise have been contrary to the constitution.

*   *   *

When it comes to a comprehensive understanding of the various Laws, Acts and Statutes that have a bearing on Irish society today, it is clear that we are subject to a mind-boggling array of overlapping rules, regulations, jurisdictions and interpretations of what can - and what cannot be done 'under the law'. In 2010 for example, 40 new or amended Public Acts came into force. In 2011 it was 41. In 2012, 53. Then 51 & 44 respectively for 2013 & 2014. Already we have some 33 entries for 2015 - and we still have a few months to go yet! That is a total of 262 changes to our laws in less than five years - and this doesn't even take into account the various attempts to amend the Constitution - sometimes repeatedly putting the same questions to the public until the 'right' decision is reached. The very fact that 'someone' has seen fit to make *"ad-hoc amendments to the Constitution"* is alarming enough in itself. It becomes even more worrying when one realizes that this is being done in order to facilitate the objectives of a government which is increasingly seen as ruthless, devious and without scruples when it comes to serving the amoral agendas of corporate interests. And if that abject 'service' requires that we tweak the Constitution a bit here or there - or bring in a few new Acts or Statutes - ah well, shur, what's the problem - because we all know by now that the Irish public will fall for anything.

In short, there are so many different laws, rules and regulations in effect, and so many *coming* into effect on a weekly basis, that for a legal professional to be able to navigate this convoluted arena with any degree of confidence or certitude is truly remarkable. In the same vein however, how on earth is an untrained lay-litigant supposed to get their heads around all these competing Acts, Laws, and Statutes - especially when the Government of the day can, apparently, 'make up' new laws at will? Well, the answer is we don't! There is one relatively simple remedy to all this that just may prevent our brains going into overload - and that is to stand by our Constitution, solidly, firmly and with confidence that if any given Law, Act or Statute is anti-constitutional in theme, process or practice, then it can (and should) be challenged on that basis.

The Acts on the following pages have been chosen due to their applicability to the main theme; that of holding erring authority figures to account - and doing so with their own rules, regulations and statutes. We recommend therefore that when compiling your Garda complaints or lodging cases in the District Court using the Common Informer process, that you add a little meat to the bones by quoting each alleged offence 'chapter-and-verse' as per the following sections.

CRIMINAL JUSTICE (THEFT AND FRAUD OFFENCES) ACT, 2001

The following excerpts from the above Act have been selected as representing those offences which have been reported to *Integrity Ireland* as being repeatedly committed against ordinary citizens - by persons in positions of power, authority and influence. These sections and subsections should be read in context of ANY instance where personal property is seized, impounded, repossessed or otherwise taken by the authorities against the will and consent of the owner, or, where ANY transaction or action by the authorities can be demonstrated to be fraudulent or deceptive. This could include (for example) deliberate lies, obstructionism or the withholding of information by agents of the State; the misuse of 'instruments' to achieve illicit ends (such as franking machines, date stamps, seals of office etc); or the fraudulent construction - or destruction - of documents such as the ten sacks of 'personal papers' shredded from the Garda Commissioner's Office perhaps? Similarly, the creation of bogus Court Orders which do NOT reflect the instructions of the judge; the repossession of people's homes or the chasing of debts on the back of dodgy business practices by the banks and their agents - or any other improper action which will result in some benefit to the perpetrators or their colleagues? All it would take is for *one* concerned citizen to seize the initiative as an 'interested party' and lodge a criminal charge in the District Court - and who knows, we might have *some* reforming effect on a justice system which is so blatantly corrupt and unfit for purpose as to beggar belief. The full Act can be viewed online on the *Integrity Ireland* website.

(2) For the purposes of this Act a person deceives if he or she—

(a) **creates or reinforces a false impression,** including a false impression as to law, value or intention or other state of mind,

(b) **prevents another person from acquiring information** which would affect that person's judgement of a transaction, or

(c) **fails to correct a false impression** which the deceiver previously created or reinforced or which the deceiver knows to be influencing another to whom he or she stands in a fiduciary or confidential relationship, and references to deception shall be construed accordingly.

(3) For the purposes of this Act—

(a) "gain" and "loss" are to be construed as extending only to gain or loss in money or other property, whether any such gain or loss is temporary or permanent,

(b) "gain" includes a gain by keeping what one has, as well as a gain by getting what one has not, and

(c) "loss" includes a loss by not getting what one might get, as well as a loss by parting with what one has.

(4) For the purposes of this Act—

(a) a person shall be regarded as owning property if he or she has possession or control of it, or has in it any proprietary right or interest (not being an equitable interest arising only from an agreement to transfer or grant an interest);

(b) where property is subject to a trust, the persons who own it shall be regarded as including any person having a right to enforce the trust, and **an intention to defeat the trust shall be regarded accordingly as an intention to deprive of the property** any person having that right;

(c) where a person receives property from or on behalf of another, and is under an obligation to that other person to retain and deal with that property or its proceeds in a particular way, that other person shall be regarded (as against the first-mentioned person) as the owner of the property;

(d) where a person gets property by another's mistake and is under an obligation to make restoration (in whole or in part) of the property or its proceeds or of the value thereof, then the person entitled to restoration shall to the extent of that obligation be regarded (as against the first-mentioned person) as the owner of the property or its proceeds or an amount equivalent to its value, and an intention not to make restoration shall be regarded accordingly as an intention to deprive that person of the property, proceeds or such amount;

4.—(1) Subject to section 5 , a person is guilty of theft if he or she dishonestly appropriates property without the consent of its owner and with the intention of depriving its owner of it.

6.—(1) A person who dishonestly, with the intention of making a gain for himself or herself or another, or of causing loss to another, by any deception induces another to do or refrain from doing an act is guilty of an offence.

7.—(1) A person who dishonestly, with the intention of making a gain for himself or herself or another, or of causing loss to another, by any deception obtains services from another is guilty of an offence.

8.—(3) Subject to subsections (5) and (6), any person may arrest without warrant anyone who is or whom he or she, with reasonable cause, suspects to be in the act of committing an offence under this section.

(5) An arrest other than by a member of the Garda Síochána may be effected by a person under subsection (3) only where the person, with reasonable cause, suspects that the person to be arrested by him or her would otherwise attempt to avoid, or is avoiding, arrest by a member of the Garda Síochána.

(6) A person who is arrested pursuant to this section by a person other than a member of the Garda Síochána shall be transferred by that person into the custody of the Garda Síochána as soon as practicable.

9.—(1) A person who dishonestly, whether within or outside the State, operates or causes to be operated a computer within the State with the intention of making a gain for himself or herself or another, or of causing loss to another, is guilty of an offence.

10.—(1) A person is guilty of an offence if he or she dishonestly, with the intention of making a gain for himself or herself or another, or of causing loss to another—

(a) destroys, defaces, conceals or falsifies any account or any document made or required for any accounting purpose,

11.—(1) A person is guilty of an offence if he or she dishonestly, with the intention of making a gain for himself or herself or another, or of causing loss to another, destroys, defaces or conceals any valuable security, any will or other testamentary document or any original document of or belonging to, or filed or deposited in, any court or any government department or office.

14.—(1) A person is guilty of robbery if he or she steals, and immediately before or at the time of doing so, and in order to do so, uses force on any person or puts or seeks to put any person in fear of being then and there subjected to force.

17.—(1) A person is guilty of handling stolen property if (otherwise than in the course of the stealing) he or she, knowing that the property was stolen or being reckless as to whether it was stolen, dishonestly—

(a) receives or arranges to receive it, or

(b) undertakes, or assists in, its retention, removal, disposal or realisation by or for the benefit of another person, or arranges to do so.

18.—(1) A person who, without lawful authority or excuse, possesses stolen property (otherwise than in the course of the stealing), knowing that the property was stolen or being reckless as to whether it was stolen, is guilty of an offence.

25.—(1) A person is guilty of forgery if he or she makes a false instrument with the intention that it shall be used to induce another person to accept it as genuine and, by reason of so accepting it, to do some act, or to make some omission, to the prejudice of that person or any other person.

26.—(1) A person who uses an instrument which is, and which he or she knows or believes to be, a false instrument, with the intention of inducing another person to accept it as genuine and, by reason of so accepting it, to do some act, or to make some omission, or to provide some service, to the prejudice of that person or any other person is guilty of an offence.

27.—(1) A person who makes a copy of an instrument which is, and which he or she knows or believes to be, a false instrument with the intention that it shall be used to induce another person to accept it as a copy of a genuine instrument and, by reason of so accepting it, to do some act, or to make some omission, or to provide some service, to the prejudice of that person or any other person is guilty of an offence.

28.—(1) A person who uses a copy of an instrument which is, and which he or she knows or believes to be, a false instrument with the intention of inducing another person to accept it as a copy of a genuine instrument and, by reason of so accepting it, to do some act, or to make some omission, or to provide some service, to the prejudice of that person or another person is guilty of an offence.

29.—(1) A person who has in his or her custody or under his or her control an instrument which is, and which he or she knows or believes to be, a false instrument with the intention that it shall be used to induce another person to accept it as genuine and, by reason of so accepting it, to do some act, or to make some omission, or to provide some service, to the prejudice of that person or any other person is guilty of an offence.

(2) A person who, without lawful authority or excuse, has an instrument which is, and which he or she knows or believes to be, a false instrument in his or her custody or under his or her control is guilty of an offence.

42.—A person who—

(a) commits in whole or in part any fraud affecting the European Communities' financial interests,

(b) participates in, instigates or attempts any such fraud, or

(c) obtains the benefit of, or derives any pecuniary advantage from, any such fraud,

is guilty of an offence and is liable on conviction on indictment to a fine or imprisonment for a term not exceeding 5 years or both.

43.—A person who commits active corruption is guilty of an offence and is liable on conviction on indictment to a fine or imprisonment for a term not exceeding 5 years or both.

44.—An official who commits passive corruption is guilty of an offence and is liable on conviction on indictment to a fine or imprisonment for a term not exceeding 5 years or both.

48.—(2) A judge of the District Court, on hearing evidence on oath given by a member of the Garda Síochána, may, if he or she is satisfied that there are reasonable grounds for suspecting that evidence of, or relating to the commission of, an offence to which this section applies is to be found in any place, issue a warrant for the search of that place and any persons found there.

51.—(1) Any person who—

(a) knows or suspects that an investigation by the Garda Síochána into an offence under this Act is being or is likely to be carried out, and

(b) falsifies, conceals, destroys or otherwise disposes of a document or record which he or she knows or suspects is or would be relevant to the investigation or causes or permits its falsification, concealment, destruction or disposal,

is guilty of an offence.

58.—(1) Where—

(a) an offence under this Act has been committed by a body corporate, and

(b) the offence is proved to have been committed with the consent or connivance of, or to have been attributable to any neglect on the part of, a person who was either—

(i) a director, manager, secretary or other officer of the body corporate, or

(ii) a person purporting to act in any such capacity,

that person, as well as the body corporate, is guilty of an offence and liable to be proceeded against and punished as if he or she were guilty of the first-mentioned offence.

59.—(1) In this section— ....the relevant person shall, notwithstanding any professional obligations of privilege or confidentiality, report that fact to a member of the Garda Síochána.

(3) A disclosure in a report made in good faith by a relevant person to a member of the Garda Síochána under subsection (2) shall not be treated as a breach of any restriction imposed by statute or otherwise or involve the person in liability of any kind.

(4) A person who fails, without reasonable excuse, to comply with the duty imposed by subsection (2) *(to report fraud)* is guilty of an offence and is liable on summary conviction to a fine not exceeding £1,500 or imprisonment for a term not exceeding 12 months or both.

* * *

CONVENTION: Drawn up on the basis of Article K.3 of the Treaty on European Union, on the protection of the European Communities' financial interests.

Article 3 - Criminal liability of heads of businesses

Each Member State shall take the necessary measures to allow heads of businesses or any persons having power to take decisions or exercise control within a business to be declared criminally liable in accordance with the principles defined by its national law in cases of fraud affecting the European Community's financial interests, as referred to in Article 1, by a person under their authority acting on behalf of the business.

NON-FATAL OFFENCES AGAINST THE PERSON ACT, 1997

The following excerpts from the above Act have been selected as representing those offences which have been reported to *Integrity Ireland* as being visited on ordinary citizens - by persons in positions of power, authority and influence - most notably (in the case of physical assaults) by members of An Garda Síochána acting outside of their statutory remits. Other sections might equally apply to the actions (or inactions) of State agencies, debt collection companies, banks or lawyers involved in the direct harassment of citizens, and the section on 'coercion' for example could equally apply to Gardaí, Registrars or Judges who attempt to intimidate law-abiding citizens into complying with unlawful or unconstitutional directions. Accordingly, these sections and subsections should be read in context of ANY instance where personal damage or hurt is suffered. This includes physical, mental, emotional or psychological damage as a result of improper treatment by authority figures. For the sake of brevity some of the penalties have been omitted. The full Act can be viewed on the *Integrity Ireland* website.

Assault.
2.—(1) A person shall be guilty of the offence of assault who, without lawful excuse, intentionally or recklessly—

(a) directly or indirectly applies force to or causes an impact on the body of another, or

(b) causes another to believe on reasonable grounds that he or she is likely immediately to be subjected to any such force or impact,

without the consent of the other.

(2) In subsection (1) (a), "force" includes—

(a) application of heat, light, electric current, noise or any other form of energy, and

(b) application of matter in solid liquid or gaseous form.

(3) No such offence is committed if the force or impact, not being intended or likely to cause injury, is in the circumstances such as is generally acceptable in the ordinary conduct of daily life and the defendant does not know or believe that it is in fact unacceptable to the other person.

(4) A person guilty of an offence under this section shall be liable on summary conviction to a fine not exceeding £1,500 or to imprisonment for a term not exceeding 6 months or to both.

Assault causing harm.
3.—(1) A person who assaults another causing him or her harm shall be guilty of an offence.

Causing serious harm.
4.—(1) A person who intentionally or recklessly causes serious harm to another shall be guilty of an offence.

Threats to kill or cause serious harm.
5.—(1) A person who, without lawful excuse, makes to another a threat, by any means intending the other to believe it will be carried out, to kill or cause serious harm to that other or a third person shall be guilty of an offence,

Coercion.
9.—(1) A person who, with a view to compel another to abstain from doing or to do any act which that other has a lawful right to do or to abstain from doing, wrongfully and without lawful authority—

(a) uses violence to or intimidates that other person or a member of the family of the other, or

(b) injures or damages the property of that other, or

(c) persistently follows that other about from place to place, or

(d) watches or besets the premises or other place where that other resides, works or carries on business, or happens to be, or the approach to such premises or place, or

(e) follows that other with one or more other persons in a disorderly manner in or through any public place,

shall be guilty of an offence.

(2) For the purpose of this section attending at or near the premises or place where a person resides, works, carries on business or happens to be, or the approach to such premises or place, in order merely to obtain or communicate information, shall not be deemed a watching or besetting within the meaning of subsection (l) (d).

Harassment.
10.—(1) Any person who, without lawful authority or reasonable excuse, by any means including by use of the telephone, harasses another by persistently following, watching, pestering, besetting or communicating with him or her, shall be guilty of an offence.

(2) For the purposes of this section a person harasses another where—

(a) he or she, by his or her acts intentionally or recklessly, seriously interferes with the other's peace and privacy or causes alarm, distress or harm to the other, and

(b) his or her acts are such that a reasonable person would realise that the acts would seriously interfere with the other's peace and privacy or cause alarm, distress or harm to the other.

Demands for payment of debt causing alarm, etc.
11.—(1) A person who makes any demand for payment of a debt shall be guilty of an offence if—

(a) the demands by reason of their frequency are calculated to subject the debtor or a member of the family of the debtor to alarm, distress or humiliation, or

(b) the person falsely represents that criminal proceedings lie for non-payment of the debt, or

(c) the person falsely represents that he or she is authorised in some official capacity to enforce payment, or

(d) the person utters a document falsely represented to have an official character.

Endangerment.
13.—(1) A person shall be guilty of an offence who intentionally or recklessly engages in conduct which creates a substantial risk of death or serious harm to another.

False imprisonment.
15.—(1) A person shall be guilty of the offence of false imprisonment who intentionally or recklessly—

(a) takes or detains, or

(b) causes to be taken or detained, or

(c) otherwise restricts the personal liberty of,

another without that other's consent.

(2) For the purposes of this section, a person acts without the consent of another if the person obtains the other's consent by force or threat of force, or by deception causing the other to believe that he or she is under legal compulsion to consent.

Abduction of child by other persons.
17.—(1) A person, other than a person to whom section 16 applies [*parents*], shall be guilty of an offence who, without lawful authority or reasonable excuse, intentionally takes or detains a child under the age of 16 years or causes a child under that age to be so taken or detained—

(a) so as to remove the child from the lawful control of any person having lawful control of the child; or

(b) so as to keep him or her out of the lawful control of any person entitled to lawful control of the child.

(2) It shall be a defence to a charge under this section that the defendant believed that the child had attained the age of 16 years.

Justifiable use of force; protection of person or property, prevention of crime, etc.
18.—(1) The use of force by a person for any of the following purposes, if only such as is reasonable in the circumstances as he or she believes them to be, does not constitute an offence—

(a) to protect himself or herself or a member of the family of that person or another from injury, assault or detention caused by a criminal act; or

(b) to protect himself or herself or (with the authority of that other) another from trespass to the person; or

(c) to protect his or her property from appropriation, destruction or damage caused by a criminal act or from trespass or infringement; or

(d) to protect property belonging to another from appropriation, destruction or damage caused by a criminal act or (with the authority of that other) from trespass or infringement; or

(e) to prevent crime or a breach of the peace.

(2) "use of force" in subsection (1) is defined and extended by section 20 .

(3) For the purposes of this section an act involves a "crime" or is "criminal" although the person committing it, if charged with an offence in respect of it, would be acquitted on the ground that—

(a) he or she was under 7 years of age; or

(b) he or she acted under duress, whether by threats or of circumstances; or

(c) his or her act was involuntary; or

(d) he or she was in a state of intoxication; or

(e) he or she was insane, so as not to be responsible, according to law, for the act.

(4) The references in subsection (1) to protecting a person and property from anything include protecting the person or property from its continuing; and the reference to preventing crime or a breach of the peace shall be similarly construed.

(5) For the purposes of this section the question whether the act against which force is used is of a kind mentioned in any of the paragraphs (a) to (e) of subsection (1) shall be determined according to the circumstances as the person using the force believes them to be.

(6) Notwithstanding subsection (1), a person who believes circumstances to exist which would justify or excuse the use of force under that subsection has no defence if he or she knows that the force is used against a member of the Garda Síochána acting in the course of the member's duty or a person so assisting such member, unless he or she believes the force to be immediately necessary to prevent harm to himself or herself or another.

(7) The defence provided by this section does not apply to a person who causes conduct or a state of affairs with a view to using force to resist or terminate it:

But the defence may apply although the occasion for the use of force arises only because the person does something he or she may lawfully do, knowing that such an occasion will arise.

(8) Property shall be treated for the purposes of subsection (1) (c) and (d) as belonging to any person—

    (a) having the custody or control of it;

    (b) having in it any proprietary right or interest (not being an equitable interest arising only from an agreement to transfer or grant an interest); or

    (c) having a charge on it;

and where property is subject to a trust, the persons to whom it belongs shall be treated as including any person having a right to enforce the trust.

Property of a corporation sole shall be treated for the purposes of the aforesaid provisions as belonging to the corporation notwithstanding a vacancy in the corporation.

Justifiable use of force in effecting or assisting lawful arrest.
19.—(1) The use of force by a person in effecting or assisting in a lawful arrest, if only such as is reasonable in the circumstances as he or she believes them to be, does not constitute an offence.

(2) "use of force" in subsection (1) is defined and extended by section 20 .

(3) For the purposes of this section the question as to whether the arrest is lawful shall be determined according to the circumstances as the person using the force believed them to be.

Meaning of "use of force" and related provisions.
20.—(1) For the purposes of sections 18 and 19—

    (a) a person uses force in relation to another person or property not only when he or she applies force to, but also where he or she causes an impact on, the body of that person or that property;

    (b) a person shall be treated as using force in relation to another person if—

        (i) he or she threatens that person with its use, or

(ii) he or she detains that person without actually using it; and

(c) a person shall be treated as using force in relation to property if he or she threatens a person with its use in relation to property.

(2) Sections 18 and 19 shall apply in relation to acts immediately preparatory to the use of force as they apply in relation to acts in which force is used.

(3) A threat of force may be reasonable although the actual use of force may not be.

(4) The fact that a person had an opportunity to retreat before using force shall be taken into account, in conjunction with other relevant evidence, in determining whether the use of force was reasonable.

Amendment of section 6 of the Criminal Damage Act, 1991 .

21.—Section 6(2) of the Criminal Damage Act, 1991, is hereby amended by the substitution for paragraph (c) of the following paragraph:

"(c) if he damaged or threatened to damage the property in question or, in the case of an offence under section 4, intended to use or cause or permit the use of something to damage it, in order to protect himself or another or property belonging to himself or another or a right or interest in property which was or which he believed to be vested in himself or another and the act or acts alleged to constitute the offence were reasonable in the circumstances as he believed them to be.".

General defences, etc.

22.—(1) The provisions of this Act have effect subject to any enactment or rule of law providing a defence, or providing lawful authority, justification or excuse for an act or omission.

(2) Notwithstanding subsection (1) any defence available under the common law in respect of the use of force within the meaning of section 18 or 19 , or an act immediately preparatory to the use of force, for the purposes mentioned in section 18 (1) or 19(1) is hereby abolished.

* * *

Whistleblowing - The Obligation and Duty to Report

Here is the legislation which obliges a person to report crimes - or, face some serious repercussions and penalties. So please, don't be shy. After all, it is your legal duty.

Section 19 of the Criminal Justice Act 2011 states:

"(1) A person shall be guilty of an offence if he or she has information which he or she knows or believes might be of material assistance in:

(a) preventing the commission by any other person of a relevant offence, or (b) securing the apprehension, prosecution or conviction of any other person for a relevant offence, and fails without reasonable excuse to disclose that information as soon as it is practicable to do so to a member of the Garda Síochána.

(2) A person guilty of an offence under this section shall be liable:

(a) on summary conviction, to a class A fine [ie not exceeding €5,000] or imprisonment for a term not exceeding 12 months or both, or

(b) on conviction on indictment, to a fine [ie unlimited] or imprisonment for a term not exceeding 5 years or both."

CRIMINAL JUSTICE (PUBLIC ORDER) ACT, 1994

The following excerpts from the above Act have been selected as representing those offences which have been reported to *Integrity Ireland* as being visited on ordinary citizens - by persons in positions of power, authority and influence - most notably (in the case of physical assaults and other instances surrounding public protests) by members of An Garda Síochána. It is interesting to note that in the preamble to the Act it is stated that the purpose of this Act is to *abolish* existing Common Law offences and replace them with Statutory offences. One reason for this (possibly) is because all Common Law offences are *indictable* offences which by rights, should be tried before a judge and jury. Reducing some of these offences to 'statutory' status provides for them to be dealt with *summarily* before a single judge - usually in the District Court.

Whilst effectively streamlining and simplifying the prosecution process, this nevertheless raises considerable disquiet about the perceived fairness of having criminal matters dealt with summarily by just *one* sitting judge. However, what is also very important to note is that Statutory law (such as is outlined in these Acts) is *subject to* Constitutional law. Therefore, if any given Act or Statute is in conflict with the Constitution - (and they very often appear to be) - then there may be grounds to challenge any subsequent conviction, or indeed, any move to charge an individual with any given offence in the first place. As with the other Acts and laws listed in this Guide, it is important to remember that just because any given Irish citizen happens to be wearing a uniform, a suit, or a wig-and-gown - does NOT place them outside of the law. There is no doubt that the statutory offences of; *'disorderly conduct; threatening behaviour; obstruction; assault; riot & affray'* were being actively committed by gangs of security personnel, backed up by Gardaí, at the Shell-to-Sea protests in north Mayo. Likewise with recent incidents at water meter installations and at scenes in the public Courts. But, because we have all been conditioned to accept that 'the authorities' are the *only* ones supposed to be taking the initiative when prosecuting crimes, we have missed repeated opportunities to insist upon our Constitutional and Statutory rights.

The fact remains however, that it obviously serves the interests of a compromised establishment to keep creating laws that empower the establishment to the detriment of the people. If we value our country, our heritage or our freedom at all, this trend to punitive over-legislation is something that we need to be fully alert to - and one of the best ways to do this is to educate ourselves as to our rights, and to respectfully but firmly, insist upon those rights being respected. Most especially, we need to insist that those in well-paid positions of authority and power respect the fundamental fact that they are being paid to serve US - the people - and *not* the vested interests of banks, corporations and multinationals.

The 'penalty' sections in each case have been included this time so that you are fully aware of the possible repercussions of falling afoul of this particular legislation. The full Act can be viewed online on the *Integrity Ireland* website.

Preamble

AN ACT TO **ABOLISH CERTAIN COMMON LAW OFFENCES** RELATING TO PUBLIC ORDER AND TO **PROVIDE CERTAIN STATUTORY OFFENCES** RELATING TO PUBLIC ORDER IN LIEU THEREOF, TO **PROVIDE FOR ADDITIONAL POWERS OF CROWD CONTROL BY MEMBERS OF THE GARDA SÍOCHÁNA** IN, OR OF CONTROL BY SUCH MEMBERS OF ACCESS TO, THE VICINITY OF CERTAIN EVENTS AND TO PROVIDE FOR OFFENCES RELATING THERETO, TO PROVIDE FOR OTHER MATTERS RELATING TO PUBLIC ORDER AND TO FINES AND TERMS OF IMPRISONMENT IN RESPECT OF CERTAIN OFFENCES AND FOR THOSE AND OTHER PURPOSES **TO AMEND THE CRIMINAL LAW AND ADMINISTRATION**. [3rd March, 1994]

BE IT ENACTED BY THE OIREACHTAS AS FOLLOWS:

Offences Relating to Public Order
Interpretation (Part II).

3.—In this Part, except where the context otherwise requires—

"dwelling" includes a building, vehicle or vessel ordinarily used for habitation;

"private place" means a place that is not a public place;

"public place" includes—

(a) any highway,

(b) any outdoor area to which at the material time members of the public have or are permitted to have access, whether as of right or as a trespasser or otherwise, and which is used for public recreational purposes,

(c) any cemetery or churchyard,

(d) any premises or other place to which at the material time members of the public have or are permitted to have access, whether as of right or by express or implied permission, or whether on payment or otherwise, and

(e) any train, vessel or vehicle used for the carriage of persons for reward.

Intoxication in public place.
4.—(1) It shall be an offence for any person to be present in any public place while intoxicated to such an extent as would give rise to a reasonable apprehension that he might endanger himself or any other person in his vicinity.

(2) A person who is guilty of an offence under this section shall be liable on summary conviction to a fine not exceeding £100.

(3) Where a member of the Garda Síochána suspects, with reasonable cause, that an offence under this section or under section 5 or 6 is being committed, the member concerned may seize, obtain or remove, without warrant, any bottle or container, together with its contents, which—

(a) is in the possession, in a place other than a place used as a dwelling, of a person by whom such member suspects the offence to have been committed, and

(b) such member suspects, with reasonable cause, contains an intoxicating substance:

Provided that, in the application of this subsection to section 5 or 6 , any such bottle or container, together with its contents, may only be so seized, obtained or removed where the member of the Garda Síochána suspects, with reasonable cause, that the bottle or container or its contents, is relevant to the offence under section 5 or 6 which the member suspects is being committed.

(4) In this section—

"bottle or container" does not include a bottle or container for a substance which is in the possession of the person concerned for a purpose other than the intoxication of that or any other person;

"intoxicated" means under the intoxicating influence of any alcoholic drink, drug, solvent or other substance or a combination of substances and cognate words shall be construed accordingly.

Disorderly conduct in public place.

5.—(1) It shall be an offence for any person in a public place to engage in offensive conduct—

(a) between the hours of 12 o'clock midnight and 7 o'clock in the morning next following, or

(b) at any other time, after having been requested by a member of the Garda Síochána to desist.

(2) A person who is guilty of an offence under this section shall be liable on summary conviction to a fine not exceeding £500.

(3) In this section "offensive conduct" means any unreasonable behaviour which, having regard to all the circumstances, is likely to cause serious offence or serious annoyance to any person who is, or might reasonably be expected to be, aware of such behaviour.

Threatening, abusive or insulting behaviour in public place.

6.—(1) It shall be an offence for any person in a public place to use or engage in any threatening, abusive or insulting words or behaviour with intent to provoke a breach of the peace or being reckless as to whether a breach of the peace may be occasioned.

(2) A person who is guilty of an offence under this section shall be liable on summary conviction to a fine not exceeding £500 or to imprisonment for a term not exceeding 3 months or to both.

Distribution or display in public place of material which is threatening, abusive, insulting or obscene.

7.—(1) It shall be an offence for any person in a public place to distribute or display any writing, sign or visible representation which is threatening, abusive, insulting or obscene with intent to provoke a breach of the peace or being reckless as to whether a breach of the peace may be occasioned.

(2) A person who is guilty of an offence under this section shall be liable on summary conviction to a fine not exceeding £500 or to imprisonment for a term not exceeding 3 months or to both.

Failure to comply with direction of member of Garda Síochána.

8.—(1) Where a member of the Garda Síochána finds a person in a public place and suspects, with reasonable cause, that such person—

(a) is or has been acting in a manner contrary to the provisions of section 4 , 5 , 6 , 7 or 9 , or

(b) without lawful authority or reasonable excuse, is acting in a manner which consists of loitering in a public place in circumstances, which may include the company of other persons, that give rise to a reasonable apprehension for the safety of persons or the safety of property or for the maintenance of the public peace,

the member may direct the person so suspected to do either or both of the following, that is to say:

(i) desist from acting in such a manner, and

(ii) leave immediately the vicinity of the place concerned in a peaceable or orderly manner.

(2) It shall be an offence for any person, without lawful authority or reasonable excuse, to fail to comply with a direction given by a member of the Garda Síochána under this section.

(3) A person who is guilty of an offence under this section shall be liable on summary conviction to a fine not exceeding £500 or to imprisonment for a term not exceeding 6 months or to both.

Wilful obstruction.
9.—Any person who, without lawful authority or reasonable excuse, wilfully prevents or interrupts the free passage of any person or vehicle in any public place shall be liable on summary conviction to a fine not exceeding £200.

Increase of penalty for common assault, etc.
10.—The Criminal Justice Act, 1951 , is hereby amended by the substitution for subsection (2) of section 11 of the following:

"(2) A person convicted of common assault or battery shall be liable to a fine not exceeding £1,000 or, at the discretion of the Court, imprisonment for a term not exceeding twelve months or to both such fine and imprisonment.".

Entering building, etc., with intent to commit an offence.
11.—(1) It shall be an offence for a person—

> (a) to enter any building or the curtilage of any building or any part of such building or curtilage as a trespasser, or

> (b) to be within the vicinity of any such building or curtilage or part of such building or curtilage for the purpose of trespassing thereon,

in circumstances giving rise to the reasonable inference that such entry or presence was with intent to commit an offence or with intent to unlawfully interfere with any property situate therein.

(2) A person who is guilty of an offence under this section shall be liable on summary conviction to a fine not exceeding £1,000 or to imprisonment for a term not exceeding 6 months or to both.

Amendment of Vagrancy Act, 1824.
12.—Section 4 (as applied to Ireland by the Prevention of Crimes Act, 1871) of the Vagrancy Act, 1824 , is hereby amended by the deletion of "every person being found in or upon any dwelling house, warehouse, coach-house, stable, or outhouse, or in any enclosed yard, garden or area, for any unlawful purpose;".

Trespass on building, etc.
13.—(1) It shall be an offence for a person, without reasonable excuse, to trespass on any building or the curtilage thereof in such a manner as causes or is likely to cause fear in another person.

(2) (a) Where a member of the Garda Síochána finds a person in a place to which subsection (1) relates and suspects, with reasonable cause, that such person is or has been acting in a manner contrary to the provisions of that subsection, then the member may direct the person so suspected to do either or both of the following, that is to say:

> (i) desist from acting in such a manner, and

> (ii) leave immediately the vicinity of the place concerned in a peaceable or orderly manner.

> (b) It shall be an offence for any person, without lawful authority or reasonable excuse, to fail to comply with a direction given by a member of the Garda Síochána under this section.

(3) (a) A person who is guilty of an offence under subsection (1) shall be liable on summary conviction to a fine not exceeding £1,000 or to imprisonment for a term not exceeding 12 months or to both.

(b) A person who is guilty of an offence under subsection (2) shall be liable on summary conviction to a fine not exceeding £500 or to imprisonment for a term not exceeding 6 months or to both.

Riot.

14.—(1) Where—

(a) 12 or more persons who are present together at any place (whether that place is a public place or a private place or both) use or threaten to use unlawful violence for a common purpose, and

(b) the conduct of those persons, taken together, is such as would cause a person of reasonable firmness present at that place to fear for his or another person's safety,

then, each of the persons using unlawful violence for the common purpose shall be guilty of the offence of riot.

(2) For the purposes of this section—

(a) it shall be immaterial whether or not the 12 or more persons use or threaten to use unlawful violence simultaneously at any place;

(b) the common purpose may be inferred from conduct;

(c) no person of reasonable firmness need actually be, or be likely to be, present at that place.

(3) A person guilty of an offence of riot shall be liable on conviction on indictment to a fine or to imprisonment for a term not exceeding 10 years or to both.

(4) The common law offence of riot is hereby abolished.

Violent disorder.

15.—(1) Where—

(a) three or more persons who are present together at any place (whether that place is a public place or a private place or both) use or threaten to use unlawful violence, and

(b) the conduct of those persons, taken together, is such as would cause a person of reasonable firmness present at that place to fear for his or another person's safety,

then, each of the persons using or threatening to use unlawful violence shall be guilty of the offence of violent disorder.

(2) For the purposes of this section—

(a) it shall be immaterial whether or not the three or more persons use or threaten to use unlawful violence simultaneously;

(b) no person of reasonable firmness need actually be, or be likely to be, present at that place.

(3) A person shall not be convicted of the offence of violent disorder unless the person intends

to use or threaten to use violence or is aware that his conduct may be violent or threaten violence.

(4) A person guilty of an offence of violent disorder shall be liable on conviction on indictment to a fine or to imprisonment for a term not exceeding 10 years or to both.

(5) A reference, however expressed, in any enactment passed before the commencement of this Act—

(a) to the common law offence of riot, or

(b) to the common law offence of riot and to tumult,

shall be construed as a reference to the offence of violent disorder.

(6) The common law offence of rout and the common law offence of unlawful assembly are hereby abolished.

Affray.
16.—(1) Where—

(a) two or more persons at any place (whether that place is a public place or a private place or both) use or threaten to use violence towards each other, and

(b) the violence so used or threatened by one of those persons is unlawful, and

(c) the conduct of those persons taken together is such as would cause a person of reasonable firmness present at that place to fear for his or another person's safety,

then, each such person who uses or threatens to use unlawful violence shall be guilty of the offence of affray.

(2) For the purposes of this section—

(a) a threat cannot be made by words alone;

(b) no person of reasonable firmness need actually be, or be likely to be, present at the place where the use or threat of violence occurred.

(3) A person shall not be convicted of the offence of affray unless the person intends to use or threaten to use violence or is aware that his conduct may be violent or threaten violence.

(4) A person guilty of an offence of affray shall be liable—

(a) on summary conviction to a fine not exceeding £500 or to imprisonment for a term not exceeding 12 months or to both,

(b) on conviction on indictment to a fine or to imprisonment for a term not exceeding 5 years or to both.

(5) The common law offence of affray is hereby abolished.

Blackmail, extortion and demanding money with menaces.
17.—(1) It shall be an offence for any person who, with a view to gain for himself or another or with intent to cause loss to another, makes any unwarranted demand with menaces.

(2) For the purposes of this section—

(a) a demand with menaces shall be unwarranted unless the person making it does so in the belief—

 (i) that he has reasonable grounds for making the demand, and

 (ii) that the use of the menaces is a proper means of reinforcing the demand;

(b) the nature of the act or omission demanded shall be immaterial and it shall also be immaterial whether or not the menaces relate to action to be taken by the person making the demand.

(3) A person guilty of an offence under this section shall be liable—

 (a) on summary conviction to a fine not exceeding £1,000 or to imprisonment for a term not exceeding 12 months or to both,

 (b) on conviction on indictment to a fine or to imprisonment for a term not exceeding 14 years or to both.

Assault with intent to cause bodily harm or commit indictable offence.

18.—(1) Any person who assaults any person with intent to cause bodily harm or to commit an indictable offence shall be guilty of an offence.

(2) A person guilty of an offence under this section shall be liable—

 (a) on summary conviction, to a fine not exceeding £1,000 or to imprisonment for a term not exceeding 12 months or to both,

 (b) on conviction on indictment, to a fine or to imprisonment for a term not exceeding 5 years or to both.

Assault or obstruction of peace officer.

19.—(1) Any person who—

 (a) assaults a peace officer acting in the execution of the peace officer's duty, knowing that he is, or being reckless as to whether he is, a peace officer acting in the execution of his duty, or

 (b) assaults any other person acting in the aid of a peace officer, or

 (c) assaults any other person with intent to resist or prevent the lawful apprehension or detention of himself or any other person for any offence,

shall be guilty of an offence.

(2) A person guilty of an offence under subsection (1) shall be liable—

 (a) having elected for summary disposal of the offence, on summary conviction, to a fine not exceeding £1,000 or to imprisonment for a term not exceeding 12 months, or to both,

 (b) on conviction on indictment, to a fine or to imprisonment for a term not exceeding 5 years or to both.

(3) Any person who resists or wilfully obstructs a peace officer acting in the execution of his duty or a person assisting a peace officer in the execution of his duty, knowing that he is or being reckless as to whether he is, a peace officer acting in the execution of his duty, shall be guilty of an offence.

(4) A person guilty of an offence under subsection (3) shall be liable on summary conviction to

a fine not exceeding £500 or to imprisonment for a term not exceeding 6 months or to both.

(5) The provisions of this section are in addition to and not in substitution of any provision in any other enactment relating to assault or obstruction of a peace officer.

(6) In this section—

"peace officer" means a member of the Garda Síochána, a prison officer or a member of the Defence Forces;

"prison" means any place for which rules or regulations may be made under the Prisons Acts, 1826 to 1980, section 7 of the Offences against the State (Amendment) Act, 1940 , section 233 of the Defence Act, 1954 , section 2 of the Prisoners of War and Enemy Aliens Act, 1956 , or section 13 of the Criminal Justice Act, 1960 ;

"prison officer" includes any member of the staff of a prison and any person having the custody of, or having duties in relation to the custody of, a person detained in prison.

PART III

Crowd Control at Public Events
Interpretation (Part III).

20.—In this Part—

"container" does not include a container for any medicinal product;

"disposable container" includes—

> (a) any bottle, can or other portable container or any part thereof (including any crushed or broken portable container or part thereof) for holding any drink which, when empty, is of a kind normally discarded or returned to, or left to be recovered by, the supplier, and

> (b) any crate or packaging designed to hold more than one such bottle, can or other portable container;

"event" has the meaning assigned to it by section 21 (1);

"intoxicating liquor" includes any container containing intoxicating liquor, whether or not a disposable container.

Control of access to certain events, etc.
21.—(1) If it appears to a member of the Garda Síochána not below the rank of superintendent that it is necessary in the interests of safety or for the purpose of preserving order to restrict the access of persons to a place where an event is taking or is about to take place which attracts, or is likely to attract, a large assembly of persons (in this Part referred to as the "event"), he may authorise any member of the Garda Síochána to erect or cause to be erected a barrier or a series of barriers on any road, street, lane, alley or other means of access to such a place in a position not more than one mile therefrom for the purpose of regulating the access of persons or vehicles thereto.

(2) Where a barrier has been erected in accordance with subsection (1), a member of the Garda Síochána in uniform may by oral or manual direction or by the exhibition of any notice or sign, or any combination thereof—

> (a) divert persons generally or particularly and whether in or on vehicles or on foot to another means of access to the event, including a means of access to that event on foot

only, or

(b) where possession of a ticket is required for entrance to the event, prohibit a person whether in or on vehicles or on foot from crossing or passing the barrier towards the event where the person has no such ticket, or

(c) indicate that to proceed beyond the barrier while in possession of any intoxicating liquor, disposable drinks container or offensive article will render such liquor, container or article liable to confiscation.

(3) A member of the Garda Síochána shall not prohibit a person from crossing or passing a barrier erected under this section save for the purpose of diverting the person to another means of access to the event, if it appears to the member that the person is seeking to do so for the purpose only of—

(a) going to his dwelling or place of business or work in the vicinity of the event, or

(b) going for any other lawful purpose to any place in the vicinity of the event other than the place where the event is taking place or is about to take place.

(4) A person who—

(a) fails to obey a direction given by a member of the Garda Síochána under subsection (2) for the purposes of paragraph (a) or (b) thereof, or

(b) fails to comply with the terms of a notice or sign exhibited under subsection (2) for the purposes of paragraph (a) or (b) thereof,

shall be guilty of an offence.

(5) A person guilty of an offence under this section shall be liable on summary conviction to a fine not exceeding £500.

Surrender and seizure of intoxicating liquor, etc.
22.—(1) Where in relation to an event—

(a) a barrier has been erected under section 21 and it appears to a member of the Garda Síochána that a person on foot or in a vehicle is seeking to cross or pass the barrier, or has crossed or passed the barrier, for the purpose of going to the place where the event is taking place or is about to take place, or

(b) it appears to a member of the Garda Síochána that a person is about to enter, or has entered, the place where the event is taking place or is about to take place,

and the person has, or the member of the Garda Síochána suspects with reasonable cause that the person has, in his possession—

(i) any intoxicating liquor, or

(ii) any disposable container, or

(iii) any other article which, having regard to the circumstances or the nature of the event, could be used to cause injury,

the member may exercise any one or more of the following powers—

(I) search or cause to be searched that person or any vehicle in or on which he may be in order

74

to ascertain whether he has with him any such liquor, container or other article,

(II) refuse to allow that person to proceed to the event or to proceed further, as the case may be, unless that person surrenders permanently to a member of the Garda Síochána as directed by the member such liquor, container or other article.

(2) Where a member of the Garda Síochána refuses to allow a person to proceed to the event or to proceed further by virtue of subsection (1) (II) and the person does not surrender the alcoholic liquor, disposable container or other article concerned, the member may require the person to leave the vicinity in an orderly and peaceful manner as directed by the member.

(3) A person who, without lawful authority or reasonable excuse, fails to comply with a requirement under subsection (2) shall be guilty of an offence.

(4) A person guilty of an offence under this section shall be liable on summary conviction to a fine not exceeding £500.

24.—(1) Where a member of the Garda Síochána finds any person committing an offence under a relevant provision, the member may arrest such person without warrant.

(2) Where a member of the Garda Síochána is of the opinion that an offence has been committed under a relevant provision, the member may—

(a) demand the name and address of any person whom the member suspects, with reasonable cause, has committed, or whom the member finds committing, such an offence, and

(b) arrest without warrant any such person who fails or refuses to give his name and address when demanded, or gives a name or address which the member has reasonable grounds for believing is false or misleading.

(3) Any person who fails or refuses to give his name and address when demanded by virtue of subsection (2), or gives a name or address when so demanded which is false or misleading, shall be guilty of an offence.

(4) A person guilty of an offence under subsection (3) shall be liable on summary conviction to a fine not exceeding £500 or to a term of imprisonment not exceeding 6 months or to both.

(5) In this section "relevant provision" means section 4 , 6 , 7 , 8 , 11 , 13 , 14 , 15 , 16 , 17 , 18 or 19 .

Continuance of existing powers of Garda Síochána.
25.—Any power conferred on a member of the Garda Síochána by this Act is without prejudice to any other power exercisable by such a member.

ETHICS IN PUBLIC OFFICE ACT, 1995

The following three paragraphs more or less cover the gist of the respective Acts concerning corruption by authority figures, and are one means by which any 'interested party' (meaning any member of the public who contributes in any way to the tax base) may initiate proceedings against corrupt officials. It is interesting to note that this form of corruption - regardless of the amounts involved - appear only to be considered a 'misdemeanour' or a 'lesser offence'.

Amendment of the Prevention of Corruption Act, 1916 — by the deletion of section 1 and by the substitution of the following section for section 2:

"2.—Where in any proceedings against a person for an offence under the Prevention of Corruption Act, 1906 , as amended, or the Public Bodies Corrupt Practices Act, 1889 , as amended, it is proved that any money, gift or other consideration has been paid or given to or received by an office holder or special adviser or a director of, or occupier of a position of employment in, a public body by or from a person or agent of a person holding or seeking to obtain a contract from a Minister of the Government or a public body, the money, gift or consideration shall be deemed to have been paid or given and received corruptly as such inducement or reward as is mentioned in such Act unless the contrary is proved.",

38.—The Prevention of Corruption Acts, 1889 to 1916, shall be amended as follows:

1. (1) Every person who shall by himself or by or in conjunction with any other person, corruptly solicit or receive, or agree to receive, for himself, or for any other person, any gift, loan, fee, reward, or advantage whatever as an inducement to, or reward for, or otherwise on account of an office holder or his or her special adviser or a director of, or occupier of a position of employment in, a public body as in this Act defined, doing or forbearing to do anything in respect of any matter or transaction whatsoever, actual or proposed, in which the said office holder or public body is concerned, shall be guilty of a misdemeanour.

(2) Every person who shall by himself or by or in conjunction with any other person corruptly give, promise, or offer any gift, loan, fee, reward, or advantage whatsoever to any person, whether for the benefit of that person or of another person, as an inducement to or reward for or otherwise on account of an office holder or his or her special adviser or a director of, or occupier of a position of employment in, any public body as in this Act defined, doing or forbearing to do anything in respect of any matter or transaction whatsoever, actual or proposed, in which such office holder or public body as aforesaid is concerned, shall be guilty of a misdemeanour.

EUROPEAN CONVENTION ON HUMAN RIGHTS ACT 2003

Like all member States of the European Union, Ireland is now subject to European Law. Over time, it is expected that the required amendments will be made to bring the justice systems of all EU member States into alignment. Some of those recently introduced to Ireland include the requirement that the DPP offers explanations for her decisions and that various other State agencies and departments (such as An Garda Síochána) are ultimately accountable to the people.

From the perspective of the *Integrity Ireland* project, any move that ensures that our fundamental rights are going to be better respected should be enthusiastically welcomed. However, we are still very much in a transition period, so it would be wise to keep ourselves informed about the timing of these amendments to our own laws, and to be ready to apply them in cases of injustice, because as things stand at the moment, a person cannot approach the European Court of Human Rights for example, until he or she has exhausted all avenues of remedy in their own country.

The disturbing case of Louise O'Keefe is a case in point, where Ms O'Keefe spent some 17 years bravely arguing her case through 24 different Irish Courts, including the Supreme Court. All of the Irish Courts ruled against her, effectively defending the State against responsibility for the crimes committed against Louise when she was a child. As a result, 135 people with similar cases against the State were told by the State Claims Agency to withdraw those cases on the grounds that those cases would fail. The European Court of Human Rights then ruled in Louise's favour, leaving us all wondering what on earth is going on in *our* Courts? Why such a disparity of opinion between our Irish Courts and the European Courts? The question remains largely unanswered. The people who dropped their abuse cases on the questionable advice of the State Claims Agency are now facing another uphill battle with the State trying to get their claims reinstated. The remaining claimants have been offered 'compensation' at some distant time in the future, which no doubt will be delivered the same convoluted way as the Residential Institutions Redress Board operated; drawing cases out for many years in some cases, cloaked in legalese and obscure formulas which did little to truly compensate the victims of abuse, and did far more to line the pockets of unscrupulous lawyers and those appointed to oversee the operation. Overall, this is not exactly the best advertisement for the probity, efficacy and integrity of our justice system - is it?

As more and more EU nationals from other EU States come to live in Ireland, the ECHR will come increasingly into play - as it will for the thousands of migrants and refugees from war-torn States - some of whom have suffered terribly in countries where basic human rights are *not* respected. The question we need to be asking ourselves is whether we are going to allow our fragile democracy to founder and descend into tyranny as well. Because each and every breach of our individual fundamental rights by compromised authorities is a step in that ominous direction.

The following list of Articles is abridged to include only those clauses that differ in some way from the Articles of the Irish Constitution and which appear pertinent to the I-I project; that of encouraging justice, transparency and accountability, and challenging corruption, cronyism and criminal cover-ups by agents or agencies of the State.

Article 1: Obligation to respect human rights
The High Contracting Parties shall secure to everyone within their jurisdiction the rights and freedoms defined in Section I of this Convention.

Article 2: Right to life
1   Everyone's right to life shall be protected by law. No one shall be deprived of his life intentionally save in the execution of a sentence of a court following his conviction of a crime for which this penalty is provided by law.

2   Deprivation of life shall not be regarded as inflicted in contravention of this article when it results from the use of force which is no more than absolutely necessary:

    a   in defence of any person from unlawful violence;

    b   in order to effect a lawful arrest or to prevent the escape of a person lawfully detained;

    c   in action lawfully taken for the purpose of quelling a riot or insurrection.

Article 3: Prohibition of torture

No one shall be subjected to torture or to inhuman or degrading treatment or punishment.

Article 5: Right to liberty and security

1   Everyone has the right to liberty and security of person. No one shall be deprived of his liberty save in the following cases and in accordance with a procedure prescribed by law:

    a   the lawful detention of a person after conviction by a competent court;

    b   the lawful arrest or detention of a person for non-compliance with the lawful order of a court or in order to secure the fulfilment of any obligation prescribed by law;

    c   the lawful arrest or detention of a person effected for the purpose of bringing him before the competent legal authority on reasonable suspicion of having committed an offence or when it is reasonably considered necessary to prevent his committing an offence or fleeing after having done so;

    d   the detention of a minor by lawful order for the purpose of educational supervision or his lawful detention for the purpose of bringing him before the competent legal authority;

    e   the lawful detention of persons for the prevention of the spreading of infectious diseases, of persons of unsound mind, alcoholics or drug addicts or vagrants;

    f   the lawful arrest or detention of a person to prevent his effecting an unauthorised entry into the country or of a person against whom action is being taken with a view to deportation or extradition.

2   Everyone who is arrested shall be informed promptly, in a language which he understands, of the reasons for his arrest and of any charge against him.

3   Everyone arrested or detained in accordance with the provisions of paragraph 1.c of this article shall be brought promptly before a judge or other officer authorised by law to exercise judicial power and shall be entitled to trial within a reasonable time or to release pending trial. Release may be conditioned by guarantees to appear for trial.

4   Everyone who is deprived of his liberty by arrest or detention shall be entitled to take proceedings by which the lawfulness of his detention shall be decided speedily by a court and his release ordered if the detention is not lawful.

5   Everyone who has been the victim of arrest or detention in contravention of the provisions of this article shall have an enforceable right to compensation.

Article 6: Right to a fair trial

1   In the determination of his civil rights and obligations or of any criminal charge against him, everyone is entitled to a fair and public hearing within a reasonable time by an independent and impartial tribunal established by law. Judgment shall be pronounced publicity but the press and public may be excluded from all or part of the trial in the interests of morals, public order or national security in a democratic society, where the interests of juveniles or the protection of

the private life of the parties so require, or to the extent strictly necessary in the opinion of the court in special circumstances where publicity would prejudice the interests of justice.

2   Everyone charged with a criminal offence shall be presumed innocent until proved guilty according to law.

3   Everyone charged with a criminal offence has the following minimum rights:

a   to be informed promptly, in a language which he understands and in detail, of the nature and cause of the accusation against him;

b   to have adequate time and facilities for the preparation of his defence;

c   to defend himself in person or through legal assistance of his own choosing or, if he has not sufficient means to pay for legal assistance, to be given it free when the interests of justice so require;

d   to examine or have examined witnesses against him and to obtain the attendance and examination of witnesses on his behalf under the same conditions as witnesses against him;

e   to have the free assistance of an interpreter if he cannot understand or speak the language used in court.

Article 7: No punishment without law

1   No one shall be held guilty of any criminal offence on account of any act or omission which did not constitute a criminal offence under national or international law at the time when it was committed. Nor shall a heavier penalty be imposed than the one that was applicable at the time the criminal offence was committed.

2   This article shall not prejudice the trial and punishment of any person for any act or omission which, at the time when it was committed, was criminal according to the general principles of law recognised by civilised nations.

Article 8: Right to respect for private and family life

1   Everyone has the right to respect for his private and family life, his home and his correspondence.

2   There shall be no interference by a public authority with the exercise of this right except such as is in accordance with the law and is necessary in a democratic society in the interests of national security, public safety or the economic well-being of the country, for the prevention of disorder or crime, for the protection of health or morals, or for the protection of the rights and freedoms of others.

Article 9: Freedom of thought, conscience and religion

1   Everyone has the right to freedom of thought, conscience and religion; this right includes freedom to change his religion or belief and freedom, either alone or in community with others and in public or private, to manifest his religion or belief, in worship, teaching, practice and observance.

2   Freedom to manifest one's religion or beliefs shall be subject only to such limitations as are prescribed by law and are necessary in a democratic society in the interests of public safety, for the protection of public order, health or morals, or for the protection of the rights and freedoms of others.

Article 10: Freedom of expression

1   Everyone has the right to freedom of expression. This right shall include freedom to hold

opinions and to receive and impart information and ideas without interference by public authority and regardless of frontiers. This article shall not prevent States from requiring the licensing of broadcasting, television or cinema enterprises.

2   The exercise of these freedoms, since it carries with it duties and responsibilities, may be subject to such formalities, conditions, restrictions or penalties as are prescribed by law and are necessary in a democratic society, in the interests of national security, territorial integrity or public safety, for the prevention of disorder or crime, for the protection of health or morals, for the protection of the reputation or rights of others, for preventing the disclosure of information received in confidence, or for maintaining the authority and impartiality of the judiciary.

Article 11: Freedom of assembly and association

1   Everyone has the right to freedom of peaceful assembly and to freedom of association with others, including the right to form and to join trade unions for the protection of his interests.

2   No restrictions shall be placed on the exercise of these rights other than such as are prescribed by law and are necessary in a democratic society in the interests of national security or public safety, for the prevention of disorder or crime, for the protection of health or morals or for the protection of the rights and freedoms of others. This article shall not prevent the imposition of lawful restrictions on the exercise of these rights by members of the armed forces, of the police or of the administration of the State.

Article 13: Right to an effective remedy

Everyone whose rights and freedoms as set forth in this Convention are violated shall have an effective remedy before a national authority notwithstanding that the violation has been committed by persons acting in an official capacity.

Article 14: Prohibition of discrimination

The enjoyment of the rights and freedoms set forth in this Convention shall be secured without discrimination on any ground such as sex, race, colour, language, religion, political or other opinion, national or social origin, association with a national minority, property, birth or other status.

Article 15: Derogation in time of emergency

1   In time of war or other public emergency threatening the life of the nation any High Contracting Party may take measures derogating from its obligations under this Convention to the extent strictly required by the exigencies of the situation, provided that such measures are not inconsistent with its other obligations under international law.

Article 16: Restrictions on political activity of aliens

Nothing in Articles 10, 11 and 14 shall be regarded as preventing the High Contracting Parties from imposing restrictions on the political activity of aliens.

Article 17: Prohibition of abuse of rights

Nothing in this Convention may be interpreted as implying for any State, group or person any right to engage in any activity or perform any act aimed at the destruction of any of the rights and freedoms set forth herein or at their limitation to a greater extent than is provided for in the Convention.

Regarding the European Court of Human Rights

Article 19: Establishment of the Court

To ensure the observance of the engagements undertaken by the High Contracting Parties in the Convention and the Protocols thereto, there shall be set up a European Court of Human Rights, hereinafter referred to as "the Court". It shall function on a permanent basis.

Article 20: Number of judges
The Court shall consist of a number of judges equal to that of the High Contracting Parties.

Article 21: Criteria for office
1   The judges shall be of high moral character and must either possess the qualifications required for appointment to high judicial office or be jurisconsults of recognised competence.

2   The judges shall sit on the Court in their individual capacity.

3   During their term of office the judges shall not engage in any activity which is incompatible with their independence, impartiality or with the demands of a full-time office; all questions arising from the application of this paragraph shall be decided by the Court.

Article 24: Dismissal
No judge may be dismissed from his office unless the other judges decide by a majority of two-thirds that he has ceased to fulfil the required conditions.

Article 32: Jurisdiction of the Court
1   The jurisdiction of the Court shall extend to all matters concerning the interpretation and application of the Convention and the protocols thereto which are referred to it as provided in Articles 33, 34 and 47.

2   In the event of dispute as to whether the Court has jurisdiction, the Court shall decide.

Article 33: Inter-State cases
Any High Contracting Party may refer to the Court any alleged breach of the provisions of the Convention and the protocols thereto by another High Contracting Party.

Article 34: Individual applications
The Court may receive applications from any person, non-governmental organisation or group of individuals claiming to be the victim of a violation by one of the High Contracting Parties of the rights set forth in the Convention or the protocols thereto. The High Contracting Parties undertake not to hinder in any way the effective exercise of this right.

Article 35: Admissibility criteria
1   The Court may only deal with the matter after all domestic remedies have been exhausted, according to the generally recognised rules of international law, and within a period of six months from the date on which the final decision was taken.

2   The Court shall not deal with any application submitted under Article 34 that

    a   is anonymous; or

    b   is substantially the same as a matter that has already been examined by the Court or has already been submitted to another procedure of international investigation or settlement and contains no relevant new information.

3   The Court shall declare inadmissible any individual application submitted under Article 34 which it considers incompatible with the provisions of the Convention or the protocols thereto, manifestly ill-founded, or an abuse of the right of application.

Article 37: Striking out applications
1   The Court may at any stage of the proceedings decide to strike an application out of its list of cases where the circumstances lead to the conclusion that

    a   the applicant does not intend to pursue his application; or b   the matter has been resolved; or

c   for any other reason established by the Court, it is no longer justified to continue the examination of the application.

However, the Court shall continue the examination of the application if respect for human rights as defined in the Convention and the protocols thereto so requires.

2   The Court may decide to restore an application to its list of cases if it considers that the circumstances justify such a course.

Article 40: Public hearings and access to documents
1   Hearings shall be in public unless the Court in exceptional circumstances decides otherwise.

2   Documents deposited with the Registrar shall be accessible to the public unless the President of the Court decides otherwise.

Article 41: Just satisfaction
If the Court finds that there has been a violation of the Convention or the protocols thereto, and if the internal law of the High Contracting Party concerned allows only partial reparation to be made, the Court shall, if necessary, afford just satisfaction to the injured party.

Article 43: Referral to the Grand Chamber
1   Within a period of three months from the date of the judgment of the Chamber, any party to the case may, in exceptional cases, request that the case be referred to the Grand Chamber.

2   A panel of five judges of the Grand Chamber shall accept the request if the case raises a serious question affecting the interpretation or application of the Convention or the protocols thereto, or a serious issue of general importance.

3   If the panel accepts the request, the Grand Chamber shall decide the case by means of a judgment.

Article 44: Final judgments
1   The judgment of the Grand Chamber shall be final.

3   The final judgment shall be published.

Article 46: Binding force and execution of judgments
1   The High Contracting Parties undertake to abide by the final judgment of the Court in any case to which they are parties.

2   The final judgment of the Court shall be transmitted to the Committee of Ministers, which shall supervise its execution.

Article 50: Expenditure on the Court
The expenditure on the Court shall be borne by the Council of Europe.

Article 53: Safeguard for existing human rights
Nothing in this Convention shall be construed as limiting or derogating from any of the human rights and fundamental freedoms which may be ensured under the laws of any High Contracting Party or under any other agreement to which it is a Party.

SCHEDULE 2

Article 1: Protection of property

Every natural or legal person is entitled to the peaceful enjoyment of his possessions. No one shall be deprived of his possessions except in the public interest and subject to the conditions provided for by law and by the general principles of international law.

The preceding provisions shall not, however, in any way impair the right of a State to enforce such laws as it deems necessary to control the use of property in accordance with the general interest or to secure the payment of taxes or other contributions or penalties.

Article 2: Right to education

No person shall be denied the right to education. In the exercise of any functions which it assumes in relation to education and to teaching, the State shall respect the right of parents to ensure such education and teaching in conformity with their own religious and philosophical convictions.

Article 3: Right to free elections

The High Contracting Parties undertake to hold free elections at reasonable intervals by secret ballot, under conditions which will ensure the free expression of the opinion of the people in the choice of the legislature.

SCHEDULE 3

Article 1: Prohibition of imprisonment for debt

No one shall be deprived of his liberty merely on the ground of inability to fulfil a contractual obligation.

Article 2: Freedom of movement

1   Everyone lawfully within the territory of a State shall, within that territory, have the right to liberty of movement and freedom to choose his residence.

2   Everyone shall be free to leave any country, including his own.

3   No restrictions shall be placed on the exercise of these rights other than such as are in accordance with law and are necessary in a democratic society in the interests of national security or public safety, for the maintenance of order public, for the prevention of crime, for the protection of health or morals, or for the protection of the rights and freedoms of others.

4   The rights set forth in paragraph 1 may also be subject, in particular areas, to restrictions imposed in accordance with law and justified by the public interest in a democratic society.

Article 3: Prohibition of expulsion of nationals

1   No one shall be expelled, by means either of an individual or of a collective measure, from the territory of the State of which he is a national.

2   No one shall be deprived of the right to enter the territory of the state of which he is a national.

Article 4: The collective expulsion of aliens is prohibited.
SCHEDULE 4

Article 1: Abolition of the death penalty

The death penalty shall be abolished. No one shall be condemned to such penalty or executed.

Article 2: Death penalty in time of war

A State may make provision in its law for the death penalty in respect of acts committed in time of war or of imminent threat of war; such penalty shall be applied only in the instances laid down in the law and in accordance with its provisions. The State shall communicate to the Secretary General of the Council of Europe the relevant provisions of that law.

SCHEDULE 5

Article 1: Procedural safeguards relating to expulsion of aliens

1   An alien lawfully resident in the territory of a State shall not be expelled therefrom except in pursuance of a decision reached in accordance with law and shall be allowed:

   a   to submit reasons against his expulsion,

   b   to have his case reviewed, and

   c   to be represented for these purposes before the competent authority or a person or persons designated by that authority.

2   An alien may be expelled before the exercise of his rights under paragraph 1.a, b and c of this Article, when such expulsion is necessary in the interests of public order or is grounded on reasons of national security.

Article 2: Right of appeal in criminal matters

1   Everyone convicted of a criminal offence by a tribunal shall have the right to have his conviction or sentence reviewed by a higher tribunal. The exercise of this right, including the grounds on which it may be exercised, shall be governed by law.

2   This right may be subject to exceptions in regard to offences of a minor character, as prescribed by law, or in cases in which the person concerned was tried in the first instance by the highest tribunal or was convicted following an appeal against acquittal.

Article 3: Compensation for wrongful conviction

When a person has by a final decision been convicted of a criminal offence and when subsequently his conviction has been reversed, or he has been pardoned, on the ground that a new or newly discovered fact shows conclusively that there has been a miscarriage of justice, the person who has suffered punishment as a result of such conviction shall be compensated according to the law or the practice of the State concerned, unless it is proved that the non-disclosure of the unknown fact in time is wholly or partly attributable to him.

Article 4: Right not to be tried or punished twice

1   No one shall be liable to be tried or punished again in criminal proceedings under the jurisdiction of the same State for an offence for which he has already been finally acquitted or convicted in accordance with the law and penal procedure of that State.

2   The provisions of the preceding paragraph shall not prevent the reopening of the case in accordance with the law and penal procedure of the State concerned, if there is evidence of new or newly discovered facts, or if there has been a fundamental defect in the previous proceedings, which could affect the outcome of the case.

Article 5: Equality between spouses

Spouses shall enjoy equality of rights and responsibilities of a private law character between them, and in their relations with their children, as to marriage, during marriage and in the event of its dissolution. This Article shall not prevent States from taking such measures as are necessary in the interests of the children.

The Magna Carta - Precedent & Repeals

The Magna Carta is of interest to us for two main reasons: (i) Because it predates current English Law and therefore has a direct bearing on current Irish Law as well, and (ii) because of the increasingly-held belief amongst certain lay-circles in particular, that the Magna Carta can be quoted as an authority when dealing with abuses of authority or attempts by the establishment to curtail the rights and freedoms of the people.

We do not at present sufficiently understand the implications of Magna Carta in context of current Irish Law, but we include these abridged articles from Wikipedia for the information of the reader in the hope that it will offer some clarity and a basic understanding of the foundations of many modern democracies.

In considering the bearing of Magna Carta on Irish Law today, two constructs need to be kept in mind; firstly the principle of 'legal precedent' which basically means that Courts rely on previous rulings or judgments in similar cases, when coming to a decision - or at least, that what we are told is supposed to happen. Secondly, the use of 'repeals' which is the removal or reversal of a law - by any given government. How exactly the Magna Carta fits into an Irish legal system which (in the experiences of I-I Members) employs or ignores legal precedent at will, and 'selectively interprets' a whole slew of rules, regulations, laws and statutes in an apparently arbitrary and chaotic fashion - well, we will have to leave that discussion for another day.

* * *

(Amended, from Wikipedia)

Magna Carta (Latin for "the Great Charter"), also called Magna Carta Libertatum (Latin for "the Great Charter of the Liberties"), is a charter agreed by King John of England at Runnymede, near Windsor, on 15 June 1215. First drafted by the Archbishop of Canterbury to make peace between the unpopular King and a group of rebel barons, it promised the protection of church rights, protection for the barons from illegal imprisonment, access to swift justice, and limitations on feudal payments to the Crown, to be implemented through a council of 25 barons.

The charter became part of English political life and was typically renewed by each monarch in turn, although as time went by and the fledgling English Parliament passed new laws, it lost some of its practical significance. At the end of the 16th century there was an upsurge in interest in Magna Carta. Lawyers and historians at the time believed that there was an ancient English constitution, going back to the days of the Anglo-Saxons, that protected individual English freedoms. They argued that the Norman invasion of 1066 had overthrown these rights, and that Magna Carta had been a popular attempt to restore them, making the charter an essential foundation for the contemporary powers of Parliament and legal principles such as habeas corpus. Although this historical account was badly flawed, jurists such as Sir Edward Coke used Magna Carta extensively in the early 17th century, arguing against the divine right of kings propounded by the Stuart monarchs.

The political myth of Magna Carta and its protection of ancient personal liberties persisted after the Glorious Revolution of 1688 until well into the 19th century. It influenced the early American colonists in the Thirteen Colonies and the formation of the American Constitution in 1787, which became the supreme law of the land in the new republic of the United States. Research by Victorian historians showed that the original 1215 charter had concerned the medieval relationship between the monarch and the barons, rather than the rights of ordinary people, but the charter remained a powerful, iconic document, even after almost all of its content was repealed from the statute books in the 19th and 20th centuries. Magna Carta still forms an important symbol of liberty today, often cited by politicians and campaigners, and is held in great respect by the British and American legal communities, Lord Denning describing it as "the greatest constitutional document of all times – the foundation of the freedom of the individual against the arbitrary authority of the despot".

Clauses remaining in English law

Only three clauses of Magna Carta still remain on statute in England and Wales.[232] These clauses concern 1) the freedom of the English Church, 2) the "ancient liberties" of the City of London (clause 13 in the 1215 charter, clause 9 in the 1297 statute), and 3) a right to due legal process (clauses 39 and 40 in the 1215 charter, clause 29 in the 1297 statute). In detail, these clauses (using the numbering system from the 1297 statute) state that:

I. FIRST, We have granted to God, and by this our present Charter have confirmed, for Us and our Heirs for ever, that the Church of England shall be free, and shall have all her whole Rights and Liberties inviolable. We have granted also, and given to all the Freemen of our Realm, for Us and our Heirs for ever, these Liberties under-written, to have and to hold to them and their Heirs, of Us and our Heirs for ever.

IX. THE City of London shall have all the old Liberties and Customs which it hath been used to have. Moreover We will and grant, that all other Cities, Boroughs, Towns, and the Barons of the Five Ports, as with all other Ports, shall have all their Liberties and free Customs.

XXIX. NO Freeman shall be taken or imprisoned, or be disseised of his Freehold, or Liberties, or free Customs, or be outlawed, or exiled, or any other wise destroyed; nor will We not pass upon him, nor condemn him, but by lawful judgment of his Peers, or by the Law of the land. We will sell to no man, we will not deny or defer to any man either Justice or Right.

* * *

Legal Precedent

In common law legal systems, a 'precedent' or 'authority' is a legal case establishing a principle or rule that a court or other judicial body adopts when deciding later cases with similar issues or facts based upon earlier trial results. The use of precedent provides predictability, stability, fairness, and efficiency in the law.

The precedent on an issue is the collective body of judicially announced principles that a court should consider when interpreting the law. When a precedent establishes an important legal principle, or represents new or changed law on a particular issue, that precedent is often known as a 'landmark' decision.

Precedent is central to legal analysis and rulings in countries that follow common law like the United Kingdom, Ireland, Australia and Canada (except Quebec). In some systems precedent is not binding but is taken into account by the courts.

Binding Precedent: Precedent that must be applied or followed is known as binding precedent (alternately mandatory precedent, mandatory or binding authority, etc.). Under the doctrine of *stare decisis*, a lower court must honour findings of law made by a higher court that is within the appeals path of cases the court hears. In the United States state and federal courts, jurisdiction is often divided geographically among local trial courts, several of which fall under the territory of a regional appeals court, and all regional courts fall under a supreme court. By definition decisions of lower courts are not binding on each other or any courts higher in the system, nor are appeals court decisions binding on each other or on local courts that fall under a different appeals court. Further, courts must follow their own proclamations of law made earlier on other cases, and honour rulings made by other courts in disputes among the parties before them pertaining to the same pattern of facts or events, unless they have a strong reason to change these rulings. One USA based law professor has described mandatory precedent as follows *(amended)*:

> Given a determination as to the governing jurisdiction, a court is "bound" to follow a precedent of that jurisdiction only if it is directly in point. In the strongest sense, "directly in point" means that:
>
> (1) the question resolved in the precedent case is the same as the question to be resolved in the pending case,
>
> (2) resolution of that question was necessary to disposition of the precedent case;
>
> (3) the significant facts of the precedent case are also present in the pending case, and
>
> (4) no additional facts appear in the pending case that might be treated as significant.

In extraordinary circumstances a higher court may overturn or overrule mandatory precedent, but will often attempt to distinguish the precedent before overturning it, thereby limiting the scope of the precedent in any event.

Precedent is not 'binding' on a judge or 'mandatory' in the same sense that laws are binding on citizens. A judge cannot be sanctioned for disagreeing with precedent. His oath is to "uphold the Constitution and the laws" which sounds like yet another ambiguous contradiction-in-terms does it not? What for example should a judge do when a colleague sets a new precedent which is clearly unconstitutional? Or when a Government brings in unconstitutional legislation - an all-too regular occurrence in Ireland in recent years. Which takes precedence - the precedent or the Constitution? Well, the answer is, and *always should be* 'the Constitution. But unfortunately, that's not how it always works. The Ten Canons of Justice' in the Judicial Code of Conduct say nothing about precedent - but the overriding emphasis is absolutely on 'allegiance to the Constitution'. And this is where we need to root our arguments against any unconstitutional rulings or decisions - whether set in precedent or not. "Is it Constitutional?"

Persuasive precedent: Precedent that is not mandatory but which is useful or relevant is known as persuasive precedent (or persuasive authority or advisory precedent). Persuasive precedent includes cases decided by lower courts, by peer or higher courts from other geographic jurisdictions, and cases made in other parallel systems. In some exceptional circumstances, cases of other nations, treaties, world judicial bodies, etc., may also be quoted as precedent. In a case of first impression, courts often rely on persuasive precedent from courts in other jurisdictions that have previously dealt with similar issues. Persuasive precedent may become binding through the adoption of the persuasive precedent by a higher court.

Custom: Long-held custom, which has traditionally been recognized by courts and judges, is the first kind of precedent. Custom can be so deeply entrenched in the society at large that it gains the force of law. There need never have been a specific case decided on the same or similar issues in order for a court to take notice of customary or traditional precedent in its deliberations.

Case law: The other type of precedent is case law. In common law systems this type of precedent is granted more or less weight in the deliberations of a court according to a number of factors. Most important is whether the precedent is "on point," that is, does it deal with a circumstance identical or very similar to the circumstance in the instant case? Second, when and where was the precedent decided? A recent decision in the same jurisdiction as the instant case will be given great weight. Next in descending order would be recent precedent in jurisdictions whose law is the same as local law. Least weight would be given to precedent that stems from dissimilar circumstances, older cases that have since been contradicted, or cases in jurisdictions that have dissimilar law.

Freedom of Information Act 2014

"On 14 October 2014, the Freedom of Information Act 2014 came into effect and repealed the 1997 and 2003 Acts. The new Act introduced a number of changes to the Freedom of Information scheme and widened the range of bodies to which the FOI legislation applies to all public bodies, unless specifically exempt. It also allows for the Government to prescribe (or designate) other bodies receiving significant public funds, so that the FOI legislation applies to them also."

(Wikipedia)

In context of I-I Members' efforts to secure information under this legislation in the past, the general experience has been one of obstructionism, frustration and non-compliance by the respective authorities. It was also a very costly exercise. As part of the European Union we are now obliged to adhere to EU FOI legislation which includes more openness and reduced costs, but as usual, the Irish establishment will no doubt be fighting tooth-and-nail to protect its 'secrets'. In one notable case recently, false allegations were made (by Gardaí and TUSLA employees) against a citizen, resulting in the citizen lodging criminal complaints and a civil claim in the High Court. In order to progress his claim however, this I-I Member needed copies of the Garda reports, which he requested under the FOI legislation. The Gardaí and the HSE engaged in the usual run-arounds, denials and deferments and refused point-blank to provide the information. A notice from the Data Protection Commissioner declaring that the Gardaí and the HSE were obliged to surrender the information simply got ignored. So, other than some more clever and misleading words on paper - what really has changed? One needs only look at the list of those who are deemed to be 'Heads of an FOI Body' to realise that getting any information out of these sources will be yet another exercise in frustration and exasperation - as each in turn does their level best to hide their agency's sins and protect the powers that be at all costs.

However, the new 2014 FOI Act is certainly a move in the right direction, with more specifics about who can, and who can not divulge information, and with certain prohibitive fees being eradicated or greatly reduced. The full Act can be viewed on the *Integrity Ireland* website.

* * *

PREAMBLE: An Act to enable members of the public to obtain access, to the greatest extent possible consistent with the public interest and the right to privacy, to information in the possession of public bodies, other bodies in receipt of funding from the State and certain other bodies and to enable persons to have personal information relating to them in the possession of such bodies corrected and, accordingly, to provide for a right of access to records held by such bodies, for necessary exceptions to that right and for assistance to persons to enable them to exercise it, to provide for the independent review both of decisions of such bodies relating to that right and of the operation of this Act generally (including the proceedings of such bodies pursuant to this Act) and, for those purposes, to provide for the continuance of the office of Information Commissioner and to define its functions, to provide for the publication by such bodies of certain information about them relevant to the purposes of this Act, to repeal the Freedom of Information Act 1997 and the Freedom of Information (Amendment) Act 2003 , to amend the Central Bank Act 1942 , to amend the Official Secrets Act 1963 , to repeal certain other enactments, and to provide for related matters. [14th October, 2014]

Head of an FOI body" means—

    (a) in relation to a Department of State, the Minister of the Government having charge of it,

    (b) in relation to the Office of the Attorney General, the Attorney General,

    (c) in relation to the Office of the Director of Public Prosecutions, the Director of Public Prosecutions,

(d) in relation to the Office of the Comptroller and Auditor General, the Comptroller and Auditor General,

(e) in relation to the Office of the Ombudsman, the Ombudsman,

(f) in relation to the Office of the Information Commissioner, the Commissioner,

(g) in relation to the Financial Services Ombudsman's Bureau, the Financial Services Ombudsman,

(h) in relation to the Office of the Local Appointments Commissioners, the Local Appointments Commissioners,

(i) in relation to the Houses of the Oireachtas Service, the Chairman of Dáil Éireann,

(j) in relation to the Houses of the Oireachtas Commission, its chairperson,

(k) in relation to the Office of the Ombudsman for Children, the Ombudsman for Children,

(l) in relation to the Office of the Pensions Ombudsman, the Pensions Ombudsman,

(m) in relation to the Office of the Legal Services Ombudsman, the Legal Services Ombudsman,

(n) in relation to the Garda Síochána, the Garda Commissioner,

(o) in relation to the Garda Síochána Ombudsman Commission, its chairperson, and

(p) in relation to any other FOI body, the person who holds, or performs the functions of, the office of chief executive officer (by whatever name called) of the body;

* * *

Freedom of Information *(from the Citizens Information website)*

Introduction

The Freedom of Information Act 1997 (FOI) as amended by the Freedom of Information (Amendment) Act 2003 obliged government departments, the Health Service Executive (HSE), local authorities and a range of other public bodies to publish information on their activities and to make the information they held, including personal information, available to citizens.

The old legislation continues to apply to any FOI request made before the new legislation came into effect in Octorber 2014. It also applies to any subsequent review or appeal.

Rules

The Freedom of Information Act 2014 provides the following statutory rights:
- A legal right for each person to access information held by a body to which FOI legislation applies

- A legal right for each person to have official information relating to himself/herself amended where it is incomplete, incorrect or misleading

- A legal right to obtain reasons for decisions affecting himself/herself.

Publication scheme

Under Sections 15 and 16 of the old FOI legislation, information about the activities of bodies covered by the Freedom of Information Acts, and the records they held, were contained in their Freedom of Information manuals, which each body was obliged to publish. These Section 15 and 16 manuals are being replaced by a publication scheme under Section 8 of the 2014 Act. Section 8 is not yet in effect.

The publication scheme will contain the same information as published in the manuals, as well as any information that may be required under a model scheme or guidelines that the Minister for the Department of Public Expenditure and Reform may set out.

Requests for information

You can ask for the following records:

- Any records relating to you personally, whenever they were created

- All other records created after a certain date

- - 21 October 1998 for the HSE and local authorities

- - 21 April 1998 for public bodies that were covered by the old FOI legislation

- - 21 April 2008 for public bodies that were not covered by the old FOI legislation

- - the date of the prescribing order (or a specified date) for prescribed bodies

A record can be a paper document or information held on computer. It includes, for example, printouts, maps, plans, microfilm, audio-visual material, disks and tapes.

Rates

Section 27 of the Freedom of Information Act 2014 provides for fees and charges. The current fees are:

- Type of request or application   Standard Fee*   Reduced Fee**

- Initial request for a record   Free (was €15)   Free (was €10)

- Internal review   €30 (was €75)   €10 (was €25)

- Review by Information Commissioner   €50 (was €150)   €15 (was €50)

- Application for amendment containing incorrect information   Free

- Application for reasons for a decision affecting individual   Free

There are no fees where you appeal a decision to charge a fee or deposit, or a fee or deposit of a specific amount.

** *Reduced fees will apply in respect of medical card holders and third parties who appeal a decision to release their information on public interest grounds.*

No fees apply where the request involves access to your personal records.

Charges for search, retrieval and copying of records

Charges may be applied by the body for the time spent finding and retrieving records, and for any copying costs incurred by them in providing you with the material requested.

It is very unlikely that any charges will be applied in respect of personal records, except where a large number of records are involved.

If the cost of search, retrieval and copying is €100 or less, no charge is applied. If the charge exceeds €100, full fees apply. You cannot be charged more than €500.

If the estimated cost of search, retrieval and copying is more than €700 the body can refuse to process your request, unless you refine your request to bring the search, retrieval and copying fees below this limit.

Type of Charge	Standard Charge
● Search and retrieval of records	€20 per hour
● Photocopying	4 cent per sheet
● CD-ROM containing copy of documents	€10
● Radiograph (X-ray) containing copy documents - €6	

How to apply

It is important to note that it may not be necessary to make a request for information under the Freedom of Information Act from a body. A considerable amount of material is already made available to the public through websites, information leaflets, publications and in response to oral and written enquiries. Most organisations have a dedicated information section, which is available to assist you with general queries, requests for information and publications.

If the information you require is not readily available, you must make your request in writing to the FOI Unit of the body and your application should refer to the Freedom of Information Act. If your application for information does not mention the Act, then your application will be dealt with as an ordinary request for information. If information is required in a particular form (for example, photocopy or computer disk) this should be specified in the application.

Try to be as specific as you can in order to enable the organisation to identify the information you require. Where possible try to indicate the time period for which you wish to access records (for example, records created between May 2012 and December 2012).

Under the Act, a request for records must be acknowledged within 2 weeks and, in most cases, responded to within 4 weeks. If a third party is involved, there may be another 3 weeks before you receive a response.

You can find more information on making a request on the foi.gov.ie website.

FOI review procedures

If you are not satisfied with the response of the body to any aspect of your request for information (for example, refusal of information, form of access, charges) you can seek to have the decision re-examined. Also, if you have not received a reply within 4 weeks of your initial application (this is deemed a refusal of your request) you can seek to have the decision re-examined.

The internal review of an FOI decision is carried out by more senior members of staff within the body and must be made within 3 weeks. An application for review of a decision should be addressed to the FOI Unit of the body involved.

Where to apply

FOI requests should be addressed to the FOI Unit of the body holding the records. Information on the FOI Act is available from:

FOI Central Policy Unit
Department of Public Expenditure and Reform
7-9 Merrion Row, Dublin 2, Ireland

Tel:+353 (0)1 631 8258   Fax:+353 (0)1 604 5750
Homepage: http://foi.gov.ie/
Email: cpu@per.gov.ie

The Universal Declaration of Human Rights

The Universal Declaration of Human Rights (UDHR) is a declaration adopted by the United Nations General Assembly on 10 December 1948 at the Palais de Chaillot, Paris. The Declaration arose directly from the experience of the Second World War and represents the first global expression of rights to which all human beings are inherently entitled. The full text is published by the United Nations on its website.

The Declaration consists of thirty articles which have been elaborated in subsequent international treaties, regional human rights instruments, national constitutions, and other laws. The International Bill of Human Rights consists of the Universal Declaration of Human Rights, the International Covenant on Economic, Social and Cultural Rights, and the International Covenant on Civil and Political Rights and its two Optional Protocols. In 1966, the General Assembly adopted the two detailed Covenants, which complete the International Bill of Human Rights. In 1976, after the Covenants had been ratified by a sufficient number of individual nations, the Bill took on the force of international law.

The Universal Declaration has received praise from a number of notable people. The Lebanese philosopher and diplomat Charles Malik called it "an international document of the first order of importance", while Eleanor Roosevelt—first chairwoman of the Commission on Human Rights (CHR) that drafted the Declaration—stated that it "may well become the international Magna Carta of all men everywhere." In a speech on 5 October 1995, Pope John Paul II called the Declaration "one of the highest expressions of the human conscience of our time". In a statement on 10 December 2003 on behalf of the European Union, Marcello Spatafora said that the Declaration "placed human rights at the centre of the framework of principles and obligations shaping relations within the international community."

During World War II, the Allies adopted the Four Freedoms—freedom of speech, freedom of religion, freedom from fear, and freedom from want—as their basic war aims. The United Nations Charter "reaffirmed faith in fundamental human rights, and dignity and worth of the human person" and committed all member states to promote "universal respect for, and observance of, human rights and fundamental freedoms for all without distinction as to race, sex, language, or religion".

When the atrocities committed by Nazi Germany became apparent after the war, the consensus within the world community was that the United Nations Charter did not sufficiently define the rights to which it referred. A universal declaration that specified the rights of individuals was necessary to give effect to the Charter's provisions on human rights.

(Wikipedia)

* * *

48 countries voted in favour of the original Universal Declaration of Human Rights.

Ireland was NOT one of those countries.

PART
4
DEALING WITH
THE
ESTABLISHMENT

Law Society of Ireland

An tSéirbhís Chúirteanna
Courts Service
IRELAND

When They Ignore, Delay, Frustrate and Obstruct You..

Most people are surprised at first by the circuitous, intimidatory and obstructive tactics deployed against them by supposed 'authority figures', and the honest citizen - usually acting alone - quickly becomes exasperated and frustrated. This is because the powers-that-be rely chiefly on the fact that you are an isolated individual with little or no understanding of the way 'the system' protects itself.

There are multiple layers of bureaucracy staffed by often-anonymous individuals who, if challenged, can either redirect you to nebulous 'statutory authorities' or quote (often inaccurately) supposed 'legislation' that apparently prevents them from being forthcoming / honest / transparent or accountable to you, the tax-paying citizen who is ultimately paying their wages. The sad fact is that a culture of protectionism and 'jobs-for-the-boys' exists in most Irish institutions, and anyone who directly challenges this culture will receive little if any cooperation, regardless of what the respective rules, regulations or codes of ethics state in public forums.

So take the initiative. Don't let them bully, frustrate or intimidate you into silence. Anticipate some of the usual disingenuous tactics being used against law-abiding citizens, and use some of those very same tactics - in a principled way - in your own defence and in defence of our fundamental rights!

SOME TYPICAL DISINGENUOUS TACTICS used against citizens

- Ignoring your correspondence

- Unsigned correspondence

- Ignoring issues or otherwise not properly responding to legitimate questions

- Sending multiple overlapping responses from different departments

- Failing to adhere to their own code of ethics or codes of conduct

- Prevaricating / running down the clock / declaring issues 'out -of-time'

- Making contradictory, inaccurate, misleading or deceptive statements

- Claiming to 'have already dealt with the matter in previous correspondence'

- Telling you they will 'be in touch in due course'.. (but then all goes silent..)

- Referring you to another agency or department.. (who never contacts you again)

- Stating 'this matter is now closed!'.. (despite your ardent protestations)

- Misquoting the contents of your own letters back to you

- Arrogance, rudeness, dismissiveness and/or general contempt

- Forgery, backdating documents, altering websites etc

- Threats or intimidation.. (often veiled or anonymous)

- Failing or refusing to turn up at Court.. (yet no-one is held accountable)

- Deception, forgery, perjury, conspiracy to pervert justice or other criminal acts

Civil Servant or Public Servant - What's the Difference?

Several of the Acts, Laws and Statutes referred to in this Guide speak of 'civil servants' and 'public servants' as well as the 'private' and 'public' sectors, and it could be important that we know the difference between them.

First of all, **the private sector** usually means private businesses (and voluntary organisations such as charities). When solicitors and barristers are NOT working for the State, they would fall into the category of 'private business'.

The public sector provides various government services and State agencies, including the military, Gardaí, public transport, roads, public education, health care and those working for the government itself, such as elected officials. Public Sector Employees include Public Servants and also employees of commercial semi-state organisations such as An Post, RTÉ, ESB, the VHI etc.

The public service comprises the civil service, the local authorities, the health services, the Defence Forces, the Garda Síochána, the education sector and non-commercial state sponsored bodies.

The term **civil service** can refer to either a branch of governmental service in which individuals are employed (hired) on the basis of professional merit as proven by competitive examinations; or the body of employees in any government agency apart from the Defence Forces.

A **civil servant** or **public servant** is a person in the **public sector** employed for a government department or agency. Workers in 'non-departmental public bodies' (sometimes called QUANGOs) may also be classed as **civil servants** for the purpose of statistics and possibly for their terms and conditions. Collectively the State's **civil servants** form its **civil service** or **public service**. **Public servants** therefore include **civil servants** but also Gardaí, nurses, Local Authority employees and employees of non-commercial semi-State organisations.

Confused - yes, so are we. But the three main points to note are:

- That all **civil servants** are also (technically) **public servants.**

- That the salaries and pensions for both **civil servants** and **public servants** are paid from OUR Central Funds.

- That the Civil Service Code of Standards & Behaviours (following) applies to both.

* * *

The Commission for Public Service Appointments is tasked with ensuring that appointments made to civil service or public service roles are free from cronyism, nepotism and bias..

"The Commission has a statutory role to ensure that appointments in the organisations subject to its remit are made on merit and as the result of fair and transparent appointment processes."

2.1 Probity: A key objective of the Commission is to ensure acceptable standards of probity in all appointment processes. The principles established by the Commission in this Code of Practice are underpinned by the core values that define probity such as integrity, impartiality, fairness, reliability and ethical conduct. The Commission is concerned to nurture a values-based culture of trust, fairness, transparency and respect for all, and to ensure that probity standards are subject to consistent, rigorous oversight through its audit function. Office holders must be committed to these values and must ensure that all aspects of the appointment process are managed ethically.

MISSION OF THE CIVIL SERVICE

"The mission of the Civil Service is the achievement of an excellent service for Government and the other institutions of State as well as for the public as citizens and users of public services, based on principles of integrity, impartiality, effectiveness, equity and accountability."

The Civil Service Code of Standards and Behaviour *(abridged)*

In the performance of their duties civil servants must:

(a) Maintain high standards in service delivery by: conscientiously, honestly and impartially serving the Government of the day, the other institutions of State **and the public; always acting within the law and performing their duties with efficiency,diligence and courtesy.**

(b) Observe appropriate behaviour at work by: **dealing with the public sympathetically, fairly and promptly** and treating their colleagues with respect.

(c) **Maintain the highest standards of probity** by: conducting themselves with honesty, impartiality and integrity; never seeking to use improper influence, in particular, never seeking to use political influence to affect decisions concerning their official positions; abiding by guidelines in respect of offers of gifts or hospitality and avoiding conflicts of interest.

Breaches of the Code will constitute a breach of the terms of employment of a civil servant and may result in disciplinary action.

6.1 The work of the Civil Service is carried out within a framework of law. It is the duty of civil servants to respect these legal constraints, in particular: **never to act in a manner which they know, or suspect, is illegal, improper, or unethical** or for which they have no legal authority and to exercise any discretion conferred by law in a bona fide manner in accordance with the intentions of the statute.

7.1 All civil servants should ensure that they **deal with queries from members of the public in an open and helpful way.** Under the Freedom of Information Acts 1997 and 2003 (FOI Acts), members of the public enjoy a legal right of access to information held by Government Departments/Offices and other public bodies, subject to certain exemptions defined in the FOI Acts.

8.1 Civil servants should: ensure that members of the public have their affairs dealt with sympathetically, efficiently and promptly; **always give their names to any member of the public with whom they are dealing**, except where given a special exemption, for example, on security grounds and ensure that members of the public are dealt with in a respectful manner.

11.1 **Civil servants should endeavour to ensure the proper, effective, and efficient use of public money.**

11.2 Civil servants are required to: **take proper and reasonable care of public funds** and departmental property and not to use them, or permit their use, for unauthorised purposes; incur no liability on the part of their employer without proper authorisation and **ensure that expenses, such as travel and subsistence payments, are not unnecessarily incurred** either by themselves or by staff reporting to them.

13. Civil servants are **not allowed** to: use their official positions to benefit themselves or others

with whom they have personal, family, business or other ties.

14.1 Civil servants **may not at any time** engage in, or be connected with, any outside business or activity which would in any way conflict with the interests of their Departments/Offices, or be inconsistent with their official positions, or tend to impair their ability to carry out their duties as civil servants.

14.2 Civil servants **must never** seek to use knowledge acquired in the performance of, or as a result of, their official duties to benefit themselves, or others with whom they have personal, family or other ties.

16.1 Civil servants **should not** receive benefits of any kind from a third party which might reasonably be seen to compromise their personal judgement or integrity.

16.3 It should be noted that, under the Prevention of Corruption Acts 1889 to 2001 as amended by the Ethics in Public Office Act 1995, the corrupt giving of gifts to, or receipt of gifts by, civil servants is a criminal offence punishable by imprisonment or fine or both. The Acts provide that money, gifts or other consideration received by a civil servant from a person holding or seeking to obtain a contract from a Government Department/Office is deemed to have been received corruptly unless the contrary is proved.

18.2 **All Departments/Offices should ensure that they have appropriate standards which have been clearly set out and made known to all staff.**

* * *

In the course of doing research for this Guide, we came across the following excerpt from *Section 23 of the Criminal Justice Act 1951* which appears to bestow upon the Government the absolute power to reverse / annul / cancel any decision by a criminal Court. This is certainly worth bearing in mind in context of repeated deferrals and denials from the Minister for Justice and the Office of the Taoiseach that they can in any way 'interfere' in the business of the Courts. The usual line is; *"judges are independent in their functions, subject only to the law and the Constitution - therefore I have no role to play in the matter."* (Or some such similar clause) But clearly, the power to 'interfere' IS there if they really want to avail of it.

Remission of punishment, forfeitures and disqualifications.

23.—(1) Except in capital cases, **the Government may commute or remit**, in whole or in part, **any punishment imposed by a Court exercising criminal jurisdiction**, subject to such conditions as they may think proper.

(2) The Government may remit, in whole or in part, any forfeiture or disqualification imposed by a Court exercising criminal jurisdiction and restore or revive, in whole or in part, the subject of the forfeiture.

(3) The Government may delegate to the Minister for Justice any power conferred by this section and may revoke any such delegation.

(4) This section shall not affect any power conferred by law on other authorities.

(5) Where a disqualification for holding a driving licence under the Road Traffic Act, 1933 (No. 11 of 1933), is remitted, in whole or in part, under this section, notice of the remission shall be published as soon as may be in Iris Oifigiúil (Irish State Gazette).

Dealing With Civil Servants and Public Servants by Phone

1. Always record your phone calls. You can erase them later if needs be.

2. You are NOT legally obliged to inform the other party that you are recording them (no matter what they tell you) as long as you are a party to the conversation.

3. Ask who you are speaking to before you engage with them. The *Civil Service Code of Standards and Behaviour* requires that they give their names to members of the public.

4. Be polite and civil, but firm if you sense that you are NOT being cooperated with.

5. If the person you are dealing with is in any way rude, uncooperative or obstructive, simply inform them that you will *not* continue the conversation on the grounds that they are in breach of the *Civil Service Code of Conduct*, and that you require to speak with their superior.

6. If you continue to have problems (and provided you have everything recorded) you can terminate the phone call advising them that you require their superior to call YOU back - at THEIR expense - to advance your complaint and pursue your original enquiry.

7. If they do not call you back, then you have every right not to have any further dealings with them. Your record of the phone call will be proof that they were unreasonable.

8. If on the other hand you need some answers to some important questions for example, and you absolutely *need* to communicate with them, then you might begin by advising them that the call is being recorded 'in the interests of transparency and accountability' and that if your queries are not dealt with in a prompt and helpful manner, that you reserve the right to bill them for your time at a rate of (name your price), and lodge a formal complaint.

9. You might also ask them to agree to this costs condition before you engage with them further, and get the name and address of their CEO/boss (not just a line manager or supervisor) so you can send a bill directly to him/her if your call isn't fruitful.

10. Letting them know that you are a member or supporter of *Integrity Ireland* may also be helpful - or maybe not? You decide. ☺

11. Finally, if you get one of those debt-collection-type calls where they open by questioning you about your details 'in order to establish who you are' then simply ask them the very same questions back, so that YOU know who it is that you are dealing with. They will, invariably tell you that they are 'not obliged to disclose personal information'.. So why on earth should you? And don't forget that it is a crime to 'harass' someone or demand payment with threats *(see ICCS list in Part 1, Nos 0331, 0333 & 0335)*.

The key point to remember folks is that your time is precious too. Why should YOU have to waste time and money trying to get information; or trying to solve problems which are often caused by the negligence or obstructiveness of the other party? You have an absolute right to fair, prompt and respectful treatment - especially from people whose wages YOU are paying.

But things will never change if we don't stand up and assert our rights in the face of rudeness or poor service from people who are being paid from the public purse. So, next time you come up against rudeness, ignorance or obstructiveness from a public servant, remind them (politely but firmly) that they are in a service role, and that you would be obliged if they remember that.

Of course, when someone is helpful and cooperative (as is most often the case) then please remember to thank them for their courtesy and helpful attitude - because as they say, "You'll catch more flies with honey, than with vinegar!"

Corresponding With the Authorities by Letters and Emails

The importance of letters cannot be overstated. The old saying, "The pen is mightier than the sword" has been proven beyond doubt on numerous occasions. However, on the flip side, once you put something 'in writing' it remains there as documentary evidence for all to see. How many of us have written something in anger or frustration that has later come back to haunt us? Even more so now, with the facility of social media at our fingertips. So before you put pen to paper (or fingers to keyboards) ask yourself why are you writing this letter, email or post?

First of all, is it absolutely necessary? Secondly, if it is necessary, then how do I compose this message to secure the result I want in the shortest time possible? And please, don't forget that you are usually up against a State agency who specialises in composing generic responses to 'concerned citizens' which do everything BUT answer your questions - by people who are trained over many years to frustrate your efforts to get speedy and efficient service. The reasons for this usually fall between three equally-unacceptable premises: (i) They simply don't care - or, they get a perverse satisfaction from having some 'control' over you. (ii) They are protecting their colleagues and superiors. (iii) There is profit in dragging out the process (e.g. for lawyers).

Another big problem facing 'ordinary citizens' when dealing with agencies of the State, corporate interests, or 'professional bodies' (such as lawyers for example) is the fact that we are usually obliged to deal with front-line staff in order to convey a message to the people who we *really* want to be dealing with; i.e. the mangers, the bosses, the senior partners, the CEOs, the TDs or Ministers etc. While some of these front-line staff can be genuinely helpful and accommodating, hundreds of reports on the I-I HAFTA database suggest that a great many are not - and we need to have an effective response for this.

The premise is relatively simple: if someone is rude, disrespectful, ignorant, unhelpful, deceptive or obstructive, or in any other way fails to provide the service they are supposed to deliver to you (according to their respective mandates or codes of conduct etc) then why on earth would you continue to deal with them? To put it another way, how many times are you going to pay for a bus journey when the bus driver never takes you to the right destination? Or how many times will you return to the baker who sells you mouldy bread? Who is the fool who keeps getting on that bus or buying that bread - eh? So why do we waste our precious time dealing with those who would make fools of us - and would do so deliberately, repeatedly, and even systematically? And to make matters worse - that they are often doing this at *your* direct expense.

So, the minute we sense that we are being messed about, we put them on clear notice that we will NOT be messed about, and we attach a 'Caveat of Affirmation' at the end of all our communications *(in very small print of course)* along the lines of one of the following examples. By doing this, you are doing three things: (i) Alerting them to the fact that you are aware of the usual tactics and will NOT be a pushover. (ii) Establishing a 'contract' of sorts whereby they ARE obliged to pay for any misconduct. (iii) Establishing the firm condition - based upon their OWN rules and regulations - where you are NOT obliged to communicate further with them.

__Statutory affirmation:__ The statutory right to fair and equitable treatment is asserted. Any individual or agency who, through the means of misinformation, evasiveness, deception or obfuscation, contrives to avoid fulfilling their constitutional mandate [as defined in the Irish Constitution, company law, respective members charters, codes of ethics, and/or terms of service] is hereby advised – without further notice to any such party or parties – of the individual's fundamental right to seek legal redress, as well as to note, report and/or publish any communications sent or received for the purposes of transparency and due accountability in the interests of natural justice—and to bill any such agents or agencies for time and costs incurred. Please be advised.

> ***Caveat of affirmation:*** *We respectfully assert our statutory right to fair and equitable treatment, and reserve the moral right to disengage communication with any individual or agency who, through the means of misinformation, evasiveness, obfuscation, deception or other disingenuous tactics, contrives to avoid fulfilling their mandate to the public [as defined in the Constitution, respective codes of ethics, oaths of office and/or terms of service] other than where we are legally obliged to do so. We further affirm our right to note, report, record and/or publish any communications sent or received for the purposes of transparency, due accountability, and in the interests of natural justice. We further reserve the right to hold responsible under the law any individual, agent or agency we deem responsible for deliberate civil, criminal or constitutional breaches, and to bill any such agents or agencies for time and costs incurred. We do not deal with anonymous, pseudonymous, allonymous or imaginary entities. Annotated emails are accepted under certain exceptional or pre-agreed circumstances, but important or legal correspondence must also be sent as hard copies, duly signed. Unsigned correspondence that is not ascribed to one authorised individual will not be responded to and may be returned for signing, with costs billed to the source thereof. For practical reasons, legal matters will be dealt with on Mondays and Tuesdays only. Please be advised.*

Using a caveat of this nature (please edit or amend as you see fit) deals with a number of irregularities often used by the establishment - especially by legal firms and authority figures - to avoid accountability for what they have, or have not done. The reference to '*anonymous, pseudonymous, allonymous or imaginary entities*' above for example, is to counteract the prevailing practice of correspondence being issued 'in someone's name' when the author of the correspondence is NOT that same person. This allows the *alleged* author to claim 'no knowledge' of that correspondence - or to blame some junior staffer if some irregularity or mistruth later surfaces. This practice also ensures of course, that YOU (the recipient) never really know who is actually responsible for the contents of any given letter - which in turn makes it almost impossible for you to hold anyone properly to account - right?

Even more alarming perhaps is when legal letters are 'signed off' in the name of the legal firm - or when generic 'signatures' are simply stamped on a letter, such as the case with Arthur Cox Solicitors for example, who continue to 'sign' their letters in the personal name of their long-dead founder - a practice that has been going on for over 40 years now. It wouldn't be a matter of such concern if it wasn't for the fact that Arthur Cox solicitors are the biggest law firm in Ireland; that they earn more from State contracts than any other law firm; that barristers and solicitors supplied by them are engaged in some of the most outrageous 'conflict-of-interest' and apparent overcharging scandals in recent history; and that they are, in effect, a 'private' de-facto arm of the Government.

To emphasise how important it is that those communicating with you sign off in their own personal names; just ask yourself if any law firm, Government Department or Court would allow another person to 'speak on your behalf' without a whole slew of convoluted legal processes first being in place? So, what's good for the goose is good for the gander - as they say.

So, make sure the other side knows that you are alert as to their usual tricks. And make sure that you do NOT communicate again with someone who is clearly messing you about. Just refuse, point blank to deal with them again, and instead go over their heads explaining to their superior why you will NOT be dealing with that person again. And if the superior does likewise, then go over their head too - until you reach the top. Then, you can hold the top person directly responsible for the activities and behaviours of their employees or subordinates... and if the boss is also uncooperative, then maybe it's time for some 'direct action' - I-I style?

Don't forget, that as a member of *Integrity Ireland*, you can make direct reference to the experiences of other members who have had dealings with problematic authority figures. In the same way that you could legitimately refuse to get on a bus after hearing reports from other passengers that the bus driver keeps going off-route; then in the same way, you can refer to the I-I complaints log and HAFTA Database as grounds NOT to engage with someone in authority or with an employee in a law firm for example, who has been registered as a serial malefactor. Even more so if criminal complaints have been lodged with Gardaí and/or in the District Court.

We have to remind ourselves folks that time is precious; that life is short; and that many, many ordinary people are spending years and decades trying to make progress in relatively straightforward cases - only to be repeatedly thwarted, obstructed and eventually exhausted by venal individuals engaging in deliberate and premeditated obstructionism.

You don't have to be rude - you don't even have to get angry with these ignorant behaviours (although it would be wholly appropriate to do so) - no, you just have to remain firm and determined. You DO have to expect them to try these underhanded tactics though - so be prepared for at least one round of frustration before advancing through the ranks to the head of department. No doubt, they will still try to re-route you back through other departments or otherwise waste your time, and you have to be ready for that as well. But whatever you do, don't back down, and do NOT under any circumstances re-engage with someone who you have previously cut off. Because if enough of us refuse to engage with these people - then eventually they will become unemployable - or, they will have to change their ways. Similarly, the hassle and difficulties caused to senior managers in dealing with determined complainants should not be underestimated. But we have to persevere - or else face this type of obstructive nonsense time and time again - and see our lives being systematically wasted dealing with people who have little or no respect for us, nor for the fact that it is us who are ultimately paying their wages.

And Then, What..?
The one great weakness in using these I-I tactics is that we will eventually run out of authority figures to deal with, especially if all of them—from bottom-to-top in any given agency—turn out to be as bad as each other (as has so often been the case) - conspiring with each other to cover-up for each others' sins. Sadly, this appears to be the general trend with State agencies in particular - as evidenced in our efforts to date to hold erring authority figures to account. With one or two notable exceptions* the overwhelming trend is to suppress, deny, cover-up and ignore serious problems, and punish any complainants or whistleblowers. But this is where we have to hope and believe that in taking direct action and in documenting and publicising the same, and finally, in generating enough public support and awareness of what is going on 'in our name' - that we will generate enough awareness and shame, for things to change.

As to the suggestion that 'they' can just ignore us after all the other options are spent. Well, they may be able to ignore us as *individuals*, but they won't be able to ignore us as *a collective* - especially when that collective is growing day-by-day into a national movement. However, it is going to take time, and patience and commitment from all of us to make this I-I project work. But the more of us that engage in these tactics of direct action, the sooner that rogue authorities will get the message..

Please feel free to use the examples in Part 7 as a template for your own letters and emails.

To contact Irish Politicians, TDs, Senators, MEPs, County Councillors or City Councillors please go to www.contact.ie which is a free bulk emailing service, ready-to-use.

---

* A recent exception to this rule is HIQA; the *Health Information and Quality Authority* who, under Mr Phelim Quinn really do seem to be on the ball regarding the appalling state of the HSE.

For Confidential Emails

CONFIDENTIALITY NOTICE: *This email transmission and any documents, files, or previous e-mail messages attached to it are confidential and intended solely for the use of the individual or entity to whom they are addressed. If you are not the intended recipient, or a person responsible for delivering it to the intended recipient, you are hereby notified that any further review, disclosure, copying, dissemination, distribution, or use of any of the information contained in or attached to this e-mail transmission is strictly prohibited. If you have received this message in error, please notify the sender immediately by e-mail, discard any paper copies, and delete all electronic files of the message. If you are unable to contact the sender or you are not sure as to whether you are the intended recipient, please call.. (your details here).*

* * *

USING POSTAL SERVICES

One of the mainstays of Court proceedings is the business of legal documents being 'served' on the opposition in any given case. We will deal with the specifics regarding different Courts' requirements later on, but in general, if you are serving Court documents by post, you are required to use 'Prepaid Registered Post' at a cost of €6.10 (for a normal letter) as supposed 'proof' that the documents have been delivered. The same applies to any other important correspondence. If you want to 'prove' that the document has been sent *and* received, then the accepted procedure is to use prepaid registered post and produce the signed receipt of delivery. However, all is not as it seems, and there are a number of serious problems regarding this service which we should all be aware of, especially if we are relying on the supposed integrity of this facility to prove or disprove that any given document has been sent or received.

First of all, it is a commonly-known fact that unscrupulous parties will claim to have sent letters to the opposition, and the opposition will in turn deny having received them. The result can be lengthy delays in proceedings going forwards - or in getting timely replies to important letters. This is why prepaid registered post is used in legal cases in particular. So, a litigant produces a Post Office receipt proving that he sent a letter to the opposition, and he has the opposition's signature to prove it was received - right? Wrong! All that has been proven is that an *envelope* was dispatched from one location and received at another. Because no-one (except the originator) knows exactly what was inside that envelope *at the time it was signed for* - right?

Now this might seem like a case of hair-splitting, but it's not. Because we have had examples where empty envelopes (or envelopes containing blank sheets of paper) have been signed for by a trusting recipient, thus apparently 'proving' that they received something. But when that 'something' later turns out to be a missing Notification to Attend Court for example - and they don't turn up - and the opposition dutifully presents a signed receipt of delivery... Well, who are *you* going to believe? **So, point number one is *never* to sign for registered post until you have opened the envelope and confirmed that the contents are genuine.**

If, for any reason an item cannot be delivered, then the Post Office attaches a pink sticker marked 'Return to Sender' giving the reason why the item has been returned. Those options are: *(a) Unknown at the address. (b) Gone away. (c) Insufficient address. (d) Refused. (e) Not called for. (f) Deceased. (g) Other.*

Unfortunately, these options allow for a range of abuses of this service, not least of all the option for the intended recipient to simply 'refuse' a letter which *you* have already paid €6.10 to be delivered!

Apparently, when registered post is 'refused' at the door by the intended recipient in person, the postman is under no obligation to insist upon delivery. This is another way that someone can simply avoid being notified of a Court appearance - especially if they are expecting those papers - and the other party then has to suffer further adjournments, delays, and the re-issue of costly summonses etc., because technically, the papers haven't been 'properly served'. More costly delays will ensue when the intended recipient of the letter *truthfully* states that he didn't receive the letter - a fact that is proven by the Post Office tracking records which state that the item was in fact 'returned to sender' - i.e. to you.

Another repeat problem is when registered letters are actually opened and read before being resealed, marked 'refused' and returned to sender - sometimes with the help of a friendly An Post employee. These are glaring anomalies in the integrity and reliability of this particular service, and we have so many examples of other abuses of this process by devious operators as to qualify our refusal to use this costly service, when a simple green 'Certificate of Posting' will suffice. A 'Certificate of Posting' (proof of postage) has several advantages over registered post:

- It costs nothing.

- It can apply to normal letters, packets or parcels, using normal postal rates.

- It definitively proves that you dispatched that item to the recipient.

- There is no requirement for a signature at the other end, and therefore no opportunity for the recipient to 'refuse' it.

- If the item does *not* come back to you, unopened, marked 'Return to Sender' or 'Moved Away' then it is safe to assume that it has been delivered to the addressee.

Another service provided by An Post which guarantees next day delivery - complete with tracking records and all the other advantages of registered post but *without* the requirement to collect a signature is '**Express Post**'. For the same price as registered post you can guarantee and *prove* that a document has been deposited in the recipient's letterbox. For an extra €2 you can even get their signature. It is bewildering to many of us why this Express Post service is not used instead by the Courts? Maybe upon reading this expose they might reconsider - or is it too cynical to suggest that it is ultimately much more profitable for unscrupulous litigants or their legal teams (and far easier to manipulate the records) to continue using registered post.

From the An Post website
Express Post promises speedy delivery for less. Pick up an Express Post label at any Post Office. Attach the label to your item and apply the appropriate postage. We will deliver your item on the next working day. You can track your items progress online and, for an additional fee of €2, a signature will be collected on delivery and insurance cover up to €350 in the Republic of Ireland will be included.

After you post:

- *Keep your receipt - it's your proof of postage*

- *Track your item online using the unique number on the receipt*

- *If you paid the additional €2 for Signature and Insurance the signature will be available online for up to a month after delivery*

- *If you require evidence of whom the item was sent to please ask for a Certificate of Posting at the time of posting. We guarantee next working day delivery to addresses nationwide. Terms and conditions apply*

As for the overall integrity of the registered post system; if you find yourself facing an opposition in Court for example, who states that they sent you documentation by registered post, and that because it was not 'returned to sender' after the statutory 3 days, that you *must* have received it - then you can make reference to those documented incidents on the I-I Database where registered mail was illegally held up for over a week in order to facilitate a 'connected' Defendant's attempts to avoid a Court case. This happened on three successive occasions over a four-week period, yet surprisingly, the subsequent An Post enquiries uncovered 'no cause for complaint'. Absurd excuses such as the letters having been 'overlooked' or having 'fallen behind the counter' were offered in a desperate attempt to protect a connected insider, and his friend the postman. On two other occasions registered mail intended for an I-I member was fraudulently signed for by two different Commissioners for Oaths, and then the 'proofs of delivery' were presented in Court as proof of service. (We are waiting for the Garda response to those incidents too). On other occasions, regular and registered mail has been illegally intercepted, opened-and-read, diverted, or returned-to-sender without proper cause or explanation - resulting in another ongoing investigation by the Post Office which has now been 'ongoing' for six months without reply.

So you can safely defend your decision to raise any questions you wish about the legitimacy or appropriateness of spending any more time, energy or money than is absolutely necessary, 'proving' that letters have been dispatched or received. So basically, don't waste your time and money on a service that can be so easily manipulated and abused for devious ends. Use the green 'Certificate of Posting' and/or the Express Post service and refer to these explanations and the history of abuses of the postal system as reasoning for your decision. And if all else fails, just send a copy of your original document to the person's place of work, and an email as back up 'cc'd' to yourself. Any authority figure facing this barrage of reasoning and genuine attempts to 'serve' the other party in face of such a compromised service, must surely accept that service has indeed been completed - and you save yourself €6.10 or several multiples thereof.

If you really want to be emphatic abut proper service having been completed, then attach a signed 'I-I proof of contents' slip (see below) with your certificate of posting - or a Statement of Delivery or Receipt (in Appendix II). This will remove any question as to what exactly was sent in that envelope, and may even dispense with the need for you to pay a solicitor or Commissioner for Oaths for the privilege of witnessing your signature when you declare to the Court that proper Notice was indeed completed.

DECLARATION OF POSTAL SERVICE

I hereby declare that I witnessed ....

place a letter dated.......................and/or an item (description)..........................

…..

into an envelope/packet addressed to ....

…..

Signed...Date...............................…..

By the way, in the event you need to have a signature witnesses by a solicitor or a Commissioner for Oaths, the standard rate is €10. If you are asked for any more, then request a receipt and send a copy to us so we have documentary proof of overcharging - and the basis for some appropriate 'direct action' - such as a complaint to the respective authorities, and a warning to the public.

THE IRISH GOVERNMENT

Several fundamental problems with our Irish political system need to be urgently addressed: Firstly, our system is neither democratic, nor representative, despite the illusion that the average citizen 'has a vote'. This is partly because the choices before us are abysmal; do we vote for this gang of self-serving rogues - or the *other* gang of self-serving rogues - either of which seems to believe they have the God-given right to treat us like medieval serfs - there merely to support their lavish and arrogant lifestyles? The Irish political system - described as 'unique' in Europe because of its numerous contradictions-in-terms - is badly and sadly broken. Once elected to government for example, the leader of the ruling party has in effect, full autocratic control through the party whip system, which penalises any party member who exercises his democratic right to differ with the leader. What the 'dear leader' says, goes! So, even if any individual politician has the genuine urge to 'do what is best for the people' - or genuinely intends to fulfil his election promises - 'the system' as it stands will not allow it. Furthermore, corrupt politicians who have been exposed as liars, fraudsters, perjurers and bribe-takers (and there are plenty to choose from folks) have nothing to fear it seems, from exposure in the media or the courts. Despite overwhelming evidence against them, they brazenly continue in office, grinning smugly all the way to the bank - which by the way is officially OUR bank now! And to top it all are the disgraceful levels of moral cowardice on display when our elected representatives are simply asked to do their jobs and 'represent' a wronged citizen.

It has to be asked folks; who are the REAL fools when we continue to elect politicians with no moral fibre, no sense of integrity, and no real vocation to serve anyone other than themselves? How much longer will we allow these scoundrels to lord it over us - at our expense, and at our children's expense? How many 'secret deals' with corporations will we turn a blind eye to whilst our heritage and our national resources are plundered?

US Ambassador Kennedy seemed to understand this when she said, *"The trouble with the Irish is that there isn't enough outrage!"*

Again, we seem - as a nation - to be suffering from some collective malaise. A certain apathy - a lack of engagement - a failure or refusal to accept that WE (collectively) are ultimately responsible for those who get elected. It is clear that most of them in turn are NOT responsible to us once they get elected - at least not until a couple of months before the *next* election. So, WE have to *make* them accountable. Not only when it comes to election time, but all the way through their tenures by challenging them openly and publicly every time they fail us or fail the high offices they are so privileged to hold.

Some have suggested that we are still suffering the effects of a national-level mental depression dating back to the famine years. Other say that its the fluoride in the water supply that is dumbing us down, and others (most notably those in positions of power and influence) are simply taking us for fools and sops - ready to be bought off every five years with a give-away budget, some hollow cheerleading and beating up of the opposition, and a number of 'sincere promises' that "..all is getting better. Really it is! I mean, would I lie to you?"

If the party political system hasn't yet demonstrated to all of us that it is no longer a workable option, then indeed we truly are fools and idiots if we let the same crowd back in to continue their lies, their deceptions and their manipulations of the public.

Perhaps it IS about time to consider an alliance of Independents. Because if they have had the strength and courage as individuals to stand up to the establishment, then just imagine what they could do in a collective. In contrast to most party politicians, the Independents have demonstrated courage, innovation and intelligence, and a loyalty to their constituents *and* their consciences. Unity of mind and purpose will come naturally amongst people of courage and integrity.

Overview of the Irish Political System

Ireland is a parliamentary democracy. The Head of the Government is the Taoiseach. The Tánaiste is the Deputy Prime Minister. There are 15 Government Departments. The Taoiseach and the Ministers collectively form the Government under the Irish Constitution, and they hold executive power.

The Parliament is called the Oireachtas. There are two Houses of Parliament: Dáil Éireann (House of Representatives) and Seanad Éireann (Senate). The Dáil has 166 members known as Teachtaí Dála (TD), who are elected using proportional representation with a single transferrable vote (PR-STV). Elections take place at least every five years. The current government, elected in 2011, is a coalition between Fine Gael and Labour. The other main political parties represented in the Dáil are Fianna Fáil and Sinn Féin.

The Seanad has 60 members, eleven of whom are nominated by the Taoiseach. The rest are elected from vocational panels and by national universities. The Seanad can initiate or revise legislation, but the Dáil can reject their amendments and proposed legislation.

The President of Ireland (Uachtarán na hÉireann) serves as Head of State and is directly elected by the people. Presidents are elected for seven years, and can serve no more than two terms. The President has a largely ceremonial role.

There are 114 local authorities in Ireland. They provide a wide range of services, including housing, transport, water supply, waste management, education, health and welfare.

The current government (2015) consists of:

Enda Kenny	Taoiseach	taoiseach@taoiseach.gov.ie
Joan Burton	Social Protection	minister@welfare.ie
Michael Noonan	Finance	minister@finance.gov.ie
Brendan Howlin	Public Expenditure & Reform	minister@per.gov.ie
Richard Bruton	Jobs, Enterprise & Innovation	minister@djei.ie
Simon Coveney	Agriculture, Food, Defence	minister@Defence.ie
Frances Fitzgerald	Justice & Equality	minister@justice.ie
James Reilly	Children & Youth Affairs	James.Reilly@oireachtas.ie
Leo Varadkar	Health	minister's_office@health.gov.ie
Charles Flanagan	Foreign Affairs & Trade	minister@dfa.ie
Jan O'Sullivan	Education & Skills	minister@education.gov.ie
Alan Kelly	Environment, Community etc	minister@environ.ie
Alex White	Communications, Energy etc	minister.white@dcenr.gov.ie
Paschal Donohue	Transport, Tourism & Sport	Minister@dttas.ie
Heather Humphries	Arts, Heritage & Gaeltacht	ministers.office@ahg.gov.ie

CODE OF CONDUCT FOR MEMBERS OF DÁIL ÉIREANN

1. Members must, in good faith, strive to maintain the public trust placed in them, and exercise the influence gained from their membership of Dáil Éireann to advance the public interest.

2. Members must conduct themselves in accordance with the provisions and spirit of the Code of Conduct and ensure that their conduct does not bring the integrity of their office or the Dáil into serious disrepute.

3. (i) Members have a particular obligation to behave in a manner which is consistent with their roles as public representatives and legislators, save where there is a legitimate and sustainable conscientious objection.

(ii) Members must interact with authorities involved with public administration and the enforcement of the law in a manner which is consistent with their roles as public representatives and legislators.

4. (i) Members must base their conduct on a consideration of the public interest and are individually responsible for preventing conflicts of interest.

(ii) Members must endeavour to arrange their private financial affairs to prevent such conflicts of interest arising and must take all reasonable steps to resolve any such conflict quickly and in a manner which is in the best interests of the public.

5. (i) A conflict of interest exists where a Member participates in or makes a decision in the execution of his or her office knowing that it will improperly and dishonestly further his or her private financial interest or another person's private financial interest directly or indirectly.

(ii) A conflict of interest does not exist where the Member or other person benefits only as a member of the general public or a broad class of persons.

6. Members may not solicit, accept or receive any financial benefit or profit in exchange for promoting, or voting on, a Bill, a motion for a resolution or order or any question put to the Dáil or to any of its committees.

7. Members must fulfil conscientiously the requirements of the Dáil and of the law in respect of the registration and declaration of interests and, to assist them in so doing, should familiarise themselves with the relevant legislation and guidelines published from time to time by the Committee on Members' Interests and the Standards in Public Office Commission as appropriate.

8. (i) Members must not accept a gift that may pose a conflict of interest or which might interfere with the honest and impartial exercise of their official duties.

(ii) Members may accept incidental gifts and customary hospitality.

9. In performing their official duties, Members must apply public resources prudently and only for the purposes for which they are intended.

10. Members must not use official information which is not in the public domain, or information obtained in confidence in the course of their official duties, for personal gain or the personal gain of others.

11. Members must co-operate with all Tribunals of Inquiry and other bodies inquiring into matters of public importance established by the Houses of the Oireachtas.

Adopted by Dáil Éireann on 28 February, 2002

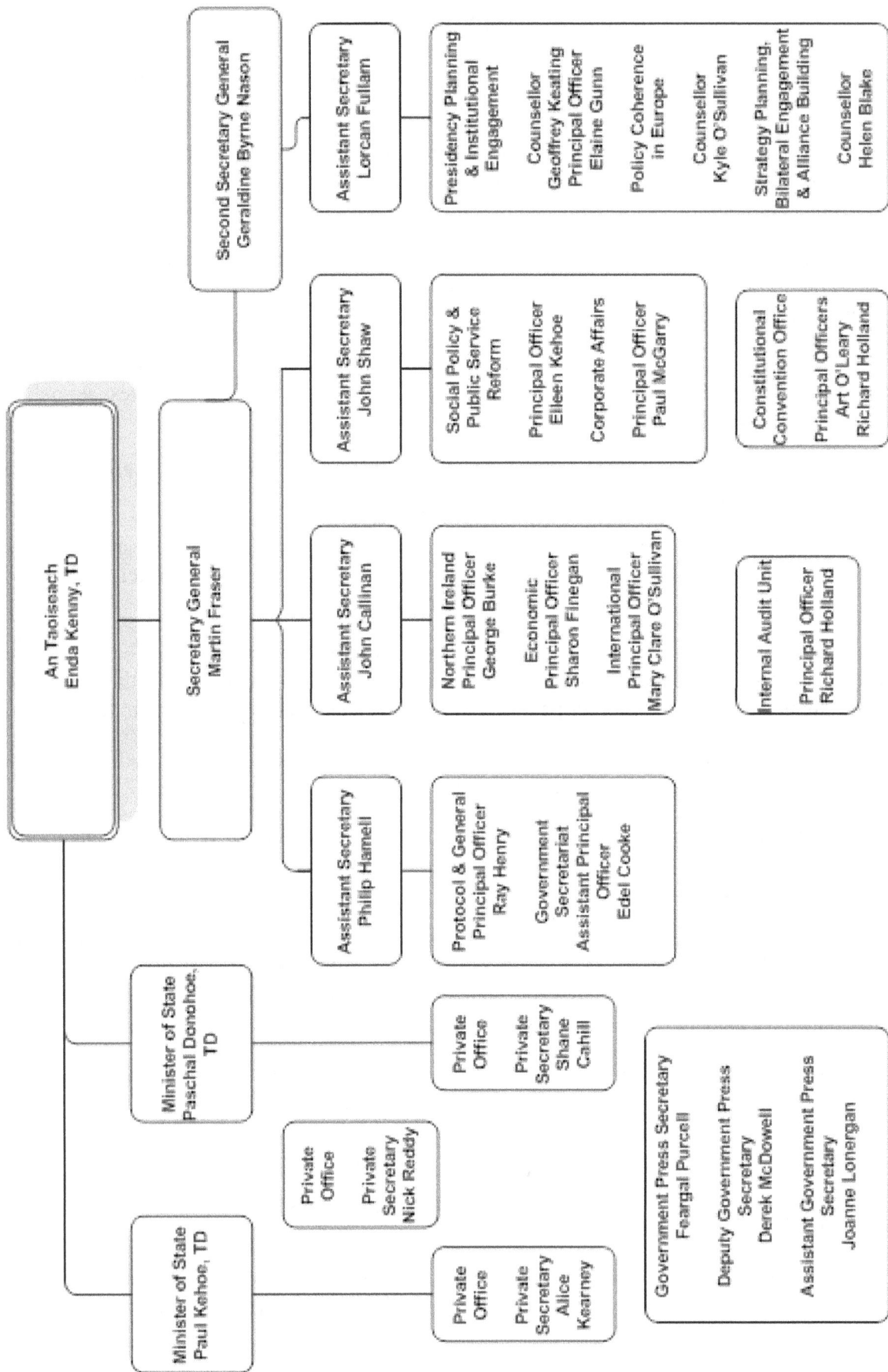

Internal Structure at the Department of the Taoiseach

An Taoiseach Enda Kenny, TD

Secretary General Martin Fraser

Second Secretary General Geraldine Byrne Nason

Assistant Secretary Lorcan Fullam
- Presidency Planning & Institutional Engagement
  - Counsellor Geoffrey Keating
  - Principal Officer Elaine Gunn
- Policy Coherence in Europe
  - Counsellor Kyle O'Sullivan
- Strategy Planning, Bilateral Engagement & Alliance Building
  - Counsellor Helen Blake

Assistant Secretary John Shaw
- Social Policy & Public Service Reform
  - Principal Officer Eileen Kehoe
- Corporate Affairs
  - Principal Officer Paul McGarry

Constitutional Convention Office
- Principal Officers Art O'Leary / Richard Holland

Assistant Secretary John Callinan
- Northern Ireland
  - Principal Officer George Burke
- Economic
  - Principal Officer Sharon Finegan
- International
  - Principal Officer Mary Clare O'Sullivan

Internal Audit Unit
- Principal Officer Richard Holland

Assistant Secretary Philip Hamell
- Protocol & General
  - Principal Officer Ray Henry
- Government Secretariat
  - Assistant Principal Officer Edel Cooke

Minister of State Paschal Donohoe, TD
- Private Office
  - Private Secretary Shane Cahill

Minister of State Paul Kehoe, TD
- Private Office
  - Private Secretary Nick Reddy

Private Office
- Private Secretary Alice Kearney

Government Press Secretary Feargal Purcell

Deputy Government Press Secretary Derek McDowell

Assistant Government Press Secretary Joanne Lonergan

To contact Irish Politicians, TDs, Senators, MEPs, County Councillors or City Councillors please go to www.contact.ie which is a free bulk emailing service, ready-to-use.

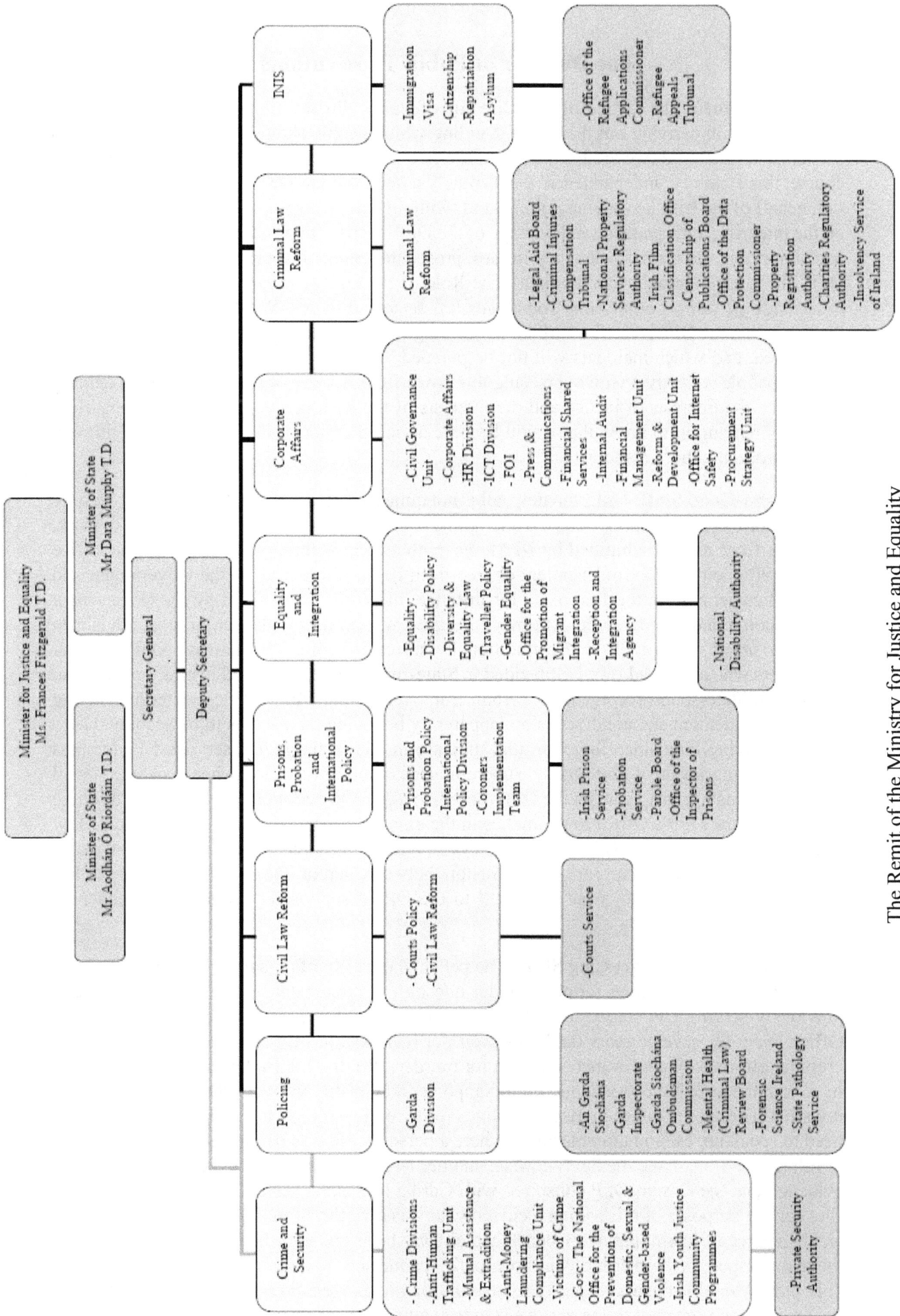

The Remit of the Ministry for Justice and Equality

Minister for Justice and Equality Ms. Frances Fitzgerald T.D.

- Minister of State Mr Aodhán O Riordáin T.D.
- Minister of State Mr Dara Murphy T.D.

Secretary General

Deputy Secretary

Crime and Security
- Crime Divisions
- Anti-Human Trafficking Unit
- Mutual Assistance & Extradition
- Anti-Money Laundering Compliance Unit
- Victims of Crime
- Cosc: The National Office for the Prevention of Domestic, Sexual & Gender-based Violence
- Irish Youth Justice Community Programme

  - Private Security Authority

Policing
- Garda Division

  - An Garda Síochána
  - Garda Inspectorate
  - Garda Síochána Ombudsman Commission
  - Mental Health (Criminal Law) Review Board
  - Forensic Science Ireland
  - State Pathology Service

Civil Law Reform
- Courts Policy
- Civil Law Reform

  - Courts Service

Prisons, Probation and International Policy
- Prisons and Probation Policy
- International Policy Division
- Coroners Implementation Team

  - Irish Prison Service
  - Probation Service
  - Parole Board
  - Office of the Inspector of Prisons

Equality and Integration
- Equality
- Disability Policy
- Diversity & Equality Law
- Traveller Policy
- Gender Equality
- Office for the Promotion of Migrant Integration
- Reception and Integration Agency

  - National Disability Authority

Corporate Affairs
- Civil Governance Unit
- Corporate Affairs
- HR Division
- ICT Division
- FOI
- Press & Communications
- Financial Shared Services
- Internal Audit
- Financial Management Unit
- Reform & Development Unit
- Office for Internet Safety
- Procurement Strategy Unit

Criminal Law Reform
- Criminal Law Reform

  - Legal Aid Board
  - Criminal Injuries Compensation Tribunal
  - National Property Services Regulatory Authority
  - Irish Film Classification Office
  - Censorship of Publications Board
  - Office of the Data Protection Commissioner
  - Property Registration Authority
  - Charities Regulatory Authority
  - Insolvency Service of Ireland

INIS
- Immigration
- Visa
- Citizenship
- Repatriation
- Asylum

  - Office of the Refugee Applications Commissioner
  - Refugee Appeals Tribunal

The Director of Public Prosecutions

The Good Stuff: The Office of the Director of Public Prosecutions (DPP) is, by statute, 'independent' in carrying out the job of deciding which people should be charged with which particular crimes, and (we are told) is therefore free from Government or Garda influence. Of course, this statutory 'independence' is absolutely essential if the DPP is to do the job properly - on behalf of the Irish tax-paying public - and 'without fear or favour'. Indeed, the public relies on the integrity, independence and courage of the DPP's Office in prosecuting serious criminals and supporting the Gardai when they in turn, prosecute less-serious crimes 'in the name of the DPP'. In their own published booklet 'The Role of the DPP' it clearly states that *"the DPP prosecutes all serious crimes and sometimes less serious crimes."* What all this amounts to is that basically, the DPP is *the* final arbiter in deciding which incidents will result in persons being prosecuted, and which incidents will not be pursued. Clearly then, it is absolutely imperative that the people we entrust with overseeing this powerful office are of the highest moral calibre, who place the interests of justice and the interests of the Irish people first and foremost. It is also very reassuring to know that if you become a victim of *serious* crimes that the DPP *will indeed* prosecute those responsible!

The Not-So-Good Stuff: Unfortunately, all is not quite as it seems at the DPP's Office. Despite all the informative brochures, booklets and online sources telling us how it is *supposed* to work, it is clear from reports submitted by I-I Members that there is little confidence that the Office of the DPP is either truly independent or free from being influenced by the Government and Garda Management. In the first place for instance, the DPP is appointed *by the Government* under recommendation from the Attorney General - who in turn is the senior legal advisor *to the Government*. The DPP is also traditionally selected from a very narrow pool of career lawmakers who are already well-embedded in State-run or State sponsored institutions. Like so many such State-sponsored agencies, certain employees at the DPP's Office suffer disquieting levels of entitlement and condescension, apparently believing themselves to be accountable to no-one - having long since forgotten that they are in fact in the *public* service. I-I Members report troubling levels of discourtesy, superciliousness and obfuscation when seeking to avail of their victims' rights to contact the DPP for information. On occasions when victims of crime have alerted the DPP's Office to anomalies in the manner in which cases are being handled by Gardai or processed at the DPP's Office, they not only get ignored or dismissed, but evidence of direct and clearly inappropriate collusion between senior DPP staff and Gardai has subsequently emerged. So, what happened to the DPP's supposed 'statutory independence' then?

The Really bad and Depressing Stuff: The personal integrity of persons in senior positions in the DPP's Office has come seriously under question in circumstances where for example, a previously-serving DPP failed to make any mention whatsoever of a case where the DPP's Office *knew* for several years (and had even put it in writing) that Gardai were engaged in criminal efforts to frame an innocent man for murder. [Re: the Ian Bailey case] This wouldn't be so bad of course if this was some sort of temporary administrative oversight. But unfortunately it wasn't. The case in question made headlines for several years, yet the DPP at the time felt no need to speak up, even in circumstances where a person's life was being destroyed day-by-day in full public view in the media. Likewise, another I-I Member reports having solid irrefutable evidence that the current DPP conspired with Gardai to make a pretence of processing *empty* files for the purposes of misleading a citizen who was a victim of multiple crimes - and where an abundance of incriminating evidence had already been given to the Gardai. Unfortunately, the main suspect in these crimes was apparently 'connected' to a senior politician which is the only plausible (albeit unacceptable) explanation for why prosecutions did not ensue. When the matter was then reported to the various statutory authorities as an allegation of 'conspiracy to pervert justice' each in turn referred to the alleged 'independence' of the DPP's Office, stating they had 'no mandate' to interfere and 'no authority' to investigate - even though both the DPP and the Chief State Solicitor were personally implicated in those very crimes? Unbelievable! Perhaps even more disturbing is the blatant and inexplicable decision *not* to prosecute a well-known, high-level international drug dealer, who already had multiple convictions against his name. Apparently this 'independent decision' of the DPP not to prosecute this individual was arrived at after alleged 'private consultations' with Garda Management who had their own reasons to want to protect this particular criminal. Again, what happened to the supposed 'statutory independence' of the DPP's Office - and being supposedly free from Garda influence? What happened to the DPP's mandate to robustly apply the law and prosecute ALL serious crimes? Is this just even more evidence of the selective interpretation of the law and the Constitution that has become routine amongst the powers that be? It seems that the DPP, like so many other highly-placed authority figures in Ireland, can do what she damn-well pleases, breaking, bending and twisting the rules at will, without fear of ever being held properly to account. Like so many other State-sponsored agencies and institutions it seems that the *primary* function and purpose for the DPP's Office is to give the misleading *impression* of being an ethical and professional instrument of the law, whilst making sure that it is in fact 'business as usual' for the protected and connected elite, and for those that so abjectly serve them.

And now, the official version of what the DPP's Office are supposed to be doing for us..

* * *

What happens when a file goes to the DPP?   *(From the website of the DPP)*
The decision to prosecute or not to prosecute is very important. Someone who is prosecuted and later found not guilty can suffer great damage. But a decision not to prosecute can cause great stress and upset to a victim. So the DPP must carefully consider whether or not to prosecute.

The DPP is independent when carrying out her job. This means that the Government or the Gardaí can neither make the DPP prosecute a particular case nor stop her doing so.

How does the DPP reach a decision to prosecute?
When the Gardaí complete their investigation, they send a file to the DPP. The prosecutor must read the file carefully and decide whether there is enough evidence to put before the court. The judge or jury has to be convinced beyond a reasonable doubt that a person is guilty. It is not enough for them to think that the accused is probably guilty.

For this reason it can be helpful to know if there is independent evidence that supports the victim's story. This could be a statement from a witness or evidence such as fingerprints or bloodstains which can provide DNA. Independent evidence makes a stronger case than a case based on one person's word against another's.

Why might the DPP decide not to prosecute a case?
Lack of evidence is the most common reason for decisions not to prosecute. If there is not enough evidence for the court to be sure beyond a reasonable doubt that a person is guilty, the prosecution will not succeed. It is not enough that the court may believe the victim's story. It has to be convinced beyond a reasonable doubt.

In a small number of cases, even though the evidence may be strong, the DPP may decide not to prosecute for other reasons. For example:

- where the offender is under 18 years of age and the case could be dealt with under the Juvenile Diversion Programme;

- where an adult is cautioned under the Adult Caution Scheme for minor offences rather than prosecuted; or

- where, in the public interest, it is better not to prosecute, for example if the offender is seriously ill.

Our publication Guidelines for Prosecutors has more detail about how the DPP makes a decision to prosecute. You may request a copy of this publication by contacting our office.

How long does it take the DPP to reach a decision?
Each case is different and has to be thought about carefully. If a case is straightforward, the DPP will generally make a decision within a few weeks. Other cases may take longer because:

- they are more complicated;

- there is a lot of evidence to think about;

- there is more than one accused person; or

- the DPP needs more information before making a decision.

Does the DPP prosecute cases on behalf of crime victims?
The DPP prosecutes cases on behalf of the people of Ireland, not on behalf of any one individual. For this reason, the views and interests of the victim cannot be the only consideration when deciding whether or not to prosecute. However, the DPP will always take into account the consequences for the victim of the decision to prosecute or not. The DPP will also consider the views of the victim or the victim's family.

Does the DPP give reasons for her decisions?
In most cases when the DPP decides not to prosecute she will tell the Garda Síochána, or other investigating agency, the reasons for her decision. These reasons are kept confidential. The DPP does not give reasons for her decisions to anyone else. This policy has been supported in recent years by a number of High Court and Supreme Court decisions.

However, the DPP introduced a pilot scheme on 22 October 2008 under which she will give reasons for her decision not to prosecute in some cases where someone has died as a result of an alleged crime. She will give a reason for her decision in these cases only if:

- the crime was committed on or after 22 October 2008; and

- a member of the family or household of the victim, or their lawyer, doctor or social worker requests the reason; and

- the DPP can give a reason without creating an injustice to someone else, for example by taking their good name.

The cases where reasons may be given include:

- murder

- manslaughter

- deaths in the workplace

- fatal road traffic incidents

Can a decision made by the DPP be changed?
Certain people may ask the DPP to review a decision she has made. These include:

- a victim of a crime;

- a family member of a victim of a crime;

- an accused person; or

- a family member of an accused person.

Doctors, lawyers and social workers can also ask the DPP to review a decision for their clients.

If the DPP changes her decision, it is usually because new evidence has come to light.

Can a crime victim meet with a member of staff of the DPP's office to discuss a particular decision?
No. The staff of the DPP's office do not meet crime victims to discuss decisions. However, crime victims may write to the DPP's office about particular decisions.

Can I get information from a prosecution file by making an application under the Freedom of Information Act, 1997?
No. Under section 46(1)(b) of the Freedom of Information Act, 1997, only records concerning the general administration of the Office of the DPP can be made public. This means you cannot get information from files relating to individual criminal cases.

* * *

[As for openness, transparency and accountability at the Office of the DPP..]

Freedom of Information: The Freedom of Information (FOI) Act 2014, asserts the right of members of the public to obtain access to official information to the greatest extent possible consistent with the public interest and the right to privacy of individuals.

The Office of the Director of Public Prosecutions makes information routinely available to the public in relation to its structure, functions and activities through the publication of its Annual Report, Strategy Statement and Statement of General Guidelines for Prosecutors. The Office will continue to expand the range of information available to the public through our website.

The DPP's Office FOI Reference Book (revised November 2010), prepared in accordance with sections 15 and 16 of the FOI Act 1997, outlines the role and functions of the Office, its structure and the procedures for making a request under the FOI Act.

It is important that the public are aware that under the Freedom of Information Act the records of the Office of the DPP are subject to the restriction provided for under section 42(f). Therefore, records held or created by the office, other than those relating to the general administration of the Office, are not accessible under the FOI Act. This means that records concerning criminal case files are not accessible under the FOI Act.

For further information on the Freedom of Information ACT, 2014 see Part 3.

* * *

What About the Government Oath of Office?
Members of the Oireachtas and of the Government **do not make any oath**. From the foundation of the Irish Free State in 1922, both had to make an oath of allegiance to the Constitution and of fidelity to King George V. This controversial provision of the 1921 Anglo-Irish Treaty contributed to the Civil War of 1922–23. The Oath was abolished by Fianna Fáil in 1932–33. Since then, Oireachtas members are required by standing orders to sign the roll before first taking their seats. The Governor-General of the Irish Free State took the same Oath of Allegiance and Oath of Office as the Governor General of Canada. This did not take place in public.

(From Wikipedia)

The Relationship Between the Public Prosecutor and the Minister of Justice

(From the Euro-justice.com website report on the Irish legal system)

No single body or person has a monopoly in the prosecution of criminal offences in Ireland. At common law any person (known as a common informer) is competent to initiate and conduct a criminal prosecution. This broad competence is now confined to minor offences which are tried summarily (Criminal Justice (Administration) Act, 1924, Sect. 9). For offences which will be tried by judge and jury (more serious offences) the common informer can still initiate the prosecution and maintain it up to the point where the defendant is sent for trial by judge and jury (State (Ennis) v Farrell, 1966, IR 107). At this point the prosecution will either be taken over by the public prosecutor or it will fall. Prosecutorial powers also vest in several statutory bodies which were created as integral parts of administrative regulatory schemes. Summary offences created in order to give effect to the objectives of such a scheme are normally prosecuted by the regulatory body entrusted with responsibility for the implementation of the scheme. Like the common informer these bodies are confined to summary prosecutions (TDI Metro Ltd (No. 2) v Judge Delap, 2000, 4 IR 337 and 520; Cumann Luthchleas Gael Teo v Windle, 1994, 1 IR 525). Where a statutory body fails to take a prosecution in any case which is within its remit the public prosecutor can step in and initiate the prosecution (Attorney General v Healy, 1928, IR 460).

The legislation establishing the Garda Siochana does not confer it or its members with prosecutorial powers. However, at common law each member of the force enjoys the status of a common informer (State (Cronin) v The Circuit Court Judge of the Western Circuit, 1937, IR 34; State (DPP) v District Justice Ruane, 1985, ILRM 349). As such they have the same competence as the ordinary citizen to initiate prosecutions which will be disposed of summarily (mostly minor offences). Unlike the citizen they also enjoy a whole range of investigative powers and resources which enhance their capacity to pursue large numbers of prosecutions. In practice that is exactly what they do. In terms of volume, members of the Garda Síochána handle by far the most prosecutions in Ireland. Many of these are taken by and in the name of the investigating officers concerned. In such cases the public prosecutor cannot intervene to terminate or take over the prosecution. Within the Dublin Metropolitan Area, as many as eighty percent of summary cases are prosecuted by the Garda Síochána, usually by the member who investigated the case. Outside of Dublin, cases are normally taken by a designated sergeant or inspector. Even where the prosecution is actually taken by a member of the Garda Sochana, it will often happen that it is taken in the name of the public prosecutor (People (DPP) v Roddy, 1977, IR 177). The latter has given a general consent to this practice (Letter from DPP to Garda Commissioner, dated January 9, 1975). His consent does not have to be sought in each case, unless it is one in which the defendant has made a complaint against the Garda arising out of the same incident which gave rise to the criminal complaint.

The Garda Commissioner lays down general guidelines for the conduct of prosecutions by members of the force (Report of the Public Prosecution System Study Group, o.c. at para.20). These guidelines are not normally made public. Nor are they absolutely binding on each member of the force in the sense that they cannot prevent a member from pursuing a prosecution if he decides in his capacity as a common informer that a prosecution is warranted. There has been greater transparency in the area of juvenile crime. Since the early 1960s the Garda have operated a juvenile liaison scheme aimed at using cautions as a means of keeping juveniles out of court in so far as possible. This scheme was originally based on guidelines laid down by the Garda Commissioner. It has since been put on a statutory footing (Children's Act, 2001, Part 4). The public prosecutor has also laid down guidelines for the conduct of prosecutions (see below). These are applicable to prosecutions taken by members of the Garda.

In 1924, the Attorney General was given a monopoly over all prosecutions on indictment (Sect. 9 subs. 1 Criminal Justice (Administration) Act, 1924). This meant that only he could initiate and maintain a prosecution all the way through to trial by judge and jury. The Attorney General is also the legal advisor to the government and is closely identified with the government of the day. Ireland's accession to the European Community in 1973 resulted in a substantial increase in his workload. This together with the recognition that the prosecution process should be insulated from even the appearance of party political influence, resulted in the creation of the new office of the Director of Public Prosecutions (DPP) to handle prosecutions on indictment. This office was created by the Prosecution of Offences Act, 1974 (Sect. 3) which also transferred most of the prosecutorial functions of the Attorney General to the DPP. The net effect is that the Attorney General's prosecutorial competence is now confined largely to a few offences which might involve sensitive political and diplomatic considerations. It is also worth noting that there is provision for the government to make a temporary transfer of prosecutorial functions back from the DPP to the Attorney General (Sect. 5 subs. 1 Prosecution of Offences Act, 1974). This transfer can be effected in relation to criminal matters of such kind or kinds as are specified in the transfer order. The government can exercise this power whenever it is of the opinion that it is expedient in the interests of national security to do so. In practice the DPP is the sole public prosecutor in prosecutions on indictment.

The office of DPP is established statutorily as a central office occupied by a single incumbent based in Dublin. He is assisted by 'officers and servants' appointed by the Taoiseach (the Prime Minister). Many of these are 'professional officers', namely barristers and solicitors to whom much of the day-to-day decision-making on prosecutions is delegated by the DPP. All of them are based in the Dublin office, although one individual is seconded on a part-time basis to Eurojust. Apart possibly from this Eurojust member, there are no specialist prosecutors or prosecutors responsible for particular crimes. Ultimately, the DPP is responsible for the decision to prosecute or not to prosecute in an individual case, irrespective of whether it is taken by him personally or by one of his staff.

There is a subdivision within the DPP's office that prepares cases for prosecution in the Dublin area once the initial decision on prosecution is taken. This subdivision comes under the general supervision of the chief prosecution solicitor. Outside of Dublin the chief prosecution solicitor's function is discharged by state solicitors. These are solicitors in private practice who provide prosecution services to the DPP pursuant to contracts with the Attorney General. It is envisaged that these contracts will be transferred from the Attorney General's office to the DPP in the near future. Where the Garda have prepared a file on a case outside Dublin which might have to be tried on indictment they will normally send it to the local State solicitor who in turn will transmit it to the DPP for a decision on prosecution. Where the DPP decides in favour of prosecution he will send the case back to the local state solicitor to prepare it for prosecution. The local state solicitor also functions as a valuable link between the Garda Siochana outside Dublin and the DPP.

The qualifications for appointment to (and procedure for removal from) the office of DPP are laid down by statute (Sect. 2 Prosecution of Offences Act, 1974). He must be a practising barrister or solicitor at the time of appointment and have practised as such for at least ten years. The incumbent is appointed by the government who must choose from a list of candidates selected by a committee composed of: the chief justice, the chairman of the Bar Council, the president of the Law Society, the Secretary of the Government and the senior legal assistant to the Attorney General (The Prosecution of Offences Act (Sect. 2) Regulations, 1974 make provision for the procedure to be followed by this committee). Before removing the incumbent from office the government must appoint a committee composed of the chief justice, a judge of the High Court and the Attorney General to investigate the health of the DPP or inquire into his conduct generally or in an individual case. The government may only remove the DPP after considering the report of this committee.

The DPP is a civil servant in the civil service of the state, as distinct from the government, (Sect. 2 subs. 4 Prosecution of Offences Act, 1974; McLoughlin v Minister for Social Welfare, 1958, IR 1). His office comes under the general remit of the Department of the Prime Minister in the sense that the annual financial estimates for the DPP forms part of the vote of the Department of the Prime Minister. There is no suggestion, however, that the DPP is in any way accountable to the Prime Minister or to any other Minister for his decisions in individual cases or even for his policies in respect of prosecutions generally. Indeed the legislation creating the office specifically states that he is independent in the performance of his functions (Sect. 2 subs. 5 Prosecution of Offences Act, 1974). It would be both improper and unlawful, therefore, for the Prime Minister or any other Minister even to attempt to apply pressure on the DPP in respect of a decision in an individual case or policy generally. There is a specific statutory outlawing representations (from persons not involved in a case) encouraging the DPP to drop a prosecution or not to initiate a prosecution (Sect. 6 Prosecution of Offences Act, 1974). Equally, the Prime Minister cannot be called to account in parliament for the decisions or policies of the DPP.

It does not follow that members of parliament do not raise prosecutorial matters from time to time and seek to put pressure on the government with respect to decisions or policies taken or adopted by the DPP. Indeed, the whole issue has come into sharp focus recently as a result of growing public concern over the DPP's long-standing policy of refusing to give reasons for deciding not to prosecute in some highly sensitive cases. Such issues are most likely to be raised with the Minister for Justice in the context of broader concerns of law enforcement, crime prevention and fairness in the criminal justice system, all of which come under the general remit of the Minister. Nevertheless, the Minister consistently refuses to entertain those questions which relate specifically to decisions taken or policies adopted by the DPP. His invariable response to attempts to drag him into discussion of such matters is that they are matters wholly within the remit of the DPP whose independence is guaranteed by law.

The DPP's primary function is to decide whether or not to prosecute in any individual case. As noted earlier, he does not normally get involved in the initiation or conduct of an investigation, although he may request further police investigations to be carried out in respect of a file which has been submitted to him. Before outlining how the DPP discharges his primary function it might be useful to quote in full the summary of the functions of his office as set out in his Annual Report for 1998. It reads:

> - the consideration of Garda criminal investigation files submitted to the Office;
>
> - the decision as to whether or not a prosecution should be initiated or as to whether a prosecution already initiated by the Garda Síochána should be maintained and the advising of any further investigations necessary for the commencement or continuation of a prosecution;
>
> - the determination of the charges to be preferred and the consideration of any charges already preferred;
>
> - the determination of the proofs and other materials to be tendered to the court and to the accused, including issues regarding the disclosure to the defense of unused material;
>
> - the issuing of decisions regarding the many questions of law and of public policy which can arise in the course of criminal proceedings;
>
> - conferring as necessary with counsel, state solicitors, members of the Garda Siochana and persons giving scientific or technical evidence;

- deciding whether appeals, including appeals by way of case stated, should be brought or contested, and the prosecution or defence of proceedings for judicial review and habeas corpus arising out of criminal proceedings;

- the consideration of complaints and allegations of the commission of criminal offences received from members of the public and where appropriate their transmission to the Garda commissioner;

- the consideration of files submitted by the Garda Complaints Board;

- the drafting or settling of documents necessary for the prosecution of requests for extradition into the State;

- the drafting of requests for international mutual assistance in criminal matters;

- serving on committees and attending meetings relating to prosecutions and criminal law and procedure; identifying operational problems arising in the administration of the criminal law and assisting on request on matters relevant to proposed criminal legislation; lecturing at the Garda Síochána Training College.

To these might be added: deciding whether certain cases should be sent for trial to the Special Criminal Court; giving consents for certain indictable offences to be tried summarily; electing between summary and indictable procedures for certain statutory offences; directing the initiation of certain types of prosecution which by law require his consent; the granting of certificates for appeal to the Court of Criminal Appeal to the Supreme Court on points of law of exceptional public importance; considering whether to seek a review of a sentence on grounds of leniency; and giving his views to the trial court on whether a custodial sentence would be appropriate.

The decision to prosecute or not to prosecute is at the centre of the DPP's prosecutorial function. Yet, there is no statutory prescription governing when he should decide for or against prosecution in any individual case. Nor is his freedom in these matters governed by any statutorily prescribed policies. As noted earlier there is no basis upon which the Minister for Justice, or any other authority can issue directions to him in such matters. Although there is statutory provision for the DPP to consult with the Attorney General from time to time it is generally recognised that this does not subordinate the DPP in any way to the Attorney General in the performance of his functions (Sect. 2 subs. 6 Prosecution of Offences Act, 1974). The legal and de facto position is that it is the DPP, and the DPP alone, who determines whether to prosecute in any case or in any type of case. In these matters he is subject only to the law.

As a general rule the DPP will require evidence sufficient to establish a prima facie case of guilt against the accused before he will decide in favour of prosecution. This means the existence of admissible evidence upon which a judge or jury could conclude beyond a reasonable doubt that the accused was guilty of the offence charged. If the evidence does not reach that standard the DPP will decide against prosecution. It does not follow, however, that the DPP will always prosecute where there is a prima facie case. He still retains a discretion over the decision to prosecute even in such cases. In deciding whether or not to prosecute he will pay particular attention to the credibility and reliability of the evidence. If he considers that the evidence is very strong and a conviction is very likely it can be expected that he will prosecute. Nevertheless, the circumstances of an individual case may be such that he considers a prosecution is merited even though the prospects of a conviction are weak. Equally, there may be factors which persuade him to exercise his discretion not to prosecute in cases where a conviction would be virtually certain.

The DPP has published a list of guidelines on the decision to prosecute. These comprise three broad groups. First there are principles governing the general duty of the prosecutor, such as the duty to act honestly, fairly, impartially and objectively (Statement of General Guidelines for Prosecutors, Dublin 2001, p. 7). Second, there is a list of 'aggravating factors' which, if present, would render a decision to prosecute more likely. These include factors such as: the likelihood of the offence attracting a severe penalty, the accused being in a position of authority over the victim and the alleged commission of the offence while on bail. The third group consists of 'mitigating factors' such as: the accused being very young or very old, the availability of alternatives to prosecution, the willingness of the victim to forgive, the length and expense of the likely trial being disproportionate to the harm caused and the willingness of the accused to assist in the prosecution of other offenders.

Ultimately, these guidelines are nothing more than what they purport to be. They are not legally binding. They are merely a policy statement issued by the DPP. No executive authority has the power to force him to alter the guidelines or to require him to follow them or to depart from them in an individual case. In the exercise of his discretion, however, the DPP is accountable to the law.

The High Court has jurisdiction to review the grounds upon which the DPP makes a decision to prosecute or not to prosecute in any individual case. If, for example, the DPP adopts a policy of refusing to prosecute in any crime against property below a fixed value the High Court would almost certainly strike down that policy, and decisions based upon it, as unlawful. Equally the High Court would strike down any prosecutorial decision taken in bad faith, such as a decision not to prosecute because the accused was a friend of the DPP or a decision to prosecute because the DPP did not like the accused's political associations. There are also indications that the High Court would strike down a decision to prosecute which departed arbitrarily from the DPP's published guidelines on prosecution (Eviston v DPP, 2002, 3 IR 260). Apart from these extreme cases, however, the High Court is most reluctant to overturn a prosecutorial decision taken by the DPP in the exercise of his discretion (State (McCormack) v Curran, 1987, ILRM 225; H v DPP, 1994, 2 ILRM 285). It is quite different if the DPP decides to prosecute in circumstances where the accused's right to a fair trial would be compromised. This might happen, for example, where the accused's capacity to prepare a defence has been irreparably damaged by excessive delay between the alleged commission of the offence and the decision to prosecute. In such cases the High Court will consider that the DPP has no discretion in the matter and it will quash his decision to prosecute (PM v District Judge Malone, 2002, 2 IR 560; PO'C v DPP, 2000, 3 IR 87; JL v DPP, 2000, 3 IR 122; PP v DPP, 2000, 1 IR 403).

Closely related to the subject of the judicial review of the DPP's discretion is the question whether he is obliged to give reasons for a decision not to prosecute. To date he has followed a consistent policy of refusing to give reasons which could make their way into the public domain. He justifies this on the basis of fairness to all parties in a criminal investigation. His position has received the endorsement of the Supreme Court which distinguishes between the role of the DPP in this matter and that of most other bodies exercising statutory powers in a manner which impact directly on specific individuals (H v DPP, 1994, 2 ILRM 285). However, the DPP is willing to give reasons for decisions not to prosecute on a confidential basis to the investigating police officers or, where relevant, the investigating officials of regulatory bodies. He also has a policy on conducting an internal review of a decision not to prosecute when requested to do so by the victim or members of the victim's family.

The criminal process in Ireland differs from the civil process in that there is no formal recognition of the practice of settling the case in advance of the trial or in the course of the trial. In theory, once the prosecution has identified the charges appropriate to the alleged offence, it will prefer those charges in a summons or indictment and prosecute then through to a formal conviction or acquittal. Admittedly, there is provision for the prosecution to change course after having preferred the charges. For example, it enjoys a broad power to amend the indictment (or summons) at any time up until the verdict is returned. This can be used to remedy defects in the indictment (or summons) and to add a new charge or substitute an existing charge. It may also enter a *nolle prosequi* [we shall no longer prosecute] on any or all of the charges at any point up until the verdict is returned. In effect this means that the charge or charges in question are dropped. That, however, would not prevent the prosecution from subsequently charging the accused with the same offences at a future date, unless the *nolle prosequi* was entered in a manner which deprived the accused of some material advantage which had accrued as a result of pre-trial decisions made by the judge (State (O'Callaghan) v O hUadhaigh, 1977, IR 42). Typically a *nolle prosequi* will be entered when it becomes apparent that the charge or charges are superfluous or that the prosecution will not be able to present evidence to support them.

Clearly, this flexibility puts the prosecution in a position where it can bargain with the accused. The bargain could take the form of agreeing to drop more serious charges in return for a plea of guilty to a lesser charge or even, in more extreme cases, agreeing to give immunity from prosecution to an offender in return for his giving evidence for the prosecution against accomplices. There are no formal legal rules governing these bargaining possibilities. Indeed, officially they do not really exist at all. In practice what is likely to happen is that the defense will approach the prosecution seeking a deal. It is entirely a matter for the prosecution whether they enter into an arrangement of the sort described above. As yet there has been no judicial decision in which any such arrangement has been declared unlawful by the Irish courts. Subject to the possibility of judicial intervention in individual cases it is a matter for the DPP's discretion whether to drop a more serious charge in return for a plea of guilty to a lesser charge or to grant immunity from prosecution in return for giving evidence against accomplices. No executive authority can override him in such decisions. Nor is he under any obligation to give reasons for such a decision or to explain it to an executive or political authority.

* * *

As of 2015, the *Victims Rights Directive 2012/29/EU of The European Parliament and of the Council of 25 October* 2012 (which was recently signed into Irish Law) provides for the right of victims and complainants to receive information about their case in an open, timely and transparent manner. This rule will apply both to An Garda Siochana and to the DPP.

* * *

From the Department of Justice's own website - August 2014

"..the (Toland) report finds fault with leadership, management and oversight systems referring particularly to the existence of "a closed secretive and silo driven culture", "significant leadership and management problems" and "ineffective management processes and structures to provide strong strategic oversight of the key agencies".

The Report found that the Department had developed a 'deferential relationship with An Garda Síochána". In response, the Minister stated that "the planned establishment of a new Independent Policing Authority will assist in providing a valuable additional layer of transparency and public accountability between the Department and Gardaí."

The Report concluded that "the overall Departmental culture has not changed or adapted to the world in which it now operates."

Minister Fitzgerald stated: "The Department of Justice and Equality must become a 21st century organisation to meet 21st century challenges."

And still... we wait.

An Garda Síochána

There is, clearly, a considerable estrangement between An Garda Síochána and Irish citizens and also widespread public distrust of the force. Such estrangement and distrust make the force 'unfit for purpose' in a, purportedly, democratic Irish society. It has been the experience of too many citizens that their ostensible protectors – their police force – became their oppressors and tormentors, with the apparent support of their political masters.

The warning of Professor Dermot Walsh – that Ireland's "huge concentration of police power in the hands of central government in the absence of adequate constitutional checks and balances is uncomfortably close to the arrangements associated with a police state" – cannot easily be ignored."

"In a democracy, there is no uglier spectacle than the power of the State being used against its own citizens. In fact, it's not even compatible with the notion of democracy. Only totalitarian states operate as if the interests of the State were more important than the needs of the people."

(Fergus Finlay, former chief adviser to Labour Party leader Dick Spring).

Excerpts from: "An Garda Síochána - an analysis of a police force unfit for purpose."
Compiled by Tom Hanahoe (former journalist, Irish Press newspaper group).
Terence Conway (Spokesperson Shell to Sea).
John Monaghan (Spokesperson Pobal Chill Chomáin).

Commissioner

Personal Assistant Private Secretary
- Garda Band
- Garda Museum

Director of Communications
- Garda Press Office

Chief Administrative Officer

Assistant Commissioner Human Resource Management
- Human Resources Administration
- Human Resource Policy and Programmes
- Recruitment and Probationer Management
- Performance Management
- Occupational Health Department

Executive Director of ICT
- Information Technology
- Telecommunications

Executive Director of Finance and Services
- Finance
- Procurement and Stores
- Services & Archives
- Fleet Management
- Estate Management

Deputy Commissioner Operations

Assistant Commissioner Eastern Region
Assistant Commissioner Southern Region
Assistant Commissioner South Eastern Region
Assistant Commissioner Dublin Metropolitan Region
Assistant Commissioner Northern Region
Assistant Commissioner Western Region

Assistant Commissioner National Support Services
- National Bureau of Criminal Investigation
- Garda Technical Bureau
- Criminal Assets Bureau
- Garda Bureau of Fraud Investigation
- Garda National Immigration Bureau
- Garda National Drugs Unit
- Operational Support

Assistant Commissioner Traffic
- Garda National Traffic Bureau

Assistant Commissioner Crime and Security
- Liaison and Protection
- Crime, Policy & Administration
- Security and Intelligence
- Special Detective Unit
- Garda Síochána Analysis Service
- Garda Internal Audit Section
- Legal Affairs Section and Human Rights

Deputy Commissioner Strategy and Change Management

Assistant Commissioner Organisation Development and Strategic Planning
- Change Management, Planning, Policy and Risk Management
- Community Relations & Community Policing
- Information Management
- Garda Information Services Centre
- Garda Central Vetting Unit

Assistant Commissioner HRM Operational Resource Allocation, Employee Development and Professional Standards
- Employee Engagement (Eg, C & A, Partnership and EAS)
- Training and Continuous Professional Development
- Internal Affairs and Overseas Office
- Garda Professional Standards
- Fleet Deployment
- Operational Resource Allocation

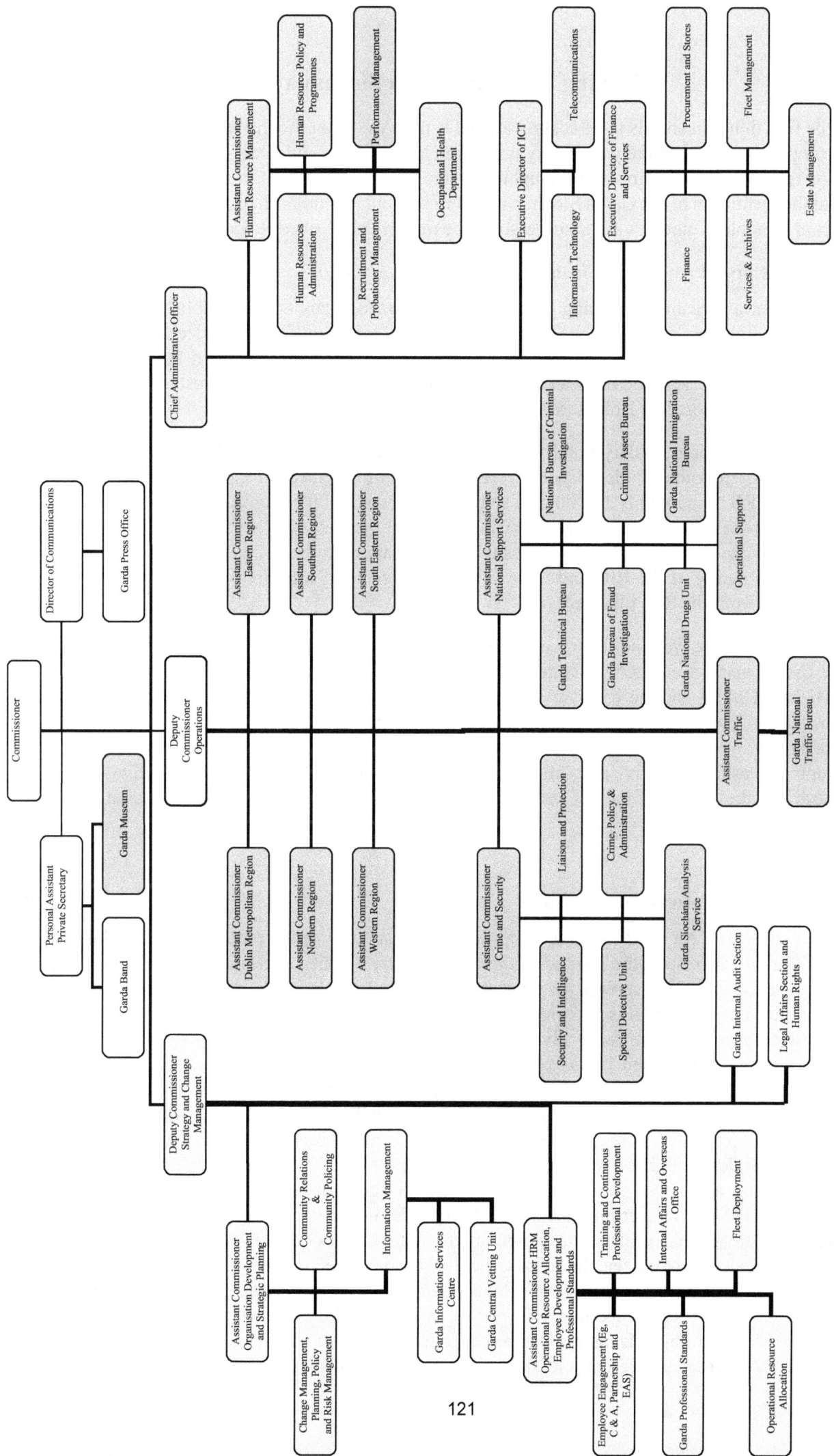

"Working with communities to protect and serve"

121

Dealing With An Garda Síochána

The first thing that needs to be acknowledged is that An Garda Síochána - when functioning properly - is an absolutely necessary institution in this State - and it has very important work do do in protecting the community and upholding the law. The reason for this I-I Guide however, is that the institution of An Garda Síochána - and in particular, Garda Management - has strayed far from its noble beginnings as the successor to the massively-resented Royal Irish Constabulary.

A Brief History of An Garda Síochána *(from the Garda Síochána website)*

The tradition of organised policing in Ireland can be traced back to the establishment of the County Constabulary in 1822. The County Constabulary was a uniformed police force formed on a regional basis. Before this there existed a basic police force known as The Peace Preservation Force. This had been set up in 1816 through an act of the Westminster Parliament. This act was sponsored by Robert Peel, the Chief Secretary for Ireland.

In 1836 the Irish Constabulary (later to be known as the Royal Irish Constabulary (RIC)) and the Dublin Metropolitan Police (DMP) were established to replace the County Constabulary. By 1900 the RIC had roughly 11,000 men stationed in about 1,600 barracks. Attacks on the RIC were widespread either in their barracks or while on patrol. Eamonn DeValera and other members of the Sinn Féin Government, "Dáil Éireann" which claimed to be ruling Ireland in absentia, urged the shunning of the RIC and their families as agents of a foreign power. Widespread resignations from the RIC followed.

Following the Civil War and the truce of July 1921 the RIC disbanded and a new police force, "The Civic Guard" (renamed the Garda Síochána na hÉireann on 8 August 1923) was formed by Michael Collins and the Irish Government. The DMP merged with An Garda Síochána in 1925. Dublin Castle, the centre of British Rule in Ireland for nearly 700 years was formally handed over on August 17, 1922 when Commissioner Michael Staines led his new police force through the castle gates. Five days after the hand-over of Dublin Castle, Michael Collins, who orchestrated the demise of the RIC and the creation of the Civic Guard was shot dead at Béal na mBlath.

The I-I Review of An Garda Síochána

The Good Stuff: 'An Garda Síochána translates as 'guardians of the peace' and we all know decent Gardaí who respect the law and do their best to carry out their duties in a fair and unbiased manner. Set up in 1923 to replace the much-resented and divisive Royal Irish Constabulary the current motto of the Gardaí is *"Working with Communities to Protect and Serve"* and each of us has a story to tell where we received personal help or assistance from honest hardworking Gardaí, 'got a break' when it was perhaps not technically deserved, or received a friendly acknowledgement in passing on the street. It is a fact that the Irish Police are regarded by most citizens as being significantly more approachable on a daily basis than many of their foreign counterparts. Certainly, the average Garda on the beat is rarely seen as a threat to the citizen or a figure to be despised, but is regarded more as a helpful member of the community who has the power and authority - when needed - to step in and take lawful action to protect the law-abiding citizen from crime or danger. All of this makes decent members of An Garda Síochána an invaluable asset in this democratic republic of ours - as long as individual Gardaí place their service to the citizen, the law and the Constitution foremost, and resist the ever-present temptation to indulge in cover-ups and protectionism when colleagues do wrong; or, succumb to pressure from peers and superiors to favour the interests of the protected elite - at the expense of ordinary law-abiding citizens. Unfortunately, the recent water charges protests have cast the Garda on the street in a different role; that of political lackeys and even occasionally, thugs.

The Not-So-Good Stuff: Like all authoritarian institutions, lower-ranking members of the Gardaí in particular are subject to the pressures of an institution that demands their complete obedience and loyalty. One's advancement through the ranks and one's pension is at stake of course if, as a ranking member of the force you incur the disapproval of your superiors. This in itself is not a problem of course, as long as Garda bosses respect the Garda code of ethics and encourage due adherence from their subordinates. It is when things go awry within the force - and especially when things go wrong amongst the higher ranks - that generic 'obedience and loyalty' issues become a problem, not an asset. When one factors in the depressing reality that favouritism, nepotism and protectionism are intrinsic features of Irish political life that extend to all but the lowest tiers of society, one begins to understand how decent Gardaí can, over time, become compromised. 'An Garda Síochána was described by a senior academic in 2009 as *"one of the most secretive police forces in the developed world."* Why would this be, one might ask? Why for example, would senior Gardaí refuse to meet law-abiding citizens making enquiries about supposed 'ongoing Garda investigations'. Why is the internal Garda Code 'confidential' and kept from public scrutiny? Why do Garda Authorities claim selective exemption from the Freedom of Information Act? How and why do they repeatedly fail to respond to Court subpoenas - and why are they allowed to do this? Why are serious complaints of criminal wrongdoing regularly suppressed or ignored? And why the pretence of a Garda Ombudsman who is in fact subject to the unchallenged directions of the Garda Commissioner? On top of this, a brief survey of recent crime statistics shows a massive increase in traffic offences and other revenue-generating arrests, while scores (literally) of unsolved murders and missing persons cases go unsolved. In conjunction with the massive deployment of Gardaí to enforce the instalment of water meters against the will of the people, one can understand the public's growing disquiet that An Garda Síochána - the 'Guardians of the Peace' - have morphed into a private, political police force whose priorities are no longer admirable, ethical or morally acceptable.

The Really Bad and Depressing Stuff: I-I members (including serving and retired members of the Gardaí) have reported internal bullying and intimidation by their Garda bosses - especially if they raise concerns. Citizens too regularly complain of apathy and disinterest, inexcusable failures or refusals by Gardaí to investigate serious complaints, or worse still, being lied to about alleged ongoing investigations. When a determined citizen presses for a response, he or she can then be subject to threats, harassment, intimidation, and even serious physical assaults and false arrests. Some of these activities have been carried out by serving Gardaí at the behest of 'connected persons' in Irish society who had a personal dispute with another citizen, or, who were involved in potentially-damaging legal action. In some cases, Gardaí have acted covertly like medieval thugs enforcing the will of their overlords; that is, the illegitimate wishes of certain 'connected persons' who are themselves, often engaged in criminal activity. But perhaps worst of all is the inexorable erosion of confidence amongst law-abiding citizens; that even those Gardaí who genuinely endeavour to do their best, cannot reverse the endemic cronyism and protectionism that has apparently filtered down from the top, and is effectively preventing An Garda Síochána from being fit for purpose. No great surprise to learn then, that senior Gardaí are NOT necessarily promoted 'on merit' and that all appointments over the rank of Superintendent are assigned by the Government. So much for the supposed 'independence' of the police and the separation of powers!

Recent Developments: As a short but clear example of the levels of 'inappropriate' behaviour and attitudes we encounter when dealing with Garda Management, we note first of all the brazen stonewalling of the current Garda Commissioner Noirin O'Sullivan in repeatedly failing or refusing to supply us with the names and badge numbers of those Gardaí involved in an operation whereby a citizen claims he was seriously assaulted and had to flee in fear of his life. Commissioner O'Sullivan has been informed that we need those details in order to lodge a criminal complaint and pursue a civil case before the statutory time limits expire, but apparently, that is none of her concern. Her ever-diligent personal assistant Superintendent Frank Walsh simply suggests that we go to GSOC instead - and enjoy the eternal run around again we suppose? Regardless of the eventual findings of any criminal investigation or Court hearing, the plain fact of the matter is that an agency of the State who has direct responsibility for policing is refusing to cooperate with a legitimate request for information in order to advance a criminal complaint. Even GSOC has complained that Gardaí are 'not cooperating' with some of their own half-baked investigations - which, interestingly, are headed up by serving Gardaí who are appointed by the Garda Commissioner. As we said before, this illustrates the prevailing mindset that they really do believe that 'the rules' simply don't apply to them.

Likewise the sudden departure of Ms O'Sullivan's predecessor Martin Callinan - he who so famously described brave, honest Garda whistleblowers Sergeant Maurice McCabe and Garda John Wilson as "Disgusting!".. before being unceremoniously sacked (or was it 'suddenly retired'?) from his position as Garda Commissioner. A somewhat tepid judicial investigation into the circumstances surrounding his untimely departure uncovered the disquieting fact that ten sacks of 'personal papers' from his Office were shredded on the day he departed, and that his official phone mysteriously 'went missing' only to eventually turn up weeks later, minus the all-important sim card. One wonders indeed if the new Commissioner Ms O'Sullivan - or even our industrious Minister for Justice Frances Fitzgerald have any personal or professional concerns about all of this secrecy and subterfuge? Well, apparently not! And this is the type of carry-on that is acceptable behaviour by the heads of policing in a so-called modern democracy? Not exactly a good example for young Gardaí to follow now, is it?

So, here are a few guidelines whenever you deal with the Gardaí.

Rule No 1: Each and every time you have any dealings with members of An Garda Síochána make sure you (politely) get their name, their badge number and the location where they work.

Rule No 2. If at all possible, never engage with members of An Garda Síochána on your own.

Rule No 3. If arrested or detained for any reason, you should immediately ask for a solicitor. When the solicitor comes, ask for another I-I member to attend as a witness as well.

Rule No 4. If attending a Garda Station for any other reason, always ensure you have at least one other person with you as a witness.

Rule No 5. If at all possible, record these exchanges. If you can't record, take written notes.

Rule No 6. Get copies of any papers you sign. There are simply too many reports of documents getting altered, rewritten or fabricated after-the-fact.

Rule No 7. If submitting a complaint, type it up beforehand using the I-I templates provided in Appendix II, and present it to your local Garda Station.

Rule No 8. If you are told that the statement HAS to be taken down in writing by a Garda (this isn't strictly true) then insist on reading out your prepared statement verbatim and check that the two statements match exactly.

Rule No 9. Get a PULSE Number for your complaint statement *before* you leave the Station. This ensures that the complaint is logged on the system and cannot later be denied.

Rule No 10. Always be polite and respectful if you can. Most ranking Gardaí are decent, and will respond better to you if treated with good manners and the expectation of fair treatment.

Possibly the most important rule of all however, is to absolutely insist on your rights, and if any member of An Garda Síochána denies you those rights or otherwise acts improperly or illegally, then take the appropriate, direct action. Given our unsatisfactory experiences with the Garda

Ombudsman, we would suggest that the 'appropriate action' is to follow the following procedure:

- Lodge a formal complaint at your local Garda Station using the Rules outlined above. If the duty Garda refuses to accept the complaint, then get his details and ask him/her to sign the appropriate I-I chit stating the grounds on which he/she is not accepting the complaint.

- If you are directed to go to GSOC because it is, *"the statutory authority that deals with complaints against Gardaí"* (etc), tell them that you ALSO wish to lodge this complaint as a criminal complaint in your local Garda station.

- Send an I-I Notification to the Garda who is the subject of your complaint. Do NOT send him/her a copy of the original complaint. Let him/her do that legwork.

- Send a copy of the I-I Notification to the Garda Commissioner - because it is only right that she should be aware of what is really going on at local levels. It is preferable if you send it to her home address (because it seems her private mail is constantly being opened by junior Officers at Garda HQ, and we are encountering considerable difficulty getting her to respond personally to anything).

- If appropriate (and it nearly always is), apply for a summons in the District Court and prosecute the Garda concerned in your own name under the 'Common Informer' legislation.

- Scour the I-I HAFTA Database for other instances where the same Garda may have acted improperly, and contact the I-I Members involved so that you have witnesses in support of your claim.

- Bill the Garda concerned for your time and costs expended on the matter.

- If the Garda doesn't pay your bill, then consider lodging a small-claims action (for €35 cost to you) and bring him/her into Court.

- Ensure you publicise your story far-and-wide, especially with *Integrity Ireland*.

- If any other person in the chain of command fails or refuses in their service to you (according to the law, the Constitution and their respective Codes of Conduct) then simply repeat the same procedure with them too.

- Finally, if you continue to have problems or difficulties with ANY other members of An Garda Síochána - including senior ranks - then put them on Notice that they are interfering with the administration of justice, and 'take the appropriate action. (Check out the list of criminal offences in Part 1 of this Guide)

If even a few resolute citizens pursue these tactics with firm determination, then something will definitely have to change - and change quickly too. As of 2015, the *Victims Rights Directive 2012/29/EU of The European Parliament and of the Council of 25 October* 2012 (which was recently signed into Irish Law) provides for the right of victims and complainants to receive information about their case in an open, timely and transparent manner. So don't be fobbed off any more folks. If you have a personal interest in a case being investigated by the Gardai or the DPP, they are now legally obliged to keep you informed. This also applies to complaints you have lodged that name Garda Management or other authority figures such as State solicitors, Registrars or Judges. The rules are now there in black-and-white for all to see. So don't take your foot off the gas (as they say). Assert your fundamnetal right NOT to be abused and mistreated by those in positions of authority and power. They are citizens of this country too, and they are obliged under law to abide by those laws and the Constitution - or, to face the same consequences as the rest of us.

Making a Statement or Lodging a Complaint

Our strong advice to anyone intending to make a statement to Gardaí is to have that statement prepared in advance, and to deliver that statement in the presence of eyewitnesses. If the Garda insists on re-taking your statement from you verbally, then simply read out verbatim what you have written. Gardaí can NOT refuse to accept a statement of complaint from a member of the public. If they try to do so, have then sign a 'refusal' chit and then go over their heads.

Paragraphs No 1 and 2 are required on a Garda complaint statement for it to be accepted at your local station. The other paragraphs listed A-F are optional, and should be used as you see fit, where appropriate. Obviously, you should edit or amend to suit your personal circumstances.

---

1. Statement of evidence of *(your name)*...D.O.B.........................

of *(address)*...

(phone):................................presented to *(name of Garda)*...

at (location) ....on *(date)*.........................

I hereby declare that this statement is true to the best of my knowledge and belief and I make this statement knowing that if it is tendered in evidence I will be liable for prosecution if I say anything in it which I know to be false or misleading or do not believe to be true.

(Body of complaint is then inserted here followed by the closing declaration and signature.)

2. This statement has been read over to me by...

at ....on ....

I have been invited to make any additions or corrections I deem necessary. I have done so.

This statement is correct.

Signed:

Date:

PULSE No:

Witnesses:

Witnesses:

Note: The addition of 'witnesses' is our idea, and you should list as many witnesses as you can so as to prevent any question that your statement is inaccurate. A witness should be allowed into the interview room with you, but if not, make sure the witness has signed your original complaint before it is submitted. Better still, arrange for the Gardaí to take the statement at your home, and make sure everything is witnessed and recorded. More examples can be found in Appendix II at the rear of this Guide.

Optional Clauses for Use in Formal Garda Complaints

(To be used or amended as you see fit)

A. It should be noted that the author of this complaint is speaking on behalf of some *30-40* members of the public *(list as attached)* who were present during these events, and that this complaint is listing *(names of authority figures here)* as primary subjects in acknowledgement of the fact that they were ultimately responsible for the actions of their subordinates, and that this complaint is being lodged by law-abiding citizens who are subject to the *Reporting Obligations* of the **Criminal Justice Act 2011** who are both legally and morally obliged (under pain of serious penalty) to report offences where, *"there is prima facie evidence of the commission of a relevant offence."*

B. In the event that Garda Management fails or refuses to act according to the Law and the Constitution in these matters, or otherwise attempts to interfere with or obstruct the lawful submission and advancement of this complaint; or if any attempt is made to suppress or otherwise improperly conceal said complaint in face of the supporting evidence; that this would constitute an additional offence against **Section 7 of the Criminal Procedure Act 2010** specifically; *"an offence against the administration of justice"* which is an arrestable offence. Accordingly, any parties so involved or implicated may be subject to another criminal complaint and/or subject to citizens arrest under **Section 4 of the Criminal Law Act 1997** whereupon said parties will be delivered to An Garda Síochána for the purposes of surrendering to due process as provided for in legislation.

C. That as a signed-up member of *Integrity Ireland*, that the Complainant *(your name here)* has access to numerous sworn complaints concerning serial acts of inexcusable malfeasance being perpetrated on ordinary citizens via the agency of the Irish Courts with the assistance of Gardaí; said complaints reflecting a pattern of deliberate and systemic contempt for the Law and the Irish Constitution. In context of the fact that this apparently-routine contempt of the Law and the Constitution by State-appointed officials can cause immense distress and damage to the lives of ordinary citizens; and in context of **Article 40:3, i & ii of the Irish Constitution** whereby the State undertakes to, *'defend and vindicate the rights of the citizen in cases where injustice is done'*; I therefore respectfully request that An Garda Síochána robustly investigates these incidents with a view to taking the appropriate action against those who have breached the Law and the Constitution as indicated in this complaint.

D. Given the collective experiences of myself and hundreds of *Integrity Ireland* Members to date; whereby formal written complaints of very serious misfeasance and malfeasance by agents and employees of the State have been reported to the Statutory Authorities without any due, proper or adequate responses – indeed, where many of those complaints (to Garda HQ, the DPP, GSOC, the Minister for Justice, the Taoiseach and the Courts for example) have been systematically ignored, deliberately suppressed, or even compounded further by additional acts of malfeasance by those agencies empowered by Statute to investigate and deal with criminality; I hereby respectfully advise that in accordance with **Article 6 of the EU Victims Directive**, the **Garda Síochána Customer Charter** and the parallel **Garda *Victims Charter*** that we will require a response <u>in writing</u> from Garda Management within 21 days please, setting out in detail what actions will be taken in this matter in accordance with the respective statutory obligations and, in the anticipated case that no proper investigations or prosecutions will (again) ensue, that we be advised <u>in writing</u> of the specific reasons thereof. I regret that verbal advices or phone calls from Gardaí or any other 'statutory authorities' will only be accepted if same are duly recorded, and followed up in writing for the purposes of accountability. Likewise, and given the proven futility of *'taking matters to the Garda Ombudsman'* – any such generic advisory from Gardaí or other Statutory Authorities to 'revert to the GSOC' will be interpreted as yet another obstructive act, and will be treated as such.

E. Although it is manifestly obvious to any right-thinking person that those entrusted with law enforcement and the administration of our Courts are morally and statutorily obliged to respect the law and treat citizens justly in accordance with the Constitution; it is regrettable to have to reiterate this fact in a complaint of this nature – where people's fundamental rights are being so abjectly and blatantly abused by those entrusted with the interpretation, administration and application of the law. In a society where ordinary citizens face serious consequences for apparent breaches of the law or for failure to adhere by Court Rules for example; surely the obligation to respect the rule of law weighs even more heavily on those entrusted with its administration and application?

F. For the avoidance of doubt and the protection of my rights, I conclude this statement as follows: I respectfully assert my statutory right to fair and equitable treatment, and reserve the moral right to disengage communication with any individual or agency who, through the means of misinformation, evasiveness, obfuscation, deception or other disingenuous tactics, contrives to avoid fulfilling their mandate to the public [as defined in the Constitution, respective codes of ethics, oaths of office and/or terms of service] other than where I am legally obliged to do so. I further affirm my right to note, report, record and/or publish any communications sent or received for the purposes of transparency, due accountability, and in the interests of natural justice. I further reserve the right to hold responsible under the law any individual, agent or agency I deem responsible for deliberate civil, criminal or constitutional breaches, and to bill any such agents or agencies for time and costs incurred. I do not deal with anonymous, pseudonymous, allonymous or imaginary entities. Annotated emails are accepted under certain exceptional or pre-agreed circumstances, but important or legal correspondence must also be sent as hard copies, duly signed. Unsigned correspondence that is not ascribed to one authorised individual will not be responded to and may be returned for signing, with costs billed to the source thereof. For practical reasons, legal matters will be dealt with on Mondays and Tuesdays only. Please be advised.

Note: The purpose of these statements is to create a firm basis upon which you can return to your original Garda complaint at a later date demonstrating that there has been a series of breaches of the law and the Constitution by those who have been charged with protecting and enforcing the same. A statement that contains a selection of these themes and elements also does the following.

- It establishes that your complaint has merit and substance,.

- It declares that your complaint is backed up by evidence and witnesses.

- It declares that you are *not* acting alone, and will *not* be ignored.

- It requires, absolutely, a written response from Gardaí.

- It establishes a solid paper record of the situation.

- It eliminates the usual tactics of delays, denials and deferments.

- It establishes the basis for future legal action - if required - to the European Court of Human Rights.

- It announces the collective efforts of *Integrity Ireland* members to challenge wrongdoing.

But.. YOU *have* to be willing to follow through when they don't respond properly according to their own codes of conduct and mandates to the public.

Garda Declaration of Professional Values & Ethical Standards

(As signed by members of An Garda Síochána)

Public Mission

Convinced that An Garda Síochána, being the national police service of the Republic of Ireland with a public mission, and acting in the public interest, has a fundamental role in protecting and vindicating the personal dignity and human rights of all members of the community;

Legal Framework

Recognising that An Garda Síochána, as a professional public body, is empowered, regulated and guided by the provisions of the Irish Constitution and subordinate Irish legislation, and International Human Rights Laws and Standards relevant to professional policing;

Rule of Law

Recognising that An Garda Síochána is committed to upholding and promoting the rule of law, which is the basis for all genuine democracies;

Legitimacy

Bearing in mind that An Garda Síochána can only carry out its functions with the consent and support of the community; is obligated to actively protect and promote this special relationship with the community through dialogue, consultation and partnership;

Trust & Integrity

Mindful that the office of Garda and its associated legal powers and authority are bestowed on officeholders as a public trust, to act on behalf of the people with integrity in the pursuit of peace and freedom and the protection of human life and property;

Diversity & Equality

Considering the diversity and equality of humanity, the requirement to accept and value differences, and the obligation to ensure that such diversity and equality is reflected in all aspects of An Garda Síochána including its professional policing practice;

Responsibility & Accountability

Recognising that officeholders in An Garda Síochána, entrusted with that office and associated powers and authority, have significantly increased responsibilities to the people, to whom they are accountable, regarding the use of such office and powers and authority;

Moral Duty

Emphasising that in the performance of our public duties, every staff member of An Garda Síochána is obligated to adhere to and be guided by the ethical, legal and professional principles which are applicable to public policing;

Commitment

An Garda Síochána and every staff member thereof, do hereby adopt, and accept and commit ourselves to this Declaration Of Professional Values and Ethical Standards.

PROFESSIONAL VALUES & ETHICAL STANDARDS
OF AN GARDA SÍOCHÁNA

Article 1 Respect the human dignity of every person.

Article 2 Uphold and protect the human rights of all.

Article 3 Respect and support the diversity and equality of cultures and beliefs in our society.

Article 4 Adhere to the principle of legality and apply the law in a fair and equitable manner.

Article 5 Be open and accountable in matters pertaining to the discharge of the professional duties and responsibilities of our public office.

Article 6 Pursue the truth by establishing and reporting all of the facts in an honest, objective, fair and impartial manner: justice being the aim.

Article 7 Maintain confidentiality in all matters, which refer to the affairs of others, unless there is a legal or compelling public interest requirement for disclosure.

Article 8 Adhere to the principles of necessity and proportionality at all times.

Article 9 Disclose immediately all conflicts of interest in accordance with our public mission as officeholders in An Garda Síochána.

Article 10 Challenge, oppose and expose illegal, unprofessional or unethical behaviour in our profession.

Article 11 Discharge our professional responsibilities and public duties with probity and integrity in the interest of the public good.

Article 12 Deliver on our employment contract obligations and commitments.

Article 13 Accept personal responsibility for the development of our professional competencies to serve the community better.

Article 14 Carry out our functions, as officeholders in An Garda Síochána, in consultation and partnership with the community.

Article 15 Apply and use Garda resources to the maximum benefit of the community

*   *   *

Important: Regarding incidences of fraud and perjury. Whose responsibility is it to investigate and prosecute? Screenshot of response received from Garda Headquarters, 26th Nov 2014.

Q1. Whose statutory responsibility is it to deal with criminal acts of fraud and perjury?
The function of An Garda Síochána is set out at Section 7 of An Garda Síochána Act, 2005. This function is to provide policing and security services for the State with the objective of, inter alia, bringing criminals to justice, including by detecting and investigating crime. Criminal acts of fraud are dealt with under the Criminal Justice (Theft & Fraud Offences) Act, 2001. Perjury is an offence under common law. Advices received by me would indicate An Garda Síochána has the statutory responsibility to deal with these criminal acts.

Q2. Why are Gardaí refusing to put in writing their decisions not to investigate crimes?
Advices received would suggest that while there is no reason such a decision would not be provided in writing, there is no legal obligation compelling same. The EU Victims Directive does state that victims should receive information on, inter alia, any decision not to proceed with or end an investigation, or not to prosecute an offender (Article 6). However, it should be noted that the Directive requires domestic legalisation to be transposed into Irish Law.

S.I. No. 214/2007 - Garda Síochána (Discipline) Regulations 2007

The following list comprises those offences for which any given member of An Garda Síochána can be *internally* disciplined. It may be useful as an indicator of when any given Garda should be sanctioned by their superiors, and these clauses should be quoted in any instance whereby members of the public have cause for complaint against a Garda.

Acts or Conduct constituting Breaches of Discipline

1. Discreditable conduct, that is to say, conducting himself or herself in a manner which the member knows, or ought to know, would be prejudicial to discipline or reasonably likely to bring discredit on the Garda Síochána.

2. Discourtesy, that is to say, failing to behave with due courtesy towards a member of the public.

3. Misconduct towards a member, that is to say -
   (a)   assaulting the member,

   (b)   oppressive or insubordinate conduct towards the member, or

   (c)   using abusive or insulting language to him or her.

4.   Neglect of duty, that is to say, without good and sufficient cause -
   (a)   failing or neglecting -

      (i) properly to account for any money or property received by him or her in his or her capacity as a member, or

      (ii) promptly to carry out any lawful order or to do any other thing which it is his or her duty to do, or

   (b)   doing anything mentioned in subparagraph (a)(ii) in a negligent manner.

5. Disobedience of orders, that is to say, wilfully disobeying any lawful order, whether written or oral, without good and sufficient cause.

6. Falsehood or prevarication, that is to say, in his or her capacity as a member -
   (a)   making or procuring the making of -

      (i)   any oral or written statement, or

      (ii)   any entry in an official document or record,

that, to the member's knowledge, is false or misleading, or
   (b)   with a view to deceiving any person -

      (i)   destroying or mutilating any official document or record, or

      (ii)   altering or erasing or adding to any entry in it.

7. (a) Breach of confidence, that is to say, making an unauthorised communication in relation to any information which comes to the member's knowledge in the course of his or her duties and was not available to members of the public.

   (b) In subparagraph (a), "unauthorised communication" means any communication other that a communication made in the execution of his or her duties or authorised by the Commissioner.

8. Corrupt or improper practice, that is to say -
   (a) soliciting or receiving as a member and without the consent of the Commissioner any gratuity, present, subscription or testimonial (other than from customary collections for such purposes as presentations on the occasion of transfer, marriage or retirement),

(b) placing himself or herself as a member under a pecuniary obligation to any person in a manner that might affect the member's ability to discharge his or her duties as a member,

(c) improperly using (or attempting to use) his or her position as a member for his or her private advantage,

(d) writing or giving, otherwise than in accordance with conditions specified from time to time by the Commissioner, any testimonial of character or other recommendation with the object of supporting an application for a licence or certificate relating to intoxicating liquor, betting or gaming,

(e) failing wilfully and without good and sufficient cause to pay any lawful debt in such circumstances as to be liable to affect his or her ability to discharge his or her duties as a member or as to be liable to compromise other members, or

(f) signing or circulating a petition or statement relating to matters affecting the Garda Síochána other than a petition or statement presented or intended to be presented to his or her superiors either directly or through a representative association.

9. Abuse of authority, that is to say, oppressive conduct towards a member of the public, including -
   (a) without good and sufficient cause, making an arrest, or

   (b) using unnecessary violence towards any person with whom the member is brought into contact in the execution, or purported execution, of his or her duties.

10. Neglect of health by a member, that is to say -
    (a) any culpable act or conduct which occurs while the member is absent from duty because of sickness and which is calculated to delay his or her return to duty,

    (b) while so absent from duty, failing, refusing or neglecting to carry out any direction of the Commissioner based on information received by him or her from the Chief Medical Officer of the Garda Síochána, or

    (c) dishonestly absenting himself or herself from duty on grounds of illness.

11. Untidiness on duty or in uniform, that is to say, without good and sufficient cause, being untidy in appearance while on duty or while not on duty but wearing uniform in a public place.

12. Misuse of money or other property belonging to a member of the public that is in the custody of the Garda Síochána, that is to say, misappropriating or wilfully or carelessly misusing, wasting, losing or damaging any such money or other property or failing, without good and sufficient cause, to report any such misuse, waste, loss or damage.

13. Intoxication, that is to say, owing to the effects of intoxicating liquor or other drugs or a combination thereof, being unfit for duty either while on duty or while not on duty but wearing a uniform in a public place.

14. Drinking on duty, that is to say, without good and sufficient cause, drinking intoxicating liquor while on duty.

15. Unauthorised entry to licensed premises, that is to say, without good and sufficient cause while on duty or while not on duty but wearing uniform, entering any premises in respect of which a licence or permit is in force, or which are registered, for a purpose relating to intoxicating liquor, betting or gaming.

16. Prohibited spare-time activity, that is to say -
    (a) identifying himself or herself actively or publicly with a political party,

    (b) behaving in relation to political matters in such a manner and in such circumstances as to give rise to reasonable apprehension among members of the public in relation to his or her impartiality in the discharge of his or her duties, or

(c) engaging (whether for reward or otherwise) in any activity which, though not mentioned in subparagraph (a) or (b), is prohibited by the Commissioner (by either general or special directive) as being -

(i) likely to interfere with the proper discharge of his or her duties, or

(ii) likely to give rise to reasonable apprehension among members of the public in relation to his or her impartiality in the discharge of those duties, or

(iii) for good and stated reasons, inappropriate for members to engage in.

17. Criminal conduct, that is to say, conduct constituting an offence in respect of which there has been a conviction by a court.

18. Failure to comply with a direction under section 39 by a member of higher rank to account for any act done while on duty where that member has informed the member concerned that such failure may lead to dismissal from the Garda Síochána.

19. Failure to comply with any specified provision of any code of ethics established under section 17 of the Act.

20. Failure to co-operate with an investigation under the law and procedure referred to in section 55(2)(a).

21. An act done by a member while on secondment to the Police Service of Northern Ireland which, if done by a member of that Service, could be the subject of disciplinary action by the authorities in Northern Ireland.

22. Failure, without reasonable excuse, to co-operate with an investigation conducted under the Act or these regulations or with a board of inquiry established under Regulation 25.

23. Failure to comply with paragraph (a) or (b) of Regulation 12.

24. Failure to co-operate with a search under section 99 of a Garda Síochána station.

25. Obstruction, that is to say, doing any act which obstructs the operation of these regulations or the operation or implementation of any official policy, directions or instructions.

26. Abuse of official communications, that is to say, using e-mail or other internet procedures contrary to official policy.

27. Accessory to a breach of discipline, that is to say, conniving at, or knowingly being an accessory to, a breach of discipline.

28. Failure to comply with a requirement under section 42(4).

29. Harassment or intimidation of a confidential reporter within the meaning of the Garda Síochána (Confidential Reporting of Corruption and Malpractice) Regulations 2007 (S.I. No. 168 of 2007).

30. Making a false allegation of corruption or malpractice within the Garda Síochána otherwise than in good faith, as provided for in Regulation 14(3) of the said Regulations of 2007.

THE GARDA SÍOCHÁNA VICTIMS CHARTER

What you can expect from the Garda Síochána

If you are a victim of a crime or traumatic incident, we will:
• respond quickly to your call and investigate your complaint;

• give you the name, telephone number and station of the investigating Garda and the PULSE incident number - this is a number given to your incident so that we can quickly find the details of your case;

• explain what will happen and keep you informed of the criminal investigation - this includes writing to you when we charge/summon or caution a suspect in relation to your incident; and

• tell you in writing about the Crime Victims' Helpline and the other services available for victims of crime or a traumatic incident. You can access a wide range of support services through this helpline.

The helpline is run by volunteers and it is independent of the Garda Síochána Crime Victims Helpline 1850 211 407

When a suspect is due to appear in court we will tell you:
• whether the suspect is being held in prison ('in custody') or on bail and any conditions of the bail, such as staying away from you or your house;

• the time, date and location of the court hearing;

• the prosecution process - if you are likely to be called as a witness, we will tell you about the support you can get from voluntary organisations which support victims of crime;

• about cases where the law allows you as a victim, to give evidence to the court about the crime's impact on you;

• about court expenses; and

• the final result of the criminal trial.

If you are a visitor to Ireland
If you are a visitor to Ireland and you are the victim of a crime or a traumatic incident we will also refer you to the services of the Irish Tourist Assistance Service Irish Tourist Assistance Service Telephone Number: 1890 365 700

We will show special sensitivity in relation to sexual offences
• we will provide a Garda of the same gender;

• we will provide a doctor of the same gender as far as possible when asked; and

• we will give you details about any local support organisations for victims of sexual offences.

Families of murder victims or victims of other unlawful killing
Your local Garda Superintendent will keep contact directly with you and any organisation supporting victims that you have asked to help you. We will keep up contact between you, the investigating Garda and any relevant support organisation through a named Garda Family Liaison Officer from the investigation team.

Victims of domestic violence

In cases of domestic violence we have a pro-arrest policy to protect spouses or partners and your family. We will also advise you about local support services.

Older people

If you are an older person who has been a victim of crime we will continue to take all reasonable steps to protect and reassure you. We will also offer you advice about home security and your safety in the community.

Special Needs

If you have any form of disability we will take your special needs or requirements into account.

If you are not fluent in English or Irish

We will provide a free translation service so that you will receive the same quality of service as any victim of crime.

Lesbian, gay, bisexual and transgender communities

If you are a member of the lesbian, gay, bisexual or transgender community we will manage your case with sensitivity. Where appropriate we will also refer you to a Gay Liaison Officer within the Garda Síochána.

Racist incidents

If you are a victim of a racist incident we will:

- accurately record the incident;

- investigate your complaint; and

- put you in contact with the Garda Ethnic Liaison Officer in your area.

Crimes committed by young people

If you are the victim of a crime committed by a young person:

• we will inform you if the person who carried out the crime is a young person;

• we will take account of any views that you, as a victim, may wish to make when a young person is being considered for the Diversion Programme; however, the decision to admit a young person to the Programme remains a decision for the Director of the Programme;

• we may invite you to be present if we are cautioning the young person;

• we may invite you to a Garda Family Conference; and

• we will uphold your interests as a victim at a Garda Family Conference, whether you are present or not.

If we do not meet your expectations

If you are not satisfied with our service - or if you have any questions, suggestions or feedback on any aspect of your treatment by members of the Garda Síochána please do not hesitate to contact: Your local Garda Superintendent. Details are available at www.garda.ie or in the telephone directory (green pages) under An Garda Síochána, or:

The Garda Victim Liaison Office, An Garda Síochána,

Community Relations and Community, Policing Section, Harcourt Square, Dublin 2

Tel: (01) 666 3880 or (01) 666 3822 or (01) 666 3882   Fax: (01) 666 3801

Email: crimevictims@garda.ie (All are monitored during business hours) We will respond to your query as fast as possible.

You may also refer a complaint to:

The Garda Síochána Ombudsman Commission (GSOC)
150 Abbey Street Upper, Dublin 1.
LoCall: 1890 600 800   Tel: (01) 871 6727   Fax: (01) 814 7023   Email: info@gsoc.ie
Website: www.gardaombudsman.ie

The Role of the Garda Síochána

We are very aware of the special place that victims have in the Garda service and within the criminal justice system. We are committed to establishing a helpful and supportive relationship with you. Looking after your dignity, concerns and needs is a high priority for us.

Professional values such as honesty, accountability, respect and professionalism and ethical standards guide us in the performance of our duties and the delivery of our public policing services.

The Garda Síochána are dedicated to:

- protecting life and property,

- detecting and preventing crime,

- preserving peace,

- maintaining public safety.

We aim to be courteous, helpful, respectful and professional. If you are upset about a crime or other traumatic incident, we will respond to your needs in a caring and sensitive manner.

When you report a crime we will investigate the matter and help to bring those responsible to justice. We do this by gathering all of the evidence surrounding the incident in a fair, honest and impartial manner. Then we will do one of the following:

- for less serious crimes bring the case before the District Court in the name of the Director of Public Prosecutions;

- if the offender is between 10 and 17 years of age decide whether that person is suitable for the Diversion Programme; or

- send a file on our investigation to the Director of Public Prosecutions (DPP) and ask for a direction on whether a criminal prosecution should take place.

All members of the Garda Síochána will treat victims with dignity and respect - whatever your gender, race, religious beliefs, ethnic origin, sexual orientation, age, nationality, disability, economic circumstances, marital or family status or if you are a member of the Traveller community.

The welfare and support of victims are central to our partnership with community groups, statutory agencies and voluntary organisations.

(Edition: June, 2010)

STANDARD ADVISORY TO GARDAÍ

(This should of course be amended to suit your situation / gender etc)

A Respectful Advisory to Members of the Garda Síochána here present:

I stand here under the Constitution, an honest man and a citizen of this State. I require that the members of An Garda Síochána here present abide by their Oath of Office in upholding the Constitution and the laws to defend and protect my human rights; specifically, that they undertake NOT to assault, restrain or otherwise unlawfully interfere with my person as long as I remain within my Constitutional remit acting and speaking as a litigant in a public courtroom. That any member of the Gardaí here present who is NOT willing to affirm their Oath of Office in this regard, immediately vacates this Courtroom on the grounds that to remain here in contempt of said Oath is to be in contempt of the Irish Constitution, the law, and the people of Ireland.

* * *

Garda Síochána Oath of Office

Section 16(1) of the Garda Síochána Act 2005 requires each member of the Garda Síochána to make the following *Solemn declaration* when they are appointed :-

"I hereby solemnly and sincerely declare before God that—

> **-I will faithfully discharge the duties of a member of the Garda Síochána with fairness, integrity, regard for human rights, diligence and impartiality, upholding the Constitution and the laws and according equal respect to all people,**
>
> **-while I continue to be a member, I will to the best of my skill and knowledge discharge all my duties according to law, and**
>
> **-I do not belong to, and will not while I remain a member form, belong to or subscribe to, any political party or secret society whatsoever."**

> Section 16(2) allows the words "before God" to be omitted from the declaration at the request of the declarant.

THE GARDA SÍOCHÁNA OMBUDSMAN COMMISSION (GSOC)

The Good Stuff: The GSOC was set up in 2008 to replace the much-criticised Garda Complaints Board after shocking revelations of Garda corruption emerged, as well as a parallel perception by the public that the G C B was 'not fit for purpose'. If the new GSOC was to function as promised; that is, as an independent *civilian* oversight that protects the public from rogue police activities (such as framing innocent citizens for murder etc), then the €11 million-a-year price tag is a real bargain for citizens. Likewise, if the three (very-well-paid) Commissioners who head up the GSOC are indeed actively and independently pursuing the declared aims and goals of the GSOC as stated in the GSOC mission statement, and are directing their 90 office staff to do likewise, then we should all be thankful to ex-Taoiseach Bertie Ahern for nominating three associates to take on this challenging enterprise - knowing of course that each would courageously and enthusiastically apply themselves to the task - *without* any hint of fear or favour, because clearly, after the debacle of blatant Garda corruption and criminality in Donegal and the findings of the Morris tribunal, it was clear that there was an immediate need for an independent statutory oversight body such as a well-functioning Garda Ombudsman that could deal robustly and effectively with systemic Garda corruption, and assuage the angst and anger of the public. In hindsight however, perhaps it wasn't the most the most well-thought out decision to appoint three Commissioners who each had parents who were Gardaí or in policing?

The Not-So-Good Stuff: Various I-I members report that it is a painfully exasperating and difficult process trying to lodge a complaint with the GSOC: They report serial difficulties in lodging their complaints, incredibly long delays, and a general perception that staff at the GSOC are either unbelievably incompetent and disorganised, or, are being deliberately obstructive, unhelpful and evasive. According to their own published records, over 11,000 complaints of various levels of seriousness were received by the GSOC in the first 4 years, as well as a further 5,300 'enquiries'. Most were automatically 'deemed inadmissible' (often without proper explanation) and only a handful of Gardaí (of the lowest rank) were ever sanctioned. As I-I members tried to approach higher-ranking GSOC staff members, they report increased levels of hubris and superciliousness which they found to be very disconcerting, and not-at-all suited to the facilitation of often very serious complaints. Most complaints submitted by I-I members were eventually 'deemed inadmissible, dismissed without due explanation, or run out-of-time'. In most cases, there is nothing to suggest that the hard evidence was ever even properly looked at, and several citizens report being treated like a criminal - rather than as a legitimate complainant.

The Really Bad and Depressing Stuff: Despite several verbal and written requests over a period of two years, we cannot secure the name of even *one* single qualified 'civilian investigator' from GSOC staff. We also cannot find any I-I member who has had dealings with the GSOC who ever met any of these enigmatic 'civilian investigators' - who appear to exist only in the imagination of the person who wrote the GSOC brochure. The evidence suggests that *all* GSOC investigators are in fact currently-serving Gardai - appointed by the Garda Commissioner, and answerable *only* to him!

The CEO of the previous Garda Complaints Board effectively runs the GSOC today as the head of administration. The three Commissioners (we have it in writing) *"..are not involved in the day-to-day processing of complaints"*. Until recently, the Chairperson of the GSOC was also an ex-policeman, whose previous job was Head of the Garda Inspectorate. So what, we might ask, has changed since the bad old days of the discredited Garda Complaints Board?

Once a Garda investigator has been appointed <u>by the Garda Commissioner</u>, he reports back to the GSOC, who in turn reports back to the Garda Commissioner. The Garda Commissioner can then make a unilateral decision on what's to be done, and he or she is, literally, answerable to no-one. Not the GSOC, not the complainant, not even to the Minister of Justice who claims (in writing) not to have any direct jurisdiction either.

And, if a Garda *is* eventually sanctioned, then those sanctions are depressingly inadequate. The worst of five possible sanctions under s.43 for example is, *"a maximum of up to two weeks reduction in pay, not to exceed 10% of salary"*. In other words, a maximum fine of a couple of hundred Euros for appalling abuses of their position of privilege and responsibility - that has probably caused an innocent citizen hell! And whilst there are other sanctions that can be applied, it would appear from members' experiences that there is a desperate resistance from staff at the GSOC into taking any real action against criminal Gardaí - especially if they are high-ranking, or otherwise 'well connected'. Clearly, the trusting public has been sold a story here that costs us over €11 million a year for what is in essence, just a smoke-and-mirrors operation designed once again, to secure 'jobs for the boys' and protect the gilded elite from further public embarrassment over the shocking levels of corruption and wrongdoing in Irish institutions.

*   *   *

And, just in case the dismal message isn't getting through, last year one of the most senior staffers at GSOC tried to raise concerns about the malfunctioning GSOC - only to be forced into resigning, as is the normal treatment being meted out to whistleblowers or conscientious sorts of any type with the courage to speak up. The *Irish Independent* had this to say.

A SENIOR Garda Ombudsman director has condemned the agency as not fit for purpose in a damning personal submission to the Oireachtas Justice Committee.

Director of investigations Ray Leonard claimed the garda oversight body lacks "effective independence" and does not represent "value for money" for the taxpayer.

Mr Leonard, who has been working for the Garda Síochána Ombudsman Commission (GSOC) for seven years, said the agency was "neither fish nor fowl" because of the legislation governing the body. "It is not an ombudsman in the ordinary meaning nor is it a law enforcement agency with the requisite tool kit," he said. His comments followed the announcement by Taoiseach Enda Kenny yesterday that the Cabinet was bringing forward legislation to give GSOC more powers. The Garda Ombudsman came under fire last week for failing to provide barrister Sean Guerin with the information he needed to investigate Sgt Maurice McCabe's allegations of garda misconduct. In his submission to the Justice Committee, Mr Leonard said his organisation could not operate independent of the State because it was financially dependent on the Department of Justice. And in a swipe at former Justice Minister Alan Shatter, he criticised the "climate" and "culture" in which "the GSOC chairman can be summoned by the minister to give an account of himself". Mr Leonard, a former Revenue Commissioner investigator, criticised several aspects of the legislation governing GSOC in his submission to the Justice Committee on the forthcoming changes to the Garda Siochana Act. Mr Leonard will today appear before the committee to answer questions on his submission. His 25-page letter to the committee is separate to a submission made by GSOC, which also put forward recommendations on legislative changes.

Meanwhile, a retired doctor has claimed there is inadequate protection for patients in garda custody. Dr Richard O'Flaherty, who worked as an on-call doctor for garda stations, made the claim in a submission to the Oireachtas Justice Committee on legislative changes to the Garda Síochána Act. Dr O'Flaherty said his 40 years of medical experience led him to conclude the "present situation is inadequate to protect patients in detention, doctors in attendance, other professionals and the silent majority of gardai". He said all garda assault allegations should be referred to the GSOC. He is a member of the victims' support group Justice4All, which forwarded allegations of garda harassment and intimidation to Taoiseach Enda Kenny. *Irish Independent*

Our recommendation? Don't waste your time. Use the Common Informer process instead.

Lawyer, Solicitor or Barrister - What's the Difference?

The term 'Lawyer' is a generic term used to describe anyone who is a Licensed Legal Practitioner qualified to give legal advice in one or more areas of law. Put simply, Solicitors and Barristers are both types of Lawyer.

What is the difference between a Barrister and a Solicitor? *(From the law library website)*
There are two types of lawyer in Ireland - barristers and solicitors. The solicitor offers legal services such as buying and selling your house, drawing up your will, advising on setting up a business, and the initial advice if you are sued by somebody or think you have a case against somebody else. This is why you go to a solicitor first. If the solicitor thinks you need specialised advice or an expert advocate to represent you in Court, the solicitor will recommend and retain a suitable barrister. There are approximately 2,300 barristers in Ireland and the solicitor can pick and choose amongst them for a particular case. In this way the solicitor (and therefore you) have available the choice of the best barrister for your case.

Barristers specialise in representing you in court (advocacy), giving you more detailed advice on your case and also advising you on more difficult areas where you (and possibly your solicitor) need more detailed advice e.g. about some complex business problem or medical negligence or a breach of your human rights or a serious crime with which you may be charged.

A fundamental distinction between a solicitor and a barrister is that the barrister does not and cannot hold any money, ever, on behalf of a client; does not and cannot handle your house purchase or sale; and does not and cannot bind you or your property by promises or undertakings to banks or financial institutions. A barrister is not and cannot be in partnership with another barrister. He or she is a sole practitioner and is entirely independent. When advising you or handling your case, your barrister is not under the influence of the Government or any public authority and will observe strict professional confidentiality about your business. He or she is a highly qualified professional and subject to a strict code of professional ethics. You thus get a totally independent, objective and specialist view of your particular problem.

The solicitor retains (or "instructs") the barrister on your behalf and furnishes him or her with a summary of the facts and the relevant documents. Normally you then have a meeting with the solicitor and your barrister who advises as to the best course to take. The barrister may give your solicitor written advice (an "opinion") on your case or on the legal issues arising. The solicitor and barrister both handle your case but do different aspects of the job. The solicitor takes your instructions, organises the witnesses, assists them in preparing their statements of their evidence, assembles the documents, corresponds with the solicitor on the other side, keeps any funds you give him in a separate account and so forth. The barrister gives the specialised advice on your case, how it should be handled, drafts the documents used in court to outline your case (the "pleadings"), drafts the written submissions to the court when this is required and argues the case for you in court. Thus the barrister and the solicitor work together on an individual case each doing a different but complementary aspect of the job of advising and representing you.

For further information please contact The Bar of Ireland Administration at 01-817 5000, email: thebarofireland@lawlibrary.ie

What Are the Main Duties of a Barrister?

(From the Law Library)

A Barrister Has a Number of Core Duties.

(a) Duty to the court.

Barristers have an overriding duty to the court to act with independence, to act in the interests of justice and to ensure that, in the public interest, the proper and efficient administration of justice is achieved. By way of example, if a client wants a barrister to lie to the court, or to mislead the court, or to hold back damaging documents which the court has ordered to be produced, the barrister is obliged not to do this under any circumstances.

(b) Duty to promote the client's interests.

Subject only to their paramount duty to the Court and the administration of justice, barristers must promote and protect fearlessly and by all proper and lawful means the best interests of the client they represent.

(c) Duty of independence.

Every barrister is completely independent. He or she is not in partnership with anybody, will not do a case if he or she has any conflict of interest and is free of any control by the Government or any outside organisation as to how he or she advises and represents you. Ensuring barristers are and remain independent has always been a key aspect of client protection, the defence of individual rights against the State and the administration of justice.

(d) Duty to represent a client irrespective of the barrister's private views

A barrister cannot refuse to take on a case in the field in which he or she practices simply because he does not like the client or his beliefs or on the basis of any opinion which the barrister may have formed as to the character, reputation, conduct, guilt or innocence of the client or the political, religious or other cause the client may be promoting.

Every client has a right of access to the courts and to the administration of justice. Every client has a right to be represented by a barrister who is entitled to be paid for his or her work. Barristers can not pick and choose which types of clients they act for if the work is within their area of expertise. Like a taxi offered a fare, the barrister has to take the passenger (i.e. the client) if he or she is free and is offered a suitable fare. The purpose of this rule is to give every client, as far as possible, an equal right of access to barristers and to legal representation in court.

What is the Relationship Between a Barrister and a Judge?

Judges in Ireland are appointed by the Government from the ranks of practicing barristers and solicitors. Judges rely on barristers appearing in Court to highlight all the relevant facts in the case and legal principles and previous cases necessary for the judge to consider before reaching his or her judgment. Part of the barrister's duty not to mislead the Court is not to put forward a legal point which the barrister knows to be wrong. The independence of the barrister is critical in ensuring that this key part of a fair and just legal system is preserved.

It is a core and valued tradition of the legal system in Ireland that barristers should never mislead the judge and a barrister who does so risks shattering his or her reputation and career.

*   *   *

Q: Is your Barrister giving you a proper service? If not, you should feel free to fire them - just as you would any other service provider who does NOT fulfil their obligations to you - the paying customer. Remember, they work for us - not the other way round!

Irish Barristers

The Code of Conduct for the Bar of Ireland says that: In Ireland, a barrister may only carry out work if instructed by specified categories of professionals, including:

- solicitors (for all types of work)

- foreign lawyers

- (in connection with *non–contentious* matters) accountants, surveyors, architects and tax experts in their areas of expertise

- any person qualified and practising as a lawyer *outside* Ireland and

- any lay client where the work originated or is to be performed wholly *outside* Ireland.

Outside Ireland, a barrister may work for:

- any qualified, practising lawyer or

- any lay client, where the matter has arisen or takes place *outside* Ireland and the United Kingdom.

In effect, this means that the average Irish citizen cannot approach a barrister directly with their case - but must first seek out and engage a solicitor. This has the effect of increasing the time, costs and complexity of cases - often unnecessarily - as well as reinforcing the elitism and classism that still pervades Irish society.

*   *   *

The Good Stuff: In part, the Barristers' Code of Conduct (2012) states: "Barristers shall uphold at all times the standards set out in the Code and shall conduct themselves in accordance with the standards of conduct expected of barristers in their practice, and it is their duty to be independent and free from any influence, especially such as may arise from their personal interests or external pressure, in the discharge of their professional duties as barristers."

The Barristers' Code of Conduct goes on to say that amongst other things: *"It is the duty of Barristers, not to engage in conduct (whether in pursuit of their profession or otherwise) which is dishonest or which may bring the barristers' profession into disrepute or which is prejudicial to the administration of justice."*

It is refreshing to be able to hold up as examples of integrity and best practice, certain members of the legal profession who do their best in difficult circumstances to service their clients honestly, to the best of their abilities. Inasmuch as the Barristers' Code of Conduct is respected and adhered to by any individual barrister, then we as citizens should be grateful and respectful of the service we receive.

But what happens when that code is *not* respected or adhered to?

The Not-So-Good Stuff: It seems once again, that the various codes of conduct; codes of ethics; or various 'declarations of professional standards' that abound nowadays in so many Irish State institutions and their affiliates - are simply there to give the misleading impression to the public and any outside observers (such as foreign governments and media) that we do actually insist upon proper professional, ethical and moral standards from our legal profession; and from State agencies and their employees.

142

Here we showcase just one example of outrageous fraud being perpetrated by a team of four barristers on the taxpayer - one of whom was a former Attorney General. *(From the Irish Examiner July 2010)*

> "A report in Thursday's Irish Times outlined how Mr Moran (the Taxing Master) had expressed his "disgust and bewilderment" at the level of costs claimed…"In my 15 years as Taxing Master or indeed in all my years involved in litigation, I have never encountered such grossly excessive fees being marked by learned counsel or solicitors," he said. Mr Moran went on to say that he could hardly "find the words strong enough to describe my disgust and bewilderment at the level of these costs being claimed".

> "This is an unconscionable situation at a time when every other section in society has endured cuts. A certain sheltered professional class which apparently has no regard for the environment in which we live is extorting extraordinary and unjustifiable fees. The Government needs to address the issue,"..

As expected, the Government did NOT 'address the issue' - and no-one in authority seems even the slightest bit concerned at such a blatant display of fraudulent extortion and profiteering at the taxpayer's expense. One of these barristers for example had charged €75,000.00 for work allegedly done, but received not a penny of it from the Taxing Master - such was the absurdity of the claim. Another bill he submitted for a similar amount was reduced by over 80%. Between them, they had attempted to claim 2.1 million! This is about as blatant an example of deliberate fraud as we are ever going to see. If we call a spade a spade, this was deliberate and premeditated theft and deception, pure and simple. But other than being reported in the press at the time, these barristers received no sanctions whatsoever. Is it too obvious a question to ask ourselves what would happen to any ordinary citizen who tried to steal even a fraction of that amount from the taxpayer's purse using fraud and deception? One imagines the Government would immediately hire some top level barristers via the Chief State Solicitors Office or the DPP to ensure that the offending criminal was punished, right? Interesting then to note that these barristers continue in practice undisturbed, and that one of them at least is now employed by the wealthiest and most influential firm of solicitors in Ireland, who receive contracts worth approximately €22,000.00 per day from the Irish Government - where opposing teams of solicitors from the *same* firm suck the public finances dry.

One of these same barristers surfaces in another I-I complaint where he engaged in further acts of fraud and deception - only this time, with the assistance and blessing of a local Court. On this occasion, he was hired 'independently' by a telephone company to prevent a citizen from securing evidence of Garda criminal activity - in a case where the CSSO is representing the Guards - 'under instructions' from the Garda Commissioner - in order to stop a private citizen securing evidence in a civil case!?

The Really Bad and Depressing Stuff: I-I members report multiple instances where barristers have lied or otherwise deliberately misled the Courts; have claimed exorbitant and unjustified fees; and otherwise acted dishonestly and violated their own code of conduct, but again, nothing ever seems to get done about it.

Solicitors - Core Values of the Profession

(From the Law Society's Guide to Good Professional Conduct for Solicitors - 3rd Edition 2013)

1.1 The Function of the Solicitor in Society

In a society founded on respect for the rule of law, solicitors fulfil a special role. Their duties do not begin and end with the faithful performance of what they are instructed to do so far as the law permits. Solicitors must serve the interests of justice as well as the rights and liberties of their clients. It is their duty not only to plead their clients' cause but also to be their adviser.

The solicitors' function therefore imposes on them a variety of legal and moral obligations, sometimes appearing to be in conflict with each other, towards:-

(a) their clients,

(b) the courts and other bodies before whom solicitors plead their clients' cause or

act on their behalf,

(c) the public, for whom the existence of a free and independent profession is an

essential means of safeguarding individual rights in face of the power of the

State and other interests in society,

(d) the legal profession in general and each fellow member of it.

Rules of professional conduct are designed to assist the proper performance by a solicitor of his duties and functions in his practice. Practising solicitors, whether in private, in-house or public service practice, share the same professional standards.

1.2 Legislation

The rules of professional conduct are derived both from statutory and non-statutory sources. The Solicitors Acts 1954 to 2011 and the regulations made under these acts are the legislative framework for the regulation of solicitors. Solicitors should also be mindful of additional statutory duties, such as those necessitated by Data Protection legislation and Anti-Money Laundering legislation.

1.3 Core Values of the Profession

In addition to the legislative requirements, solicitors are also required to observe general core principles of conduct, in particular honesty, independence, confidentiality and the avoidance of situations of conflict of interest. A solicitor should at all times observe and promote these core values of the profession and avoid any conduct or activities inconsistent with those values.

The rules of all the Bar Associations and Law Societies in the European Community are based on identical values and in most cases demonstrate a common foundation which is also reflected in the rules of Bar Associations and Law Societies throughout the world.

When the solicitor observes the highest professional standards, this is to the ultimate benefit of the client whether an individual or an organisation.

Honesty

A solicitor must be honest in his practice as a solicitor in all his dealings with others.

Independence

Solicitors must always retain their professional independence and their ability to advise their clients fearlessly and objectively. Independence is essential to the function of solicitors in their relationships with all parties and it is the duty of solicitors that they do not allow their independence to be compromised. Solicitors should not allow themselves to be restricted in their actions on behalf of clients or restricted by clients in relation to their other professional duties.

A solicitor's independence is necessary because of his various relationships of trust. The independence of a solicitor's advice is an essential value. Solicitors who are proprietors of firms are responsible for everything which happens in their firms and must retain full control of the firm at all times.

A solicitor must not allow himself to be intimidated by a client or other person, into making decisions or taking actions relating to the firm, or the legal services provided by the firm, which are illegal, breach the solicitor's professional duties or are not in the solicitor's own interests.

A solicitor should never permit his independence to be undermined by the wishes of a party who has introduced a client.

1.4 The Enforcement of the Rules of Professional Conduct

The failure of the solicitor to observe these rules, whether having a statutory basis or otherwise, could result in a complaint to the Law Society. Referral to the Solicitors Disciplinary Tribunal of the High Court may follow. Alternatively, a complaint may be made directly to the Tribunal.

The Tribunal, which sits as a division of the High Court, may upon due inquiry make a finding of misconduct. The definition of misconduct in the Solicitors Acts 1954 to 2011 provides as follows:- "misconduct" includes

(a) the commission of treason or a felony or a misdeameanour,

(b) the commission, outside the State, of a crime or an offence which would be a

felony or a misdemeanor if committed in the State,

(c) the contravention of a provision of the Solicitors Acts 1954 to 2011, or any

order or regulation made thereunder,

(d) in the course of practice as a solicitor –

(i) having any direct or indirect connection, association or arrangement with any person (other than a client) whom the solicitor knows, or upon reasonable enquiry should have known, is a person who is acting or has acted in contravention of Section 55 or 56 or Section 58 (which prohibits an unqualified person from drawing or preparing certain documents), as amended by the Act of 1994, or the Principal Act, or Section 5 of the Solicitors (Amendment) Act 2002, or

(ii) accepting instructions to provide legal services to a person from another person whom the solicitor knows, or upon reasonable enquiry should have known, is a person who is acting or has acted in contravention of those enactments,

(e) any other conduct tending to bring the solicitors' profession into disrepute.' A finding of misconduct may result in a sanction being imposed on the solicitor by the Solicitors Disciplinary Tribunal itself or by the High Court.

The requirement of standards of professional conduct which the profession sets for itself should not be confused with the requirements of the general law of contract, of tort, of criminal law or of equity, even though the requirements of conduct may in some cases follow, or closely parallel, the general legal requirements.

Irish Solicitors - The I-I Review

The Good Stuff: In the face of so much popular criticism of lawyers - and of the legal profession in general - it is refreshing to be able to hold up as examples of integrity and best practice, certain members of the legal profession who do their best in difficult circumstances to service their clients honestly, to the best of their abilities. Some I-I members are very supportive of their own legal teams and are happy to recommend them to other members, and we are privileged to count a number of such solicitors amongst our membership. Unfortunately however, those examples are very few and far between.

The Not-So-Good Stuff: According to the majority of opinion amongst I-I members, the legal profession in Ireland is a very poor reflection of what it was originally intended to be, and many citizens believe the profession has completely lost the run of itself. The overarching sense of entitlement and privilege conveyed by many solicitors when dealing with their clients for example, does not marry up with any modern concept of genuine 'service'. Members feel they are expected to go cap-in-hand when seeking legal services, and that they are in no position to question how the solicitor is operating, or why they are being charged such exorbitant amounts - often for painfully slow and shoddy work. Many people feel they are being callously exploited by self-serving, greedy and unprincipled solicitors, but that they have little choice other than to take it on the chin. The multiple instances of solicitors colluding with other solicitors in order to drag out cases and thereby increase their fees, is also extremely disturbing in a profession that is supposed to be centred on the principles of justice, and the remedies available to any citizen who has been wronged by a solicitor are also difficult and onerous to pursue - most especially if the solicitor is 'connected' in Irish society, as so many of them are.

The Really Bad and Depressing Stuff: The reports of serial frauds and deceptions by solicitors-turned-developers in recent years will not be news to anyone, nor the recent exposure that a Judge, whilst still a practicing solicitor, engaged in very serious fraud. Likewise the news that another solicitor - a prominent social figure connected to the political establishment - is now being charged with solicitation to murder three people! But what may come as a bit of a surprise to many, are the apparently-casual levels of fraud, deception and perjury engaged in by Irish solicitors on a routine basis. Most disturbing perhaps is when this happens in the Courts, whereby rogue solicitors have no apparent fear of being held to account. I-I members report that even when they can demonstrate that forged documents are being produced by dishonest solicitors, that Courts can and will simply ignore the issue. Members who have tried to bring these incidents to the attention of the Courts receive no responses to their written submissions, and cases simply 'carry on' regardless. Lodging criminal complaints with Gardaí also seems to be a pointless and fruitless exercise - especially if the solicitor in question is 'well connected'. But of course, the wronged citizen can always lodge a complaint with the Law Society of Ireland, which has a special *Complaints and Client Relations Department* set up for the specific purpose of dealing with complaints against solicitors - right? If only that were the case.

What the complainant is not told of course, is that in all but a very small handful of cases, the Complaints Department at the Law Society (which is staffed by a panel of well-connected solicitors and barristers) will first-and-foremost 'look after their own'. Some of the lawyers serving on the Complaints Department Panel for instance, are themselves the subjects of serious complaints - but no-one seems to notice the incongruity of such a situation. The current Head of the Complaints Department was recently caught lying in a High Court affidavit, and other senior Law Society officials have been accused of 'skullduggery' in an article by Village Magazine.

The fact of the matter is that the Law Society of Ireland operates in effect, as a union for solicitors (as long as those solicitors don't get too critical), and although the Society trots out the usual reassurances and codes of ethics to the public, the experience of several I-I members so far is that the Complaints Department of the Law Society is there to protect its members from being held accountable, rather than protect wronged citizens from legal malfeasance.

Likewise, the so-called 'Independent Adjudicator of the Law Society' is supposedly there to ensure the various Departments at the Law Society do *not* engage in improper conduct or procedures. Unfortunately, the individual who held that very well-paid post for several years now, has demonstrated on more than one occasion that she is neither truly 'independent' nor is she apparently willing to tackle any of the serious wrongdoing at the Law Society that has been reported to her. How for example can the Independent Adjudicator explain her statement that she *"is satisfied that all procedures were carried out properly"* when even the Complaints Department at the Law Society admitted in writing that they had closed a very serious complaint case against a Dublin solicitor - <u>without</u> notifying the complainant - and <u>without</u> producing even one iota of evidence that any investigation had ever been done? Likewise, how does the Independent Adjudicator account for the glowing personal-and-professional reference given to her by the current Head of the Complaints Department?

Independent? Trustworthy? Transparent? No, not at all!

* * *

'Unlawful Society' - Abridged from Village Magazine, April 2015

"Villager returns to the case of Kenmare-based solicitor, Colm Murphy, who was struck off from the Roll of Solicitors in 2009 on foot on foot of complaints from another solicitor, Fergus Appelbe. Murphy took a case against the Law Society which failed to investigate Appelbe until very recently when he was finally restricted as to how he can practise. Appelbe is a former member of the Law Society Conveyancing Committee and was the subject of two 'Today Tonight' investigations in 1997/8 into his conduct. He and his various companies are now also in overwhelming debt – to a sum in excess of €100m much of which will have to be borne by the state.

Allegations of "repeated skulduggery on the part of officials of the Law Society" were aired in the Supreme Court last year as part of Murphy's claim of breach of duty, negligence, defamation and misfeasance of public office against them. Murphy claimed that his striking off was based on spurious and inaccurate information provided by the Law Society to its Disciplinary Tribunal and the High Court ten years ago. Key to the decision to strike him from the roll had been a claim by a law society official, Linda Kirwan, that Murphy had breached an undertaking he had given to the President of the High Court. Kirwan insisted at various hearings against Murphy that she had been in the High Court on the day the undertaking was made. It was only after the unfortunate Murphy was struck off that she admitted that she was not in fact in the court when the supposed undertaking was made. No such undertaking is recorded in the order from the court issued on the day in question.

The three judges of the Supreme Court decided in March that the Law Society had misled Judge Hanna in the High Court. They were critical of Ken Murphy, the Society's Director General and suggested that Colm Murphy could resume practicing as a solicitor and that there would be a full hearing in respect of his compensation claim. The judges awarded costs for the Supreme Court hearing and all costs of the High Court to Murphy (Colm not Ken)."

* * *

Which leaves the obvious question: has anyone in authority considered launching a Garda investigation or issuing criminal charges 'in the public interest' as against Linda Kirwan or Ken Murphy for attempting to interfere with the administration of justice? No? Why ever not?

Making a Citizen's Arrest

(From Wikipedia - amended)

A citizen's arrest is an arrest made by a person who is not acting as a sworn law-enforcement official. In common law jurisdictions (such as Ireland), the practice dates back to medieval England and the English common law, in which sheriffs encouraged ordinary citizens to help apprehend law breakers.

Despite the practice's name, in most countries, the arresting person is usually designated as a person with arrest powers, who need not be a citizen of the country in which they are acting. For example, in the British jurisdiction of England and Wales, the power comes from section 24A(2) of the Police and Criminal Evidence Act 1984, called "any person arrest". This legislation states "any person" has these powers, and does not state that they need to be a British citizen.

(Caution) - The Legal and Political Aspect

A person who makes a citizen's arrest could risk exposing him or herself to possible lawsuits or criminal charges – such as charges of false imprisonment, unlawful restraint, kidnapping, or wrongful arrest – if the wrong person is apprehended or a suspect's civil rights are violated. This is especially true when police forces are attempting to determine who an aggressor is.

The level of responsibility that a person performing a citizen's arrest may bear depends on the jurisdiction. For instance, in France and Germany, a person stopping a criminal from committing a crime, including crimes against belongings, is not criminally responsible as long as the means employed are in proportion to the threat. Note, however, that in both countries, this results from a different legal norm, "aid to others in immediate danger," which is concerned with prevention, not prosecution, of crimes.

Ireland

Any person can arrest someone who they have reasonable cause is in the act of committing or has committed an "arrestable" offence, that is one punishable by more than 5 years in prison. *[Please see the list of indictable offences in Part 1 of this Guide].* The arrest can only be effected if the arrestor has reasonable cause that the person will attempt to avoid apprehension by Gardaí and the arrestor delivers the person to Garda custody as soon as is practicable.

"In Ireland powers of arrest are to be found both at common law and in a large number of diverse statutory provisions. These powers for the most part are exercisable only by a member of the Garda Síochána. However, as the Deputy avers, there are situations where **any person** may effect what is known as a "citizen's arrest". The basis for these important powers is set out below.

At common law **all persons**, including a member of the Garda Síochána, may arrest without warrant any person who has committed or is committing a breach of the peace in his or her presence or any person whom he or she reasonably believes is going to commit a breach of the peace in the immediate future.

Turning to the key statutory provisions in this area, the Criminal Law Act 1997 confers two distinct powers of arrest **on any person** including a member of the Garda Síochána regarding arrestable offences. "Arrestable offences" in general terms refer to offences which are punishable by imprisonment for five years or more and include an offence of attempting to commit such an offence.

Under section 4(1) of the 1997 Act **any person** "may arrest without warrant anyone who is or whom he or she, with reasonable cause, suspects to be in the act of committing an arrestable offence." Section 4(2) provides that where an arrestable offence has been committed, any person "may arrest without warrant anyone who is or whom he or she, with reasonable cause, suspects to be guilty of the offence."

Where either of these powers is exercised by a person other than a member of the Garda Síochána, two further qualifications apply: (i) the power may only be exercised if the arrestor "with reasonable cause, suspects that the person to be arrested by him or her would otherwise attempt to avoid, or is avoiding, arrest by a member of the Garda Síochána", and (ii) once an arrest has been effected by the ordinary citizen he or she must transfer the person arrested into the custody of the Garda Síochána as soon as possible. This was already the position with respect to the citizen's common law power of arrest.

Finally, under section 19 of the Criminal Law (Jurisdiction) Act 1976 **any person** may arrest a person whom he or she reasonably suspects of being in the act of committing, or having committed, any offence scheduled in that Act, these are offences of the kind associated with terrorism, if committed in Northern Ireland.

"The scope of these powers has been examined by the courts and I would refer the Deputy to Professor Dermot Walsh's text Criminal Procedure published by Thomson Round Hall 2002 for a more detailed treatment of the law relating to the citizen's powers of arrest." (Minister for Justice, Equality and Law Reform (Mr. Michael McDowell)

*   *   *

This citizen's arrest legislation is proving to be an extremely valuable tool in the face of criminal activity by authority figures, coupled with the corresponding reluctance or refusal of An Garda Síochána (or any other Statutory Authorities for that matter) to prosecute the perpetrators - or indeed, to take *any* responsibility whatsoever for crimes against the public.

Members of *Integrity Ireland* have already initiated *verbal* citizen's arrests as against members of An Garda Síochána, against County Registrars and a number of Judges, and it is a tactic that is clearly unsettling 'the powers-that-be'. However, you will note that we have, to date, only initiated *verbal* arrests and that no-one has yet been physically detained by us. This is not for any lack of courage or enthusiasm on the part of those making the arrests, but is in recognition of the fact that if we move to physically place hands on any given agent of the State, that we open ourselves to possible allegations of assault and thuggery - and this may 'justify' (in the eyes of the authorities) a violent response. As one of our members recently said on video; *"No - we won't resort to physical violence. We'll leave that up to them!"*

So what's the point of making purely *verbal* arrests you might ask? If you're *not* going to detain that authority figure, then what's the point of declaring them 'under arrest' in the first place?

Well, there are several good reasons for only initiating *verbal* citizen's arrests at this point in time - not least of which is the avoidance of any unseemly physical altercations with those being arrested - or with those who might mistakenly believe it is their duty to prevent those arrests.

Now bearing in mind that we are speaking specifically in context of the type of crimes which are being committed against the public by lawyers, Garda Management, Registrars, Judges and senior civil servants, and bearing in mind that we simply don't have the facilities at present to incarcerate these rogues pending due prosecution; then the public is left with only three choices:

- To take the abuse without complaint (not really an option for a moral person).

- To report the matter to the authorities (which we now know is a complete waste of time).

- To assume the Constitutional authority to prevent further wrongdoing and prosecute those responsible (using the same laws that they are abusing, via I-I tactics and support).

Naturally, we are advocating the third choice, which requires that we place errant authority figures technically 'under arrest' and then invite An Garda Síochána to accept jurisdiction for those arrests - something the Gardaí seem curiously reluctant to do. The fact that Garda Management have so far failed or refused to accept that jurisdiction puts all of these rogue authorities - and the compromised practices which they routinely indulge in - in a very odd predicament indeed. For not only is there the public embarrassment and private discomfiture that accompanies any direct exposure of their wrongdoing, but there is also the prospect of matters escalating to the European Courts and being reported in the international media.

In fact, these particular circumstances; whereby errant authority figures are obliged *under the law* to confront each other's wrongdoing might arguably be described as a Constitutional 'Catch 22' quagmire (for them at least) whereby, whichever way they turn, they simply dig themselves deeper and deeper into a legislative mess. That is, until *someone* somewhere along the line simply does their jobs right.

If we think about it for a moment, what we are doing in making citizen's arrests and requesting the Gardaí to accept jurisdiction is exposing the hypocrisy and duplicity of a so-called justice system whose rules do *not* apply to these particular people - just because they are part of the establishment. It is perverse, ironic and preposterous that the very people WE are paying to uphold the law and the Constitution are the ones most guilty of breaking it. It is equally absurd that we have been putting up with this for so long.

So, as long as the original citizen's arrest is valid, then the only *legitimate* way out of this mess is for the Statutory Authorities (whom you are asking to accept jurisdiction for the arrest) to simply do their jobs right; to abide by the law and accept jurisdiction for the arrest. Naturally, it then follows that they have to do an investigation and answer to you (the original arresting 'officer') as to whether or not they are going to prosecute... with all of the ramifications, uncomfortable developments and paperwork that goes along with those irksome decisions.

On the other hand, if the Gardaí (for example) refuse to accept jurisdiction for that citizen's arrest (which they have been doing so far), then technically *they too* are breaking the law and may themselves be committing an offence against the administration of justice - which is an indictable offence - and thereby subject to a citizen's arrest... etcetera.. etcetera.

In short, and in the absence or unwillingness of the various Statutory Authorities to apply the law in a fair, just and impartial way, WE (the public) will use the very legislation that was designed to oppress and exploit us to confront rogue authority figures with their own wrongdoing. In this manner, the combined use of I-I 'direct action' tactics including;

- The lodging of formal criminal complaints with An Garda Síochána;

- The issuing of private summonses under the Common Informer legislation;

- The lodging of civil claims for damages due to illicit actions;

- and the carefully-considered deployment of the citizen's powers of arrest..

..will result in a number of positive developments whereby you can then confidently assert:

- That some errant authority figure 'has been arrested!' (either by you or 'the authorities')

- Than An Garda Síochána are conducting an investigation into a *criminal* allegation.

- That said person has been summoned to a *criminal* Court and/or is facing a private damages claim in the civil Courts.

- That the rogue authority figure in question should therefore step aside from their official duties pending the investigation, and/or that you refuse to have further dealings with said authority figure until such time as the investigation by Gardaí / DPP is concluded etc.

You can see what a predicament is caused when the public seizes the initiative and decides to hold wayward authority figures to account - not only for the wrongs that are being actively committed against them (malfeasance) - but also for the additional acts of misfeasance and nonfeasance that compound the original wrongs.

- **Malfeasance:** wrongful conduct by a public official.

- **Misfeasance:** doing a proper act in a wrongful or injurious manner.

- **Nonfeasance:** A failure to act when under an obligation to do so; a refusal (without sufficient excuse) to do that which it is your legal duty to do.

On top of all this is the fact that active members of *Integrity Ireland* share their information and experiences on the HAFTA Database, thus allowing other I-I Members to use that information to object to dealing with compromised authority figures, primarily on the basis that these people have demonstrated that they cannot be trusted to carry out their duties in a lawful or Constitutional manner. A secondary objection could be the simple assertion that you believe these people to be biased or prejudiced against you because of your I-I membership, and because of our collective stance against corruption in the Irish justice system. This in turn will require that a different or more senior Garda Officer be assigned, or an alternative Judge be found to hear your case. This type of moral attrition is all part of 'the bigger picture' of making it increasingly difficult for corrupt elements in the establishment to continue to abuse their positions, and helps bring rogue authorities to account—in some direct and personal way—for their repeated misdeeds.

Eventually of course, we are going to run out of Statutory Authorities to arrest - and to refer those arrests to - and, having 'exhausted all avenues of recourse' in our own State, we will then be obliged to approach the European Court of Human Rights and other international tribunals, for some effective and longstanding solution to this particular 'Irish problem'. A problem, which, as long as we remain determined and consistent in our approach, cannot fail to garnish the attention of the mainstream media as well.

In the meantime though, it is crucial that we each take responsibility for our own situations and do not shy away from confronting wrongdoers in the system. So don't back off. Think of all the times that ordinary people have been shamed, fined, prosecuted and imprisoned because of relatively minor breaches of the law; then think of all those who have been framed, set-up or wrongly accused by errant authorities; then think of all the damage being done to our people and our Country by all this venal corruption, cronyism and abuse of power and position… and have the courage of your convictions, because as Edmund Burke said: *"Evil succeeds because 'good people' do nothing!"*

So, each and every time you are deliberately wronged by an authority figure or member of the legal profession - take the appropriate, direct action. Once 'they' realise that we will not take it anymore, who knows, maybe we might see a few changes in the way business gets done!

Power of Attorney

(From the Citizen's Information website)

Information

Power of attorney is a legal device in Ireland that can be set up by a person (the donor) during his/her life when he/she is in good mental health. It allows another specially appointed person (the attorney) to take actions on the donor's behalf if he/she is absent, abroad or incapacitated through illness. The relevant legislation is the Powers of Attorney Act 1996 and the Enduring Powers of Attorney Regulations 1996 (SI No. 196/1996) as amended by SI No. 287/1996.

If someone in Ireland is mentally incapacitated (for example, because of illness, disability or a progressive degenerative illness), all of their assets and property are normally frozen and cannot be used by anyone else unless they are jointly owned or, someone has power of attorney to deal with their property or money.

In a larger sense, power of attorney is just one of the legal arrangements that you can make during your lifetime, in the event you become incapacitated or unable to deal with your affairs. Information to help guide you in recording and registering your preferences in the event of emergency, serious illness or death is available at Thinkahead.ie, where you can also download the Think Ahead Form (pdf). Read more about the legal arrangements in the event of incapacity here.

Types of power of attorney

There are two types of power of attorney allowed under Irish law:

- Power of attorney which gives either a specific or a general power and ceases as soon as the donor becomes incapacitated

- Enduring power of attorney which takes effect on the incapacity of the donor

Both cease on the death of the donor. However, it may be difficult to prove that the donor is dead if his/her body cannot be found, for example, as in the case of a death by drowning. Once the body is found or the donor is declared to be "believed dead" by a court (usually after 7 years have passed), the power of attorney (if there was one) ends and their affairs are dealt with in the normal way by will or under intestacy law.

Power of attorney

A power of attorney can be specific (limited to a particular purpose, for example, sale of your house in your absence) or general (entitling the attorney to do almost everything that you yourself could do). For example, it may allow the attorney to take a wide range of actions on the donor's behalf in relation to property, business, and financial affairs. He/she may make payments from the specified accounts, make appropriate provision for any specified person's needs, and make appropriate gifts to the donor's relations or friends.

You do not require a solicitor to create a general power of attorney. It can be created when signed either by you or at your direction and in the presence of a witness. However, it is advisable to get legal advice before you sign a form appointing someone else to manage your affairs. You can appoint anyone you wish to be your attorney.

A form of general power of attorney is given in the Third Schedule of the Powers of Attorney Act 1996.

Enduring power of attorney

An enduring power of attorney (EPA) also allows the attorney to make "personal care decisions" on the donor's behalf once he/she is no longer fully mentally capable of taking decisions themself.

Personal care decisions may include deciding where and with whom the donor will live, who he/she should see or not see and what training or rehabilitation he/she should get. However, if the donor wants, he/she can specifically exclude any of these powers when setting up the power of attorney or can make the attorney's powers subject to any reasonable conditions and restrictions.

You can appoint anyone you wish to be your attorney, including a spouse, civil partner, family member, friend, colleague, etc. The procedure for creating an enduring power of attorney is much more complex than that for creating a general power of attorney.

Creating an enduring power of attorney
Because the enduring power of attorney involves the transfer of considerable powers from you to another person, there are a number of legal safeguards to protect you from abuses. The procedure for executing the enduring power of attorney is complex and requires the involvement of a solicitor and a doctor. The enduring power can only come into effect when certain procedures have been gone through and the courts have a general supervisory role in the implementation of the power.

The document creating the power must be in a particular format and must include the following:

- A statement by a doctor verifying that in his/her opinion you had the mental capacity at the time that the document was executed to understand the effect of creating the power

- A statement from you that you understood the effect of creating the power

- A statement from a solicitor that he/she is satisfied that you understood the effect of creating the power of attorney

- A statement from a solicitor that you were not acting under undue influence

At least 2 people must be notified of the making of an EPA, none of whom will be the attorney. One of the notice parties must be your spouse or civil partner if living with you. If this does not apply, one of your notice parties must be your child. If neither is applicable, one of the notice parties must be any relative (that is parent, sibling, grandchild, widow/widower/surviving civil partner of child, nephew or niece).

Who cannot be appointed?
An enduring power of attorney may be granted to individuals or trust corporations but may not be granted to the following people:

- People under the age of 18

- Bankrupts

- People convicted of offences involving fraud or dishonesty

- People disqualified under the Companies Acts

- An individual or trust corporation who owns a nursing home in which you live or an employee or agent of the owner, unless that person is also your spouse, civil partner, child or sibling

Registration
The EPA can only come into force when it has been registered. However, once an application to register the EPA has been made, the attorney may take action under the EPA's powers to maintain you and prevent loss to your estate. The attorney may also take action to maintain themselves and other persons, in so far as it is permitted under Section 6 (4) of the 1996 Act. The

attorney may also make any personal care decisions permitted under the powers that cannot reasonably be deferred until the application for registration has been determined.

Also, in certain circumstances before the EPA is registered, application may be made to the court to exercise the EPA's powers under Section 12 of the Act.

In order to register an EPA, the future attorney makes an application for registration to the Registrar of Wards of Court, once there is reason to believe that you are or are becoming mentally incapable. The attorney must have a medical certificate confirming that you are incapable of managing your affairs.

Five weeks before making this application, the attorney must notify you and the notice parties of his/her intention to do so. Within the 5 weeks, the donor or a notice party can lodge a notice of objection on one of the grounds given in Section 10 (3) of the Act with the Registrar of Wards of Court.

The Role of the High Court
The High Court has an extensive supervisory role in respect of the EPA. Among other things, the court has power to give directions about the management and disposal of your property. The court may confirm the revocation of a power of attorney if it is satisfied that you were mentally competent to revoke it. The court can order cancellation of the power where it is satisfied that:

- You are mentally capable and likely to remain so

- The attorney is unsuitable

- Fraud or undue pressure was used to induce you to create the power

Scope of authority of an enduring power of attorney
The EPA may give general authority to the attorney to do anything that the attorney might lawfully do or it may merely give authority to do specific acts on your behalf.

The attorney may make certain personal care decisions - these must be made in your best interests, must be in accordance with what you would have been likely to do and the attorney must consult family members and carers in making these decisions. The attorney is considered to be acting in your best interests if he/she reasonably believes that what he/she decides is in your best interests.

A personal care decision is a decision concerning one or more of the following:

- Where and with whom you should live

- Whom you should see and not see

- What training and rehabilitation you should get

- Your diet and dress

- Inspection of your personal papers

- Housing, social welfare and other benefits

The list does not include health care decisions, although the borderline between personal care and health care decisions is not always clear. However, it seems clear that the attorney does not have the power to make a decision as to whether or not a person suffering from dementia should undergo surgery.

154

Revocation of an enduring power of attorney

The donor can revoke an EPA at any time before an application is made to register it. Once the EPA has been registered you cannot revoke it even if you are, for the time being, mentally capable. To revoke it, you would have to apply to the court and the court approve the revocation.

Termination of an enduring power of attorney

An EPA ceases on the death of the donor. However, there are other circumstances in which an EPA ceases to have effect. For example, where a spouse or civil partner is the attorney, the EPA ceases where:

- The marriage/civil partnership no longer exists due to annulment, divorce or dissolution

- A judicial separation is granted or the couple enter into a separation agreement

- A protection, barring or similar order is made on the application of either spouse/civil partner

An EPA ceases where the attorney becomes one of the people listed above who cannot be granted enduring powers of attorney. The court can make an order cancelling an EPA where, for example, it finds the attorney is unsuitable.

* * *

The Power of Attorney legislation can be a very useful tool in circumstances where there is some *genuine* reason why any given individual cannot look after their own affairs. But unfortunately, it is also open to serious fraud and abuse - especially in circumstances whereby a connected litigant for example, has reasons to avoid attending Court and is receiving help 'from the inside' in doing so

In fact, in one notable case recently, an unqualified individual with a lifelong criminal record sent an email to the High Court claiming to be the 'attorney' for his older brother. No documents were registered or presented, and no notice was given to the opposition party. The older brother was the lead Defendant in a civil case that alleged conspiracy between the Gardaí, the Office of the DPP and himself in a series of disgusting and perverse anonymous attacks on a law-abiding citizen. Based on the simple claim that his older brother was 'too sick' to attend an upcoming appeal hearing, this criminal was allowed to 'represent' his brother in no fewer than eighteen hearings in the Circuit Court, the High Court and the Court of Appeal - and somehow managed to achieve this without even presenting any I.D. to the Courts. No notice whatsoever was taken of the Plaintiff's repeated objections and complaints until the President of the High Court was placed on Notice that he was facing an imminent citizen's arrest - and when the I-I Member involved called on the Gardaí to assist in that arrest.

Eventually, the circus was brought to a halt by the determined objections of the I-I Community and several approaches to senior Government Ministers, the Chief Justice and even the President of Ireland himself. But the big question remains; what on earth is going on in our so-called Superior Courts when this sort of blatant abuse of the rules and the legislation is allowed to continue ad infinitum? And where are the sanctions for those Judges, Registrars and Courts Service staff who actively engaged in what can only be described as a deliberate conspiracy to pervert the course of justice?

Well, we already know the answer to that one, don't we? But things are changing in the corridors of power. Maybe when people start using the information, tools and tactics contained in this Guide, maybe then we will see some real justice being applied equally and fairly to all.

Taking Direct Action - A Summary

Remembering that the whole purpose of this Guide and of the development of these 'direct action' tactics is to arm the ordinary citizen against serial abuses of power and position by those in authority; but in also recognising that a great many decent people employed within this wayward system are in effect, coerced into doing things which thy might otherwise morally object to; then we need to present a clear and obvious moral choice to those in authority and power - as well as to their colleagues and subordinates - who would in turn, direct any of their juniors or employees to carry out illicit or improper acts.

For example, let's say you are a solicitor who is contracted to the HSE and you are taking instructions from TUSLA personnel (the Child & family Agency) to prosecute a father in the Family Courts on the basis of an allegation which you *know* to be untrue. Naturally, the moral choice would be to refuse to act on TUSLA's behalf in that particular case, but unfortunately, you not only work in a firm of solicitors whose boss has recently been promoted to the position of Judge - (possibly because he was a close political ally of the serving Taoiseach) - but you are also married to his lovely daughter. You would normally consider yourself a moral person of course, but faced with all this subtle professional, political and personal pressure, not to mention all of the easy money to be made at this poor unfortunate's expense, you decide not to rock the boat this time, and simply get on with your job. After all, the Hearing will be held 'in camera' so no matter what you do you will hardly be held to account, and (you justify to yourself) you are only one of many solicitors and barristers whose services are being immorally deployed against ordinary citizens. In this manner, many so-called legal professionals, civil servants, social workers, Guards and Judges shelve their morality in favour of the easier option; to accommodate 'the establishment' and turn a blind eye to what is really going on. It is this fundamental lack of moral thinking - and the absence of the requisite courage to stand up and refuse to be part of it - which lies at the root of the longstanding, systemic abuse in this State.

What we have to be ready to do, is to confront these individuals with the clear and obvious moral choice whilst at the same time letting them know that any failure on their part to simply 'do the right thing' will result in direct and immediate consequences for them *personally*. It may seem a bit drastic or even overtly provocative to the uninitiated to confront these individuals in such a direct and uncompromising way, but we have to keep reminding ourselves that we have all been playing by *their* rules for years and years now, and it's simply getting us nowhere; other than deeper and deeper into debt, anger, frustration and despair.

We also need to remind ourselves of all the unnecessary pain and suffering which has been caused to otherwise decent families, whose only real crime is that they are poor or uneducated, or, that they are not politically 'connected'. The gratuitous arrogance and hubris of so many agents of the State who prey on the innocent is an appalling advertisement for the supposed "best little country in the world to do business!" It is time for us to remind those who are privileged to serve us, that there is indeed a moral aspect to what they do. Indeed, that our very Constitution is based on a collective public morality which has been recognised by all decent human beings as being the foundation of a fair and just society. In contemptuously ignoring those moral imperatives, these individuals not only heap shame and disgrace on themselves, they bring our whole society into a longstanding, historical disrepute.

It's time for a change in attitudes, in morals and in practice in the corridors of power in Ireland. And where patient dialogue, strident pleas and desperate appeals for justice have been repeatedly and contemptuously ignored, then maybe a little bit of 'direct action' might do the trick? For as John E Lewis said;

"If not us, then who? - If not now, then when?"

General Tips Regarding Direct Action

- Record everything and document everything.

- Never go to legal appointments, Garda interviews or Court appearances alone.

- Know the Constitution - especially the Articles concerning your fundamental rights.

- Advertise the fact that you are a Member (or supporter) of Integrity Ireland and use the Caveat of Affirmation (or similar statement) in all correspondence, emails, affidavits etc.

- If wronged by an authority figure (where appropriate):

  1. Take immediate, direct action. Do NOT delay. Delay plays into their hands.

  2. Make a written complaint to the head of their organisation / firm / agency.

  3. Lodge a criminal complaint statement with Gardaí.

  4. Notify the subject (using the I-I Notification) that a criminal complaint has been lodged.

  5. In the case of legal professionals, notify their professional indemnity insurers that a criminal complaint has been lodged with the authorities.

  6. Notify the Courts Service / the Law Society / the Garda Commissioner / the Minster for Justice of the same.

  7. Invoice the wrongdoer for your time and costs.

  8. If they fail or refuse to pay, lodge a claim in the Small Claims or Civil Courts.

  9. Consider placing a commercial lien on their personal property.

  10. Use the Common Informer legislation and summons them to the District Court.

  11. Report them to the I-I Database, thereby alerting the Membership of the problem.

  12. Make an I-I video of your story (with us) and we will publish it online.

  13. Canvas their neighbourhood with I-I Notification-flyers of their illicit activities.

  14. Picket their homes or businesses.

- Repeat the process with each and every individual who wrongs you or who attempts in any way to try to cover up or suppress what's going on.

*   *   *

Please remember that it is not just individual wrongdoers that we are targeting with these tactics - but the whole corrupt system that facilitates and promotes a culture of failure, apathy, abuse and exploitation. Each and every time a person takes 'direct action' in this manner, it increases the pressure on all concerned - to sit up and take notice of what's really going on.

"One by one, together, we CAN make a difference!"

157

Invoice example for I-I Members – feel free to use and amend as you wish.

To [addressee]

INVOICE

To: [addressee]

Summary: Administration, office costs and expenses, and various per-diem charges as per the caveat in formal correspondence, relating to [name your issue here]-related issues.

Ref	Item description	Rate / costs	Frequency / time	Line total €
1	Office and administration costs	€40.00 per hour	16 hours	€640.00
2	Improper correspondence received	€40.00 per item	5	€200.00
3	Letters sent to solicitor [name]	€40.00 per item	10	€400.00
4	Letters sent to other parties	€40.00 per item	**3**	€120.00
5	Personal costs / food / fuel / parking	various	various	€65.00
6	Personal attendance at Court	€210.00 per person daily	2 days x 2 adults	€840.00
7	Carer / babysitter for Children	€40 daily	2 days	€80.00
8	Carried forward from previous invoices	n/a	n/a	0
9	Interest at 1% monthly	n/a	n/a	0
10	Admin costs for updated invoice	€12.00	1	€12.00
			TOTAL:	€2,357.00

I hereby declare that the above is an accurate account of the work carried out in this matter to date, and of the related costs and expenses.

[Your name or business name]

Signed:...Date:..

Please pay the invoiced amount within 30 days. Cheques or money orders should be made payable to [insert your name or business] at the address noted below. In the event of non payment within 30 days, we reserve the right to lodge additional administration costs at €40 per hour or part thereof, and interest on the outstanding balance at 1% monthly accruing. Invoices that remain unpaid will be reported to the Integrity Ireland HAFTA Database and mayl become the subject of a Small Claims Action in the Courts. Accordingly, please consider yourself advised.

[Your contact details here]

PART

5

THE COURTS

REGISTRARS & JUDGES

The Overriding Objective - Where Is It?

For nearly 200 years, certain Common Law jurisdictions (such as the UK, Canada, Australia, New Zealand, Kenya and the United States for example) have incorporated a concept called 'the overriding objective' as the basis for their various legal systems. This concept was then refined and delivered into the UK's civil procedure rules in the mid 1990's for the purposes of ensuring that the UK's civil justice system delivered justice in a, *"fair, expedient and cost-effective manner"*. The Irish legal system on the other hand is notable amongst Common Law jurisdictions in that there is no such overriding objective or similar set of principles - all the more noteworthy perhaps when one acknowledges that, *"The modern Irish legal system is derived from the English common law tradition"* and that Irish judges regularly quote legal precedents set by their British counterparts as a basis for their rulings.

In 1996 the UK Master of the Rolls Lord Woolf published his *Access to Justice Report* in which he suggested there were *"... a number of principles the civil justice system should meet to ensure access to justice. The system should..*

(a) be just in the results it delivers;

(b) be fair in the way it treats litigants;

(c) offer appropriate procedures at a reasonable cost;

(d) deal with cases with reasonable speed;

(e) be understandable to those who use it;

(f) be responsive to the needs of those who use it;

(g) provide as much certainty as the nature of particular cases allows; and

(h) be effective: adequately resourced and organised."

Lord Woolf then went on to implement the aforesaid "Overriding Objective" which emphasised the need for Court rules to be written, *"in language that is intelligible not just to lawyers but to litigants in person also."* In short, that lay litigants would not only be able to understand what was going on in the process, but that they could be reasonably assured that they would receive an expedient and cost-effective service from the Courts, and that any decisions or rulings made by the judge would be fair and just - and perhaps more importantly - would be *seen* to be so. If such principles existed at the heart of the Irish legal system, there would be no need for a lay litigant's Guide of this nature, which simply sets out to address - in a very modest way - the extraordinary disconnect between the average citizen and the Irish legal system, and the extraordinary levels of misfeasance and malfeasance being foisted on the Irish public by certain establishment figures and their equally-venal counterparts in the so-called 'legal profession'.

Hundreds of case reports sent in to the *Integrity Ireland* database records the fact that the Irish legal system is overwhelmingly perceived by lay litigants as being convoluted, unpredictable, very costly and not at all 'user friendly' - especially given its vulnerability to abuse by compromised legal professionals and being subject as it is to the vagaries of an often-capricious judiciary. The ever-expanding *Integrity Ireland* database of serious complaints reinforces ordinary citizens' concerns about the systemic abuse, greed, collusion and exploitation which, in direct contrast with the 'overriding objective' seems to be the basis upon which most 'business' is being done in our Courts - and unfortunately, as can be seen on the *Integrity Ireland* website, the problems for ordinary citizens doesn't stop there.

It needs to be emphasised that our main critique—and the main motivation in compiling this modest Guide—is not just that the Irish justice system is obscure, convoluted and difficult to comprehend; because the same could also be said of many other jurisdictions where the police, the lawyers and the judges more-or-less abide by the rules in fair, reasonably well-functioning legal systems. No, the main problem we are facing here in Ireland is that 'the rules' (apparently) simply don't apply to a whole section of Irish society, namely, the connected elites and those who wield statutory power and authority. This makes an utter nonsense of the concept of 'justice for all' and the supposed 'equality' of every citizen, which is the very foundation of our hard-won Constitution. Arguably, nowhere is this unjust dynamic more evident than in the Irish Courts - especially when lay litigants attempt to advance their own cases. It is as if the legal profession (including the judiciary) are determined to demonstrate to those who have the audacity to try to bypass their longstanding monopoly on so-called 'legal services' that doing so will prove a *very* costly and infuriating experience. The smug direction from the bench to simply 'seek legal advice' is no longer appropriate for most people due to the outrageous costs being sought, and due to the perception that the legal profession - in general - simply cannot be trusted.

Even a cursory look at the day-to-day functioning of our Courts uncovers some glaring inconsistencies between the universally-accepted concept of 'natural justice' and the manner in which justice is applied here in Ireland. Ordinary citizens who find themselves dealing with the Gardaí, with lawyers or with the Irish Courts for example often find themselves completely and utterly at a loss as to understand what exactly is going on; why they are in such a predicament; and who they can actually trust. Overt secrecy and obfuscation belies any pretence at openness, and it is an established fact that lawyers regularly collude with each other to 'pluck' their trusting clients clean. To make matters worse, all of the 'recommended' or statutory avenues of complaint for consumers; to the Law Society; to the Bar Council or to the various Ombudsmen, are populated with insiders and colleagues of those being complained about. This includes the appeals process in the Courts whereby if one is unhappy with the decision of any given judge you must lodge an appeal to a higher Court where not only the professional performance of the complained-about judge is being questioned, but arguably, where the integrity of the whole Irish Courts system comes under scrutiny. Obviously, there is a natural tendency - even on the part of the most objective of advocates - to defend and protect one's own chosen profession.

So, despite bland Government reassurances to the contrary, it appears there are no *truly* 'independent oversight bodies' in the Irish legal system - including in the Irish Courts. This results in a scenario whereby in effect, these institutions, agencies and even individuals end up policing and investigating themselves—or, adjudicating on the performance of their own friends and colleagues—with all of the dismally-anticipated outcomes that one can expect from such a compromised process. In short, the whole Irish 'oversight' system is designed to ensure that wrongdoers in the corridors of power are insulated as effectively as possible from accountability for their actions, whilst at the same time the general public are systematically misled, deceived and tricked into believing that the opposite is the case; that we have a properly-functioning justice system which applies equally to *all* citizens. But the plain fact of the matter is that a great many of those employed in the Irish justice system are deliberately and repeatedly breaking the law; ignoring the Constitution; and perverting the course of justice on a daily basis - thereby visiting serious injustices on ordinary citizens - and are doing so with arrogant impunity. They can do this because, quite frankly, we have allowed them to get away with it for far too long.

This is why we are focusing on the *rogue* elements in the Gardaí, the legal profession and the Courts, in the hope that this will aid in the empowerment of ordinary citizens to stand up for themselves, and to encourage those good and decent souls who already exist within the system to do likewise. This *Integrity Ireland SOS Guide* is our first, modest attempt to document a process of accountability which will help restore some Constitutional authority back to the Irish people - the very people whom the law and the Constitution were designed to protect and serve.

LIST OF EXPERIENCES OF I-I MEMBERS IN IRISH COURTS
(As reported to the I-I HAFTA Database)

- Confusion and bewilderment at the various rules, processes and procedures which are each different for the District Court, the Circuit Court and the Superior Courts.
- Repeated failure or refusal of Courts Service staff, barristers, solicitors, Registrars and Judges to properly follow those rules.
- Litigants not understanding the language used in Court.
- Altered deeds and fraudulent affidavits being submitted to the Courts.
- Barristers and solicitors lying openly without sanction.
- Fraudulent documents being accepted as legitimate by Registrars and Judges.
- Public Hearings being held in private.
- Personal conflicts of interest by solicitors, barristers and Judges.
- Cases being put back to last on the list - in order to dissuade supporters and keep proceedings out of the public view.
- Court dates being changed without notifying all of the parties - (usually the lay-litigant).
- Papers being withheld / files and transcripts being altered / amended / changed.
- No effort at expediency. Lengthy delays and multiple adjournments on flimsy or non-existent grounds.
- Judges assuming or denying jurisdiction with no consistency.
- Lay-litigant's ignorance of the law being used against them.
- Members of the public being denied access to public Courtrooms.
- Intimidation by members of An Garda Síochána - some wearing firearms.
- Assaults by Gardaí and ushers & lay-litigants being filmed as if they were criminals.
- Rude, irascible and belligerent adjudicators / speaking over litigants / bullying behaviour.
- Courts Service staff refusing to give their names when asked.
- Collusion between State agencies to obstruct justice.
- Incorrect case numbers being issued / litigants being directed to the wrong Courthouse.
- Gardaí and other 'Officers of the Court' refusing to identify themselves.
- Judges & Registrars exceeding their statutory and fiscal jurisdictions.
- Inaccurate or misleading Court Orders that do NOT reflect what was said in Court.
- Failure to compensate successful lay litigants in any proper way.
- Failure to sanction instances of blatant fraud, perjury, forgery and deception.
- Judgements being prepared *in advance of* the Hearing to determine matters.
- Judges abandoning the Court when challenged on a Constitutional matter.
- Judges overstepping their jurisdiction / contradicting themselves and each other.
- Digital Audio Recording system switched off / malfunctioning / selectively edited.
- Abuse of the 'Contempt of Court' rule.
- Costly at every step of the process.

The Irish Court System
(From the Law Library website)

The Irish Courts System exists in what is called a 'common law' jurisdiction. It shares this with other English speaking countries, such as the UK, USA, Canada, Australia and New Zealand; and some non-English speaking countries, such as India.

The system originates from the English legal system. Common-law legal systems place greater emphasis on previous court decisions than do 'civil-law' jurisdictions, such as those in France and other European countries. Those legal systems originate from Roman Law and, more recently, the legal framework put in place by Napoleon Bonaparte.

This means that lawyers working in common-law jurisdictions like Ireland need to work more closely with case-law (previous cases that have come before the courts) than do lawyers operating in civil-law countries. Irish courts are bound by their previous decisions and this is known as the principle of stare-decisis.

The Irish legal system is broadly divided into two branches: the civil side and the criminal side, each with its own specialised courts.

Civil courts hear cases involving disputes between individuals, organisations or the State. These disputes may concern anything from an injury caused in a car accident to a contested corporate take-over.

In civil cases the plaintiff (someone who takes a civil action in a court of law) sues the defendant (someone against whom an action or claim is brought) for compensation for the wrong caused. The compensation for damages caused is usually money. The different courts can hear cases for compensation of certain amounts. These are:

- in the District Court claims up to €15,000

- in the Circuit Court claims between €15,000 and €75,000

- in the High Court claims above €75,000

The Criminal Courts deal with prosecutions brought by the State against people accused of anti-social behaviour – from petty theft to murder.

The Court of Appeal Act 2014 provides for the establishment of a general Court of Appeal which sits between the High and Supreme Courts. It is the default court for all appeals from decisions of the High Court and its decision is final (save in certain limited circumstances).

The Supreme Court, as a court of last resort, should only hear cases of public significance or cases where an important aspect of the law or the Constitution is in issue.

Ireland is a member of the European Union. Disputes involving European law raised in the Irish courts may be referred to the European Court of First Instance and, or, the European Court of Justice.

Generally, the same judges deal with all classes of cases, sitting from time to time for civil or criminal cases, as needed.

The Supreme Court, the Court of Appeal and the High Court are referred to as 'The Superior Courts'. Separate rules apply to the Superior Courts, the Circuit Court and the District Court. They can be found at the website for the Irish Courts Service http://www.courts.ie

Structure of the Irish Courts

Please note that the Court of Appeal now occupies the position as indicated on the diagram below. A full explanation of the role and function of the Court of Appeal is explained below.

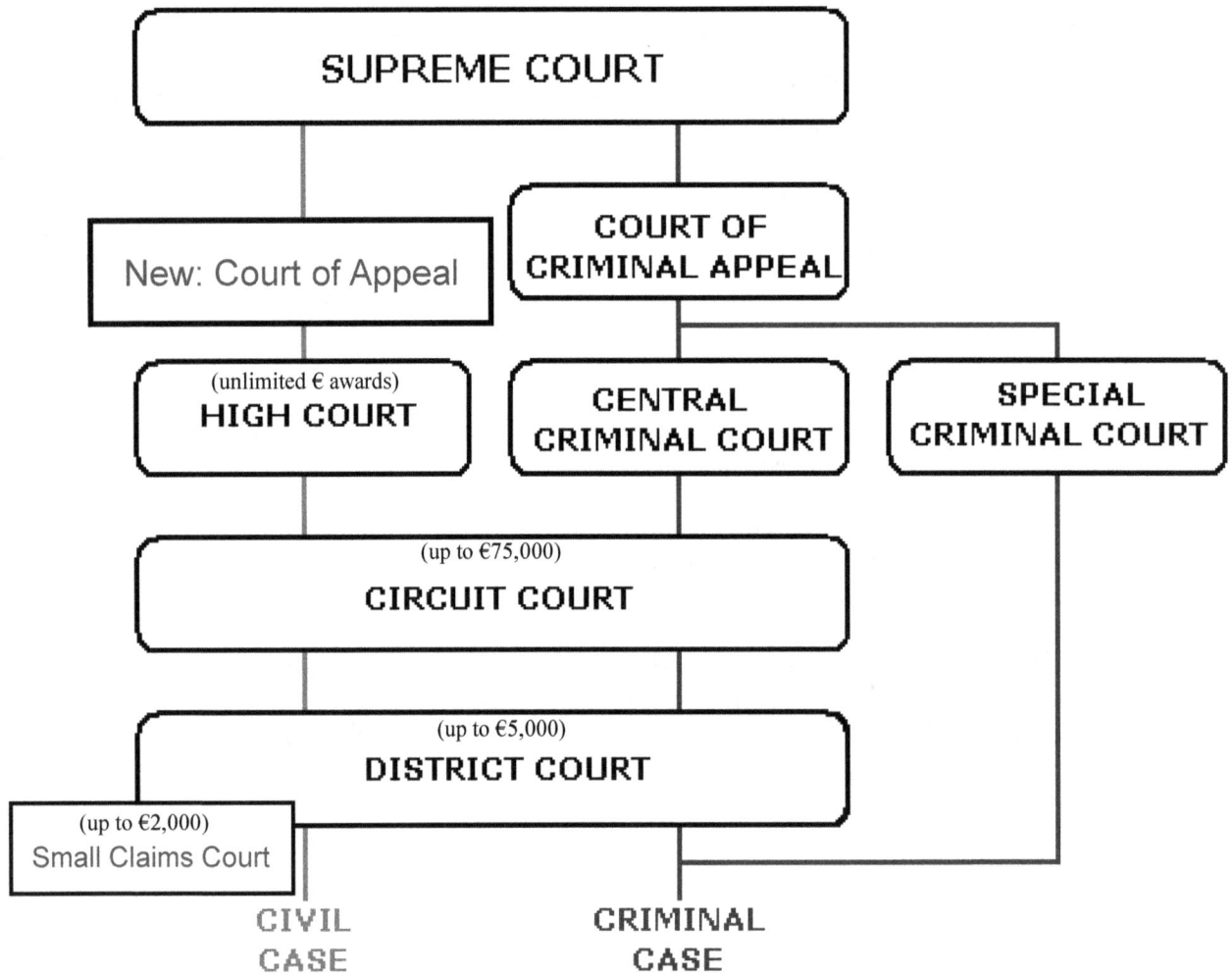

```
                    ┌─────────────────────────────────────────┐
                    │            SUPREME COURT                  │
                    └─────────────────────────────────────────┘
                          │                    │
            ┌──────────────────────┐   ┌──────────────────────┐
            │ New: Court of Appeal │   │     COURT OF         │
            │                      │   │  CRIMINAL APPEAL     │
            └──────────────────────┘   └──────────────────────┘
                    │                    │                    │
        ┌──────────────────┐  ┌──────────────────┐  ┌──────────────────┐
        │ (unlimited € awards)│ │     CENTRAL      │  │     SPECIAL      │
        │   HIGH COURT     │  │  CRIMINAL COURT  │  │  CRIMINAL COURT  │
        └──────────────────┘  └──────────────────┘  └──────────────────┘
                    │                    │
        ┌───────────────────────────────────────────┐
        │           (up to €75,000)                  │
        │             CIRCUIT COURT                  │
        └───────────────────────────────────────────┘
                    │                    │
        ┌───────────────────────────────────────────┐
        │           (up to €5,000)                   │
        │            DISTRICT COURT                  │
        └───────────────────────────────────────────┘
        ┌──────────────────┐ │                    │
        │  (up to €2,000)  │ │                    │
        │ Small Claims Court│ │                    │
        └──────────────────┘ │                    │
                        CIVIL              CRIMINAL
                         CASE                CASE
```

Important Note: The monetary jurisdiction amounts displayed above have a particular bearing on recent house repossession cases - many of which have been surreptitiously pushed through the Circuit Courts by the Banks via County Registrars/Sherriffs despite being over the €75,000 limit. (See p.180 for more on County Registrars).

The (new) Court of Appeal

The Court of Appeal, established on 28th October 2014, occupies an appellate jurisdictional tier between the High Court and the Supreme Court.

Composition of the court
The Court of Appeal is composed of a President and nine ordinary judges. The Chief Justice and the President of the High Court are ex officio judges of the Court of Appeal.

The Court may sit in divisions of three judges. Some interlocutory and procedural applications may be heard by the President alone or by another judge nominated by the President.

Jurisdiction of the court
As with the other Superior Courts, some of the jurisdiction of the Court of Appeal is conferred by the Constitution and some by legislation.

Appeals in civil proceedings

The Court has jurisdiction to hear appeals in civil proceedings from the High Court which prior to the Thirty-third Amendment of the Constitution would have been heard by the Supreme Court. Exceptions are those cases in which the Supreme Court has permitted an appeal to it on being satisfied that the appeal meets the threshold set out in Article 34.5.4° of the Constitution (a 'Leap Frog' appeal).

The Court can hear appeals from cases heard in the High Court about whether or not a law is constitutional. The Constitution provides that no laws may be passed restricting the Court of Appeal's jurisdiction to do this.

Appeals in criminal proceedings

Under the Court of Appeal Act 2014, the Court of Appeal was given the appellate jurisdiction previously exercised by the Court of Criminal Appeal.

Appeals by persons convicted on indictment in the Circuit Court, Central Criminal Court and Special Criminal Court now lie to the Court of Appeal. Appeals against the severity of a sentence imposed by those courts also lie to the Court of Appeal. The Director of Public Prosecutions may appeal a sentence to the Court of Appeal on grounds of alleged undue leniency under section 2 of the Criminal Justice Act 1993. In the case of an alleged miscarriage of justice, an appeal by the convicted person can be lodged under section 2 of the Criminal Procedure Act 1993.

The Court of Appeal was also given jurisdiction to hear appeals by the Director of Public Prosecutions on a question of law arising out of criminal trials which resulted in an acquittal.

Courts-Martial appeals

Under the Court of Appeal Act 2014, the Court of Appeal was given the appellate jurisdiction previously exercised by the Courts-Martial Appeal Court. This means that appeals from people who have been convicted by a court-martial now lie to the Court of Appeal.

The appeal is determined on a record of the proceedings at the courts-martial with power to hear new or additional evidence or to refer any matter for report to the president or the judge advocate of the courts-martial. If the appeal is against the finding and the sentence, the court may affirm or reverse the finding in whole or in part, or order a new trial or vary the sentence. If the appeal is limited to either finding or sentence, the court is confined to dealing with the matter which is the subject of the appeal. The court also has power to review a finding or sentence (which was the subject of a previous appeal) where new evidence shows that there has been a miscarriage of justice.

The decision of the Court of Appeal is final unless the Supreme Court permits an appeal under Article 34.5.3 of the Constitution.

Cases stated

Questions of law which could previously be referred by the Circuit Court to the Supreme Court for determination (a 'case stated') are now determinable by the Court of Appeal.

Appeals transferred from Supreme Court to Court of Appeal

Following the establishment of the Court of Appeal specified appeals pending in the Supreme Court which had been initiated before the establishment day and had not been fully or partly heard by that court were directed by the Chief Justice to be heard and determined by the Court of Appeal.

MODERN IRISH COURTS SYSTEM

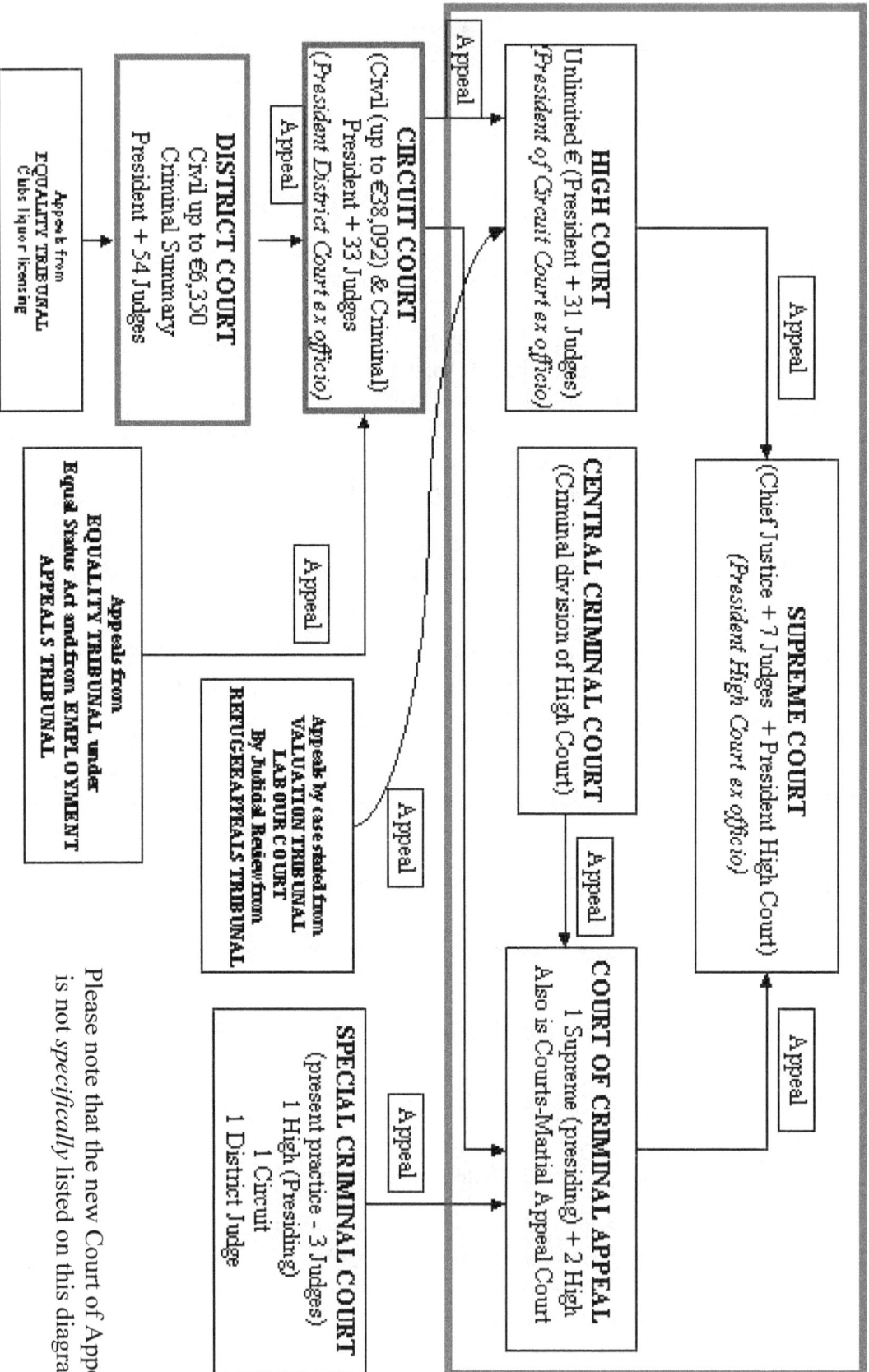

HIGH COURT
Unlimited € (President + 31 Judges)
President of Circuit Court ex officio

Appeal

CIRCUIT COURT
(Civil (up to €38,092) & Criminal)
President + 33 Judges
(President District Court ex officio)

Appeal

DISTRICT COURT
Civil up to €6,350
Criminal Summary
President + 54 Judges

Appeal

Appeals from
EQUALITY TRIBUNAL
Clubs liquor licensing

SUPREME COURT
(Chief Justice + 7 Judges
(President High Court ex officio)

Appeal

Appeal

CENTRAL CRIMINAL COURT
(Criminal division of High Court)

Appeal

COURT OF CRIMINAL APPEAL
1 Supreme (presiding) + 2 High
Also is Courts-Martial Appeal Court

Appeal

SPECIAL CRIMINAL COURT
(present practice - 3 Judges)
1 High (Presiding)
1 Circuit
1 District Judge

Appeals by case stated from
VALUATION TRIBUNAL
LABOUR COURT
By Judicial Review from
REFUGEE APPEALS TRIBUNAL

Appeals from
EQUALITY TRIBUNAL under
Equal Status Act and from **EMPLOYMENT**
APPEALS TRIBUNAL

Please note that the new Court of Appeal
is not *specifically* listed on this diagram.

166

Acting As A Lay-Litigant

The main purpose of this Guide is to arm the average citizen with the basic knowledge required to deal with improper or illegal behaviour by members of the legal profession; by An Garda Síochána; and in the Irish Courts. Some of the materials in this Guide will also be helpful in dealing with various other incidences of improper conduct by persons in positions of power, authority or influence. But as we pointed out in the introduction, this Guide is not (per se) a legal manual nor an instruction booklet to explain step-by-step how to advance one's case through the Courts. That would be an impossible task, not only because every case is different, but because the set-up in the Irish Courts is incredibly convoluted and confusing with all manner of different rules and regulations applying to each of the various Courts, and to the different types of cases being heard. Some have argued that this overt complicatedness is deliberately so, in order to maintain a cloud of mystique about all things 'legal'; to maintain the prevailing status quo; to draw out litigation and justify the exorbitant charges and fees; and to ensure that 'Paddy' doesn't wake up to the reality that it he is being taken for one prolonged, proverbial ride.

Adding to the difficulty is the fact that the responsibilities of the parties involved in any given case differ depending on whether they are a legal professional, a plaintiff, a defendant, an appellant, a respondent, a witness, a lay litigant etc etc. It really is a specialised environment and it requires a solid understanding of all of the various processes, rules and regulations if one is not to fall afoul of some obscure procedure or other, and be deemed 'out of time'; having 'not properly served' some document or other; or of 'failing to make the appropriate submissions'. And of course, any of these apparent errors or omissions on your part could very well mean the untimely end of your case - especially if the adjudicator is having a bad day - or, if there is some other undeclared reason why 'they' might want your case to simply go away!

Unfortunately, the sad fact remains that a great many people are trying to manage their own cases through the Courts only to find that they are indeed falling afoul of the various rules and regulations - (or at least that's what they are being *told* is the problem) - and, having already lost their faith and trust in the legal profession (as well as their life savings, their property and even their sanity in some cases).. these lay litigants face a steep uphill task if they hope to secure justice while managing their own cases in this alien legal environment.

Regrettably, there is no 'magic wand' solution to this problem other than to take the time to read the respective Rules & Regulations on the Courts Service website, and do your utmost to comply with those directions. You should also seek out other *Integrity Ireland* members in your area who will no doubt be able to offer some advice or assistance in this area as well.

However, in general terms, one of the main rules of the Courts is that they must 'afford a reasonable amount of latitude to lay litigants'. So, the moment that you feel that you are not being treated fairly, equitably and impartially - including not understanding fully what is going on in Court - then you have grounds to formally object; because you are ARE entitled to a fair hearing or trial under Article 6 of the European Convention of Human Rights (p.178).

Evan Bell, the Master of the Northern Ireland Queen's Bench had this to say on the matter.

JUDGES, FAIRNESS AND LITIGANTS IN PERSON

"Trying cases in which a party represents himself "can be amongst the more difficult judicial tasks". Judges who preside at trials where one party is self-represented are often faced with continuous challenges, the most vexing of which is how to ensure a fair hearing in the circumstances. The court must be sensitive to the problems facing personal litigants, some of whom may be lacking in confidence, unassertive, inarticulate and daunted at the prospect of appearing for the first time in an unfamiliar setting, and others of whom are obsessive litigants, determined to leave no procedural stone unturned."

Mr Bell explains that the common characteristics of self-represented (lay) litigants include:

(i) Lack of Knowledge. (ii) Lack of Objectivity. (iii) Difficulty with Appreciating Relevance

And he suggests that the principles that should be applied by the Court, in response, include:

(i) Fairness. (ii) A Degree of Latitude. (iii) Limited Interference (by the judge).

The full text of the article can be found on the I-I website, but Mr Bell goes on to explain that it is vitally important that the lay litigant has a clear understanding of what he or she intends to prove to the Court; that all the statements and allegations in sworn statements are backed up with actual evidence (not just hearsay); and that any examination or cross-examination of witnesses is done in a clear, concise and systematic manner. Mr Bell then concludes..

CONCLUSION

Self-represented litigants now form a prominent feature of the judicial landscape. This has caused a dramatic change in the role of the trial judge and represents a great challenge to the administration of justice. The common law has long recognised the right of litigants in civil and criminal proceedings to appear for themselves. Yet access to the courts is one thing; effective access is another. However hard the courts try to accommodate personal litigants it is unrealistic to suggest that such litigants are not often at a considerable disadvantage. So too is the court. The adversarial system depends, not only for the justice of the ultimate outcome, but also for the efficiency with which the proceedings are conducted, upon the assumption that the competing cases are being put by professionals who have the skills necessary to marshal evidence and argument, to identify the issues to be determined, to present the facts capably, and to understand and argue the law. For a system based upon that assumption, self-represented litigants are a serious problem. The common law adversarial system of litigation is a modernised version of trial by battle, the outcome of which turned on the quality of champion which each party could afford to retain.

There is more than a very serious risk that a self-represented litigant will fight the "wrong" fight against the wrong opponent on the wrong basis, will fail to call the right evidence, and will be unable by cross-examination or otherwise to meet the case made against him. The judge in the adversarial system has a very limited scope to play a part in adjusting the balance in representation of the parties. As under the rules governing trial by battle, his function is to ensure that the rules of battle are complied with by all parties and to decide the winner and loser in accordance with the rules. He cannot equalise the balance by charging into battle himself or by intervening, calling witnesses or giving directions or making the case for the disadvantaged litigant. He must take no action which might reasonably be seen as compromising his neutrality, however much he may be tempted to do so.

Although the duties of the judge in relation to self-represented litigants are discussed in numerous cases, there is no common approach as to the manner and form in which assistance is provided which can be applied in practice to all circumstances. This is unsurprising bearing in mind the myriad of circumstances in which litigants may appear in person. However, the authorities do provide general guidance as to principles which should be applied. Some jurisdictions have gone as far as to lay down formal guidelines for judges as to how cases involving personal (lay) litigants should be handled. Other jurisdictions have not been as prescriptive. For all jurisdictions, however, how to balance the competing imperatives of helping a litigant who is in need of assistance while maintaining impartiality is a recurring dilemma. Appropriate judicial assistance will usually involve fine questions of judgment. Ultimately, reasonable minds may differ as to the assistance which a personal litigant should be given and the proper scope of the court's responsibility to a litigant is necessarily an expression of a careful exercise of judicial discretion and cannot be fully described by a specific formula. *(See pp 175-179 for more on this topic)*

THE COURTS SERVICE

As with all institutions of the Irish State which are covered in these I-I reviews, the Courts Service unfortunately suffers from the same routine sense of complacency that comes with a 'jobs for life' culture. It is not the best environment for sincere persons to aspire to high levels of public service - especially when staff see their superiors (most especially certain Registrars, Judges and Office Managers) indulging in some appalling abuses of authority and power. It is remarkable therefore to be able to commend many of those who do work in these compromised environments for their cheerful and helpful attitudes - albeit officially advised by their superiors to inform lay litigants (in particular) that they are *'not qualified to give legal advice'*. Regrettably, in far too many cases reported to us, this statement seems to be getting interpreted by certain disobliging Courts Service Staff as a 'free pass' to be as unhelpful and unaccommodating as they can possibly be - and in certain notable cases - even downright obstructive. This includes repeated breaches of the Courts Service's own *Customer Service Charter* which clearly and unequivocally states:

- *"Our correspondence will identify the writer's name and/or position, the address of the court office, a direct telephone number and an e-mail address."*

- And.. *"We will promptly provide clear and correct information."*

- And.. *"In cases where we cannot release information, we will explain why."*

- And.. *"We will conduct our business to the highest standards of ethical and professional behaviour in an atmosphere of mutual respect and courtesy"* etc etc..

So, we have to ask; why is it that despite these sincere written undertakings to the public that Court Service Staff consistently refuse to identify themselves in correspondence, and consistently fail or refuse to answer legitimate questions asked of them? Indeed, in considering the explicit E U Directives regarding citizen's fundamental rights - especially in context of the justice system - (and now written into Irish law) it is very hard to account for the recent point-blank refusal of the Senior Registrar of the High Court to simply direct his staff to identify themselves either by their initials or an assigned staff number!? In face of multiple complaints of personal rudeness, stonewalling, errors, omissions, and deliberate and sustained obstructionism, the Senior Registrar's declaration that he *'doesn't see any need'* for the public to know who they are dealing with, is a very telling statement from someone who either doesn't understand the parallel concepts of 'professionalism' and 'public service' - or, who is being deliberately evasive, obstructive and obtuse. Alternatively, it could simply be that a person of his obvious importance and standing shouldn't have to condescend to deal with the lowly public - a public who are simply asking him to do his job properly in a professional and obliging manner.

It is an obvious conclusion to come to, that when 'officials' in any Semi-State Department act with such hubris and arrogance - and who refuse to be accountable to the very people who are paying their wages - that something is seriously amiss. The fact of the matter is that one small but calculated act of obstructionism on the part of a Courts Staff member can have a massively detrimental effect on a lay litigant's case - adding months and years of unnecessary frustration, costs and anxiety to their lives. Unfortunately (as usual) if you chose to lodge a complaint to the *Quality Standards Controls Officer* at the Courts Service (and no, not even the Courts Service Reception were aware the position existed when we first approached them) ..then you invariably find yourself facing the same old routine whereby another so-called *'statutory oversight body'* does exactly the *opposite* of what they are mandated to do, and simply ensures that the incoming complaint - however serious it may be - is 'dealt with' via the usual denials, lame excuses and suppression of the facts; for the purposes of ensuring that no-one is held properly to account, thereby ensuring the minimum of embarrassment to the organisation - an organisation by the way which is in fact a private registered *commercial* company. 'Public Service'? Really?

IRISH JUDGES (& Registrars)

The Good Stuff: When an Irish Judge takes office, he swears to uphold the following '*Ten Canons of Justice*' as outlined in *Article 14 of the Judicial Code of Conduct*:, declaring; *"It is to these truths and ideals that I shall hold my office and no other:"*

1. That I (a judge) shall seek to perform the duties and responsibilities of office to the best of my abilities;

2. That I (a judge) pledge my allegiance to the constitution of United Ireland and shall do all within my power to protect its sovereignty and integrity;

3. That I (a judge) pledge my honor and duty to upholding the essential rights of every human being and the values of just society;

4. That I (a judge) shall always uphold the integrity and independence of the judiciary;

5. That I (a judge) shall executive the duties of my office without fear or favour;

6. That I (a judge) shall never allow my personal life, relationships or beliefs to be associated with, or influence in my judgment in any matter before me;

7. That I (a judge) shall seek to render judgment with care, precision and without delay;

8. That I (a judge) shall refrain from extra-judicial activities excepting those that seek to enhance the status of law and administration of justice;

9. That I (a judge) shall refrain from public and political comment whilst in office;

10. That I (a judge) shall avoid impropriety and the appearance of impropriety;

Inasmuch as any of our Judges genuinely and sincerely endeavour to abide by these canons, then they should undoubtedly be respected and admired, and rewarded through the full and wholesome appreciation of Irish society for their crucial contribution in maintaining a functioning democracy.

The Not-So-Good Stuff: The *Irish Independent* newspaper recently reported that five out of six newly-appointed Judges were found to have *"close political links to the current government"* at the time they were appointed. Likewise, a study of judicial appointments since 1995 found that *at least* a third of the 168 newly-appointed judges had *"personal or political connections to political parties before being appointed to the bench"*. The added fact that at a time when the country is in a financial crisis, Irish Judges are the second-highest paid in Europe; enjoy some of the most generous privileges and benefits; and share the highest number of personal assistants, makes a judicial appointment a much-sought-after career move - for those who qualify. Unfortunately, the process of 'qualifying' individuals for appointment to the bench also raises uncomfortable questions which the government repeatedly refuses to answer. An independent TD recently stated; *"Judges do not have to be interviewed or answer specific questions and it is an advantage to have political affiliations"*. The same TD asked how judges are vetted before they get the job? He said it seemed the refusal of the Government to answer the question meant, *"the old political jobbery"* was in place. Notwithstanding the requirement that newly-appointed Judges affirm their adherence to *The Judicial Code of Conduct*, it is difficult to reconcile the notion of genuine judicial independence (or judicial competence) against the backdrop of such thinly-disguised political cronyism - especially when so many apparently-unconstitutional decisions are being made in our Courts which directly or indirectly favour the often-illegitimate interests of the connected elite.

The Really Bad and Depressing Stuff: Amongst the current members of Integrity Ireland who have taken legal action in one form or another, *not one of them* would recommend the process here in Ireland. Each reports serious inconsistencies between the activities and decisions of individual Judges at various levels, so much so that the prospect of coming before any given Judge is described at best (even by some members' legal teams) as 'a lottery'. Court rules are selectively 'dismissed' by one Judge for example - and then selectively 'enforced' by another, thus causing bewildered litigants additional costs and delays. Irrefutable evidence that implicates 'connected persons' is regularly blocked, ignored or dismissed, and no direct action is taken against blatant perjury, forgery and contempt of Court. Many such bewildering, and clearly-unconstitutional decisions are being regularly made in our Courts that can only be accounted for as acts of mind-boggling incompetence (which is very hard to believe) or, as deliberate acts of intentional bias - the private motives for which remain a disquieting area of morbid speculation. Some decisions are so obviously improper and unjust - especially when lay litigants are representing themselves - that one wonders how long this malfeasance has been going on - and at what cost to our democracy? This naturally leads the concerned citizen to question the overall integrity of a justice system that allows and encourages - and apparently even rewards - those who indulge in blatant nepotism, bias and other unconstitutional activities, ostensibly whilst 'serving the interests of justice'. Whilst it is an obvious fundamental tenet of any genuine democracy that its justice system is - in the main - beyond reproach, and that its Judges are comprised of the very best and the wisest of its citizens; it is a shameful indictment of the Irish justice system incorporating the police, the legal system, the Courts and the Ministry of Justice that so many Irish citizens express resignation and dismay at the prospect of going to Court, and have little faith that they will receive a fair and equitable Hearing. In the UK and other Common Law jurisdictions there is a concept called *"The Overriding Objective"* which ensures that cases are held in a fair, expedient and cost-effective manner. No so in today's Ireland, where the opposite seems to be the norm - where cases are so burdensome, costly and convoluted as to render the concept of 'fairness' totally redundant. The questions remain; how long before Judges are appointed on *moral* merit? And how long will we have to wait for the establishment of a *proper* judicial oversight body?

The Judicial Appointments Advisory Board (JAAB) was set up to counteract a longstanding perception by the public that Judicial appointments were overtly political. Members of the current JAA Board include the Chief Justice, the Presidents of the various Courts and the Attorney General, as well as a handful of nominees by the Minister of Justice. Despite having the resources to advertise, interview and recommend suitable individuals for nomination by the President of Ireland, it was disclosed in the Dail in Feb 2014 that in the ten years of existence of the JAAB to date, that not even ONE single interview has been conducted! Meanwhile it seems, the same old 'jobs for the boys' system continues to work behind the scenes!

The Head of the Association of Judges of Ireland has stated publicly that the creation of the Judicial Appointments Advisory Board (JAAB) in 1996 *"was done to create the semblance of independence as to how judges were appointed"* but *"the JAAB by common consent, doesn't really work."* So, why all the declarations of 'real change' and why all the pretences of some real reforms being made? Who do you think is being fooled here again folks?

Meanwhile, a letter sent 'on behalf of' the Chief Justice informs us that 'regrettably' there is no facility at present via the Chief Justice's Office to complain about judicial misconduct.. or indeed, to complain anywhere about anything worse.. And very interestingly, the Twenty-second Amendment of the Constitution Bill, 2001 [relating to the removal of a judge from office and providing for a body to be established by law to investigate or cause to be investigated conduct constituting misbehaviour by a judge or affected by incapacity of a judge] was *not* passed by the Houses of the Oireachtas.

Independence of the Judiciary

The independence of the judiciary is a cornerstone of democracy. It is a principle that is enshrined in legal systems so that judges are free from any outside influence when deciding on the matters before them. It is an obvious requirement to ensure that judges do *not* for example succumb to political pressure, and/or are *not* vulnerable to manipulation or coercion by vested interests. Now this is all very well and good if one's judges are properly selected to ensure only the *best* of us ascend to those lofty positions of authority; that only truly objective, wise, fair and impartial persons qualify for the job. But what if the very process by which judges are selected and appointed is absolutely compromised? What if prospective judges are chosen from a shallow pool of politically-connected legal professionals - many of whom have already demonstrated a fundamental lack of personal and professional integrity in their previous business lives? What if the establishment *knowingly* selects individuals to become judges based primarily upon their already-demonstrated political bias, and their already-proven deference to the powers-that-be? What if that deference constitutes, in effect, substantial grounds to argue that said persons should be *disqualified* from judicial selection precisely *because* they are embedded in the establishment; an establishment which has demonstrated time after time that one of its lowest priorities is the delivery of true, democratic, independent justice to the people?

The judicial selection process in Ireland is one of the most glaringly obvious examples of cronyism and inappropriate patronage at work, and remains one of the most conspicuous areas of much needed reform. It is no coincidence that we are directed to 'respect' the judiciary (under pain of serious penalty) whilst successive Governments make a nonsense, a sham and a travesty of the judicial selection process. Appointing one's professional friends and political colleagues to the bench is a sure-fire way for politicians in particular to ensure that if they ever fall afoul of the law - or indeed, if any of their colleagues or supporters do - that they can depend on 'the system' - in the form of grateful and compliant judges - to make the appropriate decisions.

In this manner, the authorities (including the judiciary) rely on the various Articles in the Irish Constitution and the law to demand our compliance, obedience and 'respect' while at the same time selectively ignoring all those aspects which require them to be genuinely independent and objective; to be men of 'unblemished integrity'; and to ascend to the bench via a process which is free from 'improper motives.' This leads us to ask some obvious questions: If a judge has been appointed via a process which is clearly compromised and is in violation of the universally-accepted principles of objectivity and independence (as laid out in the various Charters and Constitutions); and if the persons being chosen are likewise lacking in the requisite objectivity, impartiality and independence - then how on earth are we expected to 'respect' them let alone have faith and trust that the life-changing decisions they make, are the *right* ones?

The story of the baker and the bus driver comes to mind again. What fool is going to keep getting on a bus that never goes to the right destination? What idiot keeps returning to the baker who keeps selling him mouldy bread? It matters not how big and shiny the bus is - nor how colourful the advertisements are if the *product* is no good. There is no other scenario where the consumer (we, the public) are required to keep purchasing a product which is so obviously unfit for purpose as to render it a scam, a hoax and a deception. The bus driver might have the proper licence, but if you can't trust him to follow the scheduled route - then what's the point of getting on the bus? Similarly, the baker might be a very nice guy, but if he can't provide you with edible bread, then why would you keep returning to him? The plain fact of the matter is that the process of selecting Irish judges is so infused with insider dealings, cronyism and political patronage as to render the process itself in violation of the UN Charter. Accordingly, while exasperated citizens who disrupt a Court for example might *technically* be in violation of Article 2, the question needs to be asked again; who is ensuring that our judiciary perform in accordance with the other fundamental principles of justice? If not by us - then who will do it?

From the UN Charter, adopted by the Seventh United Nations Congress on the Prevention of Crime and the Treatment of Offenders held at Milan from 26 August to 6 September 1985 and endorsed by General Assembly resolutions 40/32 of 29 Nov 1985 and 40/146 of 13 Dec 1985

"The following basic principles, formulated to assist Member States in their task of securing and promoting the independence of the judiciary should be taken into account and respected by Governments within the framework of their national legislation and practice and be brought to the attention of judges, lawyers, members of the executive and the legislature and the public in general. The principles have been formulated principally with professional judges in mind, but they apply equally, as appropriate, to lay judges, where they exist."

Independence of the judiciary

1. The independence of the judiciary shall be guaranteed by the State and enshrined in the Constitution or the law of the country. **It is the duty of all governmental and other institutions to respect and observe the independence of the judiciary.**

2. **The judiciary shall decide matters before them impartially, on the basis of facts and in accordance with the law,** without any restrictions, improper influences, inducements, pressures, threats or interferences, direct or indirect, from any quarter or for any reason.

3. The judiciary shall have jurisdiction over all issues of a judicial nature and shall have exclusive authority to decide whether an issue submitted for its decision is within its competence **as defined by law.**

4. There shall not be any inappropriate or unwarranted interference with the judicial process, nor shall judicial decisions by the courts be subject to revision. This principle is without prejudice to judicial review or to mitigation or commutation by competent authorities of sentences imposed by the judiciary, **in accordance with the law.**

5. Everyone shall have the right to be tried by ordinary courts or tribunals using established legal procedures. Tribunals that do not use the duly established procedures of the legal process shall not be created to displace the jurisdiction belonging to the ordinary courts or judicial tribunals.

6. **The principle of the independence of the judiciary entitles and requires the judiciary to ensure that judicial proceedings are conducted fairly and that the rights of the parties are respected.**

7. It is the duty of each Member State to provide adequate resources to enable the judiciary to properly perform its functions.

Freedom of expression and association

8. In accordance with the Universal Declaration of Human Rights, members of the judiciary are like other citizens entitled to freedom of expression, belief, association and assembly; provided, however, that in exercising such rights, judges shall always conduct themselves in such a manner as to preserve the dignity of their office and the impartiality and independence of the judiciary.

9. Judges shall be free to form and join associations of judges or other organizations to represent their interests, to promote their professional training and to protect their judicial independence.

Qualifications, selection and training

10. Persons selected for judicial office shall be **individuals of integrity and ability** with appropriate training or qualifications in law. **Any method of judicial selection shall safeguard**

against judicial appointments for improper motives. In the selection of judges, there shall be no discrimination against a person on the grounds of race, colour, sex, religion, political or other opinion, national or social origin, property, birth or status, except that a requirement, that a candidate for judicial office must be a national of the country concerned, shall not be considered discriminatory.

Conditions of service and tenure

11. The term of office of judges, their independence, security, adequate remuneration, conditions of service, pensions and the age of retirement shall be adequately secured by law.

12. Judges, whether appointed or elected, shall have guaranteed tenure until a mandatory retirement age or the expiry of their term of office, where such exists.

13. Promotion of judges, wherever such a system exists, **should be based on objective factors**, in particular ability, **integrity** and experience.

14. The assignment of cases to judges within the court to which they belong is an internal matter of judicial administration.

Professional secrecy and immunity

15. The judiciary shall be bound by professional secrecy with regard to their deliberations and to confidential information acquired in the course of their duties other than in public proceedings, and shall not be compelled to testify on such matters.

16. Without prejudice to any disciplinary procedure or to any right of appeal or to compensation from the State, in accordance with national law, judges should enjoy personal immunity from civil suits for monetary damages for improper acts or omissions in the exercise of their judicial functions.

Discipline, suspension and removal

17. **A charge or complaint made against a judge in his/her judicial and professional capacity shall be processed expeditiously and fairly under an appropriate procedure.** The judge shall have the right to a fair hearing. The examination of the matter at its initial stage shall be kept confidential, unless otherwise requested by the judge.

18. **Judges shall be subject to suspension or removal only for reasons of incapacity or behaviour that renders them unfit to discharge their duties.**

19. All disciplinary, suspension or removal proceedings shall be determined in accordance with established standards of judicial conduct.

20. **Decisions in disciplinary, suspension or removal proceedings should be subject to an independent review.** This principle may not apply to the decisions of the highest court and those of the legislature in impeachment or similar proceedings.

Finally, it is worth noting that at present there is NO way to make a complaint against a judge other than to appeal to a higher Court on points of law - or, to have the offending judge impeached via a process which requires a 2/3 majority vote by the Houses of the Oireachtas. In 2013, after receiving several reports of alleged serious malfeasance by senior judges, the Office of the Chief Justice Susan Denham wrote to us stating, *"We regret at present there is no facility at this Office to process a complaint about a judge"*. Likewise, after delivering a formal petition containing thousands of signatures to the Dáil calling for the impeachment of a local Judge, Minister for Justice Frances Fitzgerald returned the petition to us stating absurdly; *"I have no role to play in this matter"*. When the Minister for Justice denies any responsibility and shows no ministerial interest in pursuing such an important matter - well, what more needs to be said?

CONTEMPT OF COURT

The contempt of Court rule is another means by which the judiciary can quash any dissent or outspoken voices. In cases of *genuine*, serious contempt of a *properly-functioning* Court, it is of course appropriate that the judge has the power to have someone removed and sanctioned. When a judge is reasonable, just and fair, it would be hard to find fault with the necessity for the contempt of Court rule. But when a judge is irascible, unjust and unfair, there is a clear Constitutional obligation on ANY law-abiding citizen to speak up in defence of justice and fundamental human rights. The problem in Ireland is that if you dare to try to assert your rights in any manner which the judge takes exception to, then you might find yourself being frogmarched to the cells. In this manner the contempt of Court rule is being seriously abused by certain members of the judiciary in order to bully and intimidate citizens into compliance, often, whilst said judges act in direct contempt of *their own* Courts, by breaching the law, the Constitution, and their solemnly-sworn Oaths of Office. To put it more plainly, the situation as it stands right now in Ireland is that if any given judge takes a dislike to anything which is said or done in the Court, then he or she can simply bark, "Contempt of Court!" (when what they *really* mean is, "YOU have offended MY sensibilities")..and the alleged offender can be whisked away to jail on a *criminal* charge, having been tried and convicted *summarily*. The only relief for the prisoner is if they 'purge their contempt' with an abject apology to the judge and give an undertaking to 'respect the Court'. In some cases that may not be enough, and some people have found themselves languishing in jail for days and even weeks on the whim of a judge, or, because that person believes they have to stand behind what they said or did - on principle.

'Contempt of Court' is defined as *'an act or omission, which interferes with the due administration of justice'* and can cover a multitude of incidents, from the failure or refusal to comply with a Court Order, to 'contempt in the face of the Court' - which is the one that most frustrated lay litigants would be familiar with. However, in taking the action to sanction someone for alleged 'contempt in face of the Court' the judge has just appointed himself judge, jury and executioner in a case where HE/SHE is the accuser - which is a clear and obvious breach of the overriding 'impartiality' rule. At the end of the day, and given the central role of our Courts in administering justice for the people, to endow our judges with this type of power is to court a Constitutional absurdity. Do we have the right to speak in Court or do we not? Have we the right to freedom of expression? Are we not under oath to state the truth, the whole truth, and nothing but the truth? What then about 'the truth' concerning the misbehaviour of judges and the endemic corruption in our Courts? Are we obliged to comply with unlawful directions or unconstitutional behaviour? And, given that 'contempt' is a *criminal* offence; what about our fundamental right to a fair trial before an impartial judge and a jury of our peers?

Thankfully, a case was brought to the European Court of Human Rights by a Cypriot lawyer who was himself jailed for contempt of Court. The following extracts from the findings of the ECHR furnish us with a legitimate objection to any *abuse* of the contempt of Court rule here in Ireland. However, it needs to be reiterated that the position of *Integrity Ireland* remains as stated in our Terms of Membership that we, *"show (appropriate) courtesy and respect for the authority figures, institutions and agencies we are dealing with.."* because as long as we remain grounded in the Constitution and continue to educate ourselves as to knowing when any given Judge, Registrar or other Court Official is in breach of the same; then there really is no need to get into any heated or contentious exchanges in Court - other than to politely, but firmly, maintain OUR Constitutional position and by refusing, absolutely, to be actively or passively complicit in any illicit or unlawful acts. In other words, if we find ourselves in a situation where the facility of the Court is being misused (for example) to prevent a legitimate prosecution going forwards, or to shield and protect 'connected' wrongdoers from due accountability, then we should feel absolutely secure in (respectfully) advising the judge of the situation, safe in the knowledge that if indeed we are then committed for contempt of Court, that we have the right to a full criminal trial where we can draw on the facts at hand - as well as the collective testimonies of hundreds of I-I Members - as to the often unconstitutional state of dysfunction in our Courts. For ultimately, the central question remains; which is the greater offence: to confront injustice or to ignore it? To act in alleged contempt of an unconstitutional and unworthy Court - or, to passively comply with the same? This could very well be the question that determines the future of the Irish legal system, so please, don't be afraid to ask it!

The findings below are explicitly pertinent to the Irish justice system, not only because we are subject to the rulings of the European Courts, but because the Irish legal system is grounded in Common Law (as is the US system) and on precedents set in the British Courts.

European Court of Human Rights - Case of Kyprianou v. Cyprus

JUDGMENT. STRASBOURG. 27th January 2004

283. In the <u>United Kingdom</u>, on whose legal system Cyprus based its own laws and practice regarding contempt of court, a *Practice Note* was issued by the Lord Chief Justice in May 2001 ([2001] 3 All ER 94), according to which a) if an offence of contempt is admitted and the offender's conduct was directed to the magistrates "it will not be appropriate for the same bench to deal with the matter", and b) in the case of a contested contempt, "the trial should take place at the earliest opportunity and should be before a bench of magistrates other than those justices before whom the alleged contempt took place. If a trial of the issue can take place on the very day of the alleged offence, such arrangements should be made taking into account the offender's rights under Article 6 of the European Convention for the Protection of Human Rights and Fundamental Freedoms".

284. In the <u>United States</u> the Supreme Court has established through its case-law that, for contempt based on intemperate remarks made during trial, a public hearing before another judge is required - *Mayberry v. Pennsylvania* (400 U.S. 455, 91 S. Ct. 499, 27 L. Ed. 2nd 532 [1971]). In *Bloom v. State of Illinois* (391 U.S. 194, 88 S. Ct. 1477) the same court found that contemnors are entitled to a jury trial for instances of serious contempt. The court stated *inter alia* as follows:

> "Even when the contempt is not a direct insult to the court or the judge, it frequently represents a rejection of judicial authority, or an interference with the judicial process or with the duties of officers of the court ... If the right to jury trial is a fundamental matter in other criminal cases, which we think it is, it must also be extended to criminal contempt cases ... We cannot say that the need to further respect for judges and courts is entitled to more consideration than the interest of the individual not to be subjected to serious criminal punishment without the benefit of all the procedural protections worked out carefully over the years and deemed fundamental to our system of justice. Genuine respect, which alone can lend true dignity to our judicial establishment, will be engendered, not by the fear of unlimited authority, but by the firm administration of the law through those institutionalised procedures which have been worked out over the centuries."

294. The Court reiterates that it is of fundamental importance in a democratic society that the courts inspire confidence in the public and, above all, as far as criminal proceedings are concerned, in the accused. To that end it has constantly stressed that a tribunal must be impartial. Whilst impartiality normally denotes the absence of prejudice or bias, its existence or otherwise can, notably under Article 6 § 1 of the Convention, be tested in various ways. It is well established in the case-law of the Court that there are two aspects to the requirement of impartiality. First, the tribunal must be subjectively free of personal prejudice or bias. Personal impartiality is to be presumed unless there is evidence to the contrary. Secondly, the tribunal

must also be impartial from an objective viewpoint, that is, it must offer sufficient guarantees to exclude any legitimate doubts (see *Sander v. the United Kingdom*, no. 34129/96, § 22, ECHR 2000-V, and *Piersack v. Belgium*, judgment of 1 October 1982, Series A no. 53, § 30).

296. The Court considers that the decisive feature of the case is that the judges on the court which convicted the applicant were the same judges before whom the contempt was allegedly committed. This in itself is enough to raise legitimate doubts, which are objectively justified, as to the impartiality of the court - *nemo judex in causa sua*.

297. For the Government to aver that the judges who convicted the applicant cannot be considered complainants in the proceedings and had no personal interest in the relevant offence, but were simply defending the authority and standing of the court, is, in the opinion of the Court, theoretical. The reality is that the courts are not impersonal institutions but function through the judges who compose them. It is the judges who interpret a certain act or type of conduct as contempt of court. Whether this is so has to be assessed on the basis of the particular judges' own personal understanding, feelings, sense of dignity and standards of behaviour. Justice is offended if the judges feel this to be so. Their personal feelings are brought to bear in the process of judging whether there has been a contempt of court. Their own perception and evaluation of the facts and their own judgment are engaged in this process. For that reason, they cannot be considered to be sufficiently detached, in order to satisfy the conditions of impartiality, to determine the issues pertaining to the question of contempt of their own court. The Court adopts in this respect the statement of the Supreme Court of the United States in the case of *Offutt v. USA* (348 U.S. 11. 75 S.Ct.11):

> "But judges also are human, and may, in a human way, quite unwittingly identify offence to self with obstruction to law. Accordingly, this Court has deemed it important that district judges guard against this easy confusion by not sitting themselves in judgment upon misconduct of counsel where the contempt charged is entangled with the judge's personal feeling against the lawyer".

298. In this connection, the Court notes that, in their decision, the judges of the Assize Court acknowledged that their "*persons*" were "*insulted gravely*" by the applicant, even though they went on to say that this was the least of their concerns, and emphasised the importance for them to uphold the authority and integrity of justice.

299. The Court considers that in situations where a court is faced with misbehaviour on the part of any person in the court room, which may amount to the criminal offence of contempt, the correct course dictated by the requirement of impartiality under Article 6 § 1 of the Convention is to refer the question to the competent prosecuting authorities for investigation and, if warranted, prosecution, and to have the matter determined by a different bench from the one before which the problem arose. In fact, with the exception of Cyprus, this is the practice in the High Contracting Parties to the Convention as regards behaviour which amounts to the criminal offence of contempt of court. The situation regarding sanctions of a disciplinary nature, in the form of fines, in connection with behaviour which cannot be considered as amounting to a criminal charge, is different (*Ravnsborg v. Sweden*, judgment of 23 March 1994, Series A no. 283-B).

303. The lack of impartiality is evidenced by the intemperate reaction of the judges to the conduct of the applicant, given their haste to try him summarily for the criminal offence of contempt of court without availing themselves of other alternative, less drastic, measures such as an admonition, reporting the applicant to his professional body, refusing to hear the applicant unless he withdrew his statements, or asking him to leave the court room. In this respect an additional important factor is the severe punishment - immediate imprisonment - which they imposed on the applicant while stating, for example:

i) "It is impossible for us to imagine another occasion of such a manifest and unacceptable contempt of court by any person..."

ii) "If the Court's reaction is not immediate and drastic, we feel that the blow to justice will be disastrous".

304. The Court also finds relevant in this connection its observations and conclusions below regarding the complaints of a breach of the presumption of innocence and insufficient information as to the nature and cause of the accusation against the applicant (paragraphs 52-58 and 65-68).

309. In conclusion, the Court considers that there has been a breach of the principle of impartiality, on the basis of both the objective and subjective tests. Accordingly, there has been a violation of Article 6 § 1 of the Convention.

FOR THESE REASONS, THE COURT UNANIMOUSLY

1. *Holds* that there has been a violation of Article 6 § 1 of the Convention;
2. *Holds* that there has been a violation of Article 6 § 2 of the Convention;
3. *Holds* that there has been a violation of Article 6 § 3 a) of the Convention;

European Convention on Human Rights

ARTICLE 6

Right to a Fair Trial *(remembering that 'contempt of Court' is a criminal offence)*
1. In the determination of his civil rights and obligations or of any criminal charge against him, everyone is entitled to a fair and public hearing within a reasonable time by an independent and impartial tribunal established by law. Judgment shall be pronounced publicly but the press and public may be excluded from all or part of the trial in the interests of morals, public order or national security in a democratic society, where the interests of juveniles or the protection of the private life of the parties so require, or to the extent strictly necessary in the opinion of the court in special circumstances where publicity would prejudice the interests of justice.

2. Everyone charged with a criminal offence shall be presumed innocent until proved guilty according to law.

3. Everyone charged with a criminal offence has the following minimum rights:

(a) to be informed promptly, in a language which he understands and in detail, of the nature and cause of the accusation against him;

(b) to have adequate time and facilities for the preparation of his defence;

(c) to defend himself in person or through legal assistance of his own choosing or, if he has not sufficient means to pay for legal assistance, to be given it free when the interests of justice so require;

(d) to examine or have examined witnesses against him and to obtain the attendance and examination of witnesses on his behalf under the same conditions as witnesses against him;

(e) to have the free assistance of an interpreter if he cannot understand or speak the language used in court.

Going Before the Court - Your Rights & Contempt

In conclusion, and in context of the current situation in the Irish Courts, where members of the public are becoming increasingly concerned and exasperated at the extraordinary abuses of the law and the Constitution; of breaches of Court Rules; of routine fraud, perjury, forgery and deception; of overt intimidation and bias by judges; of physical assaults by Gardaí; - not to mention a whole slew of other human rights violations which are occurring on a daily basis in and around and via the facility of the Irish Courts, well, it is hardly surprising that the public are finally finding their voices and challenging what's going on. Accordingly, we need to be alert as to the possibility and likelihood that judges will try to apply the contempt of Court rule in order to quell dissenting or challenging voices - and thereby intimidate us again into silence and compliance. So, if you have any reason to question the probity of the Court or the integrity of the judge that you may be facing on any given day, here are a few tips to consider:

- Be prepared. Have *at least* two people with you to take notes and to witness any shenanigans that may ensue; and to speak 'amicus curiae' on your behalf if you are silenced (p.183).

- Collect the names (politely) of any officials / lawyers / Gardaí present - especially those who are in any way connected to your case. This puts them on notice that you are well prepared, and you also have their names as possible witnesses should you need them later.

- Read out your Constitutional Affirmation and ask the Gardaí present to affirm their Oaths.

- Once you begin speaking, do NOT let the opposition or the judge interrupt you. Be firm but polite, but insist that you be allowed to finish what you have to say.

- If the opposition and/or the judge speaks incoherently / uses Latin terms / or tries to move the case on too quickly for your note-takers - then get the judge to go at YOUR pace.

- If you are threatened with contempt by the judge, remind him of Article 6 ECHR (see left) and of the 2004 and 2011 judgements of the European Court of Human Rights [App. 73797/01, *Kyprianou* v. *Cyprus*, Judgment of 15/12/2005; & *Loukis Loucaides Advocate*, Application 45/2011, Judgment of 16/5/2011] and quote at liberty from the preceding pages.

The main points to note are:
(i) That a judge *cannot* sit in judgement over his own case of alleged contempt.

(ii) That you have a right to a full criminal trial before an *impartial* judge and jury *before* you are jailed for alleged contempt. A judge cannot just jail you on a whim without due process.

(iii) That if the judge is in any way breaching the law, the Constitution, Court Rules, or his Oath of Office, that it is *the judge*, and not you, who is technically 'in contempt of the Court'.

Please remember, that 'contempt of Court' is defined as *an act or omission, which interferes with the due administration of justice.'* Obviously, this also applies to any act or omission <u>by an authority figure</u> which interferes with the due administration of justice as well - right? Don't forget, that in the event one of our members is *unjustly* put in jail or *wrongfully* put on trial for alleged contempt, that we have scores of eager witnesses willing to take the stand with hundreds of examples of deliberate, premeditated acts and omissions that have been carried out by various authority figures—including judges—for the express purposes of interfering with justice. Before any given judge considers putting any of us in jail for alleged contempt, he or she now has to consider the repercussions of opening that particular Pandora's Box / can of worms in full view of an increasingly disillusioned public. Alternatively, as long as any given judge is doing their job properly according to their solemn Oath of Office, well, then there should be no risk, nor excuse, for anyone entering into contempt of Court - should there?

The Role of County Registrars

A County Registrar is an official attached to the Irish Circuit Court who carries out a number of quasi-judicial and administrative functions regarding the functioning of the court within the county or counties to which he or she is assigned. The County Registrar has responsibility for the administration and management of the circuit court offices in each county. These quasi-judicial functions of a County Registrar in the Circuit Court are similar to those of the Master of the High Court in the High Court. Except in Dublin and Cork, the county registrar is also the sheriff and responsible for the enforcement of court orders and acts as returning officer for all referenda and elections. County Registrars are appointed by the government on the nomination of the Appointments Advisory Board. *(Wikipedia)*

County Registrars are appointed directly by the government. The Department of Justice and Law Reform advertises to fill these positions. County registrars perform a number of quasi-judicial functions which are conferred on them by statute - for example holding motions courts and case progression hearings, conducting arbitrations under the Landlord and Tenant (Ground Rents) Acts and the taxation of costs. They are independent in the exercise of these functions and appeals against their decisions are made directly to the circuit court judge. In addition, the county registrar has responsibility for the administration and management of the circuit court offices in each county. There are 14 District Probate Registries covering all counties other than Dublin. In these counties the county registrar is the district probate registrar. The district probate registry provides a local and accessible service to legal practitioners and the public whereby they can apply for and obtain grants of probate and administration in relation to the estates of deceased persons. Except in Dublin and Cork, the county registrar is also the sheriff and responsible for the enforcement of court orders and acts as returning officer for all referenda and elections. *(From the Courts Service website)*

*   *   *

What is *not* clearly articulated in the above quotes however is the astounding fact that County Registrars can preside over a house repossession hearing (for example) in their role as Registrar, and then make an Order for the Sheriff to repossess a property. Given that the County Registrar (in all locations except for Dublin and Cork) *IS* the Sheriff, then what this actually means is that the Registrar can issue Orders to himself to repossess people's homes - for which he or she receives a commission or 'poundage' from the banks. This is an appalling conflict of interest situation which absolutely flies in the face of all of the principles of fairness and impartiality. To make matters even worse, we hear that the appointment of County Registrars is another piece of thinly-veiled patronage based on a supposed 'nomination' by the Judicial Appointments Advisory Board - the same discredited Board of legal insiders whose 'nominations' can be totally and utterly ignored by the Government, making the whole set-up just another smoke-and-mirrors farce designed to mislead the public into believing that there is something genuinely open, objective and impartial about the appointment of our Registrars and Judges. Apart form a very generous salary and pension, and the commissions from house repossessions, Registrars also earn substantial fees for presiding over elections.

"County registrars, who earn a salary of up to €129,521, received on average €12,000 each for working as returning officers in elections and referendums last year. Figures obtained by The Sunday Times show that 23 returning officers and 31 assistants earned €427,917 from last year's general election, even though it is a statutory duty. At least another €232,000 will be paid to them for working on the presidential election and two referendums held on the same day last October. There are 23 returning officers in the country, and last year they employed 31 temporary assistants. Nineteen of them are county registrars paid a salary of up to €129,521." *(Sunday Times, June 2012)*

Circuit Court Rules - Order 18 - County Registrar

The following Rules are listed here in specific context of the failure or refusal of certain County Registrars to act according to their own specified rules - or in declaring they 'have no jurisdiction' to take an action - when it is clear that they actually do. Some such improper decisions can wreak havoc in a lay litigant's case and can cause endless problems for the parties involved - but as we have seen in recent months, anyone who dares to challenge the County Registrar or who speaks up in *their* Courtroom faces imminent removal from the Court - with the possibility of some physical assaults and intimidation from obliging Gardaí. It is educating ourselves to these abuses of power and position that we begin to bring an end to so many shameful and disgraceful practices that are being used against lay litigants in particular.

* * *

1. The County Registrar, within the County to which he is assigned, shall be the proper officer of the Court in respect of all its jurisdiction, and shall be responsible for the discharge of all duties imposed upon him or upon the Office, by Statute or otherwise, and for the safe custody of all documents and records of the Court. He shall cause to be kept such files and books of record, and in such form, as may from time to time be prescribed by the Minister.

In particular and without prejudice to the generality of the foregoing and without prejudice to any other provisions of these Rules, the County Registrar may, in accordance with Section 34(1) and the Second Schedule of the Courts and Court Officers Act 1995 make the following orders:

(i) Any order which may be made as of course. *[I-I Note: As long as it is under €75,000]*

(ii) Any order for a statement of the names of persons who may be co-partners in any firm suing or being sued in action or matter.

(iii) An order for enlargement of the time for doing any act or taking any step in action or matter.

(iv) An order for discovery, limited or general, or inspection of documents or real or personal property, or delivery of interrogatories.

(v) An order for the appointment or the discharge of a receiver in uncontested applications.

(vi) An order to dismiss an action with costs for want of prosecution or for failure to make an affidavit of discovery or to answer interrogatories.

(vii) An order to strike out a defence with costs for failure to make an affidavit of discovery or to answer interrogatories.

(viii) An order for the taking of evidence on commission.

(ix) An order on an application for directions as to service in case of a civil bill or other originating document not inter partes or as to other procedure in any action or matter.

(x) An order adding or substituting a party in any proceeding.

(xi) An order giving liberty to intervene and appear.

(xii) An order for the amendment of pleadings on consent.

(xiii) An order to receive a consent and make the same a rule of Court where the parties are sui juris.

(xiv) An Order under the Bankers Books Evidence Acts 1879 and 1959.

(xv) An order for payment out of Court of funds standing to the credit of an infant on attaining majority, or (if so authorised by order of a judge) for his or her benefit during minority.

(xvi) An order in uncontested cases to have an account taken or inquiry made.

(xvii) An order for the issue, for service outside the jurisdiction of a citation to see proceedings in contentious probate matters.

(xviii) An order for the issue of a citation to lodge in Court a grant of probate or letters of administration in contentious probate matters.

(xix) An order giving liberty to file a supplemental affidavit of scripts.

(xx) An order for the lodgement of scripts by any party.

(xxi) An order appointing a receiver in place of a receiver who has died or been discharged, including any necessary consequential directions as to the accounts of the deceased or discharged receiver.

(xxii) A stop order on moneys or securities in Court.

(xxiii) An order for the issue of a sub-poena under Order 39 rule 30 of the Rules of the Superior Courts.

(xxiv) An order to vacate a lis pendens on the application of the person who registered the same.

(xxv) An order under Order 33, rule 1 of the Rules of the Superior Courts, on consent, settling the issues to be tried.

(xxvi) An order giving liberty to issue execution in the name of or against the legal personal representative of a deceased party.

(xxvii) An order giving liberty to issue a new Order of Execution on the loss of the original.

(xxviii) An order for transfer of proceedings to the District Court on consent of the parties, including all ancillary orders for the transfer of monies lodged in Court.

(xxix) An order giving liberty to serve a third party notice on consent of the plaintiff.

2. The County Registrar shall take and make all such accounts and inquiries as may be ordered by the Court, and shall certify the result thereof to the Court on completion and for this purpose he shall have all the powers of the Examiner in the High Court, and he shall issue such citations and subpoenas as are necessary to implement the jurisdiction of the Court.

3. If any matter appears to the County Registrar proper for the decision of the Judge, the County Registrar may refer the same to the Judge who may either dispose of the matter or refer the same back to the County Registrar with such directions as he may think fit.

4. The County Registrar shall have power to settle all necessary advertisements, and arrange for the insertion thereof in such publications as he shall think right.

5. The County Registrar may summon to attend before him, and may examine on oath any party to any proceeding, or any witness whose attendance in connection with any of the duties or powers conferred upon him by statute, or otherwise, he may deem necessary.

6. The County Registrar shall have power, when directed by the Judge or empowered by these Rules, to tax all Bills of Costs, including costs as between solicitor and client, and shall certify

the amount properly due thereon. In every case he shall measure the costs by fixing a reasonable sum in respect of the entire Bill or any particular item therein.

7. Any party dissatisfied with any certificate, ruling or decision of the County Registrar, may, within ten days from the date of such certificate, ruling or decision, apply to the Judge by motion on notice to review such certificate, ruling or decision, and the Judge may thereupon make such order as he shall think fit.

8. In the absence of any order of the Court, or of a direction or request by a person entitled to make the same, as to the investment of sums of cash paid into Court, the County Registrar shall apply to the Judge for directions as to the investment thereof.

9. In the absence of the Judge the County Registrar shall have power to declare the Court adjourned for such period, or to such date, as may be necessary.

10. The County Registrar in each County may from time to time carry over to a general ledger account for dormant balances the balances of funds to the credit of any ledger account which have not been dealt with for fifteen years or upwards; and he may carry to the credit of the same general ledger account the interest or dividends from time to time accruing upon the balances of funds which have been so carried over. When an order dealing with funds carried over under this Rule is to be acted upon, the County Registrar shall carry back such funds, and any interest or dividends accrued thereon, to the credit of a ledger account in the same title as the account from which they were so carried over, and shall deal therewith as directed by such order.

11. On or before the 31st day of December in every third year the County Registrar shall prepare a list or statement of the accounts in the Office carried over to the general ledger account under the next preceding Rule. The said list or statement shall be filed and exhibited in the Office, and a copy thereof shall be published in Iris Oifigiúil.

*   *   *

Amicus Curiae - Friend of the Court

In the event that someone sees or hears something amiss in a Courtroom - and provided that person is NOT a party to the case, they can (and arguably should) stand up and address the judge stating 'Amicus Curiae - Friend of the Court'. This is another useful tool for bringing public attention 'on the record' whenever there appears to be a breach of process or protocol - or, more importantly perhaps, when a miscarriage of justice is afoot.

(From the Law Dictionary): Literally, friend of the court. A person with strong interest in or views on the subject matter of an action, but not a party to the action, may petition the court for permission to file a brief, ostensibly on behalf of a party but actually to suggest a rationale consistent with its own views. Such amicus curiae briefs are commonly filed in appeals concerning matters of a broad public interest; e.g., civil rights cases. They may be filed by private persons or the government. In appeals to the U.S. courts of appeals, an amicus brief may be filed only if accompanied by written consent of all parties, or by leave of court granted on motion or at the request of the court, except that consent or leave shall not be required when the brief is presented by the United States or an officer or agency thereof.

An amicus curiae educates the court on points of law that are in doubt, gathers or organizes information, or raises awareness about some aspect of the case that the court might otherwise miss. The person is usually, but not necessarily, an attorney, and is usually not paid for her or his expertise. An amicus curiae must not be a party to the case, nor an attorney in the case, but must have some knowledge or perspective that makes her or his views valuable to the court.

The McKenzie Friend

A McKenzie friend in the Irish Courts is, basically, when a lay litigant in a civil case has a friend or colleague sit beside them as 'moral support'. There doesn't appear to be any formal rules laid down in this regard, but the general understanding is that the McKenzie friend can assist the litigant in preparing the case and drawing up documents, but he or she is not allowed to speak on the litigant's behalf in Court unless invited to do so by the Judge. This is what Wikipedia says on the subject:

"A McKenzie friend assists a litigant in person in a court of law in England and Wales. This person does not need to be legally qualified. The crucial point is that litigants in person are entitled to have assistance, lay or professional, unless there are exceptional circumstances.

Their role was set out most clearly in the eponymous 1970 case McKenzie v McKenzie. Although in many cases a McKenzie friend may be an actual friend, it is often somebody with knowledge of the area, and the trend is heavily in favour of admitting McKenzie Friends. He or she may be liable for any misleading advice given to the litigant in person but is not covered by professional indemnity insurance.

The role is distinct from that of a next friend or of an amicus curiae.

McKenzie v. McKenzie was a divorce case in England. Levine McKenzie, who was petitioning for divorce, had been legally aided but the legal aid had been withdrawn before the case went to court. Unable to fund legal representation, McKenzie had broken off contact from his solicitors, Geoffrey Gordon & Co. However, one day before the hearing, Geoffrey Gordon & Co. sent the case to an Australian barrister in London, Ian Hanger, whose qualifications in law in Australia did not allow him to practise as a barrister in London. Hanger hoped to sit with his client to prompt him, take notes, and suggest questions in cross-examination, thereby providing what quiet assistance he could from the bar table to a man representing himself. The trial judge ordered Hanger not to take any active part in the case (except to advise McKenzie during adjournments) and to sit in the public gallery of the court. Hanger assumed his limited role was futile and did not return for the second day of the trial.

The case went against McKenzie, who then appealed to the Court of Appeal on the basis that he had been denied representation. On 12 June 1970, the Court of Appeal ruled that the judge's intervention had deprived McKenzie of assistance to which he was entitled, and ordered a retrial.

In English courts, where a case is being heard in private, the use of a McKenzie friend has sometimes been contentious. This is a particular problem in family court hearings, where it has been held that the nature of the case is so confidential that no one other than the litigants and their professional legal representatives should be admitted to the court.

A 2005 Court of Appeal case, In the matter of the children of Mr O'Connell, Mr Whelan and Mr Watson, clarified the law in this area. The result of the appeal has legitimised the use of McKenzie friends in the family court and allowed the litigant to disclose confidential court papers to the McKenzie friend.

England and Wales allow fee charging McKenzie Friends, who may charge for their services, including the giving of legal advice. A recent report by the Legal Service Consumer Panel found that fee charging McKenzie Friends were a net benefit. The report stated, "They should be viewed as providing valuable support that improves access to justice in the large majority of cases."

Recording of Proceedings - What's The Law?

One of the most questionable aspects of engaging in Court proceedings in Ireland - and one that raises serious questions about the underlying philosophy of our judicial system - is the prohibition on making private recordings in the Courts. Given that so many other Common Law jurisdictions either have public cameras in their Courts (except for certain special cases) and/or make recordings available to the public on request for a nominal fee, the stance of the Irish Courts on this matter is quite telling. I mean - these are *our* public Courts after all - right?

You see, the Irish Courts are *very* insistent indeed that no-one but themselves can make digital, audio or video recordings of proceedings. So much so in fact, that if you attempt to do so, you may find yourself charged with contempt of Court and hauled off to the cells - as some I-I Members recently discovered. But what most people have not questioned is the fundamental contradiction between having 'open, public hearings' and having rules imposed on people that prevent them from collating accurate records of those hearings in a format that cannot be disputed.

People are allowed to take notes of course, and may refer to the various Court-generated documents if they wish to review an issue. But this is unsatisfactory for a number of practical and cost-related reasons. Firstly, no-one except a trained stenographer could possibly keep up with the pace of exchanges in a Courtroom. Secondly, when the Courts hold all the original records and recordings, then any argument that their records are inaccurate can be summarily dismissed. Thirdly, if you want to challenge the authenticity of those records, then you are faced with a very onerous task involving multiple applications and fees. Adding to the overall suspicion as to why exactly these 'no recording' rules are being imposed on the Irish public in supposedly 'public' hearings, is the fact that the Courts Service charges exorbitant fees for transcripts of their Digital Audio Recordings (DAR). On one occasion for example, a lay litigant who was challenging some very influential people on points of evidence in an apparent attempted murder case ended up paying over €4,000 for a much-altered transcript of proceedings. The first quote he received was for 'only' €250 but by the time he had jumped through all the necessary legal hoops, the costs had increased 16-fold. That was over 16 years ago, and no, the case was never resolved, other than the connected perpetrators walking away with his very lucrative business.

The financial motivation for creating these 'no recording' rules in 2013 is self-evident, if also a touch unsettling. Because as we all well know, when profit becomes the motivating factor, then justice and human rights are the first things to be dumped. The official line for having these 'no recording' rules in Court is that this somehow protects the integrity of the Courts process, and serves to protect the innocent from defamatory or injurious reports being circulated via social media by reckless observers, for example. Well, that's all very plausible - and highly convenient - for a legal system that is so steeped in duplicity and double-dealing that one does have to wonder if there might be some other, less noble motivation for all this secrecy and subterfuge? Given that so many perfected Court Orders do NOT reflect what actually happened in Court; and given the often outrageous and unconstitutional behaviour of certain judges and registrars; and given the multiple instances of fraud, perjury, deception and abuse of process which make up the bread and butter of an utterly compromised legal and judicial system - well, is it really any wonder that they don't want it all broadcast abroad?

On the other hand, there are some very solid reasons why we *should* be allowed to make recordings of proceedings - not least of all because this would help all parties involved to keep subsequent hearings concise and expedient. Imagine for example the removal of all instances of argument about what was, or was not said in a previous hearing - or better still, what the judge did, or did not direct on the day? Of course, this would not be nearly so profitable for a legal system that thrives on confusion, deception and obfuscation, but that brings us back to the original question; are we really going to Court to secure justice - or are we just unwitting participants in a scam and a pretence, designed to part us from our money at all costs - while keeping the proverbial lid on the tin and the proverbial genie in the bottle? To add more meat to the argument, we also have documented incidents of the DAR system failing or being switched off - sometimes for weeks at a time - as well as reports of transcripts being altered, amended or otherwise interfered with at source. Similarly with CD disks containing the DAR recordings that have been reluctantly divulged to persistent lay-litigants where files cannot be opened or accessed by normal computers. All-in-all, not a very reassuring set of reasons for insisting that *only* the Courts Service (or whatever armed Gardaí may be present) may make recordings in Court. Meanwhile, no-one seems to be asking the crucial questions; is this prohibition lawful? Is it even Constitutional? Or is it in fact a breach of our fundamental right to a fair hearing?

Well, the following pages detail an interesting conundrum. Because according to the Law Reform Commission it appears that there is in fact no *law* (per se) that prohibits recording in Court.

> *"No statute regulates in express terms the use of tape recorders (or other sound recorders) in court." (1991)*

However, there are Court Rules that were brought in in April 2013 which declare that the public cannot record in Court. These rules have been given some level of legitimacy with the signature of a judge - albeit one with a notorious 'insider' reputation. But again we return to the basic question of what is the *real* standing of these rules if they are in fact unconstitutional at source?

You see, the Courts Service is a <u>private commercial company</u> (CRO number 194696). But apart from their headquarters in Dublin (which are only part-accessible to the public) they 'do business' out of our *public* Courthouses and that is where all of their revenue is generated. Given that these public Courthouses are funded by the taxpayer, then arguably we should have all the rights available to members of the public who are using public facilities - including the right to meet, speak and record what's happening - right? But somewhere along the road the lines have gotten crossed, and we now have a situation where a private company can dictate the rules in a public facility - and those rules are not necessarily serving the public, nor the legitimate interests of justice. They are however contributing to a nice little earner for a Court Service which makes millions in profits each year.

In 1991, the Law reform Commission authored a 440 page report which covered the issues of recording in Court. This, in part, is what they had to say:

"The Case in Favour of a Wide-Ranging Entitlement to Make Sound Recordings
The general principle that justice should be administered in public is one that has the support of the Constitution. Street CJ, of the New South Wales Supreme Court, put the matter well:

> "It is a deeply rooted principle that justice must not be administered behind closed doors – court proceedings must be exposed in their entirety to the cathartic glare of publicity. There are limited exceptions to the observance of this principle but these are well defined and sparingly allowed. Statutes are made by public processes. They are judicially administered in public proceedings. It is only thus that the right of representation and of due hearing of all legitimate submissions can be seen to have been accorded to parties subjected to the judicial process. Moreover, publicity of proceedings is one of the great bastions against the exercise of arbitrary power as well as a re-assurance that justice is administered fairly and impartially."

If the principle of open justice is to be given full effect it should not be subject to limitations unless they are essential in the interests of justice. It may be suggested that the concerns about the risks of abuse of sound recordings are somewhat fanciful, at all events to the extent that they would imply a general rule of exclusion."

The Commission went on to discus various pro's and cons, but in context of our primary concern that lay litigants in particular should be allowed to record their own proceedings, this was the Commission's conclusion:

"A strong case may be made in favour of the parties and their legal representatives being permitted to make sound recordings. The benefits, in terms of exactitude, speed and cost, seem considerable. The possible disadvantage, to which we have already referred, is the enhanced capacity it confers on legal representatives to coach witnesses. As we have already indicated, the reply to this concern is that it can be mitigated by giving the judge power to prohibit the making of sound recordings by parties or the representatives in cases where, either in the particular circumstances or by reason of the general category of proceedings, the judge considers this desirable.

..We think it plain that *some* controls must exist, and equally plain that a complete embargo on their use is not called for. Within these parameters two competing strategies may be considered. One would have the legislation prescribe in detail the circumstances in which sound recording is permissible and the consequences of breach of these rules."

The various Court Rules governing the prohibition of public recordings can be found under the Courts.ie website under Order 12B District Court Rules, and S.I. No. 100/2013 - Circuit Court Rules (Recording of Proceedings) 2013. In brief, they can be summarised as follows:

"No person, other than the Courts Service or a person authorised by it on its behalf, shall make any record of proceedings otherwise than by written or shorthand notes."

You can however make an application to the Court to receive a transcript of the DAR - provided you jump through all the necessary hoops and pay the appropriate fees (of course) or, you might get a copy for free on the basis of impecunity (being poor). But before you receive any transcripts, the Court is allowed to have a quick look at the contents - just to make sure all is in order.

"The Court may, for the purposes of considering any such application, review privately the contents of the relevant record... (and) ..the Court may, where it considers it necessary in the interests of justice so to do, permit the applicant to have such access to all or such part of the relevant record concerned as is specified in the order made on the application, by such means and at such time or times as may be specified in that order and on such terms and under such conditions (including terms restraining the publication, dissemination or further disclosure of all or any part of the relevant record by the applicant, and the giving of an undertaking to such effect) as the Court may direct. (and) Unless the Court otherwise directs, access to the relevant record concerned shall, where permitted under sub-rule (6), be afforded solely by the provision to the applicant of a transcript of all or any part of that record, on payment by the applicant to the transcript writer of the transcript writer's fee for producing the transcript."

Our position is that we should by rights be allowed to record our own hearings, especially when there is no specific law expressly forbidding it, and it is clearly in the interests of justice and expediency that we can do so. (Remember the absent Overriding Objective?) But, while we are waiting for the judiciary and the Courts Service to get in line with the recommendations of the Law Commission of some 25 years ago, we suggest that you make a verbal request at the start of every Court hearing listing all of the reasons why you should be allowed to record including the acknowledged failures of the DAR system; the documented instances of questionable Court records; and your general lack of confidence in the probity of the Irish justice system. At least then it is 'on the record' that you have formally asked to record - and have been refused. Who knows, you might just get lucky, and some anonymous source might find it in their heart - in the overall interest of justice and transparency of course - to send you a recording free of charge.

Prohibiting Recording in Court: Another Arrow in our Quiver?

An article by Dr Finabr Markey of the National Land League

As many well-versed Lay-litigants know there is no actual statute or Court rule prohibiting the use of a recording device by a Defendant for the purpose of assisting himself/herself in their case. There is however an unspoken rule that it is never allowed. Indeed, I once witnessed a free-lance journalist prostrating himself before a Judge of the High Court to let him know someone might be recording in the court, and the Judge making a gloating speech about his "inherent jurisdiction" to find out who was recording and demand it stop. So why stop Defendants recording proceedings that our Constitution states must be publicly heard and fair (not to mention numerous other international agreements)?

Well one shot probably not far off the mark is that the recording systems in the courts are a great money spinner, and who wants to damage industry eh? There's a recession on. No thought is spared for the lay-litigant homeowner and their inability to access expensive court recordings. Meanwhile, the banks can well afford multiple copies, can afford to have them digitally remastered and released as a Christmas album if they so desire.

Currently it would appear no-one is taking this serious prejudice against the lay-litigant homeowner very seriously and yet it is at the very least another ground for appeal into the future if denied the right to record. Some might even be cheeky enough to seek an indefinite adjournment of their cases until such matters are deliberated in a Higher Court: if of course someone files such a case.

What would it look like? How would one introduce the matter in let's say the Circuit Court and in doing so at the least set on record for the future your request to record proceedings on your own device. Well it might begin by the lay-litigant politely letting the court know (maybe even in a bridging affidavit) that as a litigant representing him/herself and a novice note-taker the defence would be best served by recording proceedings.

I can imagine the Registrar or Judge making utterances to the effect, *"it is not allowed"* - the lay-litigant in reply asking if there is any other way to obtain recordings?

"You can get the DAR (Digital Recording System) recordings" says the Judge in a hurried fashion - such matters being beneath Judges of course.

"Is there a cost to that Judge?" says the Lay-litigant innocently.

"Oh I don't know. What matter! You are not recording in this court!!" says the Judge.

"Is that your last word on the matter Judge - that you are stopping me from recording my own matters in Court in the knowledge that I cannot afford access to the DAR?" Says the Lay-litigant calmly.

"Erm, yes, it is." says the Judge edgily, and after a long suspicious squint down on the Lay-litigant.

"Thank you Judge".

Now refusal may not be the outcome and the Judge—maybe seeing the fix he is getting caught up in, or maybe genuinely listening—might say that you *can* record. It's highly unlikely however, and you have just established grounds for an appeal and/or if you feel up to it a judicial review, either of which may be used by all other Lay-litigants into the future.

Our friends at the National land League can be contacted at www.nationallandleague.org

Rules Regarding the Clearing of a Court & Prohibition of Reports

Criminal Justice Act, 1951: Clearing of court and prohibition of reports of proceedings.

20.—(1) On the preliminary investigation of an indictable offence the Court may, if satisfied that it is expedient for the purpose of ensuring that the accused will not be prejudiced in his trial, do any one or more of the following:—

(a) subject to subsection (4), exclude the public or any particular portion of the public or any particular person or persons except bona fide representatives of the Press from the court during the hearing;

(b) prohibit the publication of information in relation to the proceedings or any particular part of them;

(c) impose restrictions or limitations on publication.

(2) An order of the District Court under paragraph (b) or paragraph (c) of subsection (1) shall cease to be in force—

(a) if the accused is dealt with summarily—at the conclusion of the proceedings in the District Court;

(b) if informations are refused—on the expiration of one month after such refusal unless, within that month, the accused is sent forward for trial by direction of the Attorney-General;

(c) if the accused is sent forward for trial—on the conclusion of the trial or the entry of a nolle prosequi.

(3) In any criminal proceedings for an offence which is, in the opinion of the Court, of an indecent or obscene nature, the Court may, subject to subsection (4), exclude from the Court during the hearing all persons except officers of the Court, persons directly concerned in the proceedings, bona fide representatives of the Press and such other persons as the Court may, in its discretion, permit to remain.

(4) In any criminal proceedings—

(a) where the accused is a person under the age of twenty-one years, or

(b) where the offence is of an indecent or obscene nature and the person with or against whom it is alleged to have been committed is under that age or is a female, a parent or other relative or friend of that person shall be entitled to remain in Court during the whole of the hearing.

(5) A person who contravenes an order or direction of the Court under this section shall, without prejudice to his liability for any other offence of which he may be guilty, be guilty of an offence under this section and shall be liable on summary conviction thereof to a fine not exceeding one hundred pounds or, at the discretion of the Court, to imprisonment for a term not exceeding six months or to both such fine and imprisonment.

(6) The powers conferred by this section are in addition to any other power of the Court to do all or any of the things which this section authorises.

*   *   *

In short, that there are strict conditions under which a judge or registrar can clear a Court, and that, (a) people simply expressing their Constitutional rights to a fair hearing - or (b) objecting to breaches of the law and the Constitution - or (c) lay litigants trying to advance civil cases.. do NOT appear to be among those conditions. We also need to remember that (with a few special exceptions) that Court hearings *must* be heard in public, otherwise they are illegitimate / unconstitutional / bogus & null-and-void - as are any findings, Orders or directions issued at any such unconstitutional hearings. Similarly, removing the public is clearly unconstitutional.

Disclosure, Discovery - and the Gary Doyle Order

In simple terms, the Gary Doyle Order is a means by which any person arrested or charged with a criminal offence can demand to see all of the evidence which the State intends to use in their prosecution. It is an incredibly valuable tool to counteract questionable evidence, unsound procedures or abuses of process by the authorities. We need to remember that the bulk of prosecutions through the Courts are minor traffic offences or other 'crimes' such as not paying your TV licence which generate a great deal of revenue both for the Courts Service (which is listed as a private company in the Companies Registration Office under number 194696) and for the State. The irony is that most of these charges relate to the non-payment of something - usually because these people simply cannot afford it in the first place. With the highest rates of motor tax and insurance in Europe, is it any wonder that people struggle to pay these 'statutory charges'? And what's the response of the Courts? To fine those people even more money! A more cynical observer might even suggest that the principal work of the Gardaí and the Courts is *specifically* to raise funds from an unwitting public - and NOT necessarily to combat *real* crime. If this is the main motivation for designating the non-payment of motor tax for example, and routine traffic offences as 'criminal offences'; thereby allowing Courts to jail people if they fail or refuse to pay the fines imposed; and if some of those alleged 'offences' are being substantiated only on the word of a Garda - who may or may not be one of the good guys out there - then clearly there is an argument for educating the public as to any way that they can properly defend their rights, and thus remove some of the incentive for 'the establishment' to continue to create more and more laws and statutes resulting in hundreds of thousands of traffic fines and other minor offences - which in turn is generating an unhealthy profit for the powers that be - at OUR direct expense. We have a right to know what the evidence is against us - but most ordinary citizens often aren't aware of this, and they surrender meekly to the charges against them - usually out of fear, embarrassment or shame, or because of the legal ignorance of the bewildered accused. Often, these prosecutions succeed on spurious grounds, based as they often are on falsified evidence or contrived Garda statements. But if we each asked for a Gary Doyle (discovery) Order every time we were charged with an offence, and if we challenged each and every abuse of process with resolve, then it wouldn't be too long before the accountants at Pheonix House began to realise that the profit was quickly going out of the process.

So, next time you are charged with an offence - and most especially if those charges are false, erroneous, inaccurate, exaggerated or fabricated, then ask for a Gary Doyle Order. If the resultant disclosure of documents reveals ANY deliberate breaches of the law or the Constitution; then make sure that you take 'the appropriate action' and that you do so with courage and conviction!

* * *

(From the DPP website, in context of discovery, disclosure, and the Gary Doyle Order)
9.1 The constitutional rights to a trial in due course of law and to fair procedures found in Articles 38.1 and 40.3 of the Constitution of Ireland place a duty on the prosecution to disclose to the defence all relevant evidence which is within its possession. That duty was stated by McCarthy J. in The People (Director of Public Prosecutions) v. Tuite (Frewen 175) as follows:

"The Constitutional right to fair procedures demands that the prosecution be conducted fairly; it is the duty of the prosecution, whether adducing such evidence or not, where possible, to make available all relevant evidence, parol or otherwise, in its possession, so that if the prosecution does not adduce such evidence, the defence may, if it wishes, do so".

9.2 In Director of Public Prosecutions v. Special Criminal Court [1999] 1 IR 60, Carney J. (at p.76, in a passage subsequently approved by the Supreme Court at p.81) defined relevant material as evidence which "might help the defence case, help to disparage the prosecution case or give a lead to other evidence".

"the prosecution are under a duty to disclose to the defence any material which may be relevant to the case which could either help the defence or damage the prosecution and that if there is such material which is in their possession they are under a constitutional duty to make that available to the defence"- McKevitt v. Director of Public Prosecutions (Supreme Court, 18 March 2003, Keane C.J.).

9.3 The prosecution is therefore obliged to disclose to the defence all relevant evidence which is within its possession. A person charged with a criminal offence has a right to be furnished, firstly, with details of the prosecution evidence that is to be used at the trial, and secondly, with evidence in the prosecution's possession which the prosecution does not intend to use if that evidence could be relevant or could assist the defence. The extent of the duty to disclose is determined by concepts of constitutional justice, natural justice, fair procedures and due process of law as well as by statutory principles. The limits of this duty are not precisely delineated and depend upon the circumstances of each case. Further, the duty to disclose is an ongoing one and turns upon matters which are in issue at any time.

9.4 Article 5 of the European Convention of Human Rights also guarantees a person charged with a criminal offence the right to a fair hearing and:

"to be informed promptly in a language which he understands and in detail, of the nature and cause of the accusation against him".

The Convention provides guidance concerning the minimum rights of accused persons as they are guaranteed throughout Europe and has been incorporated into Irish domestic law by the European Convention on Human Rights Act 2003.

9.5 The precise scope of the duty to disclose differs as between cases which are triable summarily in the District Court and those triable on indictment and are discussed separately below at paragraph 9.6.

Summary Prosecutions
9.6 The scope of the duty of disclosure in summary prosecutions has been defined by the Supreme Court in Director of Public Prosecutions v. Gary Doyle [1994] 2 IR 286. In the light of that judgment the following principles should be observed by the prosecution:

there is no general duty on the prosecution in a summary case to furnish in advance the statements of intended witnesses whether or not there is a request for them from the defence. However, if there is some reason arising from the particular circumstances of a case why advance disclosure of the details of the case, whether by furnishing statements or otherwise, is necessary in the interest of justice, this should be done whether or not there is a request;

the test to be applied by a court on an application by the defence to be furnished pre-trial with the statements on which the prosecution case will proceed is whether "in the interests of justice on the facts of the particular case" this should be done (Gary Doyle's case, at p.301). The requirements of justice must be considered in relation to the seriousness of the charge and the consequences for the accused. Very minor cases may not require that statements be furnished. Complexity of the case is also a factor. Amongst the matters which the Supreme Court in Gary Doyle identified as possibly relevant to the court's decision were:

(a) the seriousness of the charge;

(b) the importance of the statements or documents;

(c) the fact that the accused has already been adequately informed of the nature and substance of the accusation;

(d) the likelihood that there is no risk of injustice in failing to furnish the statements or documents in issue to the accused.

Gary Doyle's Case

In making a decision whether to furnish statements the prosecutor should have regard to the principles set out in Gary Doyle's case and referred to above; a request for statements made by the defence should be considered in the context of the witnesses whom it is proposed to call at the trial and whether the Gary Doyle principles require disclosure. It is primarily a matter for the defence, when requesting statements in summary cases, to advance the reason or reasons why the accused considers that statements should be furnished. If the defence does not advance any adequate reason for disclosure, and the case does not appear to be one where the Gary Doyle principles require disclosure, then they need not be furnished without an order of the court; statements or information not intended to be tendered at a summary trial should be furnished to the defence where it is necessary in the interest of justice. This should be done with or without a request. This includes statements or information which, even if the prosecutor does not regard them as reliable, might reasonably be regarded as of assistance to the defence; while the Gary Doyle case arose from indictable offences which were being dealt with summarily, the principles set out in that case are applicable to all offences being tried summarily.

PROSECUTIONS ON INDICTMENT

The Book of Evidence

9.7 Where an offence is to be disposed of by trial on indictment the prosecution has a statutory duty pursuant to sections 4B and 4C of the Criminal Procedure Act, 1967 as inserted by section 9 of the Criminal Justice Act, 1999, to furnish the accused with certain materials setting out the evidence intended to be adduced against the accused. The documents provided under section 4B are usually referred to collectively as the book of evidence. This essentially comprises the evidence which the prosecution intends to adduce at the trial. The following documents should be included in the book of evidence:

- a statement of the charges against the accused;

- a copy of any sworn information in writing upon which the proceedings were initiated;

- a list of the witnesses whom it is proposed to call at the trial;

- a statement of the evidence that is expected to be given by each of them;

- a copy of any document containing information which is proposed to be given in evidence by virtue of Part II of the Criminal Evidence Act, 1992;

- where appropriate, a copy of a certificate pursuant to section 6(1) of the Criminal Evidence Act, 1992; and

- a list of exhibits (if any).

9.8 These documents are required to be served on the accused person within 42 days of the accused's first appearance in the District Court. An application to extend this time period may be made which must be grounded on sufficient reasons such as complexity of the case, large number of witnesses, or other such reason which may cause delay. Because of the short time for service of the book of evidence it may be more convenient not to charge an accused until the book of evidence is prepared unless there is some reason why such a course of action would be inappropriate.

Further evidence

9.9 Pursuant to section 4C of the 1967 Act, as inserted by section 9 of the Criminal Justice Act, 1999, if the prosecutor proposes to call further evidence or additional witnesses or evidence has been taken on deposition, the prosecutor should serve the accused and furnish the court with the following applicable documents:

- a list of any further witnesses the prosecutor proposes to call at the trial;

- a statement of the evidence that is expected to be given by each witness whose name appears on the list of further witnesses;

- a statement of any further evidence there is expected to be given by any witness whose name appears on the list already served under section 4B(1)(c);

- any notice of intention to give information contained in a document in evidence under section 7(1)(b) of the Criminal Evidence Act, 1992 together with a copy of the document;

- where appropriate, a copy of a certificate under section 6(1) of the Criminal Evidence Act, 1992;

- a copy of any deposition taken under section 4F;

- a list of any further exhibits.

Obligation by the prosecution to disclose material not intended to be used at the trial

9.10 There may also be other material of an evidentiary nature which the prosecution has decided not to use at trial. Some of this evidence may neither add to nor detract from the case against the accused, in which case it is not relevant and need not be disclosed. Other evidence may undermine some aspect of the prosecution case or in some other way be of assistance to the defence.

9.11 In the ordinary course disclosure of evidence should be made, without a request, if the evidence is relevant. In this regard relevant evidence includes information which may reasonably be regarded as providing a lead to other information that might assist the accused in either attacking the prosecution case or making a positive case of its own. The following information should ordinarily be disclosed if relevant:

- information not in statement form of which the prosecution is aware whether intended to be used by the prosecution or not and whether considered reliable or not;

- in the case of material not in the possession or procurement of the prosecution but of which it is aware the existence of that material should be disclosed;

- information regarding proposed prosecution witnesses which might reasonably be considered relevant to their credibility, such as criminal convictions, an adverse finding in other proceedings, relationship with a victim or another witness or any possible personal interest in the outcome of a case;

- details of any physical or mental condition which may affect reliability;

- details of any immunity from prosecution provided to a witness with respect to his or her involvement in criminal activities. Where a witness is admitted to a witness protection programme the fact of such an admission should be disclosed;

- where the witness participated in the criminal activity the subject of the charges against the defendant, whether the witness has been dealt with in respect of his or her own involvement and, if so, whether the sentence imposed on the witness took into account any cooperation with law enforcement authorities in relation to the current matter;

- statements not included in the book of evidence which could be of assistance to the defence;

- the unedited version of statements prepared for inclusion in the book of evidence;

- items not included in the list of exhibits in the book of evidence which could reasonably be of assistance to the defence;

- sworn information and warrants where relevant;

- particulars of the accused's prior convictions;

- any prior inconsistent statements of witnesses whom the prosecution intend to call to give evidence;

- copies of all electronically or mechanically recorded statements obtained from the accused;

- copies of any photographs, plans, documents or other representations that might be tendered by the prosecution at trial or which, even though not intended to be so tendered, might reasonably be relevant to the defence. The defence should also be provided with reasonable access to inspect exhibits and, where it is practicable to do, photocopies or photographs of such exhibits;

- where the prosecutor declines to call a witness whose statement is contained in the book of evidence, the defence should be given details of any material or statements which may be relevant and if requested the prosecution should make the witness available for the defence to call (see paragraph 8.6 to 8.8);

- any other relevant document.

9.12 Where it is feasible to do so the defence should be provided with copies of relevant unused material. However, where that is not feasible (for example because of the large quantity of material involved) the defence should be provided with an opportunity to inspect it.

9.13 The investigating agency should, as early as possible:

- inform the Director's Office of the existence of any material not included with the file that it considers is potentially relevant. In cases of doubt the investigating agency should err on the side of informing the Director of the existence of the particular material;

- inform the Director's Office of the existence of any potentially disclosable material of which it is aware and which is in the possession of a third party (that is, a person or body other than the prosecution or the investigating agency);

- provide the Director's Office with copies of potentially disclosable material unless that is not feasible, (for example, because of the bulk of the material. In such a case it may be necessary for arrangements to be made to enable the prosecutor to view the material before such a decision can be made whether it has to be disclosed to the accused).

Material in the possession of third parties
9.14 Following the decision of the Supreme Court in the case of The People (Director of Public Prosecutions) v. Sweeney (2001 4 IR 102), to the effect that the civil procedure known as 'third party discovery' has no application in criminal proceedings, defendants cannot utilise this procedure to ensure production of material in the hands of third parties.

9.15 This does not, however, have as a necessary consequence an erosion of the fair procedures to which the defendant is entitled. The following observations are relevant:

- the Criminal Justice Act, 1999 provides for the possibility of taking evidence by way of sworn deposition in the District Court at any stage after the return for trial and it is open to the accused to ensure that any relevant records or notes in the possession of a witness are produced;

- alternatively it is open to the accused to require witnesses to attend at the trial and produce any relevant documents by the issue of a subpoena duces tecum.

The duty to retain and preserve evidence

9.16 A number of principles can be determined from decisions of the High Court and Supreme Court in:

- Director of Public Prosecutions v. Daniel Braddish (2001 3 IR 127);

- Director of Public Prosecutions v. Robert Dunne (2002 2 IR 305);

- Director of Public Prosecutions v. Bowes and McGrath (Supreme Court unreported 6 February 2003);

- Director of Public Prosecutions v. Ian Connolly (High Court 15 May 2003); and

- Michael Scully v. Director of Public Prosecutions, (unreported 21 November 2003).

The following guidelines are drafted in the light of these cases.
9.17 Evidence relevant to guilt or innocence must, so far as necessary and practicable, be kept until the conclusion of a trial. This principle also applies to the preservation of articles which may give rise to the reasonable possibility of securing relevant evidence. The fact that evidence is not to be used by the prosecution does not justify its destruction or unavailability or the destruction of notes or records about it. Where the evidence gives rise to a reasonable possibility of rebutting the prosecution case it should be retained.

9.18 There is a duty to seek out evidence having a bearing on guilt or innocence. The obligation does not require the investigator to engage in disproportionate commitment of manpower or resources in an exhaustive search for every conceivable kind of evidence. The duty must be interpreted realistically on the facts of each case. The obligation to seek out and preserve evidence is to be reasonably interpreted and the relevance or potential relevance of the evidence needs to be considered. There is an obligation and responsibility on defence lawyers to seek material they consider relevant.

9.19 While observing the foregoing principles the Garda Síochána must have regard to the rights of the owner of stolen goods. Where they possess evidence which it is not proposed to use at the trial and which they intend to return to the owner or otherwise dispose of, they should inform the accused of this fact beforehand so the defence may have the opportunity to examine the items before their return to the owner.

9.20 The defence should be afforded a reasonable amount of time in which to carry out such an inspection. A record should be retained of any communication with the accused or the accused's representatives inviting access to the item and the time limit allowed for such access should be recorded. Where the Garda Síochána have recovered stolen property used in criminal offences the main consideration is relevance to the offence which is being investigated. The item has to be considered with regard to the overall nature of the investigation. If a third party is seeking the return of the item, but no suspect has been identified, the question should be asked as to whether forensic examination, sampling or other tests need to be carried out beforehand to rebut any possible prejudice which may arise from the disposal of the item.

9.21 Where the Garda Síochána or another investigating agency is in doubt whether material should be retained they should seek the advice of the Director's Office.

Limitations on the Duty to Disclose

9.22 The prosecution is under no obligation to disclose irrelevant material to the defence. If the material is irrelevant in the sense that it is not relied on by the prosecution and does not appear to assist the defence then it is neither appropriate nor necessary to disclose it. However, as a general guideline if it is reasonably possible that something is relevant and if there is no other obstacle to disclosure the balance is in favour of disclosure. It must be borne in mind that the prosecution may not be aware that a particular defence will be put forward by the accused. In cases of doubt concerning either relevance or a competing claim of privilege the prosecutor should consider seeking a ruling from the court.

9.23 The prosecution is not obliged to disclose:

- a confidential statement made by a Garda informant where such statement would identify the informant;

- the identity of a potential witness who has assisted the Garda Síochána without intending to be a witness and the prosecution has agreed not to call the person unless that person has evidence which would assist the defence.

- 9.24 In deciding whether to disclose material the prosecutor must also have regard to any other issues of the public interest which might arise. In such cases, however, the defence should be informed that material has been withheld on such grounds so as to enable the accused to seek a court ruling on the matter. Some relevant factors to be considered are:

1. whether the material is protected by legal professional privilege. The public policy which protects communications between lawyer and client extends to communications between the Director and his professional officers, solicitors and counsel as to prosecutions by him which are in being or contemplated;

2. whether the material, if it became known, might facilitate the commission of other offences or alert a person to Garda investigations;

3. whether the material would be of assistance to criminals by revealing methods of detection or combating crime;

4. whether the material involves the security of the State;

5. whether disclosure of the document would lead to the publication of the names of others in respect of whom further investigative discussions are to take place or in respect of whom enquiries have been made in certain circumstances where all the parties involved have an entitlement to the presumption of innocence;

6. where the circumstances require, a prosecutor may seek an undertaking that the material will not be disclosed to parties other than the accused's legal advisers and the accused.

9.25 The privileges or exemptions outlined at 9.23 and 9.24 are subject to the 'innocence at stake' exception where the disclosure of the material concerned or of the identity of the informant or witness is necessary or right because the evidence in question if believed could show the innocence of the accused.

"If upon the trial of a person the judge should be of opinion that the disclosure of the name of the informant is necessary or right in order to show the person's innocence, then one public policy is in conflict with another public policy, and that which says that an innocent man is not to be condemned when his innocence can be proved is the policy that must prevail" - Lord Esher MR in Marks v. Beyfus (1890 25 QBD 494).

If the prosecution is nonetheless unable to disclose the material concerned then it may be necessary to discontinue the prosecution.

The Timing of Disclosure
9.26 As a general rule disclosure should be made sufficiently in advance of the trial to enable the accused to consider the material disclosed. Primary voluntary disclosure of all disclosable material then in the possession of the prosecution should be made at the time of the return for trial of the accused. Any further material subsequently coming into the possession of the prosecution or specifically requested by the defence should be disclosed in a timely fashion.

*   *   *

The Small Claims Procedure

The following procedure directions from the Courts.ie website are listed as another effective means of holding erring authority figures to account. In combination with; (i) the lodgement of criminal complaints with the Gardaí; (ii) with the publication of those complaints and stories online; (iii) with the use of Common Informer legislation and/or claims in the civil Courts, the lodgement of a small claims action for your costs and expenses should also give rouge authorities some food for thought.

For example, let's say you have been falsely charged with some offence, and in your struggle to clear your name you get obstructed or are denied proper service by some State Official. This could be their refusal to disclose evidence, or some other petty abuse of power and position that ends up costing YOU a great deal of time and money, and causing you considerable distress. Well, YOUR time is precious too. Why should THEY be allowed to take months and years out of your life without any cost to them *personally*? How is it that THEY can claim State wages or fees while visiting this abuse on you? Why is it that only THEY get costs awarded to them at the end of a case? Why is it that there seems to be NO effective sanction of disincentive for lawyers and civil servants in particular NOT to misuse their favoured positions?

Well, here is your chance to make them pay *personally* for their actions. A small claims action only costs the claimant €35 to lodge and you can claim up to €2,000, and even if you don't ever get properly compensated for all the time, costs and inconvenience suffered at these people's hands, then at least you will have forced the opposition into a public Courtroom to account for their misfeasance. And in the event you did actually win some compensation, then you can pursue those individuals further through the Courts - and in public - until they pay up.

The process is relatively straightforward if, for example, you have purchased a 'service' (such as from a solicitor) and you did not get your money's worth. Arguably, the fact that you are a taxpayer but have been failed by some Government agency or State body should, technically, also qualify as 'a failure of service' if for example, the Gardaí or the Garda Ombudsman does not deliver. Similarly, if you have used a 'caveat' or a simple declaration in your correspondence that you reserve the right to charge for time and costs wasted due to improper actions - then technically, they have engaged in an agreed contract with you, and you have a legitimate right to seek compensation. In any event, the technicalities can be argued in open Court where the opposition will face - at the very least - some uncomfortable questions about their methods of operation. This is a simple but practical way of ensuring that there is *some* accountability of *some* sort, for people who have long since forgotten the true meaning of 'value'.

(From the Courts.ie website) The Small Claims procedure is an alternative method of commencing and dealing with a civil proceeding in respect of a small claim and is provided for under the District Court (Small Claims Procedure) Rules, 1997 & 1999 as amended by Statutory Instrument No. 519 of 2009, Order 53A. It is a service provided by District Court offices and is designed to handle consumer claims and business claims cheaply without involving a solicitor. To be eligible to use the procedure, you, the 'consumer' must have bought the goods or services (or the service) for private use from someone selling them in the course of business. As a 'business' you must have bought the goods or services (or the service) for use in business from someone selling them in the course of business. The District Court Clerk, called the Small Claims Registrar, processes small claims. Where possible, the registrar will negotiate a settlement without the need for a court hearing. If the matter cannot be settled the registrar will bring your claim before the District Court.

Type of claims dealt with

(a) a claim for goods or services bought for private use from someone selling them in the course of a business (consumer claims)

(b) a claim for goods or services bought for business use from someone selling them in the course of a business (business claims)

(c) a claim for minor damage to property (but excluding personal injuries)

(d) a claim for the non-return of a rent deposit for certain kinds of rented properties. For example, a holiday home or a room / flat in a premises where the owner also lives

provided that a claim does not exceed €2,000.

Claims in respect of other matters relating to rented accommodation must be brought to: Private Residential Tenancies Board, 2nd Floor, O'Connell Bridge House, D'Olier Street, Dublin 2. Website: www.prtb.ie

Excluded from the small claims procedure are claims arising from:

(a) a hire-purchase agreement

(b) a breach of a leasing agreement

(c) debts

A word of warning

Deciding on whether or not to make a claim is a matter for yourself and only you can be the judge of that. In making a claim you must be sure of the name and address of the person or company against whom you want to make a claim. These details must be accurate in order to enable the Sheriff to execute the Court Order (Decree).

When a Respondent is a company, rather than an individual, it is important to ascertain the correct title of the company. This may be obtained from the Companies Registration Office, telephone no. 01- 804 5200/1, or Lo Call 1890 220 226. Clarifying this may entail some research on your part.

Remember, there is little satisfaction to be gained from winning your case if the Respondent has no money to pay a judgment debt. Consider carefully before deciding to make a small claim but remember that the procedure is there to help you to make your small claim with a minimum of procedural red tape and at little cost.

The 'In Camera' Rule - and the Family Courts

'In Camera' is Latin for "in the room" or "in private" - and should not be confused with the notion of having cameras in Court, although there is an obvious connection between the two. Most family law cases are dealt with 'in camera' where only the parties involved are allowed to witness proceedings. The general public is most definitely *not* allowed to attend 'in camera' proceedings, and anyone reporting on family law matters is obliged to adhere to some pretty strict confidentiality rules. All this (we are told) is to protect the identities of any children who may be involved or affected. But the big problem we are facing once again, is that all this secrecy and suppression of information behind closed doors plays right into the hands of errant authorities who can, basically, say or do what they like during these hearings safe in the knowledge that it cannot be reported, and safe in the knowledge that any legal challenges or appeals against what is going on 'in camera' will in turn, have to be dealt with 'in camera'. In short, the foundational principle that justice needs to be conducted in open, public Courtrooms has been sidelined by persons who may have reasons for *not* wanting their activities and practices to be too closely scrutinised. According to many reports received from I-I Members, this lack of public scrutiny of what is going on in family Courts has resulted in the wholesale destruction of what otherwise would be happy family units, along with the accompanying emotional and psychological distress and turmoil in the lives of those affected. Apparently, there is a lot of money to be made out of Government contracts for those solicitors working for the HSE or TUSLA for example, and the fostering-out of children during contentious litigation between parents - or when the HSE unilaterally deems it necessary - has been described by some as a massive money-making racket. Indeed, the sheer volume of complaints coming in about arrogant and out-of-control social workers interfering with families and colluding with State agencies to build damaging Court cases is so overwhelming as to raise serious questions about whatever alternative agendas might be going on behind the scenes. Our 'official record' in Ireland when it comes to protecting the young, the disadvantaged and the vulnerable is so shockingly deplorable as to lead one to wonder how on earth this type of underhandedness, secrecy and subterfuge is still allowed to carry on behind closed doors - without our knowledge - yet at our direct expense?

In June 2012 for example, a headline on The Journal.ie reported that; *"Children's Ombudsman criticises application of 'in camera' rule on child cases."* The article continued: "The Children's Ombudsman has said that her office spent three years investigating one case involving a child in state care because of "resistance" in the system and the lack of access to information.

Emily Logan was speaking to RTÉ's This Week in response to the publication of an independent report on the deaths of children in state care between 2000 and 2010. The report found that of 196 deaths of children known to State child protection services, 112 were attributed to "non natural causes". Speaking of her office's investigation into one of the cases covered by the report, Logan said that she "couldn't progress the investigation because of resistance" in the child care system. She said that the in camera rule was given as one of the reasons to challenge her inquiry. The application of the rule "remains problematic" she said, adding that for as long as this is permitted, the childcare system "will remain as invisible" as it is now."

Another well-known voice has added to the debate. During a recent visit to Dublin TV personality Judge Judy Sheindlin of New York remarked on her astonishment that the public recording of cases was forbidden in Ireland saying; "Closed courtrooms only protect bad judges and lawyers. They also protect bad institutions that serve those courts, such as social services. Cameras should be there as the norm. If you have a specific exclusion, then you make it."

Finally, former Chief Justice Ronan Keane noted that; "The most benign climate for the growth of corruption and abuse of powers, whether by the judiciary or members of the legal profession, is one of secrecy."

Behind the Veil – A New Era Has Begun for Family Courts
(Abridged, from an article in the Journal.ie January 2014)

The easing of the in camera rule in Irish family courts will see many social issues come to light – many of which may have been hidden behind from the public for generations, writes Katherine Irwin.

Sunday 12th January marked the first of many legal changes in 2014, as the in camera rule was eased in family law courts. The lifting of the veil on family law proceedings means that for the first time members of the media have access to report on family law cases before the courts. Before now the in camera rule was exacting and strictly enforced, allowing none but a limited group of people, including the parties involved, into a court where family law matters were being heard. Debate has raged for years over the restriction of access by the public to the family law courts. Accusations of collusion between judges and solicitors in the making of orders and a level of distrust have grown up between the public and the legal system over the operation of the courts. An attempt at alleviating this gulf between the public's perception of the legal system and the reality was the implementation of Section 4(3) of the Civil Liability and Courts Act 2004. This allowed limited access to family law cases by allowing a number of categories of people to attend a court where family law proceedings are being heard and to report on the proceedings. Journalist Carol Coulter was one such person who was engaged by the Courts Service to prepare such reports. But in recent years it had become inevitable that the move towards greater openness would result in further changes to the law.

Public interest v private interest

Weighing up the demands of the public for knowledge and the right to privacy for those engaged in the legal system on family law matters is a fine balancing act. Crucially the tensions between the private interest and the public interest have resulted in this reform which it is hoped will balance the family's right to privacy with the public's right to know. The Courts and Legal Services Act, 2013 (Part II) allows a bona fide representative of the press to be present in court during these proceedings. The anonymity of parties will be preserved in all cases.

Relying on the quality of media reports

In addition, the amendment provides that it would be an offence to broadcast or make public any information that would be likely to lead members of the public to identify the parties to the family proceedings or any children to whom the proceedings relate. The fine on conviction could amount to €50,000 or imprisonment for a term not exceeding three years, or both. The Minister for Justice has stated that the changes were a part of the government's commitment in the programme for government to reform and modernise aspects of family law.

There is a surely a degree of fear present when it comes to the lifting of the in camera rule. Families involved in such court proceedings and members of the legal profession will need to adjust to this new era. Essentially we will be relying on the quality of reporting by the members of the media to maintain the standard and the dignity of those utilising the justice system for such sensitive matters. On a positive note, in the first report of its kind on Tuesday January 14, Fiona Gartland in the Irish Times provided a largely balanced description of cases before the Circuit Court and District Court. One of the issues reported on related to domestic violence. We can be sure that we will see many social issues come to light in the coming months and years, many of which may have been hidden behind the veil of the in camera rule for generations.

Raising the awareness about these issues through its reporting in the press can only have positive effects. The insight and ability of our experienced judiciary can also be highlighted for what it is with the benefit of such measured reporting. Let's hope the Minister has gotten the balance right.

Findings of the Judicial Appointments Review Committee

In an interesting development which occurred in and around the same time that the *Integrity Ireland* project was beginning to garnish widespread support from a very disillusioned public, the Judicial Appointments Review Committee (comprising several of our senior judges) took it upon themselves to draw up a submission for the attention of the Minister for Justice, that basically, underscores all of the issues and failings within the justice system - and the judiciary in particular - that are articulated in this Guide. Let's hope that Minister Fitzgerald will now pay a bit more attention, and take these recommendations seriously. Here's what they had to say:

* * *

Judicial Appointments Review Committee Preliminary Submission to the Department of Justice and Equality's Public Consultation on the Judicial Appointments Process

RECOMMENDATIONS OF THIS PRELIMINARY SUBMISSION

1. The present system of judicial appointments is unsatisfactory. The opportunity should now be taken to appoint a high level body to carry out research, receive submissions and within a fixed timescale develop comprehensive detailed proposals in a structured, principled and transparent way to make a radical improvement in the judicial appointments process in Ireland.

In advance of any such comprehensive review there are a number of steps which can and should be taken immediately:

2. As a matter of principle, political allegiance should have no bearing on appointments to judicial office. Early acceptance of this principle is essential to a transformation of the appointments process.

3. The merit principle should be established in legislation.

4. A properly resourced judicial education system should be established without delay with a mandate to provide education to members of the judiciary on all matters bearing on the administration of justice.

5. The creation of a Judicial Council is a much needed reform to support the judiciary. A Judicial Council should be established forthwith, with responsibility for representation of the judiciary, an independent disciplinary process, judicial education, and the judicial involvement in the appointment process. However, judicial appointments need not be part of a Judicial Council but can be conducted by a committee as envisaged in the European Network of Councils for the Judiciary "Dublin Declaration" of May 2012.

6. The key to reforming the judicial appointments system rests on reform and development of the Judicial Appointments Advisory Board.

7. The process of judicial appointments should first and foremost enhance the principle of judicial independence, upon which the rule of law in our democracy is built.

8. The Committee believes that all judges should be capable of performing and be seen to perform the full functions of their colleagues of the same court jurisdiction. Variations and inconsistency lead to lack of clarity and confusion where such should be avoided.

9. The number of candidates for a single judicial post submitted by the Judicial Appointments Board for Governmental decision should be reduced to three. Where there are multiple vacancies in a Court, the number of candidates should be increased by no more than the number of additional vacancies.

10. Where it is proposed to fill a judicial position by promotion, including the positions of Chief Justice and Presidents of the other Courts, the candidates should also be subject to the advisory process of the Judicial Appointments Advisory Board. Applications from serving judges to advance between different courts should be processed through application to the Judicial Appointments Advisory Board.

11. The Judicial Appointments Advisory Board should be empowered to rank candidates and to designate any particular candidate as "outstanding".

12. The Judicial Appointments Advisory Board should be specifically empowered to inform the Government when it considers that there are either no, or no sufficient candidates of sufficient quality.

13. The Judicial Appointments Advisory Board requires adequate financial resources to enable it to carry out its functions. A reformed appointments system will require adequate resources. It is recommended that there be consultation with the Judiciary on this matter.

14. The current statutory minimum periods of practice as a barrister or solicitor for appointment to all Courts should be extended to fifteen years.

15. It is essential that high quality experienced candidates are attracted to the bench. Recent changes to pension provisions, both public and private, as they apply to entrants to the judiciary, may have little fiscal benefit to the State, yet create a wholly disproportionate disincentive to applicants for judicial posts, and deter high quality applicants from seeking appointment. It is desirable that such provisions should be immediately reviewed to assess the benefit if any to the State, and assessing their impact on the quality of candidates for appointment to the judiciary.

16. The current requirement for Judges of the District Court to apply for yearly renewal from age sixty five to age seventy should be abolished. Judges of all jurisdictions should have the same retirement age on judicial appointment.

Membership of the Committee

Court Presidents
- The Hon. Mrs. Justice Susan Denham, Chief Justice of Ireland, Chairperson
- The Hon. Mr. Justice Nicholas J. Kearns, President of the High Court
- The Hon. Mr. Justice Raymond Groarke, President of the Circuit Court
- Her Honour Judge Rosemary Horgan, President of the District Court

Committee members representing colleagues
- The Hon. Mr. Justice Donal O'Donnell, The Supreme Court
- The Hon. Mr. Justice Peter Kelly, The High Court and President of the Association of Judges of Ireland
- The Hon. Mr. Justice Paul Gilligan, The High Court and President of the European Network of Councils for the Judiciary
- Her Honour Judge Jacqueline Linnane, The Circuit Court
- Judge Cormac Dunne, The District Court

Secretary to the Committee
- Mr. Richard McNamara, Solicitor, Executive Legal Officer to the Chief Justice

"Judges Aren't Rotten, the Appointment System Is"

An article by TD Shane Ross published in the Sunday Independent 09/08/2015

Her words fell on deaf ears: Chief Justice Susan Denham chaired a committee which reported that "the relative success of the administration of justice in Ireland has been achieved in spite of, rather than because of the appointment system". The politicians have responded with delaying devices like a public consultation process, designed to ensure that no decisions to dilute their powers of patronage are made before the General Election.

There was a shock hook against the head in the Supreme Court 10 days ago. Normally, official Ireland might have expected the beaks on the bench to close ranks. On July 31 they confounded convention. The five-member court made a 4-1 finding against a member of the inner circle. They rapped one of their own mates on the knuckles.

Admittedly, Judge John Cooke has retired. But the Supreme Court's findings will not have made pleasant reading for his lordship. John Cooke was a shareholder in giant conglomerate CRH when he was sitting in judgment over a serious case being taken against the elite Irish company by a tiny rival, Goode Concrete, for alleged uncompetitive practices. Cooke made three rulings in favour of CRH -and against Goode - between 2010 and 2012. His bosses on the bench have now decided that there was a reasonable apprehension of objective bias because of his CRH holding. Cooke told the court in November 2010 that he had "a very small number" of CRH shares "somewhere in my pension fund". Two years later, it emerged that he held CRH shares to the value of €135,000. He insisted that he was unaware that further shares had been bought for him by his advisers in late 2010.

The Supreme Court has set aside Cooke's decisions in the Goode case. Chief Justice Susan Denham was emphatic that judges should not "generally" hear cases if they held shares in companies involved in the litigation. It would be different if the shares were held in a pension scheme or a unit fund over which they had no control. In Cooke's case, he held the shares directly. Cooke must have a red face this weekend. Other judicial colleagues may be reflecting nervously on whether they have ever been compromised in their judgments by their personal financial interests.

How many other judges are conflicted in their work by their assets and liabilities? Are many silently in hock to the banks after being burned in property transactions? Fortunately for their lordships, we will never be sure. Judges do not have to make a declaration of personal interests. They are expected to recuse themselves from cases if they feel they are conflicted by any material debts, assets or other obligations.

Judges are not subject to the same regime as politicians. In today's supposedly open and transparent world, all politicians must rightly make a clear declaration of all interests above a certain value. They must reveal external earnings, gifts, sources of income, property, shares or any asset that could influence their behaviour as advocates or executives in the public interest. Other public servants are obliged to go through similar hoops.

Not judges. As citizens they are suddenly above reproach the moment they don the big wig. Ordinary solicitors or barristers miraculously morph into people whose honour is beyond question. Some of them have even been politicians in a previous life. Others have been close to ministers or even to taoisigh. No doubt they have been subjected to rigorous processes to ensure that their integrity is unimpeachable, their record beyond question? No point in having accident-prone types on the bench. Ahem.

The bad news is that the judiciary (particularly at District Court level), can be very ordinary human beings. One politically nominated judge, Heather Perrin, has been jailed in recent years.

Worse still is that none of them are subject to interview. Worst of all is that every single judge is the beneficiary of an act of political patronage. The selection system is rotten. That does not mean that the judges themselves are rotten, just that the chance of a political insider charging through the system is even greater than a party foot soldier securing a job as a postman or a local garda. The pattern of promotions from recent appointments is disturbing.

Two weeks ago, the government made several new appointments. It promoted Iseult O'Malley to the Supreme Court and Richard Humphreys to the High Court. Neither went through an interview. Humphreys was a barrister, a Labour Party Councillor until recently and was a special adviser to an earlier coalition government. Iseult O'Malley was lifted into the High Court only three years ago by the same coalition. She is the grand-daughter of Kevin O'Higgins, a Free State minister, and a sister of Finbarr O'Malley, another former Labour Party adviser. It would be unfair to cast aspersions on the undoubted abilities of both appointees, but it is fair to question whether either would have been given such preferment under Fianna Fail. Iseult is, very appropriately, replacing one-time Fianna Fail Dail candidate, Fianna Fail adviser and Fianna Fail Attorney-General John Murray.

Four years ago, under the present Fine Gael government, Mayo solicitor Patrick Durcan was appointed to the District Court. Durcan had served in various capacities for Fine Gael, not least as a four-time running mate of the current Taoiseach and a senator under Garret FitzGerald. Two years ago, barrister Colm MacEochaidh was appointed to the High Court. The same man had run for Fine Gael in the 2002 General Election in Dublin South East.

The examples of such political appointments are legion - under all administrations. A fig leaf called the Judicial Appointments Advisory Board - known as JAABs - masks the decisions. It receives applications and passes a selected list of at least seven names to the minister for justice. He or she recommends a name to the Government. Absurdly, ministers can ignore the list if no names please them. They can simply parachute in someone more politically palatable. The Cabinet then recommends to the President, who announces the favoured winner. Sadly, the JAABs (now derided as "Jaabs for the boys" down in the Law Library) consists of three political nominees, plus the politically-appointed Attorney-General and the politically-appointed Presidents of the Supreme, High, Circuit and District Courts. Add the nominees of the Bar Council and the Law Society and you have a web of comfortable insiders who are hardly likely to rock the designs of the Department of Justice. The current coalition is making up for lost ground. After Fianna Fail had their way for 14 years, Fine Gael and Labour have treated vacancies on the bench as the spoils of war.

Eighteen months ago, the judges themselves lashed out at their own indefensible appointments system. "It is increasingly clear" stated a damning report from the committee chaired by Chief Justice Susan Denham, "that the relative success of the administration of justice in Ireland has been achieved in spite of, rather than because of the appointment system". The report pointedly declared that political allegiance should have no bearing on appointments to judicial office. The Chief Justice's words have fallen on deaf ears. The politicians have responded with delaying devices like a public consultation process, designed to ensure that no decisions to dilute their powers of patronage are made before the General Election. Meanwhile, their friends will be further favoured; judges will need nothing but basic legal qualifications; they will not be interviewed for their jobs; they will not be compelled to make a declaration of interests; they will remain self-regulated.

It is easier to topple a government than to fire a judge. It only takes a simple majority vote in the Dail to bring down a government but it needs a vote of both Houses to remove a judge.

The first is not unknown, the second has never happened.   *Sunday Independent*

A Summary of the Most Expensive Legal System in Europe
(As submitted to Integrity Ireland by a journalist and law graduate, July 2015)

1. Ireland has the highest legal costs in the world.

2. Ireland (consequently) has the lowest level of *civil* litigation in the western world. Ireland has just one sixth the average number of judges per capita in the 47 Members of the Council of Europe. This, I suggest, is reflective of the very high legal costs which deters public participation in civil litigation.

3. Irish courts are somewhat secretive. There is generally no access to court documents. Only High Court/Appeal Court/Supreme Court decisions are published, but not consistently. It is now clear that some judgements are never published. The majority of decisions (99.9%) of the Circuit Court–whose money limit was doubled last year to €75,000– are not published. The published judgements are not comprehensive (and may not detail all arguments advanced), and 95% of the time these do not detail any information regarding costs, which are usually burdened on the loser. Some 97% of costs dispute outcomes at higher court level are kept secret, as are 99.9% of Circuit Court costs outcomes.

4. Lawyer overcharging is rife, with very few sanctions. The overcharged litigants are effectively punished for challenging lawyers' excessive fees. The Challenger has to pay 8% stamp duty to the government, even when the lawyer seeks five times the so-called going rate. If a client seeks to challenge their own lawyers' excessive fees, the client will have to pay *all* of the legal costs of the adjudication hearing *plus* an 8% tax, unless he/she succeeds in dropping the bill by 20% or more. Even still, the client will get *no* costs themselves even if they establish a [20% plus] overcharge.

5. The system of high legal costs is quite complex and has been honed over hundreds of years. There are a number of elements to the cartel:

   (i) The 'tying' of lawyers. The profession of lawyers is divided into three sections: Solicitors, Junior Barristers and Senior Barristers (aka 'Counsel'). In theory, a solicitor *could* represent a client alone, thus constricting costs. In practice this rarely happens, as the Judges (secretly) enforce the cartel, making it clear to any errant solicitors that it would be "foolish" and not in their client's interest to breach the established etiquette of using 3 or 4 lawyers at the higher courts. Most judges (98.4%) are selected from the barrister profession with most High Court judges from the Senior Counsel ranks. The government appoints all Senior Counsels, and later selects some of these to become judges, and retains the power to promote judges thereafter.

   (ii) No advertising is allowed by barristers.

   (iii) Fee-splitting arrangements between lawyers are overlooked and are not outlawed.

   (iv) Incumbent barristers are isolated from competition by the 'culling' of new entrants – new barristers have to effectively 'pay to work' for up to seven years. The first year, a new barrister has to pay €3,100 to register and practice, while primarily working for free for his or her 'master'. These registration fees drop to €1,500 for year 2, but increase to €7,500 over time. The result is that 60% of new entrants drop out after four years – struggling to survive, while prevented from advertising to expand their customer base.

   (v) There is near zero level of enforcement of competition law.

6. Competition Law - The Story: The Irish Competition authority produced a report in 2006 which recommended many reforms. The Chairman resigned (c. 2007) because the government refused to implement most of the report. The OECD *[Organisation for Economic Co-operation*

and Development] produced a report in 2007 which highlighted the fact that Ireland prohibited advertising by barristers. In 2011, following intervention in Ireland by the IMF/EU Commission/ ECB (the Troika), reform of legal services in Ireland was identified as <u>a priority reform issue</u>. A pretend–reform Bill was then drafted in Ireland *[The Legal Services Regulation Bill 2011]* and is still glacially working its way through parliament. I lodged a formal complaint with the EU Commission in February 2013, alleging breaches of, (a) competition law, (b) freedom of establishment rules, and (c) human rights. In May 2014, the Commission dismissed my complaint. However, the EU Ombudsman Office got the Commission to concede that the Commission had, in fact, issued a formal 'Infringement Notice' on foot of my complaints against Ireland (though the Commission initially claimed that the action was *not* as a result of my complaint). The EU Ombudsman's office refused to publish a summary of my compliant to her office (including her decision). In January 2015, the [New] Commission, wrote to me and informed me that a second Infringement Notice had been served on Ireland in relation to restrictions of advertising of the Solicitor profession, and clarified that this was as a result of my complaint. [The previous Commission refused to acknowledge this]. I was advised by an EU civil servant (in an email) that political pressure was been applied on Ireland to reform (to allow direct access to barristers and advertising). Last month, the *Irish Independent* newspaper announced that the Troika had given up trying to get Ireland to reform the legal professions.

7. Conflicts: *The New York Times* previously reported on the issue of judges pay in the EU. In 2009, following the initiation of the Lisbon Treaty, judges' pay was harmonised for EU judges to a very high level – coincidentally pitched at a level in-between Irish and UK judges' salaries, at about €238,000 (incl. relocation allowance). So here is the potential conflict of interest: The salaries of EU judges (of the Court of Justice of the European Union [CJEU]) appear to be pinned to a level between the two highest paid judiciaries in the EU. {Note- the salaries of MEP's were also raised to fall between the highest and second highest paid parliamentarians in the EU}. It is unclear how this benchmarking was arrived at, but it appears problematic. Salaries of MEPs (members of the EU parliament) are set at 38.5% of EU judges' salaries. Salaries of Commissioners are set at 112% of EU judges salaries. Salaries of leading (if not all) EU civil servants are similarly linked to a certain fraction of EU judges salaries. If it is the case that the salaries of UK and Irish judges influenced the upgrading of EU judges salaries in 2009, (which on the face of it seems apparent), then clearly, there are several conflicts of interest established: The EU Commission is charged with enforcing competition law, freedom of movement (of lawyers) and human rights within the EU, and they rely on the advices of top civil servants in the EU Commission – for example, as in DG Competition. MEPs are supposed to hold the Commission to account for failing to enforce EU law. The salaries of both Irish and UK judges are directly benchmarked to those of the Senior Barristers in each country, which are evaluated via 'secret reports' produced by the respective Bar Councils. Hence, the salaries of Irish and UK judges are significantly inflated by anti-competitive restrictions operated by the Barristers in both countries. These restrictions are both covertly and overtly enforced by the judges, with regular warnings that 'second-rate' judges will be appointed if judges' salaries are not kept in step with those of top barristers. Thus, it appears that the prosecutors of EU competition law (the Commissioners) appear to have their salary inflated by the anti-competitive practices of the Barristers in Ireland and the UK. The complaint system to the EU Commission is totally secretive. The Commission has only *once* prosecuted a member state legal profession for violation of competition law. In that case, against Italy (in 2011), the Commission sought to remove a fee-cap system that was an encumbrance to lawyers in seeking higher fees. [This sole prosecution was taken, despite a similar action failing about five years earlier, when taken by an Italian Lawyer]. In other words, the only time the Commission has taken legal action is when it directly served the interest of lawyers. It has also never intervened in a case, in support of a litigant, to remove a restrictive practice by a legal profession.

Judicial Council 'imperative', says Chief Justice: Justice Susan Denham says Ireland's reputation is being damaged by delay in setting up council

(Irish Times, Oct 2015)

Ireland's reputation is being damaged due to the continuing delay in establishing a judicial council, whose functions would include setting out a code of conduct for judges, Chief Justice Ms Justice Susan Denham has said.

It was "imperative" a council was established, she said.

"The hard won standard of the administration of justice in Ireland is being affected in terms of reputation, internationally, due to the long-fingering of this much needed infrastructure."

Noting almost 15 years had passed since the 2000 report of the Committee on Judicial Conduct and Ethics recommended establishment of a council, she welcomed the priority listing of the Judicial Council Bill in this session of the Oireachtas.

Ms Justice Denham, who was secretary to the committee, said it had recommended a judicial council be set up to establish best practice for the education, support and training of judges; a code of conduct; and a complaint structure for people who felt a judge had departed from acknowledged standards of judicial conduct.

In a statement marking the opening of the new legal year, the Chief Justice also said new court rules and case management systems were part of continuing efforts to combat delays and improve access to justice.

She was very conscious of the saying "justice delayed is justice denied" and was pleased the new approach and rules allowed for speedier access to appeal structures "at the highest level of our legal system".

She said 236 cases were dealt with by the Supreme Court in the first half of 2015 when the court also published 89 judgments and 24 written determinations.

At every level of court and court administration across the country, reorganisation and modernisation were being undertaken to ensure less delays and improved access to justice, she said.

Litigants in the High Court could now expect a hearing date for many matters in a timescale ranging from immediately to 16 weeks while delays had also been reduced in many areas in the circuit and district courts, she said.

"There will always be areas we need to improve upon," she added.

Her statement came as the new Court of Appeal, which began work last year, continues to work to clear an inherited backlog of hundreds of cases from the Supreme Court, while also coping with hundreds of new appeals entering its list.

The Supreme Court is dealing with hundreds of new appeals as well as appeals dating back several years which have not been transferred to the new appeal court.

The fact a significant number of appeals before both courts are brought by personal litigants, most of whom are not familiar with the required appeal processes, has added to the delays.

*   *   *

The Association of Judges of Ireland

(See www.aji.ie)

The Association of Judges in Ireland (AJI) was formed on the 18th of November 2011. It is a representative body and represents the interests of its members. Although it does not represent the judiciary as such, the AJI's membership comprises the vast majority of the judges in the Supreme Court, the High Court, the Circuit Court and the District Court. The AJI's mandate is set out in detail in its Constitution and includes the protection and enhancement of judicial independence, the improvement of the administration of justice and the promotion of a better public understanding of the role played by the judiciary both within the justice system and as an arm of government.

Foundation

The background to the foundation of the AJI was concern that, in the absence of an independent judicial council established by statute, no satisfactory mechanism existed for the judiciary as a whole to convey its point of view on matters of concern to it, when appropriate, and in a manner consistent with the judicial function.

Existing channels for communication between the executive and the judicial branches of government, respectively, were perceived to be inadequate; in particular, it was felt that established protocols for consultation between the executive and the judiciary about matters of mutual interest were ineffective, alternatively too slow, and in any case no longer fit for purpose in the second decade of the 21st century.

The AJI was established as a vehicle to facilitate its members in addressing such issues, both those of urgent and immediate concern, and those that might arise in the future.

The AJI was founded on the 18th of November, 2011 at the 2011 National Conference of the Judiciary hosted by the Committee for Judicial Studies at Dublin Castle. On that occasion some 113 members of the Irish judiciary, drawn from every jurisdiction, and representing approximately 77% of total number of serving judges in Ireland, signed the Constitution of the Association of Judges of Ireland as founding members. Membership is voluntary but has grown to the point where the AJI now represents in excess of 90% of the serving judiciary. In addition, a number of retired judges have joined the AJI as Honorary Members.

The aims and objectives of the AJI are set out in Part B of the Constitution of the Association of Judges of Ireland. They are:

a. To maintain and promote the highest standards in the administration of justice.

b. To promote the interests of its members in their professional capacity.

c. To promote the independence of the judiciary.

d. To promote the highest standards of judicial conduct amongst its members.

e. To promote the general interests of its members, including those interests arising upon retirement from the Bench.

f. To promote the exchange of ideas on the administration of justice.

g. To further the cultural intellectual and legal proficiency of its members.

h. To promote and maintain contacts with judges and magistrates abroad, with national and international associations and in particular national and international associations of judges.

i. To represent its members in any forum where that is necessary.

Notable Quotes & Statements by Irish Judges and Registrars

(as reported by eyewitnesses, or as per written statements, news articles or recordings)

* * * * *

"Court Rules are only guidelines and I can overrule them if I wish."

Circuit Court Judge Raymond Groarke, 24th April 2012

On the occasion of allowing a 'politically connected' defendant to come back into a case, against the repeated objections of the Plaintiff, after an Order for judgment had already been issued against the Defendant.

* * * * *

"It may be that these legal rules (from 1936) may no longer be appropriate in modern Ireland, but I'm afraid we do have to stick to them.."

High Court Judge Barry White, High Court on Circuit, Sligo, Nov 8th 2012

On the occasion where a Plaintiff arrived for a High Court Appeal Hearing only to be met by seven Senior and Junior Counsel representing the State who argued that the case had to be heard in Dublin.

* * * * *

"As counsel has explained, I do not have the jurisdiction to hold this hearing, therefore I cannot make any such Order."

High Court Judge Barry White, High Court on Circuit, Sligo, Nov 8th 2012

On the occasion of being asked by the Plaintiff for an Order that would 'preserve' phone data held by Eircom-Meteor that was central to proving criminal allegations against agents of the State. The data was subsequently erased despite Court Orders seeking discovery, and despite the statutory requirement that evidence that is material to a Garda investigation <u>must</u> be preserved. Oh, and by the way, a Judge *can* make any Order he or she sees fit to make.

* * * * *

"The Order as issued does not have to represent what the Judge said."

County Registrar Fintan Murphy, Castlebar, Co. Mayo, December 2012

..after being challenged by the Plaintiff on the wording of an apparent bogus Order (see above) that Mr Murphy had constructed after a High Court hearing where Mr Murphy was *not* even in attendance!

* * * * *

"I am not sure that I have the jurisdiction to issue any such Order."

County Registrar Fintan Murphy, Castlebar, Co. Mayo, 2012

On the occasion of being asked by the Plaintiff to Order that the Defendant appears in Court to be cross-examined on a fraudulent defence statement. *[County Registrars' first rule is that they may make <u>any</u> Order they deem fit to issue.]* The Order was *not* issued despite this being a fundamental right articulated in Court Rules.

* * * * *

"Inconsistencies sometimes occur in litigation. Tell it to the Judge at the next hearing – and you might get your costs."

County Registrar Fintan Murphy, Castlebar, Co. Mayo, 2012

On the occasion of being informed by the Plaintiff that a defence solicitor had just entered two fraudulent documents into evidence in order to forestall a legitimate judgement against a connected Defendant. The case continues..

* * * * *

"There are penal sanctions for people who commit perjury!"

Mr Justice John Hedigan, Dec 2014

Speaking to a witness in the Ian bailey case against the State. (Someone needs to tell the Guards – and Mr Murphy..)

"That is of little consolation to the victim. You did not make sufficient efforts to get the right person!"

Circuit Court Judge Anthony Hunt, 2011

On the occasion of sentencing a hired 'heavy' who had carried out a punishment beating on an innocent party, and was claiming it was a case of mistaken identity.

* * * * *

"I want to make it clear that when a Court makes orders, compliance is not optional. If people did not comply with Court Orders, there would be anarchy."

High Court Judge Brian McGovern, Nov 2013

On the occasion when protestors occupied farm lands belonging to farmer Eugene McDermott to try to prevent repossession by the banks.

* * * * *

"I am not dealing with this today. It has been adjourned. Guards, remove him from the Court!"

Circuit Court Judge Margaret Heneghan, Castlebar, Feb 18th 2014

After being told that the Defence had completely ignored a Circuit Court Order and had held a fraudulent and preemptive Hearing a week earlier <u>without</u> notifying the Plaintiffs.

* * * * *

"Well if the Defendant says he is sick, then what can we do? We will just have to adjourn the matter."

Circuit Court Judge Donagh McDonagh,Castlebar, 2013

Referring to the last-minute production of a handwritten sick note from a Defendant who had already avoided several previous 'mandatory' Court appearances using a variety of other excuses.

* * * * *

"Sometimes the law is subject to the Constitution, and sometimes it's the other way round."

Judge Rory McCabe, April 2012

On being asked for clarity on the matter by a confused Plaintiff. The confusion remains although the facts are now clear; the law is in fact subject to the Constitution.

* * * * *

"Power of Attorney does <u>not</u> entitle you to represent your brother in Court."

High Court Judge David Keane, Oct 2014

On the occasion when a criminal tried for the 16th time in a row, to 'legally represent' his brother, the Defendant in a civil case. He *had* been allowed (illegal) audience by several other judges on those 15 previous occasions.

* * * * *

"You are not allowed audience in this Court."

Justice Nicholas Kearns, President of the High Court.

On another occasion, with the same litigants, and after a letter of complaint to the Chief Justice. But it was Justice Kearns who granted this criminal access to the High Court as a self-professed 'attorney' in the first place.

* * * * *

"We are not here to discuss that matter today. That is a matter for another Court. The documentation looks legitimate to me."

Circuit Court Judge Karen Fergus, July 2015

Even after being told that the criminal who was posturing as an attorney in her Court (again) had already been refused the right to speak in the High Court and in the Court of Appeal. He was *still* allowed to continue.

"One judge of the High Court can <u>not</u> make an order against a decision by a fellow High Court judge."

Justice Nicholas Kearns, President of the High Court, Nov 2014

Oh really? Would someone explain that to Justice Sean Ryan then please? (See below)

*   *   *   *   *

"I am making an Order to set aside the Judgment..." (of fellow High Court Judge O'Malley)

High Court Judge Sean Ryan, March 31ˢᵗ 2014

On the occasion when a completely illegitimate hearing was held in the High Court <u>without</u> the Plaintiff being present, and without due Notice being served. An email into the Court explaining that the Plaintiff was abroad and could not attend was also ignored. Judge Ryan is now the President of the Appeals Court.

*   *   *   *   *

"I have read the Defence affidavit. I will not need to hear from you Mr ** (Plaintiff). I have made a decision.."

Justice Nicholas Kearns, High Court, Nov 2014

After having been notified that the Plaintiff had <u>not</u> seen the contents of the Defence affidavit and that it had <u>not</u> been served on the Plaintiff - which is in breach of Court Rules. The Judge continued with his delivery nevertheless.

*   *   *   *   *

"I have read the submissions from the Defence and I have made a decision.."

Justice Mary Finlay Geoghegan, Court of Appeal, Jan 2015

After having been notified that the Plaintiff had <u>not</u> seen the contents of the Defence affidavit and that it has <u>not</u> been served on the Plaintiff - which is a clear abuse of process. The Judge continued nevertheless.

*   *   *   *   *

"You are not here to lecture the Court... I am going to rise and exit this Courtroom. If you are still here in two minutes I will take the appropriate action!"

High Court Judge Larfhlaith O'Neill, October 2013

After being asked by the Plaintiff why the Plaintiff was not being awarded his expenses according to *Rule O 27 r 9(3) RSC* when the opposition barrister admitted that *'it was a deliberate tactic'* of the Defence solicitor not to respond to the Plaintiff's sixteen formal correspondences over a period of eleven months.

*   *   *   *   *

"It's time for more force to be used on these fellows... (these knackers). Maximum force should be used."

District Court Judge Geoffrey Browne, Jan 2013

Referring to burglars from the Travelling Community.

*   *   *   *   *

"Neanderthal men... abiding by the laws of the jungle"

Judge Seamus Hughes, 2012

Also referring to Travellers.

*   *   *   *   *

"A Polish charity? There is. It's called the social welfare."

Judge Mary Devins, Aug 2012

No comment.

*   *   *   *   *

"Have a word with your client. He's just perjured himself."

Judge Gerald Keys, 2012

To the Defendant's Barrister, on the occasion when a 'connected' businessman lied during evidence. Despite proving his case beyond question, the lay litigant still lost the case. There was no sanction for the perjury.

211

"Shut up! Shut up! Shut up! Shut up! Shut up!...(16 times in succession)

District Court Judge John Coughlan, Wexforrd, April 2013

To a lay litigant attempting to defend himself against HSE/Garda charges.

* * * * *

"I think I might serve womankind if I could stop people wearing those shoes - but that is not my function"

Referring to high hells, in a High Court claim for damages. *Justice John Hanna, June 2015*

* * * * *

*"..it would be most unjust for this court to imprison these two gentlemen when it seems to me a State agency has led them into error and into illegality. So I'll adjourn the matter.. ..to assess both Mr ** and Mr ** as to suitability as to community service."*

Judge Martin Nolan, April 2014

On the occasion of the criminal sentencing hearing of two Anglo-Irish executives who were found guilty of massive financial fraud .

* * * * *

*"Ms ** has listed her professional qualifications, and she is speaking under oath. That is good enough for me."*

Judge Rory McCabe, July 2014

On the occasion when a lay litigant told the Judge that Ms ** (a social worker from the HSE/TUSLA) was lying under oath. When asked if a digital recording that proved the facts could be read into the record, the Judge refused.

* * * * *

" (silence)"

High Court Judge Michael White, July 2015

On the occasion when I-I members read out a Constitutional declaration of non-cooperation before exiting the Courtroom en masse.

* * * * *

If you have any unusual, interesting, odd, contradictory or outrageous quotes or decisions made by judges in your case – please feel free to forward them to 'sos@integrityireland.ie' for inclusion in Version 2 of this Guide, due out in Spring 2016.

Extra Court-related Information

Request to Record: "I respectfully request permission to record these proceedings on the basis of expediency and transparency, in circumstances where there are numerous documented incidents of inaccurate Court Orders being issued; of official interference with DAR recordings and transcripts after-the-fact; and of other incidents whereby the DAR was switched off or inoperable. This combination of; (i) unreliable Courts Service processes; (ii) the costs and complications involved; and (iii) the deliberate interference with 'official' records, requires that we make our own independent recording of this hearing - in the overall interests of justice."

Opposition not cooperating? In the event the opposition fail to respond to a Motion you have brought or fail to adhere to an Order of the Court - and especially if this is done by deception, trickery, fraud or by any other abuse of Superior Court Rules - then the following rule might apply: *"Rule O 27 r 9(3) Rules of the Superior Courts provides that the defendant must pay to the Plaintiff a set sum (Euro 750.00) for the costs of the motion for judgment."* (Para 7.8.2)

PART
6

GLOSSARY & DICTIONARY
of
LATIN & LEGAL TERMS

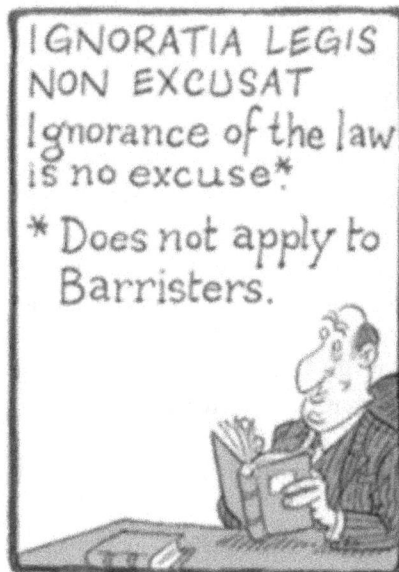

Glossary & Dictionary of Legal Terms (in English)

Some of the more common Latin terms are also included in this list. A full list of Latin legal terms follows.

Abatement: Reduction or rebate of an amount owed, usually by agreement with the person to whom the debt is owed. Debts or claims may be abated pro rata if there is not enough money to meet them all.

Acceptance: One of three requirements for a valid contract under common law (the other two being offer and consideration). A contract does not become legally binding until one party has made an offer and the other party indicates his readiness to accept the terms of the offer. Acceptance must be unconditionally communicated to the offeror while the offer is still open. Acceptance of an offer can, in certain circumstances, be implied by conduct.

Accord and Satisfaction: A contract may be discharged if one party, who has complied with his part of the contract, accepts compensation from the other party instead of enforcing the contract. The accord is the agreement by which the obligation is discharged. The satisfaction is the consideration (usually money and of a lesser value) which makes the agreement operative.

Acquiescence: Action or inaction which legally binds someone, even unintentionally. For example, an action such as accepting goods from a supplier will be binding if it implies recognition of the terms of a contract.

Act of God: An event resulting from natural causes, without human intervention (such as floods or earthquakes). Insurance policies often exclude acts of God.

Action: Proceedings in a civil court.

Adjournment: Postponement of a hearing by a judge on whatever terms he sees fit.

Administrative law: Law which applies to hearings before quasi-judicial or administrative tribunals. Such hearings must be conducted in accordance with the principles of natural justice, such as audi alteram partem and nemo judex in sua causa.

Administrator: A person appointed to manage the property of another (such as the administrator of the estate of someone who has died without leaving a will).

ADR: Alternative dispute resolution (such as arbitration, mediation and conciliation).

Adverse possession: Possession of land, without legal title, for long enough - normally 12 years - to be recognised as the legal owner ("squatter's rights").

Adversarial: when two or more parties are putting their case and the judge's role is like that of a referee.

Advocacy: the skills of arguing and explaining a client's case in court.

Affidavit: Sworn written statement signed by a deponent, who swears that its contents are true to the best of his knowledge and belief. It must be witnessed by a practising solicitor or commissioner for oaths.

Agent: Person with power to contract on behalf of others, binding them as if they were signing the contract themselves. The person represented by the agent is called the principal.

Aggravated damages: Exceptional damages awarded by a court where a defendant's behaviour towards the plaintiff or victim has been particularly humiliating, malicious or vindictive.

Alternative dispute resolution: Method by which conflicts and disputes are resolved privately, other than through litigation, usually by mediation or arbitration. ADR involves the appointment of a third-party to preside over a hearing between the two sides. The advantages of ADR are privacy and speed. The disadvantage is that ADR may involve compromise of legal rights.

Antedate: To date retroactively, before a document was drawn up.

Appeal: Challenge to a court decision in a higher court.

Appearance: The act of replying to a summons or turning up in court and accepting its jurisdiction to try proceedings. A barrister or solicitor may make an appearance on a client's behalf.

Appellant: Person who makes an appeal.

Arrears: Accumulated debt which has not been paid on the due date.

Assault: Touching - or threatened touching - of another person, without that person's consent.

Assign: To give or transfer responsibility to another person. The person who receives the right or property is the assignee; the assignor is the person giving.

Attachment and committal: Bringing a person before a court, with a threat of imprisonment for failure to obey a court order.

Attachment of earnings: Court order for deduction of salary at source in order to pay, for example, maintenance or a debt.

Attorney General: Legal adviser to the government, appointed by the President on the advice of the party in power.

Bailee: Person who accepts property through a contract of bailment, from the bailor, and who has certain duties of care while the property remains in his possession.

Bailment: Temporary transfer of goods by a bailor to a bailee (for example, for storage), after which theproperty is either returned to the bailor or disposed of according to the contract of bailment.

Barrister: Specialist in litigation and advocacy who receives instructions from a solicitor. **Barrister** – a lawyer who specialises in advocacy and has the right to speak in the High Court. A barrister is usually instructed to act in a case by a solicitor on behalf of the solicitor's client. Barristers may not normally deal directly with members of the public.

Beneficiary: Person who receives a gift under a will, or for whose benefit property is held by an executor or trustee.

Bill of exchange: Written, signed instrument requiring the person to whom it is addressed to pay on demand (or on a future date) a fixed amount of money either to the person identified as payee or to anyone presenting the bill of exchange. A cheque is a form of bill of exchange.

Bill of lading: Document used in foreign trade, acknowledging that a company has received goods for transportation. The Bill serves as title to the goods until they have reached their destination.

Breach of contract: Failure or refusal to fulfil a term of a contract. The injured party may bring an action for damages, for enforcement or for cancellation of the agreement.

Burden of proof: A rule of evidence that requires a party to a court action to prove something, otherwise the contrary will be assumed by the court. For example, in criminal trials, the prosecution has the burden of proving the accused guilty beyond a reasonable doubt (because of the presumption of innocence).

Call-over: an occasion in court where dates for all the cases in the next few months are fixed. It is important for the parties or their lawyers to attend the call-over.

Case: the proceedings, arguments and evidence in court and the court hearing.

Case law: Published court decisions which establish legal precedents, binding lower courts.

Caveat: (Latin: let him beware.) A formal warning.Caveat emptor (let the buyer beware) is a warning to buyers to check for themselves things which they intend to buy, so they cannot later hold the vendor responsible for the faulty condition of the item. The Sale of Goods and Supply of Services Act 1980 extends the rights of consumers in this area.

Central Criminal Court: The High Court sitting to deal with serious criminal offences, such as rape and murder.

Certificate of readiness: a document prepared by all the parties to a case jointly, confirming that all the necessary steps have been taken for the case to be heard.

Certiorari: Form of judicial review whereby a court is asked to set aside the decision of an administrative tribunal, judicial officer or public organisation. Certiorari may be used where the decision of the lower tribunal was made in breach of the rules of natural justice. An application for certiorari must normally be made within six months of the decision.

Chambers: Judge's personal rooms, where he may hear matters in private.

Charge: Form of security for payment of a debt.

Chattels: Moveable items of property which are neither land nor permanently attached to land or a building. (Land or buildings are described as "real property".) Chattels are also known as personal property (or personalty). A freehold property is not a chattel, but a leasehold is.

Cheque: Form of bill of exchange where the order to pay is given to a bank holding the payor's funds.

Child: Person under 18.

Circuit Court: Court above the District Court and below the High Court, with power to award damages in civil cases up to €75,000 (or €60,000 in personal injury cases).

Circuit Judge: Judge of the Circuit Court, addressed as "Judge".

Civil case: any type of case which is not a criminal case.

Class action: Legal action taken by a number of different persons where the facts and the defendants are similar. Class action lawsuits may occur, for example, after a public transport accident or in the case of a faulty drug, where all the victims sue the same defendant.

Clayton's Case: This English case established a presumption that money withdrawn from an account is presumed to be debited against the money first deposited (first in, first out).

Close of Pleadings: pleadings are deemed to be closed 21 days after service of the reply, or, if there is no reply, after service of the defence to any counterclaim.

Clinical negligence case: A civil claim for damages where negligence by a doctor, dentist or other healthcare professional is alleged.

Codicil: Written amendment or addition to an existing will.

Collateral: Property committed to guarantee a loan.

Collusion: Illegal and usually secret agreement between two or more people to deceive a court or defraud another person.

Common law: Judge-made law which has developed over centuries, also referred to as "unwritten" law. Common law (as practised in Ireland, England and the USA) is often contrasted with civil law systems (such as in France or Germany) where laws are set down in a written code.

Company: Legal entity which permits a group of shareholders to create an organisation to pursue set objectives. A company may have legal rights which are usually reserved for individuals, such as the power to sue and be sued, own property, hire employees or lend and borrow money. The main advantage of a company structure is that it gives shareholders a right to participate in profits (through dividends) without any personal liability.

Consent order: Court order agreed between all sides.

Consideration: Defined as "some right, interest, profit or benefit accruing to the one party, or some forbearance, detriment, loss or responsibility given, suffered or undertaken by the other". At common law, any binding contract must have some consideration, no matter how small. The courts will not normally inquire into the adequacy of the consideration; a "peppercorn rent" would be sufficient.

Consign: To leave property in the custody of another. An item can be consigned to a transport company, for example, to move it from one place to another. The consignee is the person who receives the property and the consignor is the person who ships the property to the consignee.

Construction: Legal process of interpreting a phrase or document. If a term is unclear or ambiguous, lawyers and judges must try and interpret (or construct) its probable intention and purpose. This may be done by referring to other parts of the document, by reference to the known intentions of those who drew up the document or, in the case of statutes, by referring to an interpretation law which gives guidelines for construction.

Constructive trust: Trust imposed by a court in certain circumstances, regardless of the intention of the parties involved (such as where a trustee has improperly profited from his position).

Contempt: Deliberate disregard of a court order.

Contract: Agreement between two or more persons which obliges each party to do (or refrain from doing) a certain thing. A valid contract requires an offer, acceptance of that offer and consideration.

Contract law: Contract law is the basis of all commercial dealings. The terms of a contract may be express or implied. Express provisions may be varied by statute. Unfair contract terms are excluded by legislation and, in areas such as employment and the sale of goods, the law imports a wide range of implied terms into new and existing contracts.

Contributory negligence: Negligence which is not the primary cause of a tort, but which combined with the act or omission of another person to cause the damage. In the case of a car crash, for example, an injured driver who was not wearing a seat belt may be found contributorily negligent for his injuries.

Conversion: Legal proceeding for damages by a property owner against a defendant who found property and converted it to his own use - that is, retained it or otherwise interfered with it.

Conveyance: Written document transferring property from one person to another. Conveyances are usually rafted by solicitors.

Costs: The legal expenses of an action, such as lawyers' fees, witness expenses and other fees paid out in bringing the matter to court. The rule is generally that "costs follows the event", which means that the loser normally pays the legal costs of both sides. The judge has the final decision and may decide not to make an order on costs.

Counsel: Barrister(s). 'JC'= Junior Counsel. 'SC'= Senior Counsel.

Counterclaim: a claim for damages or another remedy by a defendant against a person who has sued him.

Court of Appeal: Court which will deal with appeals from the High Court, although the Supreme Court will still consider appeals on a matter of general public importance or in the interests of justice. The Court of Criminal Appeal and the Courts-Martial Appeal Court will be abolished.

Court order: the enforceable decision of the court.

Covenant: Written document in which signatories either commit themselves to do (or not to do) something, or in which they agree on a certain set of facts. Covenants are very common in leases where a landlord will usually covenant to give the tenant "quiet enjoyment" and the tenant covenants to pay the rent, keep the premises in good repair and deliver them up at the end of the tenancy.

Creditor: Person to whom money, goods or services are owed by a debtor.

Crime: Act or omission forbidden by criminal law. The commission of a crime is punishable by a fine, imprisonment or some other form of punishment. Crimes are divided into minor offences (which may be tried in the District Court) and indictable offences, which are tried by a judge and jury in the Circuit Court or Central Criminal Court.

Creditor: a person who is owed money by a debtor.

Criminal case: a case about whether someone is guilty of a crime and, if so, how they should be punished.

Cross-examination: In a trial, each side calls its own witnesses and may also question the other side's witnesses under oath. Examination-in-chief is the questioning of a party's own witnesses; cross-examination involves questioning the other side's witnesses. A party may not put leading questions (which suggest the answer, or require a simple yes or no) to his own witness, but he may ask such questions in cross-examination.

Curtilage: Land around a dwelling house, used by the occupants for their enjoyment or work. Curtilage may be enclosed by fencing and includes any outhouses such as sheds, garages or workshops.

Damages: money paid to one party by the other to compensate for a wrong. Damages are referred to as liquidated, where they are easily calculated, such as a debt owed or the cost of repairing a car, or unliquidated, where they are less easily calculated, for example compensation for pain, suffering and injury.

De facto: (Latin: in fact) Something which exists in fact, though not necessarily approved by law (de jure). A common law spouse may be referred to as a de facto spouse, although not legally married.

De novo: (Latin: anew) Used to refer to a trial which begins all over again, as if any previous partial or complete hearing had not occurred. A District Court appeal is heard by the Circuit Court de novo, with the court considering afresh all the law and facts.

Debtor: Person who owes money, goods or services to a creditor. If a court judgment has been registered against the person owing the money, he is known as a judgment debtor.

Deed: Written and signed document which sets out the agreement of the signatories in relation to its contents. Under common law, a deed had to be sealed - marked with an impression in wax. A deed is delivered by handing it to the other person. Usually a deed (or some other written evidence) is required in relation to actions involving land.

Defence: Response to claim by plaintiff.

Defendant: Person, company or organization which defends a civil action taken by a plaintiff and against whom the court is asked to order damages or corrective action to redress some unlawful or improper action alleged by the plaintiff. Also a person charged with a criminal offence.

Delegatus non potest delegare: (Latin: a delegate cannot delegate) A person to whom authority or decision-making power has been delegated by a higher source, cannot delegate that power to someone else, unless the original delegation explicitly authorised it.

Deponent: Person who swears an affidavit or deposition.

Descendant: Persons born of, or from children of, another. Grandchildren are descendants of their grandparents, as children are descendants of their natural parents. The law distinguishes between collateral descendants, such as nephews and nieces, and lineal descendants, such as sons and daughters.

Detinue: Tort involving the defendant's retention of property belonging to the plaintiff after the plaintiff has demanded its return. The plaintiff may seek damages for the period of possession, even without proving any actual loss.

Devise: Transfer or conveyance of real property by will. The person who receives such property is called the devisee.

Director of Public Prosecutions: Independent official who decides whether to prosecute in criminal cases and in whose name all criminal prosecutions are taken.

Disclosure: giving access to a document or other evidence relevant to a case to other parties in advance of the hearing.

Discovery: Notifying the other parties about a list of the documents (including paper and electronic documents, maps and photographs, sound and video recordings and information stored in any other way) which are or have been in your possession, custody or control and which are relevant to the case and are not protected by privilege. The duty to make discovery is continuous, so if further relevant documents come into your possession after the exchange of lists, you need to notify other parties about them too. Certain types of document which are "privileged" need not be discovered, but they must be identified to the other side.

Distraint: Seizure of personal property to compel a person to fulfil a legal obligation. Formerly landlords had the power to distrain against the property of a tenant for arrears of rent or other default, but such action is now forbidden in relation to premises let solely as a dwelling. A legal action for the restoration of goods that have been distrained is called replevin.

District Court: Lowest court in the Irish judicial system, with power to award damages up to €15,000 in civil cases.

District Judge: Judge of the District Court, addressed as "Judge".

Dividend: Proportionate distribution of profits made by a company in the form of a money payment to shareholders. Dividends are declared by the board of directors at the annual general meeting. The shareholders decide the dividend at the meeting, but it must not exceed the directors' recommendation.

Domicile: A person's fixed and permanent residence; a place to which, even if he is temporarily absent, he intends to return. Legally, a person may have many residences or several nationalities, but only one domicile.

Dominant tenement: Property or land that benefits from, or has the advantage of, an easement, such as a right of way.

Donee: Beneficiary of a trust or person given a power of appointment.

Donor: Person who gives property for the benefit of another, usually through a trust. Sometimes referred to as a "settlor". Also used to describe the person who signs a power of attorney.

Duces tecum: (Latin: bring with you) Type of subpoena which requires a person to appear before a court with specified documents or other evidence.

Duress: Threats or force preventing - or forcing - a person to act other than in accordance with free will. A contract signed under duress is voidable at the option of the person forced to sign it. Duress may invalidate a marriage.

Easement: A right over a neighbour's land or waterway. An easement is a type of servitude. For every easement, there is a dominant and a servient tenement, or piece of land. Rights-of-way are the most common easements, but others include the right to tunnel under another's land, to emit smoke or fumes, to access a dock and to use a well. An easement that is not used for a long time may be lost.

Emolument: Wages, benefits or profits received as compensation for holding office or employment.

Endorsement: Writing on a document. With a bill of exchange, an endorsement is a signature on the back of the bill by which the person to whom the note is payable transfers the right of payment to the bearer or to a specific person. An endorsement may restrict payment to one person only, and prohibit any further endorsements.

Endorsement of claim: Concise summary of the facts supporting a legal claim.

Endowment: Transfer of money or property (usually as a gift) to a charitable organisation for a specific purpose, such as research or a scholarship.

Enforcement: the processes for making sure that a court order is obeyed.

Equity: The law of equity developed to temper the rigid interpretation given by medieval English judges to the common law. For hundreds of years, there were separate courts in Ireland for common law and equity (known as courts of Chancery). Where decisions conflicted, equity prevailed. In 1877, the two systems were merged. The principles of equity, based on fairness, include "equity will not suffer a wrong to be without a remedy" and "equity looks on the intent, rather than the form".

Estoppel: Rule of evidence which prevents a person from relying on facts when, by deed, word or action, he has led another person to act to his detriment on those facts. Estoppel is a defence, not a cause of action. Anyone who wishes to rely on the defence of estoppel to defend an action must plead it.

Evidence: Testimony of witnesses at a trial, or the production of documents or other materials to prove or disprove a set of facts. Evidence may be direct or circumstantial (that is evidence from which a fact may be presumed). The best evidence available - such as original, rather than copy, documents - must generally be presented to a court.

Ex aequo et bono: (Latin: in justice and fairness) Most legal cases are decided on the strict rule of law. But, where a case is decided ex aequo et bono, the judge may make a decision based on what is just and fair in the circumstances.

Ex parte: (Latin: on the part of) Court application made without notice to the other side. One party is therefore neither present nor represented.

Ex post facto: (Latin: after the fact) Ex post facto legislation retrospectively makes acts illegal which were committed before the law was passed.

Ex turpi causa non oritur actio: (Latin: No action arises from an illegal cause) A person may not sue for damage arising out of an illegal activity. A person may not sue on an illegal contract, because it is void from the time of its creation.

Examination-in-chief: Questioning of witnesses under oath by the party who called those witnesses (also called direct examination). After the examination-in-chief, the other side's lawyer may question the witnesses in cross-examination. Thereafter, the first party may re-examine them, but only about issues raised during the cross-examination.

Executor: Person appointed by a testator to administer a will. The executor is a personal representative whose duties include burying the dead, proving the will, collecting in the estate, paying any due debts and distributing the balance according to the wishes of the deceased.

Exhibit: Document or object shown to a judge or jury as evidence in a trial. Each exhibit is given a number or letter as it is introduced, for future reference during the trial.

Expert report: a report about medical, accounting, engineering or other specialist technical evidence, prepared by a professional with expertise in that area. An expert is the only type of witness who can give evidence about his or her opinion.

Express trust: Trust specifically created by a settlor, usually in a document such as a will, although it can be oral. An express trust which deals with land must be in writing.

Extradition: The arrest and handover of a person wanted for a crime committed in another country, usually under the terms of a extradition treaty. A person may not be extradited from Ireland for a purely political offence.

Fee simple: Freehold estate in land, the most extensive tenure allowed under the feudal system. A person who owns a fee simple estate may sell it, convey it by will or it may be transferred to an heir if the owner dies without leaving a will. For a fee simple estate to be conveyed in a will, the proper words of limitation must be used: either "To X in fee simple" or "To X and his heirs".

Fee tail: Form of tenure that can only be transferred to a lineal descendant. In feudal times, if there were no lineal descendants, the land reverted to the lord on the death of the tenant.

Fiduciary: Person (such as a trustee, company director or executor) who exercises rights and powers for the benefit of another person, but without being under the control of that person. A fiduciary must not allow any conflict of interest to affect his duties and would not normally be allowed to profit from his position.

Fieri facias: (Latin: cause to be made) A writ of fieri facias commands a sheriff to take and auction off property to pay a debt (plus interest and costs) owed by a judgment debtor.

Foreclosure: Forfeiture of a right of redemption on a property (generally when someone fails to pay a mortgage). Even if there has been no payment, the borrower normally retains a equitable right of redemption if he can raise the money to exercise the right. To clear the title of this potential right, a lender can apply to court for a date to be set, by which the entire amount becomes payable. If payment is not made, the property belongs entirely to the lender, who is then free to go into possession or to sell it.

Fraud: Dishonest conduct designed to persuade another person to give something of value by lying, repeating something that is or ought to have been known by the fraudulent party to be false or suspect, or by concealing a relevant fact from the other party. Fraud allows a court to void a contract or to set aside a judgment, and can result in criminal liability. A person who defrauds creditors of a company may be held personally liable.

Freehold: Right to the full use of real property for ever (as opposed to leaseholds or tenancies, which allow possession for a limited time). Varieties of freehold include fee simple, fee tail and life estate.

Freeholder: Person who owns freehold property rights.

Garnishee: Person who owes a third party a debt which is attached by court order for the benefit of a judgment creditor.

Goodwill: Intangible business asset based on the good reputation of a business and resulting attraction and confidence of repeat customers and connections. Part of the sale price of a business may be for goodwill, in which case the seller may not solicit former customers for his new business.

Gross negligence: Act or omission in reckless disregard of the consequences for the safety or property of another; more than simple carelessness or neglect. Gross negligence by an employee may justify summary dismissal.

Guardian ad litem: a relative or friend who defends a case on behalf of a person under a disability named as a defendant or third party. In the Family Division, a guardian ad litem is also the name for the independent social worker who represents the interests of the child in difficult cases.

Guarantor: Person who pledges collateral for another's contract.

Hearing: the trial of a case or preliminary issue in court.

Hearsay evidence: Evidence of a statement someone made which is presented in court in some other way than by their direct spoken evidence or affidavit. A previous written statement or a description by someone else of what that person told them would both be hearsay. Hearsay evidence is usually, but not always allowed, but it may have less weight than a statement given by someone in court whose evidence can be tested by cross-examination. Hearsay evidence is normally only admissible in court proceedings to show that a statement was made, not to prove the truth of the contents of the statement.

High Court: Court above the Circuit Court with full jurisdiction to decide all matters of law and fact. High Court judges - male and female - should be addressed as "Judge".

Incorporeal: Intangible legal rights, such as copyrights or patents.

Incorporeal hereditament: Intangible property rights which may be inherited, such as easements and profits à prendre.

Injunction: Court order that forbids a party to do something (prohibitory injunction) or compels him to do something (mandatory injunction). It may be enforced by committal to prison for contempt.

Insolvent: Person not able to pay his debts as they become due. Insolvency is a prerequisite for bankruptcy.

Inter alia: (Latin: among other things) Used to precede a list of examples covered by a more general descriptive statement.

Interim order: Temporary court order of very limited duration, usually until the court has heard the full facts of a case.

Interlineation: Addition to a document after it has been signed. Such additions are disregarded unless they are initialled by the signatories and, if necessary, witnessed.

Interlocutory application: a procedural matter which has to be decided by a judge (usually a Master) before the final decision can be made in a case. For example, a challenge to one party's refusal to give discovery, or an application for substituted service are interlocutory applications.

Interlocutory injunction: An injunction which lasts only until the end of the trial during which the order was sought, when it may be replaced by a permanent injunction.

Inter partes: Latin: between the parties.

Inter vivos: (Latin: between living persons) An inter vivos trust is set up to take effect while the settlor is still alive (as opposed to a testamentary trust, which takes effect only on the settlor's death).

Intestate: Person who dies without making a valid will.

Invitation to treat: An offer to receive an offer. Goods advertised by a shopkeeper are open to offers from customers. If goods are mistakenly marked with the wrong price, the retailer is not bound to accept that price because he has not offered the goods at that price: he has invited members of the public to make him an offer which he is entitled to accept or reject. A retailer who deliberately or consistently misprices goods, however, may be committing an offence under the Consumer Information Act.

IOU: A written confirmation of a debt, signed by the debtor, which implies an undertaking to pay the sum owed at some future date. An IOU is not a negotiable instrument and may not be passed on to a third party.

Joint and several liability: Liability of more than one person, under which each may be sued for the entire amount of damages due by all. The obligation may arise by agreement or may be imposed by law.

Joint tenancy: Ownership of property by two or more people with a right of survivorship. If one owner dies, his share passes to the surviving owners so that, eventually, the entire property is held by one person. A valid joint tenancy requires the four unities: unity of interest (each joint tenant must have an identical interest, including equality of duration and extent), unity of title (the interests must arise from the same document), unity of possession (each joint tenant must have an equal right to occupy the entire property) and unity of time (the interests must have arisen at the same time). Married couples and trustees are frequently joint tenants. (Contrast with tenancy-in-common.)

Judgment: the judge's statement of the court order and his or her reasons for making it. A judgment can be spoken or in writing.

Judicial Review: an action taken in the High Court to challenge the decison of some statutory body; a lower Court; or quasi-judicial tribunal. Judicial review is not usually limited to errors in law but may be based on alleged errors on findings of fact or unfair procedures. Judicial review proceedings may not be brought in the area of private law where the disputed decision is a matter of contract or agreement between two sides.

Junior counsel: Barrister who has not "taken silk" or been called to the Inner Bar.

Jurisdiction: Power of a judge or court to act, limited by a defined territory (the jurisdiction of the District Court is restricted to offences committed in that district), by the type of case (the jurisdiction of a criminal court is limited to criminal cases) or to certain persons (a court martial only has jurisdiction over military personnel).

Kin: Relationship by blood.

King's Inns: The body responsible for the training of all barristers in Ireland.

Knock-for-knock: An arrangement between insurance companies whereby each company pays the claim of its own insured, on the basis that neither party will pursue a claim against the other.

Laches: Doctrine whereby those who delay too long in asserting an equitable right lose their entitlement to bring an action.

Landlord: Owner of a building or land who leases the land, building or part thereof, to another person, who is called the tenant or lessee.

Lay litigant: Non-lawyer who brings a legal action without the assistance of a barrister or solicitor.

Lease: Contract between a property owner and another person for temporary use of property, in exchange for rent.

Legal aid: Government scheme providing advice or assistance from a solicitor or barrister free or at a reduced rate.

Legal professional privilege: Confidential communications between a lawyer and client may not be revealed in court unless the client, expressly or impliedly, waives the privilege. The communications must relate to court proceedings or intended litigation.

Liability: Any legal obligation or duty, now or in the future. A person who is liable for a debt or wrongful act is the person responsible for paying the debt or compensating for the wrongful act. If a court finds a person to be contributorily liable, he will bear part of the responsibility for the act or omission.

Licence: Permission to do something on or with someone else's property which, if it were not for the licence, could be legally prevented or could give rise to an action in tort or trespass. A common example is allowing a person to cross the licensor's lands, which would otherwise constitute trespass. Licences, unlike easements, may be revoked at will, unless supported by some form of payment or consideration. Licences which are not based on a contract and which are fully revocable are called simple or bare licences.

Lien: Right to hold property which has been sold, but not finally paid for. It may involve possession of the object until the debt is paid or the lien may be registered against the object (especially land). Ultimately, a lien can be enforced by a court sale of the property to which it is attached, and the debt is paid out of the proceeds of sale.

Life estate: Right of a tenant to use land during his lifetime. The estate reverts to the grantor (or some other person) on the death of the life tenant. A property right which lasts until the life tenant dies is called an estate pur sa vie (French: for his life). If it is for the duration of the life of a third party, it is called an estate pur autre vie (French: for another's life). The life tenant is not allowed permanently to change the land or structures on it.

Life tenant: Beneficiary of a life estate.

Lineal descendant: Direct descendant (for example, the child of his natural parent).

Limitation of actions: The Statute of Limitations sets down times within which proceedings must be brought. If no action is taken within the prescribed time limits, any future action is said to be statute-barred. In negligence claims, where there is no personal injury, the limit is six years. Where there is personal injury, the limit is three years (reduced to one year by the introduction of a bill in 2004). In a fatal injury case, it's three years from the date of death. In a claim involving breach of a simple contract (not under seal), the limit is six years. With personal injury arising from breach of contract, it's three years (or three years from the date of death). With a specialty contract (under seal), the period's 12 years, as it is for actions involving land. The maximum period for recovery of arrears of tax or rent is six years.

Liquidation: Sale of all the assets of a company or partnership by a liquidator and use of the proceeds to pay off creditors. Any money left over is distributed among shareholders or partners according to their interests or rights.

Lis pendens: (Latin: pending action) Registration of a pending action against the owner of land. It does not bind any subsequent purchaser of the land until a memorandum is registered in court

Litigant: a person who is a party in a case.

Locus standi: (Latin: place of standing) Person's right to take an action or be heard by a court.

Lodge documents: send documents to the court office.

Lodgement: payment of money into court which the payer believes is a reasonable figure to settle a case, but which the other party will not accept. If the other party does not "beat the lodgement" by being awarded a higher sum by the judge, they may not have all their costs paid by the losing party and may have to pay the costs of the other party arising after the date of the lodgement.

Mandamus: (Latin: we command) High Court order commanding an individual, organisation, administrative tribunal or court to perform a certain action - usually to correct an earlier illegal action or failure to fulfil some statutory duty.

Master: a statutory civil procedure judge who deals with certain types of cases in the High Court.

Mediation: Form of alternative dispute resolution involving an agreed mediator acting as a facilitator to help the parties negotiate an agreement. The mediator does not adjudicate on the issues or force a compromise; only the parties involved can resolve the dispute. The result of a successful mediation is called a settlement.

McKenzie friend: a person who supports and advises a personal litigant in court, but does not speak on their behalf.

Mens rea: (Latin: guilty mind) Most crimes require proof of guilty intention before a person can be convicted. The prosecution must prove either that the accused knew his action was illegal or that he was reckless or grossly negligent. Some offences (such as drunken driving) are matters of strict liability, which means that the intention or state of mind of the person committing the offence is irrelevant.

Minor: Person under the age of 18 who is not married (or has not been married). A minor may only enter into certain contracts, such as those for necessaries or an apprenticeship. An Irish resident under the age of 18 may not legally marry without the permission of the Court, even if the ceremony takes place somewhere (such as Northern Ireland) where the minimum age for marriage is under 18.

Misfeasance: Improperly doing something which a person has a legal right to do. Contrast with nonfeasance.

Misjoinder: When a person has been wrongly named as a party to a law suit, a court will usually amend the proceedings to strike out the name of the misjoined party and substitute the person who should have been joined.

Misrepresentation: False material statement which induces a party to enter into a contract; grounds for rescission of the contract.

Mitigation: Facts which, while not negating an offence or wrongful action, tend to show that the defendant may have had some excuse for acting the way he did. For example, provocation may constitute mitigating circumstances in an assault action.

Mitigation of damages: A person who sues another for damages has a duty to minimize his loss, as far as reasonable. For example, in a wrongful dismissal suit, the person who was fired should make some effort to find another job, to minimize the economic damage to himself.

Moiety: Half of anything. For example, joint tenants each hold a moiety of the property.

Money in court: money is paid into court when, for example, a party makes a lodgement of a sum they believe is reasonable to settle a case, or where the person to whom damages should be paid is a person under a disability.

Mortgage: An interest given on land, in writing, to guarantee the payment of a debt or the execution of some action. It automatically becomes void when the debt is paid or the action is executed. The person lending the money and receiving the mortgage is called the mortgagee; the person who concedes a mortgage as security upon his property is called a mortgagor. The three types of mortgage are a legal mortgage (involving a transfer of the legal interest in the property), an equitable mortgage (by depositing the title deeds) and a judgment mortgage (following a court judgment).

Natural justice: The requirement for application of the tenets audi alteram partem (hear the other side) and nemo judex in causa sua (no-one may be a judge in his own case). The principles of natural justice were derived from the Romans, who believed that some legal principles were natural or self-evident and did not need a statutory basis.

Natural person: Human being with legal and Constitutional rights and duties, including the right to life, right to information, right to travel, right to a good name, right to earn a living, right to sue and be sued, to sign contracts, to receive gifts and to appear in court either by himself or through a lawyer. Individuals are persons in law unless they are minors or under some other type of incapacity, such as a court finding of mental incapacity. Contrast with a company, which is a legal person.

Negligence: Carelessness. A person who owes a duty of care to someone else and breaches it by lack of reasonable care may be liable in damages for negligence. The negligence may involve a positive deed or a failure to act. If no damage results, there can be no action. The standard of care required is usually that of the reasonable man, but a person who claims to have special skills (such as a surgeon) owes a higher duty of care.

Nemo judex in sua causa: (Latin: nobody may be a judge in his own case) Principle of natural justice. A judge must be seen to be free of bias and may not have any interest - personal, pecuniary or otherwise - in a case he is deciding. Also referred to as nemo debet esse judex in propria causa.

Next friend: a relative or friend who brings a case on behalf of a person under a disability.

Next of kin: Person's nearest blood relation. The expression has come to describe those persons most closely related to a dead person and therefore due to inherit his property if there is no will.

Non est factum: (Latin: not his deed) Defence in contract law which allows a person to avoid liability because he was mistaken about the nature of the contract. For example, a person who signs away the deed to a house, thinking that the document was only a guarantee for a debt, might be able to plead non est factum. Failure to read the terms of a contract will negate this defence.

Nonfeasance: Not doing something that one is bound to do by law. Compare with misfeasance.

Non-joinder: If a person who should have been a party to legal proceedings has been omitted, the court may amend the pleadings to include the non-joined party.

Notice Party: someone who is not a party but who the court decides has a proper interest in the proceedings and should be notified about the hearing so that they can ask the judge's permission to participate.

Novation: Substitution of a new contractual debt for an old debt by agreement between the debtor, the creditor and a third party who takes on responsibility for the original debt.

Nuisance: Substantial unlawful use of one's property or interference with another's property to the extent of unreasonable annoyance or inconvenience to a neighbour or to the public. Private nuisance might be caused by smells, noise, smoke, dust, fumes, vermin, obstruction or a wide range of other activities or inactivity. The remedies would include abatement (an order to cease the nuisance), damages and/or an injunction.

Obiter dicta: (Latin: sayings by the way) Observations by a judge on law or facts not specifically before the court or not necessary to decide an issue. An opinion which does not form part of the judgment for the purposes of stare decisis. Such opinions are not binding in future cases.

Offer: Definite proposal to contract which, if accepted, completes the contract and binds both the person that made the offer and the person accepting the offer to the terms of the contract. The offer may be express or implied. The person making the offer is called the offeror, and the person to whom the offer is made is the offeree.

Order: Formal written direction by a judge. Once a final order is made, it may only be amended if there has been an accidental slip in the judgment.

Originating motion: A document which starts some kinds of High Court cases

Originating summons: a document which starts some kinds of High Court cases.

Out-of-court settlement: Agreement between two litigants to settle a matter privately before a court has heard the matter or given its decision. Most personal injuries cases settle before reaching court.

Pari passu: (Latin: with equal step) Often used in bankruptcy proceedings where creditors are said to rank pari passu, which means the assets are distributed without preference between them.

Partition: Division of jointly-owned land or property between the respective owners.

Partnership: Two or more persons carrying on a business together. Partners are each fully liable for all the debts of the enterprise but they also share the profits exclusively. Their rights are regulated by their partnership agreement.

Party: the plaintiff, defendant or third or other party in a court case.

Patent: Exclusive privilege granted to an inventor to make, use or sell an invention for a period of years. A renewal fee must be paid every year.

Payee: Person to whom a bill of exchange is made payable. On an ordinary cheque, the name preceded by the words "pay to the order of" identifies the payee.

Payor: Person who makes a payment on a cheque or bill of exchange.

Perjury: Deliberate lie under oath or in a sworn affidavit.

Perpetuity: Forever, of unlimited duration. The law leans against against agreements that are to last in perpetuity because they may hinder commerce by impeding the circulation of property. The rule against perpetuities says that a limitation of any interest in land is void if it can vest outside the perpetuity period, which is a life plus 21 years. For example, if a will proposes the transfer of an estate at some uncertain future date, which is either more than 21 years after the death of the testator or more than 21 years after the life of a person identified in the will, the transfer is void.

Personal litigant (or la litigant): a person who is a party in a case and does not have a lawyer.

Personal representative: Person who administers the estate of a deceased person. Where a person dies without a will, the court appoints an administrator. A personal representative named in a will is called an executor.

Person under a disability: a person under 18 years old or a person with mental incapacity, who cannot be a party in a court case without the help of a next friend or guardian ad litem.

Petition: the document which starts a divorce or civil partnership dissolution case, and some other kinds of cases.

Petition: Formal, written submission to court, seeking redress of an injustice. Petitions set out the facts, identify the law under which the court is being asked to intervene, and end with a requested course of action for the court to consider (such as payment of damages). Petitions are normally used to institute proceedings in the areas of bankruptcy, patents, professional disciplinary bodies and family law matters.

Picket: Peaceful public demonstration, on or near an employer's premises, in furtherance of an existing or proposed trade dispute. Picketers may not threaten, insult or abuse other workers.

Plaintiff: Person who brings a case to court. (Also called the petitioner or applicant.) The person being sued is generally called the defendant or respondent.

Pleadings: Written allegations or claims delivered by one claimant to another which formally set out the facts and legal arguments supporting his position. High Court pleadings might include an originating summons, statement of claim, defence, counterclaim and reply - or a petition and answer.

Power of attorney: Document under seal which gives a person the right to make binding decisions for another, as an agent. A power of attorney may be specific to a certain kind of decision or general, in which the agent makes all major decisions for the subject of the power of attorney.

Pre-action Protocol: a court document setting out the steps the court expects the parties to take before a court case is started.

Precatory words: Words that express a wish, hope or desire rather than a clear command. Precatory words in trusts or wills can cause problems when the courts have to decide the real intention of the settlor or testator. If a gift is given, with the addition of precatory words, the courts tend to construe the words as expressing the reason for the gift, rather than a restriction on its use or the establishment of a trust.

Precedent: Court judgment which is cited as an authority in a later case involving similar facts. Precedent cannot bind a higher court (for example, a Circuit Court decision cannot bind a High Court judge). A Supreme Court judgment binds all courts - although it does not bind the Supreme Court itself in future cases. The system of precedent forms the basis of the policy of stare decisis which helps litigants to predict the outcome of a case in a given situation.

Preference shares: Shares in a company that have some kind of special right or privilege over other shares. The most common special right is a preference over holders of ordinary shares when dividends are declared. Dividends on preference shares are presumed to be cumulative, in the absence of any agreement to the contrary, so unpaid dividends are payable before any ordinary dividends.

Prescription: Way of acquiring property rights, such as an easement, by long and continued use or enjoyment. The required period of continued use or enjoyment, before legal rights are enforceable, is set out in the 1832 Prescription Act.

Prima facie: (Latin: at first sight) A prima facie case is one which, at first sight, seems to support the allegation or claim made. If a prima facie case is not made out in the early stages of proceedings, the other side may apply to the court to dismiss the action without hearing the rest of the evidence.

Principal: Person from whom an agent has received instructions and for whose benefit the agent acts and makes decisions. The principal has a duty to pay the agent any agreed sum or commission, and to indemnify him against any losses in the course of his agency.

Private law: Domestic law which regulates the relationships between individuals and in which the State is not directly concerned. Family, commercial and labour law are examples of private law because their focus is the relationships between individuals or between corporations or organisations and individuals.

Privilege: Special legal right such as a benefit, exemption, power or immunity. One example is the right of the media to publish contemporaneous reports of court proceedings without fear of an action for defamation, even if the matters published would ordinarily constitute libel. Also, the rules of law which protect a document, recording or other information from being disclosed to the other party to proceedings, for example because it is correspondence between a lawyer and his client.

Pro rata: (Latin: in proportion) Division proportionate to a certain rate or interest. For example, if a company with two shareholders, one with 25% and the other with 75% of the shares, declared a dividend of €1,000 to be split pro rata between the shareholders, the one with 25% of the shares would receive €250 and the other €750.

Probate law: That part of the law which regulates wills and other subjects related to the distribution of a deceased person's estate.

Proceedings: a shorthand term for all the court procedures and documents before the final court order.

Process server: a professional who serves documents.

Profit à prendre: (French: profit to be taken) Right which allows the holder to enter the land of another and to take some natural produce, such as fish, game, timber, sand, crops or pasture.

Prohibition: Legal restriction on the use of something or on certain conduct.

Promissory note: Unconditional, written and signed promise to pay a certain amount of money on demand or at a certain defined date in the future. Unlike a bill of exchange, a promissory note is a promise - rather than an order - to pay.

Proof on the balance of probabilities: the standard of proof in a civil case – "more likely than not", or more than 50% likely.

Proof beyond reasonable doubt: the standard of proof in a criminal case – not proof beyond the shadow of a doubt, but leaving the judge or jury without the sort of doubt that would affect their decisions in their ordinary life.

Property: Property is commonly thought of as something which belongs to a person and over which he has total control. But it is more correctly defined as a collection of legal rights over a thing. These rights are usually enforceable by the owner or the State against others. The most common classifications of property are between real or immovable property (such as land or buildings) and chattels or personal property (such as stock or a leasehold), and between public property (belonging to everybody or to the State) and private property.

Prospectus: Document or notice in which a company sets out details of a proposed share or bond issue, inviting the public to invest by purchasing the financial instruments. It must specify the nominal capital of the company, the names, addresses and descriptions of the directors, when the subscription lists open, the amount payable on application and on allotment of shares, and the rights in respect of different classes of share.

Proxy: Agent who votes on behalf of another. Any shareholder who is entitled to vote at a meeting of a company is entitled to appoint a proxy to vote in his place. The member may direct the proxy which way to vote.

Punitive damages: Special, exceptional damages ordered by a court where an act or omission was of a particularly serious, extensive or malicious nature. (Normally damages are awarded to compensate, not to punish.) Also known as exemplary damages.

Real property: Immovable property such as land, buildings or an object that, though at one time a chattel, has become permanently affixed to land or a building.

Rebuttable presumption: Presumed fact based on the proof of other facts. Most presumptions are rebuttable, which means that the person against whom the presumption applies may present evidence to the contrary, thus nullifying the presumption. If a person has not been heard of for seven years by people who should have seen him, he may be presumed dead - but this presumption is rebutted if he turns up!

Redemption: Repayment of a mortgage, so the equitable estate of the lender and the legal estate of the borrower merge in the mortgagor.

Rent: Money or other consideration paid by a tenant to a landlord in exchange for the exclusive possession and use of land, buildings or part of a building. Under normal circumstances, rent is paid at regular agreed intervals, but it may be paid in kind or by the provision of services. A peppercorn rent is a nominal sum (perhaps a penny a year) as an acknowledgement of the tenancy.

Replevin: Legal action to recover goods which have been distrained. The applicant must give an undertaking to keep the goods safe, to continue with his court action and to return the goods if ordered to do so.

Replies: As well as its usual meaning, this is a technical legal term for the pleading in which a defendant to a case in the Queen's Bench Division replies to the Statement of Claim.

Res ipsa loquitur: (Latin: the thing speaks for itself) Situation where negligence is presumed against the defendant since the object causing injury was under his control. This is a presumption which can be rebutted by showing that the accident was inevitable and had nothing to do with the defendant's control or supervision. An example of res ipsa loquitur might be where a motorist hits a stray cow. The event itself imputes negligence by the farmer and that presumption may only be defeated if the defendant proves that the land was properly fenced.

Rebuttal: evidence, or a pleading, which tries to show that the other party's evidence and arguments are not accurate.

Rejoinder: the pleading in which the plaintiff to a case in the Queen's Bench Division replies to the defendant's Replies.

Rescission: Abrogation or cancellation of a contract, putting the parties in the same position they would have been in, had there been no contract. Rescission can occur because of some defect in the formation of the contract (such as misrepresentation, duress or undue influence) or by agreement of the parties - for example where they reach a new agreement.

Reserved costs: Apportionment of payment of legal fees to be decided at a later stage.

Reserved judgment: Decision to be given at a later date.

Residence: Place where someone usually - but not necessarily permanently - lives.

Respondent: Person against whom a summons is issued, or a petition or appeal brought.

Resulting trust: Trust which comes into being when an express trust fails. It is similar to a constructive trust but the court will presume an intention to create a trust. The court will assume that the possessor of property is only holding it in trust for the rightful owner. (In constructive trusts, the courts do not presume any intention to create a trust.)

Reversion: Future interest in property retained by a transferor or his heirs (for example, the interest left when the owner of a fee simple grants a life estate in the property).

Review hearing – a hearing at which a judge / master / registrar will ensure that the case is proceeding as efficiently and proactively as it should, and will help the parties define what work still needs to be done.

Right of audience – the right to speak in a particular court.

Riparian rights: Rights of owners of land on a river bank. Riparian rights include the right of access to, and use of, the water for domestic purposes (bathing, cleaning and navigating). The owner of the rights may take action to prevent damming, diversion or pollution of the water.

Sanction: To ratify, to approve or to punish.

Scienter: (Latin: knowledge) Common law rule that the owner of a vicious dog must keep it secure. A person bitten by such an animal may bring an action, even if the dog has never bitten anyone before.

Search warrant: Written order (normally issued by a judge or peace commissioner) giving gardai permission to enter private property, to search for and seize evidence of the commission of a crime, the proceeds of crime or property that they suspect may be used to commit a crime.

Senior counsel: Barrister who has "taken silk" or been called to the Inner Bar.

Sequestration: Temporary confiscation of property by court order until the owner purges his contempt by obeying an earlier court order.

Serve – court documents are served when they are sent to a person or company in a way required by court rules, so that it can be proved to the judge that the person to whom they are addressed actually received them.

Service: Delivery of court documents by one party to the other, personally or by post.

Servient tenement: Land subject to an easement. The beneficiary of the easement is called the dominant tenement.

Set off: a claim by a defendant that the person who sued them owes them an amount of money which should be "set off" against the sum the person is suing them for.

Setting down: telling the court office a case is ready for hearing.

Settlement: A solution to a case agreed by the parties before the hearing, usually involving the payment of damages.

Settlor: Person who creates a trust by donating property to be administered by a trustee.

Share: A portion of a company. A share certificate constitutes proof of share ownership. Those owning shares in a company are called members or shareholders. There are two basic kinds of shares: ordinary and preferred. A shareholder is not normally liable for the debts or other obligations of the company, except to the extent of any commitment made to buy shares. Two other benefits of shares include a right to participate in profits (through dividends) and a right to share the residue of assets of the company if it is dissolved, once liabilities have been paid off.

Silent partner: Person who invests in a company or partnership, shares in the profits or losses but takes no part in administering or directing the organisation.

Skeleton argument: a summary of the arguments a party will make before the Court.

Slander of title: Falsely and maliciously denying someone's title to property including real property, a business or goods (the latter might also be called "slander of goods"). The tort is only actionable if damage has been suffered.

Solicitor: a lawyer who has an office and meets directly with the public. Some solicitors are trained as solicitor-advocates and have the right to speak in the High Court.

Special Criminal Court: Non-jury court with three judges, set up to deal with mainly terrorist offences. To be abolished by Court of Appeal.

Statement of claim: the pleading in which the person bringing a claim in the Queen's Bench Division sets out in detailed summary the claim they are making

Stay of enforcement: part of a court order which stops it coming into effect as long as a condition (such as making regular payments of a debt) continues to be met.

Strict liability: Liability in tort without need to prove wrongful intent, negligence or fault.

Sub judice: (Latin: under trial) Matter still under consideration by a court. Any action which may interfere with the proper administration of justice while a matter is sub judice may be a contempt of court.

Submissions: the speeches that lawyers or personal litigants make to the court.

Subpoena: an order from the court requiring a person to attend for a case, either as a witness or in order to bring a specific document to court.

Subrogation: Substitution of one person or thing for another by operation of law, without the agreement of the person from whom the rights are transferred.

Substituted service: If a party appears to be avoiding service of legal documents, the court may be asked to direct that, instead of personal service (that is giving the documents directly to the person), they should be served in a different way, perhaps by posting them to the defendant's home or office or leaving them with a member of his family.

Successor: Person who takes over the rights or property of another.

Sui juris: (Latin: of his own right) Person who has full legal rights and is not under any incapacity, such as being bankrupt, a minor or mentally incapable.

Summons: Written command to a person to appear in court.

Supreme Court: Final court of appeal in Ireland, headed by the Chief Justice. Most appeals are on matters of law or procedure. The Supreme Court will not normally reverse a finding of fact by a lower court, unless the decision was so perverse that no ordinary person could have come to such a finding on the facts.

Surety: Person who has pledged himself by deed to ensure that another person fulfils an obligation - such as appearing in court or paying back a loan.

Tenant: Person to whom a landlord grants temporary and exclusive use of land or a building, usually in exchange for rent. The contract for this type of legal arrangement is called a lease.

Tenancy in common: Tenants-in-common share property rights, but may hold different parts of a piece of land, or unequal shares. On the death of either of them, that person's share does not pass automatically to the surviving tenant but becomes part of the deceased's estate.

Tender: Unconditional offer of a party to a contract to perform his side of the bargain. For example, with a loan contract, a tender would be the debtor's offer to repay the amount owing to the creditor. If the tender is refused, the contract comes to an end.

Tenement: Property that could be subject to common law tenure, such as land, buildings or apartments. In relation to business tenants, a tenement is a defined portion of a building held by the occupier on a tenancy and not dependent on the continued employment of the tenant.

Tenure: Right to hold or occupy land or a position for a certain amount of time.

Testator: Person who dies after making a valid will.

Testimony: Verbal presentation of evidence in court.

Tort: Non-contractual breach of duty which allows the injured person to claim compensation (or damages) from the tortfeasor. Torts include wrongs such as negligence, nuisance, defamation, false imprisonment and trespass.

Tortfeasor: Person who commits a tort.

Tracing: Equitable right of a plaintiff to reclaim specific property, through the court, where the property has passed on to others. This procedure is frequently used by a trust beneficiary to recover misappropriated trust property. Property may not be recovered from a person who has bought it for value, without notice of the circumstances.

Transferee: Person who receives property being transferred.

Transferor: Person who transfers property.

Trespass: Unlawful interference with another person or his property or rights. Trespass is a civil, not a criminal, offence and is actionable without proof of any actual damage. Section 13 of the Criminal Justice

(Public Order) Act 1994 makes it an offence to trespass on any building or its curtilage in a way which may make another person afraid.

Trust: Property given by a donor or settlor to a trustee, for the benefit of another person (the beneficiary or donee). A trustee manages and administers the property. A will is a form of trust but a trust can be formed during the lifetime of the settlor, in which case it is called an inter vivos or living trust.

Trustee: Person who holds property rights for the benefit of another through the legal mechanism of the trust. A trustee usually has full management and administration rights over the property, which must be exercised to the advantage of the beneficiary. All profits from the trust go to the beneficiary, although the trustee is entitled to recover administrative costs.

Undertaking: Enforceable promise given to court.

Undue influence: Unfair pressure which may invalidate a contract.

Unjust enrichment: Profit unjustly obtain by a wrongdoer. To obtain reimbursement, the plaintiff must show an actual benefit to the defendant, a corresponding loss to the plaintiff and the absence of a legal reason for the defendant's enrichment.

Usury: Excessive or illegal interest rate.

Variation: Alteration of term of court order.

Verdict: Decision of a jury. In criminal cases, this is usually expressed as guilty or not guilty and may be unanimous or by a majority of 11-1 or 10-2. In a civil case, the verdict would be a finding for the plaintiff or for the defendant by at least nine of the 12 jurors.

Vicarious liability: Responsibility for the tort of another, even though the person held responsible may not have done anything wrong. This is often the case with employers who may be held vicariously liable for damage caused by their employees.

Void: Without legal effect. A document that is void is worthless. An anti-competitive agreement or contract in restraint of trade may be void. A "marriage" involving a person under the age of 18 would be void in Ireland.

Voidable: The law distinguishes between void and voidable contracts. Some contracts have such a fundamental defect that they are said to be void. Others have more minor defects and are voidable at the option of the innocent party.

Voire dire: (French: To speak the truth) Separate trial within a trial, generally in the absence of the jury, on the admissibility of contested evidence.

Waiver: Renunciation of a right or benefit. Waivers are not always in writing. Sometimes actions can be interpreted as a waiver.

Waste: Abuse, destruction or permanent change to property by a person who is merely in possession of it, such as a tenant or a life tenant.

Words of limitation: Words in a conveyance or will which limit the duration of an estate. If a testator leaves property "to X and his heirs", the words "and his heirs" are words of limitation because they indicate that X gets the land in fee simple and his heirs get no interest.

Words of purchase: Words in a conveyance or will which specifically name the person to whom land is being conveyed.

Witness: someone who has personally seen, heard, or otherwise experienced the events which the case is about, such as someone who saw a car crash. A witness can only report what they saw, heard or experienced and the inferences they draw from those facts. They cannot give evidence of their opinion.

Writ: A document which starts a case.

Year: When used without any other qualification, a 12-month period beginning on January 1.

Young person: Person under 16, whose regular, full-time employment is forbidden by the 1996 Protection of Young Persons (Employment) Act. A child over 14 may do light work during school holidays, but a child under 14 cannot be employed at all.

Zero hours: If an employee is available for work but there is no work for him to do, the zero hours provision of the Organisation of Working Time Act 1997 requires the employer to compensate him for one quarter of the time for which he had to be available.

Explanation of Latin Legal Terms

A fortiori: Even more so; with all the more force.

Ab Absurdo: an evidentiary suggestion or statutory interpretation that is, or leads to, an absurdity.

Aberratio Ictus: the accidental harm to a person; perpetrator aims at X but by chance or lack of skill hits Y.

Ab Initio: from the start; from the beginning.

Accusare Nemo Se Debet Nisi Coram Deo: no man is obliged to accusehimself except before God.

Acta Exteriora Indicant Interiora Secreta: The outward acts show the secret intentions.

Actio Personalis Moritur Cum Persona: any right of action dies with the person.

Actus Curiae Neminem Gravabit: An act of the court shall prejudice no one.

Actus Dei Nemini Facit Injuriam: An act of God causes legal injury to no one.

Actus Regis Nemini Est Damnosa: The law will not work a wrong.

Actus Reus: a prohibited act.

Actus Reus Non Facit Reum Nisi Mens Sit Rea: conviction of a crime requires proof of a criminal act and intent.

Ad Colligendum Bona: for the collection of the goods of the deceased.

Ad Damnum: to the damage.

Ad Hoc: limited in time; to this point.

Ad Infinitum: forever; without limit; indefinitely.

Ad Litem: for the suit.

Ad Proximum Antecedens Fiat Relatio Nisi Impediatur Sententia: relative words must ordinarily be referred to the last antecedent, the last antecedent being the last word which can be made an antecedent so as to give a meaning.

Ad Quaestionem Facti Non Respondent Judices, Ad Quaestionem Juris Non Respondent Juratores: The judge instructs on points of law and the jury decides matters of fact.

Aequum et bonum: what is right and just..

Agnatio: members of a group having a common male ancestor.

Alea jacta est: the die is cast.

Alia Enormia: The catch-all phrase in trespass pleadings to refer to all such other harms and damages that may have been caused by the alleged trespasser other than those specified.

Alibi: A defence to a criminal charge to the effect that the accused was elsewhere than at the scene of the alleged crime.

Alieni juris: under the legal authority of another.

Aliunde: otherwise.

Amicus Curiae: friend of the court.

Animus: intention.

Animus Contrahendi: an intention to contract.

Animus Furandi: an intent to do wrong.

Argumentum Ab Inconvenienti Plurimum Valet In Lege: An argument drawn from inconvenience is forcible in law.

Audi Alteram Partem: literally 'hear the other side'. A principle of natural justice which requires that, where a decision may affect an individual's rights, that person has a right to be heard. It includes the right to receive notice of a hearing and to be legally represented.

Audita Querela: An application to a court after judgment seeking to avoid execution of that judgment because of some event intervening between judgment and execution which compromises the judgment creditor's entitlement to execution.

A Vinculo Matrimonii: of marriage.

Avunculus: a mother's brother.

Bona Fide: good faith.

Bona Vacantia: Property that belongs to no person, and which may be claimed by a finder.

Boni Judicis Est Ampliare Jurisdictionem: good justice is broad jurisdiction.

Bonus pater familias: the good family man.

Casus Foederis: treaty event.

Causa Causans: The real, effective cause of damage.

Causa Proxima Et Non Remota Spectatur: the immediate, not the remote cause, is to be considered.

Causa Sine Qua Non: An intervening cause of loss which, though not direct, may nonetheless contribute to the loss.

Caveat: let him beware. A formal warning.

Caveat Emptor: buyer beware.

Certiorari: A formal request to a court challenging a legal decision of an administrative tribunal, judicial office or organization (eg. government) alleging that the decision has been irregular or incomplete or if there has been an error of law.

Cessante Ratione Legis, Cessat Ipsa Lex: The reason for a law ceasing, the law itself ceases.

Cestui Que Trust or Cestui Que Use: the beneficiary of a trust.

Ceteris Paribus: all things being equal or unchanged.

Comitatus: a contract of personal services between a land lord and his men.

Commodum Ex Injuria Sua Nemo Habere Debet: a wrongdoer should not be enabled by law to take any advantage from his actions.

Commorientes: Two or more persons dying at about the same time, usually in the same event, but in circumstances in which it is impossible to determine the order of death.

Communis Error Facit Jus: Common error makes right.

Consensus: A decision achieved through negotiation whereby a hybrid resolution is arrived on an issue, dispute or disagreement, comprising typically of concessions made by all parties, and to which all parties then subscribe unanimously as an acceptable resolution.

Consensus Ad Idem: a meeting of the minds.

Consensus Tollit Errorem: Consent obviates errors in the course of judicial proceedings.

Consortium: Companionship, love and affection and intimacy between husband and wife within a mariage.

Consuetudo Volentes Ducit, Lex Nolentes Trahit: Customs leads the willing, law drags the unwilling.

Contemporanea Expositio: That the meaning of words in a document are to be understood in the sense which they bore at the time of the document.

Corpus Delicti: the body of the offense.

Crimen Omnia Ex Se Nata Vitiat: property obtained by crime is tainted (vitiated).

Cuicunque Aliquis Quid Concedit Concedere Videtur Et Id Sine Quo Res Ipsa Esse Non Poluit: Whoever grants a thing is supposed also tacitly to grant that without which the grant itself would be of no effect.

Cuius Est Solum Ejus Est Usque Ad Caelum: whose is the soil, his it is even to the skies and to the depths below.

Cuius Est Solum Ejus Est Usque Ad Coelum Et Ad Inferos: for whoever owns the soil, it is theirs up to heaven and down to hell.

Cujus Est Commodum Ejus Debet Esse Incommodum: Whose is the advantage, his also should be the disadvantage.

Culpa Lata: gross negligence.

Cursus Curiae Est Lex Curiae: The practice of the court is the law of the court.

Custodia Legis: In the custody of the law; the taking, seizing or holding of something by lawful authority.

Damnum Absque Injuria: harm absent a wrong.

Damnum Injuria Datum: wrongful injury to the property of another.

De Bene Esse: To take something for what it is worth, such as evidence collected for the time being, in the absence of, but in anticipation of, litigation, admissibility to be determined when such thing is sought to be used against another at trial.

De Bonis Non: assets not yet administered.

Decree Nisi: A provisional decision of a court which does not have force or effect until a certain condition is met such as another petition brought before the court or after the passage of a period time.

Dedimus Potestatem de Attornato Faciendo: to substitute an attorney.

De Facto: in fact.

De Fide et Officio Judicis non Recipitur Quaestio, sed de Scientia Sive sit Eror Juris sive Facti: The bona fides and honesty of purpose of a judge cannot be questioned, but his decision may be impugned for error of law or of fact.

De injuria sua propria absque tali causa: of his own wrong (or injury) without any other cause.

De Jure: of the law.

Delegatus Non Potest Delegare: a delegate cannot delegate.

Delict: A civil law term which imposes liability on a person who causes injury to another, or for injury caused by a person or thing under his custody.

De Minimis Non Curat Lex: the law does not concern itself with trifles. A common law principle whereby very minor transgressions of the law are disregarded. Under the Consumer Information Act 1978, for example, a description must be false "to a material degree" to constitute an offence.

De Non Apparentibus Et De Non Existentibus Eadem Est Ratio: What is not juridically presented cannot be judicially decided.

De Non Sane Memorie: of insane memory.

De Novo: new.

Dicta or Dictum: saying.

Dies Dominicus Non Est Juridicus: Sunday is not a day for judicial or legal proceedings.

Divorce a Mensa et Thoro: An obselete form of divorce order which did not end the marriage but allowed the parties to reside separate; in effect, a legal or judicially-sanctioned separation of two married persons.

Dolus Eventualis: Awareness of the likely outcome of an action.

Dominion Utile: the property rights of a tenant; exclusive right to use a thing

Dominium Directum: qualified ownership of a land: not having possession or use of property but retaining ownership.

Domitae Naturae: Animals which are of a nature easily tamed and may be readily domesticated.

Domus Sua Cuique Est Tutissimum Refugium: Every man's house is his refuge.

Donatio Mortis Causa: gift due to death. Gift made by a dying person with the intent that the person receiving the gift shall keep it if the donor dies from his existing complaint. Such a gift is excluded from the estate of the deceased, as the property is automatically conveyed on the donor's death.

Duces Tecum: bring with you.

Dum Casta: for so long as she remains chaste.

Dum Sola: for so long as she remains unmarried.

Dum Sola et Casta Vixerit: for so long as she remains single (unmarried) and chaste.

Dum Vidua: for so long as she remains a widow.

Ejusdem or Eiusdem Generis: of the same kind or nature.

Emptio or Emtio: for 'purchase' or referring to the contract in which something is bought.

En banc: (French) As a full bench.

Error In Objecto: A mistake by a perpetrator as to the identity of the victim; an error as to the object of his act.

Erunt animae duae in carne una: two souls in one flesh.

Et. al.: and others.

Et Impotentia Excusat Legem: The law excuses someone from doing the impossible.

Ex Aequo Et Bono: in justice and fairness.

Exceptio Non Adimpleti Contractus: exception of a non-performed contract.

Ex Debito Justitiae: as of right.

Executio Juris Non Habet Injuriam: The execution of the law does no injury.

Ex Juris: outside of the jurisdiction.

Ex officio: by virtue of office.

Exordium: introduction.

Ex Parte: outside the awareness of a party; for one party only.

Ex Patriate: A person who has abandoned his or her country of origin and citizenship and has become a subject or citizen of another country.

Ex Post Facto: after the fact.

Expressio Unius Est Exclusio Alterius: the expression of one thing is the exclusion of the other.

Ex Rel: on the relation of, or the information of.

Ex Turpi Causa Non Oritur Actio: Of an illegal cause there can be no lawsuit.

Falsa Demonstratio Non Nacet: A wrong description of an item in a legal document (such as a will) will not necessarily void the gift if it can be determined from other facts.

Fiat Justitia Ruat Caelum: do justice though the heavens fall.

Fieri Facias: that you cause to be made. Mostly used to refer to a writ of judgment enforcement obtained under the old common law of England.

Functus Officio: an officer or agency whose mandate has expired either because of the arrival of an expiry date or because an agency has accomplished the purpose for which it was created.

Furiosi Nulla Voluntas Est: mentally impaired persons cannot validly sign a commit their will.

Furtum: theft or a thing stolen..

Habeas Corpus: a court petition which orders that a person being detained be produced before a judge for a hearing to decide whether the detention is lawful.

Hereditas: the estate of a deceased person.

Hereditas Damnosa: an inheritance that is more of a burden than a benefit.

Hereditas Jacens: an unclaimed estate.

Hostis Humani Generis: the enemy of mankind.

Ignorantia Juris Non Excusat: ignorance of the law is no excuse.

In Absentia: in the absence of.

In Camera: A closed and private session of Court or some other deliberating body.

In Fictione Juris Semper Aequitas Existit: With legal fictions, equity always exists.

In haec verba: verbatim.

In Jure Non Remota Causa Sed Proxima Spectatur: In law the near cause is looked to, not the remote one.

In Limine: at the beginning or on the threshold.

In Loco Parentis: A person who, though not the natural parent, has acted as a parent to a child and may thus be liable to legal obligations as if he/she were a natural parent.

In Pari Delicto: If two parties are equally to blame for a situation (such as both failing to comply with the terms of a contract), a court could refuse to provide a remedy to either of them because they are in pari delicto.

In Personam: All legal rights are either 'in personam' or 'in rem'. An in personam right attaches to a particular person; regarding a person; a right, action, judgment or entitlement that is attached to a specific person(s).

In Rem: against the thing. In rem rights relate to property and are not based on any personal relationship.

Inter Alia: 'among other things', 'for example' or 'including'.

Interest Reipublicae Ut Sit Finis Litium: in the interest of society as a whole, litigation must come to an end.

Inter Partes: between, among parties.

Interpretatio Cessat in Claris: Interpretation stops when a text is clear.

In Terrorem: in terror, fright, threat or warning.

Inter Se: as between or amongst themselves.

Inter Vivos: from one living person to another living person.

In tota fine erga omnes et omnia: for all purposes, in regards to all and everything.

In Toto: in total.

Intuitu Personae: Because of the person.

Ipso facto: By the act itself.

Ipso jure: by operation of law.

J. D: Abbreviation for juris doctor or doctor of jurisprudence and the formal name given to the university law degree in the United States.

Judex: A form of judge in early Roman law.

Jura Regalia: Rights which belong to the Crown or to the Government.

Jurat: The written certification by a judicial officer that a deponent or affiant recognizes and endorses all parts of an affidavit he or she proposes to sign, and confirms that an oath has been administered in this regard to the affiant.

Jure: by right, under legal authority.

Jure Coronae: A right of the Crown.

Juris Utriusque Doctor: a combined law degree, in both civil and canon law.

Jus: the law or a legal right.

Jus Ad Bellum: the legal authority to wage war.

Jus Cogens: peremptory law.

Jus Detractus: The right to deduct.

Jus Disponendi: The right to dispose of a thing.

Jus Dispositivum: Law adopted by consent.

Jus Ex Injuria Non Oritur: a legal right or entitlement cannot arise from an unlawful act or omission.

Jus Publicum: legal rights enjoyed by all citizens; more recently used in reference to the right of the public to access shorelines for fishing, boating, swimming, water skiing and other related purposes.

Jus Spatiandi Et Manendi: the right to stray and remain.

Justiciar: An obsolete judicial position of English nobility; that of chief justice of the realm.

Jus Vitae Necisque: Power of life and death.

Leges Posteriores Priores Contrarias Abrogant: Later laws abrogate prior contrary laws.

Lex Causae: law of the cause.

Lex Fori: for the law of the forum.

Lex Loci Contractus: the law of the place where the contract is made.

Lex Loci Delecti: the place of the wrong.

Lex Non Cogit Ad Impossibilia: The law does not compel a man to do that which is impossible.

Lex Non Scripta: Unwritten law; the common or custom law.

Lex non scripta, diuturni mores consensus utensium comprobati: Law derived from custom must be firmly entrenched in practice and adopted and followed by tradition.

Lex Scripta: Written law; statutes.

Lex Situs: A conflict of law rule that selects the applicable law based on the venue or location of something.

Lis Pendens: a dispute or matter which is the subject of ongoing or pending litigation.

Locus: the place; venue.

Locus Regit Actum: The law of the place where the facts occurred.

Locus Standi: legal standing before a court.

Lubricum Linquae Non Facile Trahendum Est In Poena: the law tends to overlook rash or inconsiderate language spoken in the heat of the moment.

Mala Fides: bad faith.

Malum in se: something wrong in itself.

Malum prohibitum: wrong because prohibited.

Mandamus: A writ which commands an individual, organization (eg. government), administrative tribunal or court to perform a certain action, usually to correct a prior illegal action or a failure to act in the first place.

Mansuetae Naturae: animals which are now generally domestic, presumed gentle and readily tamed, such as dogs, cats, cows and horses.

Mea Culpa: I am guilty.

Melius Est Petere Fontes Quam Sectari Rivulos: it is better to seek the sources than to follow the tributaries.

Mens Rea: for guilty mind; guilty knowledge or intention to commit a prohibited act.

Mobilia Sequuntur Personam, Immobilia Situa: movables follow the person, immovables their locality.

Modus Operandi: method of operation.

Mortis Omnia Solvit: Death puts an end to everything.

Mutatis Mutandis: with changes on points of detail.

Necessitas Indicit Privilegium Quoad Jura Privata: From necessity spring privileges upon private rights.

Nemo Debet Bis Vexari Pro Una Et Eadem Causa: No-one shall be tried or punished twice in regards to the same event.

Nemo Debet Locupletari Ex Aliena Jactura: no one should be enriched by another's loss.

Nemo Judex In Parte Sua: no person can judge a case in which he or she is party or in which he/she has an interest.

Nemo Patriam In Qua Natus Est Exuere, Nec Ligeantiae Debitum Ejurare Possit: No one can renounce the country in which he was born nor the bond of allegiance.

Nimia subtilitas in jure reprobatur, et talis certitudo certitudinem Confundit: too much subtlety in law is condemned, and so much certainty confounds certainty.

Nisi Prius: unless, before. More commonly, a civil jury trial.

Nolle Prosequi: no prosecution.

Nolo Contendere: I will not defend.

Non Compos Mentis: Not of sound mind.

Non Est Factum: not his deed.

Non Potest Adduci Exceptio Ejusdem Rei Cujus Petitur Dissolutio: A plea of a matter sought from a court, cannot be contradicted by the same litigant.

Non Potest Rex Gratiam Facere Cum Injuria Et Damno Aliorum: The king cannot confer a favor on one subject which occasions injury and loss to others.

Non Sequitur: it does not follow.

Noscitur a sociis: that the meaning of a word may be known from accompanying words.

Nota Bene: note well.

Nova Constitutio Futuris Formam Imponere Debet, Non Praeteritis: a new law ought to be construed to interfere as little as possible with vested rights.

Nudum Pactum: an empty pact; a contract for which there is no consideration. An agreement without consideration, such as a unilateral undertaking, which may bind a person morally, but not under contract law, unless the agreement is under seal.

Nullum Tempus Occurit Regi: time does not run against the King.

Nunc Pro Tunc: deemed retroactive.

Nuptias non concubitus sed consensus facit: consent, not physical intercourse, constitutes marriage.

Obiter Dictum: an observation by a judge on a matter not specifically before the court or not necessary in determining the issue before the court.

Omne Majus Continet In Se Minus: The greater contains the less.

Omnia praesumuntur contra spoliatorem: All things are presumed against the individual who destroys evidence.

Omnis Innovatio Plus Novitate Perturbat Quam Utilitate Prodest: The disturbance resulting from an innovation is so great an evil as to outweigh any benefit that might arise from it.

Onus: the burden.

Pacta Sunt Servanda: agreements must be kept.

Parens Patriae: literally, father of the country. Refers to the inherent jurisdiction of the courts to make decisions concerning people who are not able to take care of themselves.

Pari Delicto: of equal fault.

Pari Passu: Equitably and without preference.

Pater est quem nuptiae demonstrant: The father is he who is married to the mother.

Patrocinium: A contract under Roman law where a man agrees to be another's servant in exchange for food and shelter.

Peccatum illud horribile: that horrible crime.

Pendente lite: during litigation. If the validity of a will is challenged, a court may appoint an administrator pendente lite with limited powers to preserve the assets of the deceased until a hearing on the validity of the will.

Per Capita: by the head.

Per Curiam: on behalf of the court.

Per Incuriam: through want of care.

Per Infortunium: by misadventure.

Per Quod Consortium Amisit: whereby he loses the company of his wife.

Per Quod Servitium Amisit: (Latin: by which he lost the service) Action for damages by an employer for the loss of services of an injured employee, against the person responsible for the injury.

Per Se: of itself.

Per Stirpes: by the plant or by stocks. Inheriting 'per stirpes' means the division of a deceased's estate among his descendants, with the children of a deceased son or daughter dividing their parent's share equally among themselves.

Pia Causa: charitable purposes.

Piracy Jure Gentium: Piracy according to the law of nations.

Plene Administravit: for administration (is) complete.

Præcipe or Precipe: an initiating document presented to a court clerk to be officially issued on behalf of the court or a the covering memo or letter from the lawyer (or plaintiff) which accompanies and formally asks for the writ to be issued by the court officer.

Praemunire: An offence initially to prefer the Pope or his authority as against the King of England or Parliament, but later included a wide assortment of offenses against the King and always leading to serious penalties.

Precarium: the giving of land as a reward or to secure a debt.

Prima Facie: A legal presumption which means on the face of it or at first sight.

Pro Bono: for the good.

Pro Forma: for the sake of form.

Pro Jure Patrio Stamus: we will defend our rights.

Pro Possessore: a person who holds something only as possessor, not necessarily as owner.

Pro Possessore Habetur Qui Dolo Injuriave: he whose possession is taken away by fraud or injury will be deemed to continue to possess.

Proprio Motu: of one's own initiative.

Pro Rata: to divide proportionate to a certain rate or interest.

Pro Se: on one's own behalf.

Pro Socio: on behalf of a partnership.

Pro Tempore: something done temporarily only and not intended to be permanent.

Quaere: for "query" as in an issue on which some doubt or question exists.

Quaestor: In ancient Roman law, senior legal advisor.

Quam legem exteri nobis posuere, eandem illis ponemus: What law is imposed by foreign powers on our merchants, we will impose on their's.

Quando Jus Domini Regis Et Subditi Concurrunt, Jus Regis Praeferri Debet: When the right of the sovereign and that of a subject conflict, the right of the sovereign is to be preferred.

Quantum: amount or extent.

Quantum Meruit: as much as is deserved.

Quicquid Plantatur Solo, Solo Cedit: whatever is planted in the ground, belongs to the ground.

Quid Pro Quo: something for something.

Qui Facit Per Alium Facit Per Se: he who acts through another, acts himself.

Qui Jure Suo Utitur Neminem Facit Injuriam: he who exercises his legal rights harms no one.

Qui Jussu Judicis Aliquod Fecerit, Non Videtur Dolo Malo Fecisse, Quia Parere Necesse Est: One who does a wrongful act by order of a Court having jurisdiction, is not liable in tort, because he must obey the law.

Qui Non Obstat Quod Obstare Potest, Facere Videtur: an individual who does not prevent something which he/she could of prevented, is taken to have done that thing.

Qui Prior Est Tempore, Potior Est Jure: he who is earlier in time is stronger in law.

Qui Tam: who as well.

Quod Ab Initio Non Valet In Tractu Temporis Non Convalesait: That which was originally void does not by lapse of time become valid.

Quod Remedio Destituitur Ipsa Re Valet, Si Culpa Absit: That which is without a remedy is valid by the thing itself, if there be no fault.

Quorum: The minimum number of voting members that must be in attendance at a meeting of an organization for that meeting to be regularly constituted.

Quo Warranto: legal procedure taken to stop a person or organization from doing something for which it may not have the legal authority, by demanding to know by what right they exercise the controversial authority.

Rapina: to take away forcefully.

Ratio Decidendi: reasons for a decision.

Ratione Loci: by reason of the place.

Ratione Personae: by reason of his person.

Ratione Soli: In relation to territory, land.

Rebus Sic Stantibus: changed circumstances.

Reddendum: that part of a lease which sets out the amount of rent and when it is payable.

Remanet: an action that has been put over, deferred to a later time.

Res Derelicta: a thing abandoned.

Res Gestae: things done.

Res Ipsa Loquitur: the thing speaks for itself.

Res Judicata: already subject to judicial determination.

Res Noviter Veniens Ad Notitiam: Fact(s) newly coming to knowledge.

Respondeat superior: let the principal answer.

Restitutio In Integrum: restitution to the original position. In a breach of contract case, the injured party may ask the court to restore the parties to the positions they were in before the contract was signed. But if the court finds that restitutio in integrum is not possible because of subsequent actions or events, it may order payment of damages instead.

Retraxit: a withdrawal of a legal action.

Rex Debet Esse Sub Lege, Quia Lex Facit Regem: The king should be subject to the law for the law makes the king.

Salus Populi Est Suprema Lex: the welfare of an individual yields to that of the community.

Scienter: actual or guilty knowledge; knowingly.

Scintilla Juris: a spark of legal right.

Se Defendendo: self-defence.

Sic Utera Tuo Ut Alienam Non Laedas: use your property in such a fashion so as to not disturb others.

Sine Die: without a day. Taken to mean without fixing a day for continuation.

Sine Qua Non: without which, not.

Situs: location.

Stare Decisis: stay with what has been decided. To stand by decisions. Policy whereby, once a court has made a decision on a certain set of facts, lower courts must apply that precedent in subsequent cases which embody the same facts.

Statuta Suo Clauduntur Territorio, Nec Ultra Territorium Disponunt: Statutes are confined to their own territory and have no extra-territorial effect.

Statutes in Pari Materia: Statutes sharing a common purpose or relating to the same subject and which are construed together.

Strictissimi Juris: the strictest letter of the law.

Sub Judice: under judicial consideration.

Subpoena: an order of a court which requires a person to be present at a certain time and place or suffer a penalty (subpoena means, literally, under penalty).

Sui Generis: of its own kind.

Sui Juris: one's own law; having full capacity.

Summa Ratio Est Quae Pro Religione Facit: The best rule is that which advances religion.

Tenendum: to be held. In law, that part of a contract in which an interest in real property is created that sets out the extent or limitations of that interest.

Tractatus de legibus et consuetudinibus regni Angliae: 1188 statement of English common law.

Transit In Rem Judicatam: The cause of action is changed into matter of record, which is of a higher nature, and the inferior remedy is merged in the higher.

Uberrimae Fidei: of the utmost good faith.

Ubi Eadem Ratio, Ibi Idem Jus: Where there is the same reason, there is the same law

Ubi Jus Ibi Remedium: For every wrong, the law provides a remedy.

Ultra Petita: beyond that which is sought.

Ultra vires: beyond the powers. An action which is invalid because it exceeds the authority of the person or organisation which performs it. A company cannot normally be bound by an act which it is not empowered to do by its memorandum of association.

Use: trust.

Usufruct: The rights to the product of another's property.

Usury: Excessive or illegal interest rate.

Utile Per Inutile Non Vitiatur: That which is useful is not vitiated by that which is useless.

Ut Res Magis Valeat Quam Pereat: It is better for a thing to have effect than to be made void.

Vacatur: to set aside a judgment.

Valeat Quantum Valere Potest: it shall have effect as far as it can have effect.

Vana Est Illa Potentia Quae Nunquam Venit In Actum: power is vain if never put into action.

Venditio: a sale.

Venditio Bonorum: sale of goods.

Verba Fata: faded, obsolete words.

Verba Fortius Accipiuntur Contra Proferentem: a contract is interpreted against the person who wrote it.

Videlicet: (Latin: that is to say) The abbreviation of videlicet (viz.) is commonly used in legal documents to advise that what follows provides more detail about a preceding general statement.

Vigilantibus Et Non Dormientibus Jura Subveniunt: the law assists those that are vigilant with their rights, and not those that sleep thereupon.

Vinculum Juris: a legal bound.

Vir: man or husband.

Viva Voce: by voice.

Viz: to wit, that is to say.

Volenti Non Fit Injuria: Defence in tort which prevents a person who knowingly and voluntarily assumes a risk (by, for example, engaging in a dangerous sport) from later seeking compensation for any injury suffered.

Notes:

Notes:

PART 7

LETTERS TO THE AUTHORITIES

Letters to the Authorities

We open Part 7 of this Guide with a selection of letters recently sent to Garda Commissioner Noirin O'Sullivan; to Chief Justice Susan Denham; to the Minister for Justice Frances Fitzgerald; to the Taoiseach Enda Kenny and to the President of Ireland, Michael D. Higgins. These letters are just a very few from amongst hundreds of correspondences sent to various authority figures during the past few years, as we struggled - mostly in vain - to receive some open, honest and helpful responses from the powers-that-be. They are published here as a statement of fact and as a firsthand testimony of this very troubling state of affairs. Regardless of the personal qualities of any of these particular individuals (which some of them undoubtedly have) the fact remains that each heads up some senior aspect of the Government such as the judiciary, the executive or the legislature - and as such, they are either directly or indirectly responsible for what is currently going on under their watch. Needless to say, the responses we received (on those occasions when we *did* receive a response) are not worthy of further mention except as typical examples of the very problems we are complaining about in the first place.

Although these letters refer chiefly to issues in 'the Manning case', they nevertheless represent the type of difficulties being experienced by ordinary people on a daily basis in their dealings with the establishment. In publishing these letters here in this Guide, we hope to inspire and encourage others to have the pluck and determination to name and shame those who would rely on our lack of fortitude in holding them to account. Theirs is a privileged world where they can (they believe) continue to act with disdain and contempt towards the public - and can do so with a cosy impunity - safe in the knowledge that their colleagues and subordinates will cover-up their transgressions and protect their venal interests. But not any more! And not on *our* watch!

In publishing these letters in this Guide, a gauntlet is being thrown down to all those who would make a career out of systematic exploitation, deception and abuse: Abuse of their privileged positions; abuse of their authority; and abuse of their fellow citizens. And whilst we can of course admire and respect whatever leadership skills—or indeed whatever personal or professional integrity—that any given authority figure may have; the purpose of this Guide is not to butter up to errant authorities, but to challenge them to reform and improve, or, to face the consequences. Likewise, some of the generic criticisms of various Departments of State for example, may not necessarily, nor directly relate to the Head of that Department, who may, or may not be doing their level best to introduce reform. But in the repeated failure or refusal of more junior agents to accept responsibility for the changes that the public so desperately requires, we can but go to 'the top' with our concerns, because the buck just *has* to stop somewhere.

The letters that follow make a declaration of sorts; (i) That there are a number of serious problems in our so-called justice system. (ii) That these problems are being exacerbated by a culture of secrecy and suppression; (iii) That the inaction and complacency of statutory authorities is making matters even worse. (iv) That we (the public) are becoming increasingly aware of what is going on and are becoming increasingly annoyed at the fact; and (v) that we are no longer scared or intimidated by the threat of 'unknown consequences' as and when we speak out.

In fact, it would appear that things have already started to change. Not least of all because of the I-I tactic of keeping a confidential database of complaints - and a secondary database of witnesses to those complaints. Because should it ever become necessary to defend our position in the media or in the Courts, there will be an unending troop of all-too-willing witnesses who are eager for the opportunity to share their personal experiences with the world.

The battle lines have already been drawn. Errant authority figures have now been publicly put on notice that if they continue to make a mockery of ordinary decent citizens, of our law and the Constitution - and in particular, if they target I-I Members for any more abuse - then they can be absolutely assured of one thing. There WILL be consequences.

To Michael D Higgins, President of Ireland

Dear President Higgins,   January 2015

We respectfully write to you today in your role as President of Ireland regarding a grave moral and legislative crisis which threatens to undermine all of the stated values and fundamental principles of our Constitution. We write after having exhausted all other possible avenues of approach to the various 'Statutory authorities' and their respective agents, including multiple formal approaches and written complaints to the so-called 'statutory oversight bodies'(most notably An Garda Síochána, the Garda Ombudsman Commission and the Irish Courts) who have, without exception, utterly failed in their respective mandates to serve the public and protect and safeguard the Irish Constitution.

I approach you today Sir as a law-abiding Irish citizen, as a concerned husband and father of three children (one with special-needs) and as an active member of the *Integrity Ireland* community, to seek your personal intervention in a series of alarming incidents and events which are being perpetrated illegally by various agents of the State, including by several persons in high office who are embroiled in so many acts of serious and inexcusable malfeasance, misfeasance and nonfeasance as to render their positions in any legislative, service-related or governance roles to be absolutely unconstitutional and illegal, and therefore utterly untenable.

The immediate matters referred to include a succession of criminal acts committed against myself and my family since 2009 including an extended campaign of harassment; intimidation; defamation; physical assaults; death threats and other serious attacks (one of which is linked to an 'unsolved' murder which Gardaí have failed to properly investigate) – as well as to the subsequent *proven* cover-ups and collusion by agents of the State – which (either before or after-the–fact) have been committed with the direct personal knowledge of senior Gardaí up to and including current and previous Garda Commissioners Martin Callinan and Noirin O'Sullivan; with the full knowledge of DPP Clare Loftus and senior members of her staff including the current Chief State Solicitor Eileen Creedon; with the knowledge of Ministers of Justice Alan Shatter TD and Frances Fitzgerald TD; and with the full knowledge of Taoiseach Enda Kenny TD who has, for a period of at least three years, repeatedly failed or refused to meet with us to discuss matters. This, despite us articulating our serious concerns that the lead instigators of the criminal attacks are personally related to Mr Kenny and/or are aligned with prominent members of local Fine Gael, and are it seems, receiving 'protection' and assistance in their criminal activities from State agents, including being apparently immune from criminal prosecution and being facilitated time-after-time in serial abuses of our Courts, while they continue to make an absolute mockery of our so-called justice system.

In context of the above, and in addition to scores of similar sworn complaints as recorded on the *Integrity Ireland* database, I wish to draw your particular attention to the fact that we have, as of December 23rd 2014, lodged a criminal complaint with An Garda Síochána (copied to Garda Headquarters) under the reporting obligations of *Section 19 of the Criminal Justice Act 2011*; and in context of Articles 34 & 35 of the Irish Constitution naming the President of the High Court Justice Nicholas Kearns, and the newly-appointed President of the Appeals Court Justice Sean Ryan (amongst certain others) as being knowing parties to an ongoing conspiracy to pervert the course of justice; incorporating the commission of—and/or the *knowing* facilitation of—serial incidences of fraud, deception, perjury, contempt of Court, and other unlawful breaches of the Constitution, of the law and of their respective Oaths of Office; as outlined (in part) in the copy of said criminal complaint attached.

Furthermore, inasmuch as I have received notification (as the Plaintiff in a High Court action) to attend an Appeal hearing on Friday January 30th next; and inasmuch as that hearing is scheduled to be heard in utterly improper circumstances that are predicated on an indefensible series of frauds, deceptions and other calculated abuses of position and authority which have been 'facilitated' (at the very least) by various agents of the State and members of the Judiciary; and inasmuch as it would now constitute _knowing_ complicity on my part if I were to participate further in these illegal and unconstitutional activities; and inasmuch as we have written scores of formal letters and complaints to all parties concerned concerning the affiliated criminal activities of agents of the State (such as collusion and conspiracy to pervert justice for example); and given we cannot secure any proper responses from those whom we have approached to date; then I write to you Sir as the current President of Ireland, to respectfully advise that if I am to abide by the law and the Constitution, that I cannot – indeed absolutely should not – participate further in these illegal activities such as those which are currently being perpetrated by Judges Nicholas Kearns and Sean Ryan (and affiliated others) in our Superior Courts.

However, as a courtesy to the Court and as a gesture of respect to the law of the land as it is _supposed_ to be administered– it is my intention to attend the Appeals Court on January 30th next so as not to be adjudged in contempt of Court. As a law-abiding citizen however, I also understand that it is my solemn duty NOT to knowingly participate in illegal, fraudulent or criminal activities – even if instructed to do so by any given Judge (Article 35.2) – and I am therefore stating my position in advance 'for the record' and copying the same to the respective parties so that there is no misunderstanding of the position. I therefore respectfully advise of my intention to initiate a citizen's arrest of any Irish citizen (including any member of the Judiciary) who knowingly participates in or facilitates criminal activity (under the respective legislation) and I now seek your personal assurance that I will receive the full protection of your Presidential Office should any further unconstitutional abuses be visited upon us.

We further seek your assurances that a *Presidential Commission of Enquiry* will be immediately set up to enquire into the matters referred to herein; to ascertain as to whether or not Judges Nicholas Kearns and Sean Ryan (amongst others) should be the subjects of impeachment proceedings – and whether other named persons in the employ of the State should be removed from Office and prosecuted for criminal offences – to which end we undertake to cooperate fully with any such legitimate enquiry.

It is probably pertinent and appropriate Sir to note that I am fully aware of the terms and conditions of the *Defamation Act 2009* and of the consequences of publishing anything which I know to be untrue, and it is in this specific context that I advise of my intention to make this letter—and all materials in my possession that relate to it—freely available for inspection by any investigative, private or public source.

Thank you for your time and consideration Sir. Given the pressing timeline, I respectfully invite a timely response, and commit to being available to meet you personally at short notice.

Yours,

Stephen Manning (etc)

A Member of Integrity Ireland

NO RESPONSE

To Michael D Higgins, President of Ireland

Dear President Higgins,   February 2015

We respectfully write to you again in context of our previous important letter to you of January 3rd last. We acknowledge a generic advisory from Ms Linda Farrell, your Secretariat, dated January 7th stating that our letter had indeed been received, but we regret to note that despite our very best efforts to solicit some proper response from your Offices since, that we have it seems, been subjected to the very same disingenuous tactics of contempt, evasiveness and repeated circuitous deferments – tactics which we had highlighted in our January 3rd letter as being a fundamental aspect of the multiple Constitutional 'difficulties' we were experiencing in our so-far depressingly-pointless efforts to deal legitimately and lawfully with the Gardaí, the Courts, and other Irish State agencies this past six years ongoing.

To clarify sir; following the generic acknowledgement signed by Ms Linda Farrell on Jan 7th– and having received no other responses – I phoned your Offices in mid-January whereby Ms Farrell assured me that my letter was receiving 'due attention' from the Secretariat, and that a response would be forthcoming 'next week'. But that promised response never came. I had explained to Ms Farrell that I had <u>not</u> written to the Secretariat, but had written to you personally as the President of Ireland, and that I would require at the very least an assurance that you had in fact received said letter. Indeed, having received no response as promised we called a second time and spoke to Ms Farrell again on Friday January 23rd who advised us that Mr Conor O'Reilly (of whom we can find no official record as a member of your staff) was *personally dealing with the matter'* and that *'he would get right back'* to us. But Mr O'Reilly did <u>not</u> get back to us. I then left a polite and respectful phone message on Mr O'Reilly's answer machine explaining the urgency of the situation; how we required an answer as to our request for the protection of your Constitutional Office from certain criminals and various agents of the State who were engaged in criminal activities—including members of the Judiciary—and that we were fast approaching the crucial appearance in Court. But again, no response was forthcoming. We then sent the attached email-letter to Mr O'Reilly on January 28th last, which is self-explanatory, but again, there was absolutely no response or acknowledgement whatsoever; not by phone, not by email, not by letter – nothing!

You will no doubt understand our consternation and dismay sir, and our urgent need for some rational explanation? The said Appeal Hearing went ahead yesterday as scheduled *without* any due or proper response from the Presidential Office, so I phoned again at 4.20pm that day and spoke to John Ahern who claimed to be your aide-de-camp (of whom we can also find no official record) who advised me that Ms Linda Farrell and Mr Conor O'Reilly had already left for the day, and that John would 'take a message'. After I had explained the situation in some detail (including the fact that some 20,000 persons had viewed the public video version of the letter of January 3rd) John then advised me that he would pass my message 'up the chain of command' on Monday next. But then, incredibly, John Ahern categorically refused (three times) to disclose either the name, rank or position of the supposed 'superiors' to whom he was going to relay this supposedly 'important message'. Frankly, we were left utterly bewildered at all the secrecy and evasiveness on display – not to mention the near-farcical irony of the Presidential Office failing or refusing to respond to a sincere plea for Constitutional protection for a law-abiding citizen – a citizen who is being subjected to multiple serious abuses of the law and the Constitution by senior agents of the Irish State.

Naturally President Higgins, as trusting law-abiding people who came to you in all sincerity in extremely trying and traumatic circumstances for myself, my family and a great number of other 'concerned citizens' we are appalled and dismayed at this inexcusable display of unprofessional behaviour and believe we have a right to ask for an explanation as to what exactly is going on at the Presidential Offices? What sort of 'professional standards' are required in the highest Office of the land sir? Are we to believe that this level of deception, evasiveness and equivocation is routine – because certainly, it would be absolutely unacceptable in any truly professional environment? Your staff had almost a month to answer a clear and legitimate request for clarity on an important Constitutional question – that of senior Judges repeatedly engaging in unconstitutional activity to the detriment of law-abiding citizens – but your staff have not only utterly failed to deal with that question, but they have it seems, purposefully engaged in the same old discredited practices which underlie a prevalent lack of transparency in Irish State institutions; which in turn fosters widespread corruption, cronyism and a lack of any real accountability – the very same type of 'serious Constitutional issues' which prompted us to approach you in the first place. More troubling perhaps is the fact that these behaviours are being carried out 'in your name' under the auspices of the Presidential Offices and under the Constitutional authority thereof. We do sincerely hope that the irony of the situation is not lost in the fog of equivocation and evasiveness.

The fact that the highest Office in the land would deliver us the same levels of contempt is more than disturbing. It is alarming and profoundly unsettling to any person who believes in the principles of justice and in the democratic foundations of the Irish State – not to mention the overt serial breaches of the ***Civil Service Code of Standards and Behaviour*** as laid out in the ***Standards in Public Office Act 2004*** which (the official mission statement unequivocally declares) *"are based on the principles of integrity, impartiality, effectiveness, equity and accountability."* In particular, we note the requirement for civil servants to *'respect the law, disclose information and deal with the public sympathetically, fairly and promptly.'* *"Standards of probity are high.."* (it states without any apparent insincerity) *"..and must be maintained."* So why, we might ask, is our personal experience and that of so many other citizens so very contrary?

Accordingly, and in light of the fact that we deferred, as a courtesy, to the request of the Court that we submit a written account of our stated position 'within two weeks', we ask you again Mr Higgins for your personal assurance as the Guardian of our Constitution that we will receive the full protection of your Presidential Office should any further unconstitutional abuses be visited upon us via the agency of the Courts – as outlined in our letter of January 3rd last. For it should remain explicitly clear sir, that the scandal wherein senior Courts Service Staff and members of the Judiciary are at the very least *knowingly complicit* in a series of criminal acts has not 'gone away' simply because there has been no proper response from your Office – nor because we have decided to co-operate to the next stage—as a gesture of good faith—with the otherwise questionable directions of the Court. 'Questionable' that is – in specific context of these particular criminal circumstances.

Perhaps it is prudent here to note 'for the record' sir, that on January 30th last, in the absence of a proper response from your Offices, that we alerted the Gardaí in advance as to the circumstances in order to protect us from the expected unconstitutional actions of the Court – and from further intimidation from the politically-connected criminals at the centre of these matters. Indeed, we would discover upon arrival at Court that plain-clothes Gardaí had already been dispatched to the Court in advance of the Hearing (as ordered by their superiors) and that photos were reportedly taken of all *Integrity Ireland* Members present. Later, two of us were subjected to some serious verbal abuse and very convincing death threats from the aforesaid politically-connected criminals (not for the first time), and we can only hope that *this* time, with everything captured on the Four Courts CCTV that the perpetrators will in fact find themselves being duly prosecuted by the DPP. But based on or previous experiences, we are not holding our breath.

Likewise, in the absence of any proper action from the respective Statutory Authorities; that the unseemly spectacle of a Superior Court Judge being placed under citizen's arrest remains a regrettable, but very real possibility at the upcoming Hearing on Thursday February 12th next in the High Court. Indeed, the prospect of an arrest becomes all the more likely in context of the fact that the Judge currently scheduled to adjudicate on the day has already been named in a criminal complaint as a direct result of his improper actions and inactions in regards to these very cases – actions which suggest either inconceivable incompetence on his part, or, that he is *knowingly* conspiring against a law-abiding citizen.

We therefore seek your assurances sir, that you will meet with us as a matter of urgency to discuss this very serious situation; that you will either furnish us with clear written affirmations or commit to sending a delegate to the Court on Feb 12th to represent the Constitutional position. We also request again (in our own names and that of the collective Membership of *Integrity Ireland*) that a *Presidential Commission of Enquiry* be immediately set up to enquire into the matters referred to; to ascertain as to whether or not certain named Judges should be the subjects of immediate impeachment proceedings – and whether other named persons in the employ of the State should be removed from Office and prosecuted for criminal offences – to which end we undertake to cooperate fully with any such legitimate enquiry.

It is no doubt appropriate to note again that I am fully aware of the terms and conditions of the *Defamation Act 2009* and of the consequences of publishing anything which I know to be untrue, and it is in this specific context that I advise of my intention to make this letter—and all materials in my possession that relate to it—freely available for inspection by any investigative, private or public source.

Thank you for your time and consideration sir. Given the pressing timeline and these most unfortunate circumstances, I must respectfully insist upon my Constitutional right of response in an expedient and fulsome manner at your very earliest convenience, as laid out in the **Standards in Public Office Act 2004**.

We respectfully refer your staff to the caveat below and trust the position is clear.

Yours,

Stephen Manning (etc)

A Member of Integrity Ireland

NO MEANINGFUL RESPONSE

(Abridged) *" We acknowledge receipt of your letter. Full stop."*

Caveat of affirmation: *We respectfully assert our statutory right to fair and equitable treatment, and reserve the moral right to disengage communication with any individual or agency who, through the means of misinformation, evasiveness, obfuscation, deception or other disingenuous tactics, contrives to avoid fulfilling their mandate to the public [as defined in the Constitution, respective codes of ethics, oaths of office and/or terms of service] other than where we are legally obliged to do so. We further affirm our right to note, report, record and/or publish any communications sent or received for the purposes of transparency, due accountability, and in the interests of natural justice. We further reserve the right to hold responsible under the law any individual, agent or agency we deem responsible for deliberate civil, criminal or constitutional breaches, and to bill any such agents or agencies for time and costs incurred. We do not deal with anonymous, pseudonymous, allonymous or imaginary entities. Annotated emails are accepted under certain exceptional or pre-agreed circumstances, but important or legal correspondence must also be sent as hard copies, duly signed. Unsigned correspondence that is not ascribed to one authorised individual will not be responded to and may be returned for signing, with costs billed to the source thereof. For practical reasons, legal matters will be dealt with on Mondays and Tuesdays only. Please be advised.*

An Open Letter to the Judges of Ireland

January 2015

I respectfully write to you today as a law abiding citizen and father of three children who, because of the improper, illegal and unconstitutional actions of various agents of the State, find myself in the impossible position where—if I am to abide by the law and the Constitution, and specifically to the *Reporting Obligations* of the **Criminal Justice Act 2011**—that I have no alternative but to bring the following grave matters to the direct attention of the Irish Judiciary in this public letter.

I have, for the past six years engaged truthfully, openly and in good faith with the Irish statutory authorities and the Courts in *attempting* to secure justice for myself and my family in the wake of over seven hundred incidents of harassment, intimidation, defamation, death threats, physical assaults and more, all of which have either been reported to the Gardaí or have formed the subject matter of civil cases which we have taken through our Courts. Yet despite overwhelming evidence in support of the facts and despite having named the perpetrators openly in formal criminal complaints and in sworn affidavits, not a single individual has been prosecuted by the Gardaí or has otherwise held accountable in the Courts. Indeed, all the indicators are, that the perpetrators of these crimes are being actively protected from prosecution through the illegal and improper activities of agents of the State – including (we regret to say) by Gardaí, senior civil servants and members of the Judiciary.

It is not our wish or intention to disrespect our Courts nor to impugn the good name of any member of the Judiciary who is carrying out their duties justly, diligently and 'without fear or favour', but some serious questions have to be asked when a law-abiding citizen is repeatedly thwarted, obstructed and denied justice over a period of several years; by the very people entrusted with the administration of the law and the protection of our Constitution.

In the experience of myself and a great many other citizens including scores of *Integrity Ireland* Members (who have documented their experiences in sworn affidavits currently before the Minister for Justice); the general perception is that our Courts are simply 'unfit for purpose' – unless that 'purpose' is to protect the establishment at all costs - even at the direct expense of truth and justice.

Given that our Judges are absolutely required to operate *'according to the law and the Constitution'* and have each sworn a solemn oath to adjudicate matters *'without fear or favour'* it is a scandal of alarming proportions that so many of our Judges are perceived as being unpredictable and inconsistent or, as mere puppets of the political establishment. With all due respect to the *best* of our Judges, it is unsettling to any right-thinking person that five out of six judicial appointments for example are politically motivated and that the JAAB (*the Judicial Appointments Advisory Board*) has failed to conduct even one single interview in over eleven years of existence. How is the public supposed to have confidence in a judicial appointments system that is so overtly compromised as to engender astonishment in the eyes of outside observers? And whilst it does not necessarily follow that Judges so appointed are *not* doing an excellent job, only a fool would not entertain the possibility in our Ireland of today that Judges so appointed would not feel politically and personally inclined to favour those whose patronage delivered them to their lofty positions. In this manner, the insidious tentacles of cronyism, nepotism and political patronage undermine the public's confidence in the essential 'independence' of the Judiciary – not to mention other obvious issues of concern such as having no special training for prospective Judges – and having no workable mechanism by which erring Judges can be effectively curbed – because the current appeals system is so onerous to negotiate and so open to abuse as to be no effective deterrent to Judicial misfeasance, malfeasance or incompetence. And if the common man loses confidence in the judiciary then arguably the judiciary have lost their moral authority. And without a moral dimension, authority quickly descends into tyranny.

The courts are our very last refuge. If they are <u>not</u> solidly rooted in the principles of justice, and if the ordinary citizen cannot rely on fair and expedient treatment then this is no 'justice system' worthy of the name. All we are asking for is fair treatment – as laid out in the respective legislation. It is all there in black and white. We have an absolute right to be treated with dignity, fairness and respect – especially by those who have been gifted so much power and authority and are being paid from the public purse. Surely it is not too much to ask that our Judges honour the principles of justice, and treat all men fairly, as laid down in our Constitution and in the Judges Oath of Office?

Anyway – to the matter at hand: Although we could quote literally scores of examples of improper conduct by senior Court Service Staff and members of the Judiciary as listed on the *Integrity Ireland HAFTA database* I will just highlight one particular issue concerning a matter coming before the new Appeals Court on January 30th next, where a non-national who has a longstanding criminal record in another jurisdiction has, with the apparent direct facilitation and support of a number of Court Registrars and Judges, made an absolute mockery and a farce of the Irish justice system, so much so that we took it upon ourselves to send a circular to the respective Courts Service Offices (in early November 2014) advising them that this individual was a criminal who had been refused audience by two Judges of the superior courts, on the grounds (as stated by us) that his multiple appearances in court were predicated on serial misrepresentations, deceptions and frauds including dozens of incidences of blatant perjury and forgery, and other criminal acts which, despite our most strident efforts are drawing no appropriate responses from the so-called 'statutory authorities'. Clearly something is very seriously amiss here.

In my own case, it seems pointless trying to engage with the judicial process 'in good faith' while so many blatant breaches of the law and the Constitution are allowed to continue. Instead of remedying these flagrant offences when the cases come before them, certain Judges have either completely ignored blatant acts of perjury, fraud, deception, forgery and collusion, or, have further compounded matters by issuing oral 'directions' in open Court in order to temporarily appease those present and avoid any uncomfortable developments – and then, afterwards, signing off on perfected Orders which bear little or no resemblance to the directions given in Court! When we then seek clarifications or explanations, we are variously ignored, rebuked or otherwise treated with contempt by certain Courts Service Staff who clearly struggle with any proper understanding of the concept of genuine 'public service'. A simple analogy would be to ask how you would react if, when waiting for a bus, the driver failed to stop; or, took you to the wrong destination; or, mounted the pavement and tried to run you over!? Don't you think you would have a right to report that driver? Should he not be sacked for failing to do his job properly? Why then, do we continue to put up with a so-called 'Courts Service' – that is anything but!

On Friday January 30th an Appeal by the aforesaid criminal is scheduled to be brought before the Court. He has absolutely no right of audience in these cases, yet several Judges and Registrars have it seems knowingly allowed him to bully and barge his way from hearing to hearing, making an absolute mockery and disgrace of our so-called justice system. In light of our numerous letters and notices to all parties concerned, any person – including any Courts Service Staff or member of the Judiciary who facilitates the progression of this utterly illegitimate Appeal on January 30th is clearly and demonstrably complicit in facilitating a criminal who is engaged in a longstanding fraud on the Irish people and the Irish Courts. Accordingly, we respectfully ask each of the Presidents of the various Courts as listed below to ensure that all Judges and Courts Service Staff under their jurisdiction are alerted as to the facts of this particular case so that further abuses, and the resultant costs and embarrassment to our justice system, may be avoided.

I therefore respectfully reiterate my intention to maintain Constitutional integrity at the Appeal hearing scheduled for January 30th by declaring as absolutely illegal any attempt by Courts Service Staff or members of the Judiciary to facilitate said criminal other than by denying him the right of audience in the Irish Courts, as dictated by the law, by the Constitution, and by Superior Court Rules. In the event that said criminal is indeed further facilitated in this blatant and recurrent fraud, then any person so engaged will be invited to surrender themselves into custody under the terms of ***Section 4(1) of the Criminal Law Act 1997*** for the arrestable offence of, *'obstructing or attempting to obstruct, interfere with, or pervert the course of justice'*.

It remains only for me to emphasise most sincerely on a personal level, that this open letter to our Judges is <u>not</u> an attempt by me to *inappropriately* affect the progress of any case wherein I am a named party – other than to respectfully insist that my *'inalienable fundamental rights'* – as per the law and the Constitution – are duly and properly respected. I believe it is fair to say that I speak for the great majority of the Irish public in drawing these matters to the public attention of our Judiciary – albeit through the vehicle of my own personal experiences in the Courts – for, based on the avalanche of complaints which continue to arrive for the *Integrity Ireland HAFTA Database*, there can no longer be any doubt that there is a major moral and Constitutional crisis in the manner in which thousands of legitimate cases are being dealt with, and adjudicated in our Courts.

We can but appeal to those members of the Judiciary who would act in good faith and conscience to redress these fundamental wrongs; please, please deliver us justice.

Yours,

Stephen Manning (etc)

A Member of Integrity Ireland

To Chief Justice Susan Denham

    Justice Nicholas Kearns, President of the High Court

    Justice Raymond Groarke, President of the Circuit Court

    Judge Rosemary Horgan, President of the District Court

    Judicial Advisory Appointments Board

    Mr Brendan Ryan, CEO Courts Service

NO RESPONSE

To Justice Sean Ryan, President of the Court of Appeal

For the personal attention of Justice Sean Ryan;   January 2015

Previous correspondence refers. We respectfully write as a professional courtesy to inform you that as of December 23rd 2014, a formal criminal complaint was lodged with An Garda Siochána under the auspices of the reporting obligations of *Section 19 of the Criminal Justice Act 2011* in particular context of *The Criminal Justice (Theft & Fraud Offences) Act 200, The Non-Fatal Offences Against the Person Act 1997*and in context of your professional and judicial obligations under *Articles 35.2* and *35.4.1 of the Irish Constitution.* The text of that criminal complaint in part, reads as follows:

> **12. (vii) Justice Sean Ryan, President of the Appeals Court:** (a) On March 31st 2014, whilst operating as a High Court Judge, Justice Ryan facilitated a Hearing in the High Court wherein the Plaintiff Stephen Manning had (again) NOT been notified of said Hearing as required by law, and where Paul Collins again fraudulently purported to be 'an attorney'. (b) That Justice Ryan continued with said Hearing in circumstances where the Plaintiff (Stephen Manning) had emailed the Court in detail advising that he was abroad and therefore <u>not</u> in a position to attend; that he had NOT received any proper Notice of the Hearing, and was seeking an adjournment on the basis that Paul Collins was engaged in an overtly fraudulent exercise. (c) That in a subsequent Hearing Justice Ryan also failed to act when confronted with deliberate and repeated oral and written perjuries by Paul Collins in open Court, and after the Plaintiff formally requested that he do so. (d) That upon another patently fraudulent application by Paul Collins, that Justice Ryan not only improperly assumed jurisdiction in a matter which was—(according to yet another misleading 'Court Notice' sent by Paul Collins)—apparently listed to go before the Master of the High Court; but Justice Ryan then overruled and struck out a completely legitimate 'Order of Judgment' by Justice Iseult O'Malley (as against the Defendant George Collins) in circumstances where Justice Ryan had absolutely <u>no authority or mandate to do so</u> as articulated in Superior Court Rules and demonstrated in the following quote by the President of the High Court Nicholas Kearns: *"One judge of the High Court cannot make an order against a decision made by another judge of the High Court."* Irish Times, Irish Independent, Nov 19th 2014.

A copy of the full 5-page criminal complaint has been forwarded to Garda Headquarters c/o Commissioner Noirin O'Sullivan, and we have also written openly to President Michael D Higgins advising him of the situation, and requesting a Presidential enquiry.

Under the circumstances, we trust that you will take the appropriate action.

Yours,

Stephen Manning (etc)

A Member of Integrity Ireland

NO RESPONSE

To Chief Justice Susan Denham

To Chief Justice Susan Denham,   February 2014

Further to our correspondence of February 17th last, we write in respect of the Hearing held yesterday at Castlebar Circuit Court which was overseen by Judge Margaret Hedeghan – Judge Hedeghan having advised us that Judge Raymond Groarke was 'unable to attend' as scheduled.

On November 26th 2013 Judge McDonagh adjudicated over a hearing in Case 559/11 whereby my wife and myself appeared before him as Plaintiffs in a hearing for 'assessment of damages'. A sick note addressed to Mayo County Registrar Fintan Murphy was presented to Judge McDonagh at the very last minute (without any advance notice to us) stating that the Defendant Mr George Collins was 'too sick' to attend Court. Judge McDonagh Ordered that the Hearing be adjourned to February 18th 2014 (yesterday) and explicitly declared said Order to be 'peremptory' as against the Defendant.

At the hearing yesterday before Judge Hedeghan, it was confirmed that Judge Rory McCabe had already facilitated a 'Motion to Set Aside Judgement' Hearing in this matter on Tuesday February 11th last. As previously explained, we were not advised nor put on Notice of that Hearing – including not even receiving the usual notification from Castlebar Court Office. We logically conclude therefore, that said hearing was purposefully conducted in our absence, without Notice to us, in direct contravention of Court Rules.

Furthermore, a certain 'Mr Paul Collins' who refers to himself as *'the Attorney to George Collins'* was apparently present at the Hearing of February 11th claiming to 'represent' the Defendant George Collins. Paul Collins will not respond to our requests that he properly identify himself and furnish his credentials. Neither will he forward requested legal documents and will not account for the fact that we were not formally notified of the Hearing of Feb 11th before Judge Rory McCabe wherein Judge McCabe apparently ruled that 'the matter' be adjourned to April 1st next, and allegedly 'issued instructions' to Paul Collins to write and inform us of his decision. Despite Judge Hedeghan ratifying those 'instructions' of Judge McCabe yesterday, those instructions remain in direct contradiction to two letters recently received from the President of the Circuit Court Judge Raymond Groarke – letters which we were not even allowed to present to Judge Hedeghan yesterday when we attempted to seek some clarity on the situation.

We did our best yesterday to raise the twin issues of; (i) the Hearing of Feb 11th going ahead in our absence, and (ii) Judge McDonagh's Order of Nov 26th 2013 being explicitly 'peremptory' but Judge Margaret Hedeghan would not let us address these matters, and instead ordered the Gardaí (who were quite obviously standing by 'at the ready' right behind me) to escort me out of the Courtroom. In our opinion, it was an appalling display of pre-emptive, unjust and injudicious conduct, and clearly in direct breach of our Constitutional right to a fair hearing.

We are left increasingly dismayed, bewildered and appalled Judge Denham by this litany of apparent 'irregularities', breaches of due process, and abuses of power and position that continue to be visited with impunity upon a law-abiding citizen and his family. We have toiled long and hard at great financial and emotional expense to simply avail of our Constitutional right to fair and equitable treatment in the Courts, but at every step and turn we are being systematically deprived of due process in a scenario whereby certain members of the judiciary in particular seem to be basically 'making it up as they go along' changing, bending or manipulating the rules at will – often in explicit contradiction of each other – and doing so without any proper regard to our fundamental rights in clear and obvious contravention of Court Rules. What is an ordinary citizen to do in circumstances whereby even the Judges do not respect the law or their own Judicial Code of Conduct? It is a disgraceful set of circumstances altogether that shows no sign of improving with each insidious contrivance that is deployed against our interests, and we respectfully ask again Judge Denham, that in your role as the Chief Justice that you immediately step in and put an end to this increasingly farcical situation that can only undermine the public's confidence in the overall integrity of our justice system.

In the absence of any proper explanation from the respective parties, we respectfully advise that it is our intention to lodge a formal criminal complaint with An Garda Siochána naming Mr Paul Collins and any other parties whom we can demonstrate were complicit – either before or after the fact – in facilitating the fraudulent Hearing of February 11th in direct contravention of our statutory rights.

Given that the legitimate Order of Judge McDonagh of November 26th 2013 was apparently ignored/overruled/set aside or otherwise contemptuously disregarded by other Circuit Court Judges, we would be obliged for official clarification on the position Judge Denham, so we may advance our cases appropriately.

Thank you kindly for your time and consideration Judge.

Sincerely

Stephen Manning (etc)

A Member of Integrity Ireland

(The cartoon was *not* sent to Justice Denham, despite our
sneaking suspicion that she might have found it quite funny)

To Chief Justice Susan Denham

Dear Chief Justice Denham;   May 2015

Previous correspondence refers. Speaking again as a private citizen, as a father and husband, as a lay litigant in Case 559/11, and as the Administrator of the *Integrity Ireland* association; I respectfully approach you again in your capacity as Chief Justice of Ireland to first of all request a response to my unacknowledged letter of April 23rd last, and to alert you as to the highly inappropriate behavior and demeanour of Judge Raymond Groarke, President of the Circuit Court at two Hearings in Castlebar Circuit Court on Wednesday 6th May last where, in the opinion of 19 members of *Integrity Ireland* present, Judge Groarke acted in a manner wholly unbefitting his Office inasmuch as:

In the McDonnell case: Judge Groarke repeatedly refused to acknowledge the Plaintiffs' assertions that the Circuit Court did <u>not</u> have the jurisdiction to deal with a Constitutional matter. Despite the CSSO having no contrary argument, Judge Groarke repeatedly ignored or circumvented the McDonnell's pointed questions, requests and objections, and then assigned another Hearing date <u>in the Circuit Court</u>.

That Judge Groarke led the McDonnells to believe that he was going to listen to the DAR of a previous Court Hearing over lunch 'in order to gain clarity' on contested matters, but bluntly refused the McDonnell's request that said DAR be heard by all present in Court.

In the Manning case: That Judge Groarke refused my request that an assessment of damages Hearing (now scheduled for July 21st next) be made 'peremptory' as against the Defendant George Collins (who was not present nor represented) – the very same George Collins who was allowed to rejoin another case by Judge Raymond Groarke even after judgement had been legitimately awarded against him and where Judge Groarke stated, *"Court Rules are only guidelines and I can overrule them if I wish."* This is the same George Collins who (along with his criminal brother Paul Collins) has been actively facilitated by the Courts Service and various members of the judiciary in multiple and repeated abuses of due process since 2009 ongoing – as reported to you personally on several occasions now. This latest 'non-appearance' by George Collins by the way, is the 17th such failure or refusal to appear at a scheduled Hearing *in this case alone* – and yet *still* Judge Groarke refused to make Mr Collins' next attendance peremptory. Are we the only people raising questions about this apparent chronic failure of due process and this refusal by various judges to sanction repeated acts of contempt of Court by the Collins fraternity?

That Judge Groarke also failed to properly acknowledge my request that Judges McCabe, Heneghan, McDonagh and himself be recused from adjudicating on July 21st on the grounds that each was conflicted in these matters, due to each being named as parties in certain criminal complaints lodged with An Garda Síochána which allege a general conspiracy as against the administration of justice.

That Judge Groarke hurriedly exited the Courtroom while I was still speaking and instructed Gardaí to be called, whereupon nine members of the *Emergency Response Unit* filed into the rear of the Court in what we all interpreted as an overt act of intimidation.

That upon returning to the bench, Judge Groarke embarked on an indignant tirade directed at me, stating vehemently that I had issued *"an outrageous calumny"* that placed me in contempt of Court. It appears that Judge Groarke was just about to issue an ultimatum to me to retract what I had said when I stepped forwards and interrupted him twice in succession stating that I *"absolutely"* stood behind everything I had said – whereupon Judge Groarke seemed to have no reply, other than indicating that he was now going to proceed with the next case. We have interpreted this tirade by Judge Groarke as yet another failed attempt at intimidation, and another misjudged attempt to suppress the truth being heard.

That when I sought clarity again after lunch about the matter of making the Hearing of July 21ˢᵗ peremptory – based on the defiant and contemptuous history of non-compliance and non-attendance of George Collins to *any* of these Hearings since 2010, Judge Groarke again refused to explain his refusal, instead barking orders at me to, *"shut up and sit down"*.

That when I pressed him for clarity on the issue of alleged contempt of Court, that he again refused to engage with me, repeating in a somewhat juvenile manner, *"I am ignoring you Mr Manning.. I am ignoring you.."* and waving the next litigant forwards. I then advised Judge Groarke that we had already reported the allegation of contempt to the local Gardaí, and that they would be investigating the matter. Judge Groarke then began to publicly mock me saying (abridged), *"Oh yes, and don't forget to write now to the Minister for Justice, to the Attorney General and to all of the Judges of Ireland with your complaints Mr Manning."* When I began to respond, Judge Groarke then said, *"I don't want to hear from you Mr Manning, you've had your say."* But I told him he had reopened the conversation and I was going to exercise my right to reply in a public Courtroom. Judge Groarke then tried to intimidate me again, saying, *"Be very careful Mr Manning. I am warning you. You'd better be very careful. You're on very thin ice."* (etc etc) Whereupon I said, *"Or what, Judge? What's going to happen?"* Judge Groarke's only answer was to respond, *"I know what you want and I'm not going to make a martyr out of you."* Before leaving the Court, I stated again that I absolutely stood behind my allegations of a conspiracy amongst certain members of the judiciary.

I believe it is fair to say that there can be only two credible explanations for Judge Groarke's refusal to clarify matters on the day – and both of them are utterly unacceptable. Either, (a) that he is harbouring personal animosity against me and is deliberately being as obdurate and obstructive as possible, and/or; (b) that he is indeed ensuring that George Collins will likely never have to answer for his crimes against our family in an open Court. If, as I suspect, the latter is true Justice Denham, then that absolutely supports my contention that because George and Paul Collins are 'personally connected' to a senior Mayo politician, and because they are implicated in solicitations to commit serious crimes which have been deliberately and systematically covered-up by senior Gardaí, the DPP's Office, by GSOC and by various other agents of the State; that we suspect that covert 'instructions' have been sent out that these cases are NOT to be allowed to progress so as to avoid massive embarrassment to the establishment, and thereby prevent the public exposure of endemic corruption in agencies of the State. Other than incredible incompetence on the part of some of our most senior judges, including the Presidents of the Circuit, High Court and Appeals Court – there really is no other plausible explanation. And given that such levels of incompetence are, literally 'incredible' amongst men who are clearly very well educated and are no strangers to the law or to Court Rules – then we are left with only one conclusion; that of a deliberate conspiracy to pervert the course of justice.

In our own family situation Justice Denham, we wish it clearly and specifically noted 'for the record', that there have now been 17 Court Hearings *in this one case alone* where George Collins has either failed or refused to appear, and that judgement was awarded against Mr Collins in June 2013 after 23 other acts of contempt of due process on his part beginning August 2011. That even in context of this truly extraordinary display of 40 combined incidences of contempt for due process, that we *still* cannot get this man into an assessment of damages hearing! We hope you'll agree that something very, very suspicious is going on here Justice Denham. The fact that Judge Raymond Groarke has been at the centre of a number of controversies involving our litigation against George Collins has not only resulted in us having lodged personal letters of complaint and formal appeals in the High Court regarding several disputed decisions Judge Groarke has made in the Circuit Court, but as you know, we have also named him in criminal complaints lodged with the Gardaí. What on earth he was doing adjudicating in these matters under these particular circumstances raises again, the awkward question of an obvious personal conflict of interest on Judge Groarke's part, and supports our formal request to you Justice Denham, as the current Chief Justice, that Judge Raymond Groarke is immediately prohibited from adjudicating in any further matters whereby myself or my family are litigants. We are aware of discussions ongoing in the Superior Courts about how to curb the excesses of wayward judges, and we hope you will take these matters into account when deciding what steps to take to protect the Irish people from irascible and inconsistent adjudicators, who, the evidence suggests, seem to have completely forgotten the contents of the Judges Oath of Office and of their solemn obligations to administer justice 'without fear or favour'.

Finally Justice Denham, I reiterate that I remain fully aware of the contents of the Defamation Act 2009, and repeat here in this formal correspondence my sincere assertion that in matters where I personally have been a litigant since 2009, that certain senior members of the Irish judiciary have engaged in appalling acts of misconduct which can only be explained in context of incredible incompetence, prejudice and/or bias on their part, and/or of deliberate attempts to interfere with the proper administration of justice.

Given that this letter will be placed in the public domain in due course, I actively encourage Judges Raymond Groarke, Nicholas Kearns or Sean Ryan in particular, to issue proceedings against me for defamation if they sincerely believe that anything I have stated herein (or in any previous correspondence) is actionable, for we would wholeheartedly welcome the opportunity to defend our position in public, and thereby prove these allegations 'beyond a reasonable doubt'. Who knows, this might help bring some attention to bear on a scandal which is causing major upset and trauma in the lives of ordinary citizens, and maybe even encourage some urgent and radical reform of a clearly-compromised judicial system.

Thank you kindly for your time and consideration.

Sincerely

Stephen Manning (etc)

A Member of Integrity Ireland

RESPONSE

(Abridged) *"We regret there is no facility at this Office to complain about the conduct of a Judge. Perhaps when the Judicial Council eventually gets set up…?"*

(We've been waiting over 25 years for that one to materialise..)

To Garda Commissioner Noirin O'Sullivan

Dear Commissioner O'Sullivan;   January 2015

Previous correspondence refers. Irrespective of your failure to respond to the questions raised in my correspondence of January 3rd last; I write to you today at the request of Mr Joseph Doocey, of Ballina, Co. Mayo, in context of an armed raid on his private residence at 7.50am on Saturday January 17th last, where some 20 Gardaí in riot gear stormed Mr Doocey's house, arrested Mr Doocey and removed a range of personal items, apparently without displaying any warrant or due legal authority, and without supplying any inventory of the items seized.

Based on the sworn statements of Mr Doocey, his wife and elderly father who were all present at the time, this shameful 'raid' was conducted in such appalling circumstances as to suggest that it was not only absolutely unlawful, but that it comprised an act of premeditated criminal intimidation and harassment by agents of the State incorporating verbal abuse, physical assaults and several other serious breaches of the Doocey family's fundamental rights.

Given Mr Doocey's membership of *Integrity Ireland*, we have also been informed that sensitive data that is 'strictly private and confidential' to the I-I Membership has been seized without due process, and I write as the Administrator of the I-I website to respectfully advise that neither you, nor any of your subordinates, agents or affiliates (unless they are signed-up active Members of I-I) have permission or authority to view said information. Given there is no apparent *legitimate* reason for the seizure of said confidential information (seized without due process and without our express permission), and given that Mr Doocey likewise asserts that said 'raid' was conducted in the most shocking and degrading circumstances,complete with this histrionic display of armed Gardaí descending vigilante-like on a peaceful Mayo home conducting themselves to all intents and purposes as if they were engaged in a large-scale international crime-busting operation that most people would associate with serious criminal or terrorist activity. Indeed, even Osama Bin Laden only warranted 23 US Special Forces to end the biggest international man-hunt ever – and here we have five Garda vehicles and some 20 Gardaí and armed detectives descending on a sleepy County Mayo farmhouse!?

In context of the subsequent questionable explanation that said 'raid' was prompted by some allegedly-offensive email sent by Mr Doocey in mid-December 2014 – and given the 'coincidental' posting of a public video (on January 15th last) of Mr Doocey's personal testimony of serious Garda corruption and criminality covering some 15 years, surely, this belated military-style response by Dublin-based armed detectives where all of Joe's original evidence against the Gardaí was seized, as well as his confidential *Integrity Ireland* files which detail our collective anti-corruption efforts, raises some serious questions as to why such Stasi-type tactics are being deployed by a State organisation whose official mandate is supposedly "to protect and serve" the public, to eradicate crime, and defend our Constitutional rights?

Accordingly Commissioner, you will understand the disquiet that has been generated within the *Integrity Ireland* community and the public at large by this apparent 'over-the-top' militant reaction by Gardaí to the posting of Joe's forthright video – not to mention the effect of the raid on Joe's immediate family, who have been left absolutely emotionally distraught at these events. We therefore respectfully seek answers to the following questions as a matter of urgency, so that Joe and his family may accurately present their case before the Courts:

i. Please furnish Mr Doocey with a copy of the search warrant, the sight of which was denied him and his family on the day of the raid.

ii. Please clarify upon what grounds Mr Doocey was arrested.

iii. Please explain what exactly Gardaí were doing during the 3 hours when they were in the Doocey house unsupervised.

iv. Please supply an inventory of all materials seized in said raid.

v. Please explain why no video footage of the event was taken by Gardaí, and why Mrs Doocey was ordered to stop filming and had her phone seized.

vi. Please explain why both Mrs Doocey and Mr Dermot Doocey Snr were threatened with arrest if they did not 'cooperate' and were then unlawfully detained for 3 hours.

vii. Please confirm that all materials improperly seized during said raid will be returned within 48 hours in the same condition as when they were seized.

viii. Please confirm that the confidentiality of any and all *Integrity Ireland* related materials will be absolutely respected.

Thank you for your time Commissioner. For the purposes of transparency and accountability, this letter has been copied to various 'interested parties' including the Minister for Justice Frances Fitzgerald, An Taoiseach Enda Kenny, and to the Membership of *Integrity Ireland*.

Trusting the position is clear

Yours,

Stephen Manning (etc)

A Member of Integrity Ireland

THE RESPONSE FROM GARDA HQ

(Abridged) *"Blah, blah, blah. Blather, blather.. You're not entitled.. Misdirection etc.. Section a,b,c, of the 2005 Act states we can do what we like with impunity.. But you can go to GSOC if you like (ha, ha).. and NO we are NOT going to answer your questions even though we'll make a farcical pretence of doing so."*

Caveat of affirmation: *We respectfully assert our statutory right to fair and equitable treatment, and reserve the moral right to disengage communication with any individual or agency who, through the means of misinformation, evasiveness, obfuscation, deception or other disingenuous tactics, contrives to avoid fulfilling their mandate to the public [as defined in the Constitution, respective codes of ethics, oaths of office and/or terms of service] other than where we are legally obliged to do so. We further affirm our right to note, report, record and/or publish any communications sent or received for the purposes of transparency, due accountability, and in the interests of natural justice. We further reserve the right to hold responsible under the law any individual, agent or agency we deem responsible for deliberate civil, criminal or constitutional breaches, and to bill any such agents or agencies for time and costs incurred. We do not deal with anonymous, pseudonymous, allonymous or imaginary entities. Annotated emails are accepted under certain exceptional or pre-agreed circumstances, but important or legal correspondence must also be sent as hard copies, duly signed. Unsigned correspondence that is not ascribed to one authorised individual will not be responded to and may be returned for signing, with costs billed to the source thereof. For practical reasons, legal matters will be dealt with on Mondays and Tuesdays only. Please be advised.*

To Garda Commissioner Noirin O'Sullivan

Commissioner O'Sullivan,   August 2015

Previous correspondence refers. We write again in specific context of our letters to you dated July 1st and August 3rd last, as well as nine letters previously sent which have either been ignored, deferred, not properly responded to – or otherwise redirected down the proverbial 'bottomless rabbit hole' at Garda HQ.

The so-called 'responses' issuing at the hand of Superintendent Frank Walsh and others at Garda HQ ostensibly 'on your behalf' are so blatantly contemptuous, contrived, evasive and calculating, that to refer to them in any other format would be an affront to decency. Reinterpreting our legitimate requests for information as 'complaints' – so they can then be redirected to a toothless GSOC (where YOU assign the Garda Investigating Officers) is a ploy that has worn far too thin Ms O'Sullivan. As Garda Commissioner, you have NO lawful excuse for NOT providing us with the information required to lodge criminal complaints and a civil action in the Courts. Redirecting our correspondence elsewhere without answering any of our questions is a clear and blatant attempt to interfere with justice. Likewise, you have NO excuse for NOT tackling the multiple instances of criminality and cover-ups by Garda Management ongoing under your watch.

We have no intention of continuing this farcical merry-go-round with supposed 'public servants' while multiple abuses of the law and the Constitution get swept under the carpet. These thinly-veiled efforts by you and your subordinates to avoid accountability for this shambolic state of affairs are not going unnoticed by the public, nor is your obvious scorn for the people whom you have solemnly sworn to 'protect and serve.' You are a citizen of this country too Ms O'Sullivan, and if you perpetrate crimes against other citizens – or in any way direct or facilitate the same – then you too may expect to be held accountable under the law.

Accordingly, and for the purposes of transparency and accountability, this letter is being copied to your private residence, along with a copy of our letter of August 3rd last, so there can be no doubt or discussion that you *personally* have been fully apprised of the situation.

We also attach a copy of the Power of Attorney letter as signed by Mr Joe Doocey so as to eliminate any further excuses you may attempt to deploy for NOT providing us with the information required to make a formal criminal complaint and take action in the Courts.

We now formally place you on Notice that any failure or refusal to furnish us with the required information within seven days, will result in you *personally* facing criminal charges in the Courts for interfering with, obstructing and/or perverting the course of justice.

Trusting the position is clear.

Yours,

RESPONSE

Stephen Manning (etc)

A Member of Integrity Ireland

(Abridged) *"We didn't receive any POA - honestly! Wrote back to you since, but the letter was returned to us marked 'moved away'. Hope this one gets to you okay because it's really important to us that we deliver a professional service to you.."*

To the Minister for Justice Frances Fitzgerald T.D.

Dear Minister Fitzgerald;   August 2015

We acknowledge receipt of a letter from your Department dated 8th August 2014—generically 'signed' by your Private Secretary Mr Christopher Quattrociocchi—and thank you for the timely response. However, in particular context of my own previous submissions to your Department as well as in my role as the administrator of the *Integrity Ireland* website, I feel it incumbent to note the following facts 'for the record'.

Firstly, we reiterate the respectful sentiments in our letter of August 1st, but regret to note that you have apparently decided not to respect our position regarding corresponding with Mr Quattrociocchi – and we would ask again that you please sign off personally on any letters coming from your office, so that we can be assured that you are indeed personally receiving our correspondences; that the responses sent 'in your name' are in fact coming from you; and that Mr Quattrociocchi is not again indulging in the same underhanded, evasive and obstructive tactics which he previously engaged in when serving under Mr Shatter. In this particular matter Minister, we are simply exercising our right not to continue to engage with persons in the employ of the State who variously mislead, obstruct or deceive citizens in direct contravention of their mandate to serve the people; for to continue to do so would in effect, make us complicit in that wrongdoing – something we are not prepared to facilitate.

Secondly, we note that your letter dated August 8th is identical in content to scores of letters sent out recently to persons who have submitted complaints under the umbrella of the *'Justice 4 All'* campaign – which includes several signed-up Members of *Integrity Ireland*, such as myself and my wife. We also note that a similar generic letter has been dispatched from the Taoiseach's Department and likewise forwarded to those who submitted complaints and affidavits directly to Mr Kenny. As such, neither of those generic letters recently received by us addresses any of the issues raised by us in any specific manner, so we would respectfully ask again that you please respond to the contents of our letter of August 1st, and properly address the matters raised therein.

In the meantime, and regarding your reported proposal to create an 'independent review mechanism' to look into the complaints and affidavits submitted, there are certain pertinent facts that need to be noted as well as certain issues of concern which we believe need to be placed 'on the record' so as to ensure that the proposed 'independent review' is indeed thorough and transparent, and genuinely serves the interests of justice in the eyes of all concerned. In this regard, we refer to a recent front-page article in the Irish Examiner entitled, "Justice Review of Gardaí Meaningless" which outlines some serious concerns about this proposed review process which are shared by a good many Integrity Ireland Members – not least amongst which is the fact that you are conducting a 'paper-only' review without personally interviewing any of the complainants, and that you have staffed the review panel with seven barristers – in the pay of the Government – one of whom at least appears to have a demonstrable personal conflict of interest. You will no doubt understand Minister the legitimate concerns of citizens who have already been so disrespectfully and contemptuously treated by Government agencies; that a Government-sponsored 'paper-only' review process that answers to the very same Government Department that has been so heavily criticised of late for ignoring, suppressing and/or dismissing scores of legitimate citizen's complaints; is wholly inadequate in dealing with issues that have, quite literally, destroyed so many people's lives. Indeed, it could reasonably be argued that this seemingly-superficial 'review process' is just another case of a Government Department investigating itself before the inevitable finding of 'not guilty' on all counts.

Accordingly, it should perhaps be clarified at the outset Minister that from our (citizens) perspective, there are already sufficient 'mechanisms' presently in place to identify and deal with criminal activity or serious malfeasance by Irish Government employees – and that the respective Irish and EU laws already provide the Irish Government and Courts with all the tools and sanctions it needs to deal with endemic abuses of power and position. In other words, if only our State institutions and authority figures were doing their jobs properly in the first place, then there would be no need whatsoever for the Government to establish any special 'independent review mechanism' under duress at this belated stage – especially after so much irreparable damage has already been done to so many people's lives. Indeed, we believe it should simply be a case of 'the authorities' properly applying the law and respecting the Constitution without fear or favour, and applying the appropriate sanctions on State agencies or agents who have acted improperly or illegally – such as would be visited on any ordinary citizen who committed similar acts. That being said however, we now find ourselves in a position where the Government has – at long last – apparently committed to investigate hundreds of these complaints at this preliminary level, in which context we respectfully offer the following important facts for your consideration.

Many of the complaints and affidavits submitted to you and Mr Kenny's Department have come from signed-up Integrity Ireland Members whose complaints have already undergone a strict qualifying process conducted by us using the following criteria:

- Does the prospect have legitimate cause for complaint?

- Are there verifiable proofs to substantiate their complaint?

- Has the prospect already engaged with the respective statutory authorities in pursuing their complaint? (i.e. various authority figures or agencies such as An Garda Siochána; the Garda Ombudsman; the Law Society; the Department of Justice; the Courts etc).

- Was the response of the various statutory agencies inadequate / inappropriate / dismissive / meaningless / unsatisfactory / unacceptable – or otherwise patently unconstitutional?

On the basis of these questions and criteria, as well as personal interviews (some of which can be viewed online at http://www.integrityireland.ie/videolog.html) we respectfully suggest Minister that any 'paper-only' review (at least in those particular cases which have come from signed-up Members of Integrity Ireland) will be wholly inadequate if the investigative panel does not also consult with us on these cases, and/or include a personal interview with the subject.

We also respectfully suggest that any expenses incurred by complainants in preparing and submitting said complaints or attending any scheduled interviews should be covered by the State, and that where appropriate, that legal aid is made available in those cases where there are grounds for taking subsequent civil action against the State. In this regard, we note with some considerable dismay the ridiculously prejudicial situation where the resources of the State can be deployed against a law-abiding, tax-paying citizen who takes legitimate civil action against State employees who have committed (in some cases) very serious crimes indeed. It is highly offensive to any right-thinking person that State employees can engage in illicit activities with apparent impunity – safe in the knowledge that a raft of 'professional' legal experts in the pay of the State will rally to their defence, and that the perpetrators personally will never have to bear the costs – or indeed suffer any real inconveniences for their improper actions – even after causing so much damage in the lives of ordinary law-abiding citizens. We hope that you will agree Minister that this is a shocking and indefensible scenario – and one that deserves your very serious attention if you, your Department and the Government as a whole, are to maintain any sense of legitimacy or credibility.

We also enclose a 5-page document which lists 25 complaints against members of the Gardaí which was first sent to the Garda Ombudsman Commission in 2011 without any proper response, as well as details of another serious complaint (on our own personal behalf) which names senior Gardaí and staff at the DPP's Office in serial acts of deception which, by any understanding of the term, constitute a clear conspiracy to pervert the course of justice. These issues have been repeatedly sent to the various 'authority figures' and 'statutory oversight bodies' (including to Mr Shatter and Mr Kenny personally) – again, without any proper response. Indeed, not only was there no proper response, but these particular complaints were variously suppressed and ignored (by Garda HQ and the GSOC) in a contrived attempt to try to run them 'out of time', and our subsequent efforts to appeal to the GSOC (which is our statutory right under the respective legislation) was completely and utterly ignored. We would ask therefore, that these enclosures be assigned new reference numbers and be delivered to the 'independent review panel' for their consideration.

We respectfully ask Minister that you personally confirm that these additional complaints have been accepted for consideration by the panel, and that you will at least give some consideration to our suggestion that said 'independent review panel' needs to include direct consultation with representatives from the Integrity Ireland and/or Justice 4 All groups (of our own nomination), and that once the initial paper review has been completed, that the Government will robustly apply the rule of law in sanctioning and removing from office those who have engaged in gross negligence, collusion or criminal activities, and that from now on the resources of our Justice Department (under your remit) will be properly deployed in defence of citizens' rights as per the respective Articles of the Irish Constitution. In this latter matter, we also seek clarity on the specific Terms of Reference under which the panel intends to operate, thank you.

Finally, we reiterate our sentiments of our letter of August 1st last; noting that there was no inclusion of any representatives from either the Justice 4 All or the Integrity Ireland groups on the panels who prepared the recent Government-sponsored Geurin and Toland Reports. Given the amount of time and effort that has been expended by us to date in our efforts to expose the endemic corruption, cronyism and cover-ups at the heart of so many of our State agencies, may we respectfully suggest Minister that for any Government-sponsored panel to be able to form a comprehensive and balanced view of the real state of affairs, that they need to consult directly and personally with those who have been most adversely affected.

Yours,

Stephen Manning (etc)

A Member of Integrity Ireland

RESPONSE (Abridged) *" We acknowledge receipt of your letter. Full stop."*

Caveat of affirmation: We respectfully assert our statutory right to fair and equitable treatment, and reserve the moral right to disengage communication with any individual or agency who, through the means of misinformation, evasiveness, obfuscation, deception or other disingenuous tactics, contrives to avoid fulfilling their mandate to the public [as defined in the Constitution, respective codes of ethics, oaths of office and/or terms of service] other than where we are legally obliged to do so. We further affirm our right to note, report, record and/or publish any communications sent or received for the purposes of transparency, due accountability, and in the interests of natural justice. We further reserve the right to hold responsible under the law any individual, agent or agency we deem responsible for deliberate civil, criminal or constitutional breaches, and to bill any such agents or agencies for time and costs incurred. We do not deal with anonymous, pseudonymous, allonymous or imaginary entities. Annotated emails are accepted under certain exceptional or pre-agreed circumstances, but important or legal correspondence must also be sent as hard copies, duly signed. Unsigned correspondence that is not ascribed to one authorised individual will not be responded to and may be returned for signing, with costs billed to the source thereof. For practical reasons, legal matters will be dealt with on Mondays and Tuesdays only. Please be advised.

To the Minister for Justice Frances Fitzgerald T.D.

Dear Minister Fitzgerald;   September 2015

Previous correspondence refers. We note that other than a generic acknowledgement of receipt, that we received no responses from you to our important letters of September 2nd and November 4th 2014, and ask that you please respond without delay regarding the following important matters:

- Please confirm receipt of the complaints previously submitted to your offices.

- Please confirm that said complaints have been forwarded to the 'Review Panel' for consideration.

- Please confirm that you accept that all complaints and affidavits submitted to you via the *Justice 4 All* campaign which were previously vetted by *Integrity Ireland* will <u>not</u> be dismissed, ignored or otherwise deemed 'inadmissible'.

- Please advise of the steps you have taken to ensure there is no 'conflict of interest' in barrister Mr Conor Devally being the lead member of a Justice Department Review Panel which is 'investigating' a serious case wherein Mr Devally is one of the subjects being complained about.

Impeachment of Judge Mary Devins

Secondly, we refer to our formal request for the impeachment of District Court Judge Mary Devins which was submitted to you *personally*—in your role as Minister for Justice and as a senior member of the Government—by TDs Clare Daly and Mick Wallace on 27th April this year. We note that you returned all of the accompanying documentation including several hundred original signatures and the records of several thousand additional digital signatures, along with a letter to TDs Clare Daly and Mick Wallace dated August 4th last wherein you bewilderingly declare that you *"have no role in the matter"*!?

You will forgive our puzzlement and confusion at this seemingly bizarre statement Mrs Fitzgerald, because clearly, your remit as Minister for Justice (as stated on the Department of Justice website) is to oversee your Department's supervision of policing and the Courts, specifically including issues of law and order and, *"constitutional and legislative matters related to judicial appointments"*. You are also a senior member of Government and a member of Dail Eireann are you not?

Accordingly, we are completely bewildered as to why you would misleadingly quote Article 35.4 of the Constitution to us, when it clearly states that, *"judges can be removed from office for stated misbehaviour or incapacity.. upon resolutions passed by Dail Eireann.."* etc., etc. In context of the fact that you ARE a member of Dail Eireann and that you ARE the current Minister for Justice, your closing declaration that you have *"no role in the matter"* seems absolutely incongruous and absurd, does it not? Especially as this is the contrived premise upon which you have taken NO action, other than to simply return all of the documentation to us?

Perhaps you can advise us Minister who on earth we are supposed to make an approach of this nature to – if not the Minister for Justice? Indeed, we might also be asking why you, as Minister for Justice, are NOT looking into this matter 'in the public interest'? For clearly Mrs Fitzgerald, if several thousand people have taken the trouble to sign a petition to have a judge impeached – then surely you will have deduced that something is amiss here?

If you have somehow failed to make that deduction because of the pressures of your Office in dealing with the hundreds of formal complaints *still* allegedly being 'reviewed' by the Review Panel (whose sterling work will no doubt be applauded when/if ever we receive any solid conclusions) then may we respectfully suggest that you urgently take a second look at the circumstances under which thousands of citizens have raised another justice-related matter of very serious concern – only to be blithely and contemptuously dismissed and ignored – as per usual. Leaving this problem to fester (while ordinary peoples' lives are being drastically affected) without taking *any* action whatsoever seems like an abrogation of responsibility on your part does it not? Others with a more suspicious mindset might even see yet another attempted cover-up here? Perhaps you will be good enough to clarify so that there is no misunderstanding on the part of an increasingly cynical public?

While we are on the subject, let me also draw your attention to the ongoing saga revolving around scores (literally) of improper and illegal acts being committed by certain senior Gardaí and judges on a routine basis – and the fact that no matter which 'statutory oversight body' we approach for redress, that all, without exception, are absolutely failing in their mandates to respect the law and the Constitution – and that all of these bodies come under the direct remit of *your* Department.

Indeed, we now find ourselves facing the grim reality that a section of Irish society – most notably those who hold privileged positions of power and authority, appear to believe themselves above the law. Given the clarity in *Article 40 of the Constitution* that, *"all citizens are equal before the law"* (yes, apparently that includes Garda Management, senior civil servants, judges and even Government Ministers) then we are left in the difficult position Mrs Fitzgerald of advising you personally that if you continue to fail in your duty to the people, the law and the Constitution, and continue to facilitate serial cover-ups and other serious wrongdoing by agents and employees of the State, that you, and any others so involved, each face the very real prospect of criminal charges and/or citizens' arrests being deployed by an increasingly exasperated public, who are thoroughly and utterly fed-up with the corruption and hubris of a wholly discredited so-called 'justice system' – and of the arrogance and contempt of those who purport to administer it.

I therefore now respectfully request a formal meeting with you, in person, to discuss several urgent matters of concern as indicated herein – including allegations of official cover-ups of some very serious crimes – including murder, assaults and criminal conspiracy – and I look forwards to your prompt and accommodating response. We request again Mrs Fitzgerald that you sign off *personally* on any correspondence which claims to be sent 'on your behalf' so as to avoid any doubt or misunderstandings as to who in fact is reading and responding to these important letters.

Yours,

Stephen Manning (etc)

A Member of Integrity Ireland

RESPONSE (Abridged) *" We acknowledge receipt of your letter. Full stop."*

To the Taoiseach, Enda Kenny T.D.

Dear Taoiseach / Mr Enda Kenny,   June 2014

Previous correspondence refers. We note that we have received no acknowledgement or response at all to our recent letter of May 29th last, and, (other than the usual dismissive one-liner) no proper response or follow-up to our letter of May 15th last, which was copied to your constituency office; to Government buildings; to your home address; as well as by email.

We note (again) Mr Kenny that you continue to avoid answering our questions; that you have yet to address any of the very serious matters raised in our correspondence to date; and that you seem determined to continue avoiding and evading these issues, and avoiding us, your constituents, ad-infinitum. In short, that you are engaging in the very same obstructive and discredited practices highlighted recently in the Sean Geurin Report – practices which you *personally* denounced in the Dail – when you inferred (misleadingly) that you had 'only recently become aware' that such practices were apparently 'routine' in the Ministry of Justice and at Garda Headquarters.

We repeat 'for the record' Mr Kenny; this cowardly and contemptuous tactic of evasiveness and circuitous deferrals is not going to work. This matter is NOT going away, and each and every time you attempt to sidestep the issue or otherwise shirk your responsibilities, it only exposes you further to ridicule and accusation. We note that we have written some sixteen letters to you regarding this specific matter over a period of over two-and-a-half years without any proper response from you to date. It is time that you stood up to your responsibilities both as our constituency TD and as Taoiseach, and simply do what you are being paid to do.

We are now making a pointed request that you meet with us without delay to clarify for us – in the context of ongoing criminal complaints that have been lodged with An Garda Síochána – what *your* personal role and relationship is with certain persons whom we allege have engaged in serious criminal acts and cover-ups, under the apparent protection of senior civil servants, Gardaí and State agencies.

In light of the obstructionism and evasiveness encountered to date; any failure to respond in the affirmative within 3 days will be taken as a refusal sir, and will be published to national and international media; to the members of the Oireachtas; to the EU parliament, and online. We also formally put you on Notice that in the overall interests of justice, transparency and accountability, that we will subpoena you *personally* to open Court to account for the serial acts of misfeasance, nonfeasance and malfeasance which appear to be emanating 'under your instructions' and acted upon by agents of the State in direct contravention of our fundamental human rights; of the Irish Constitution and of EU Law.

We await your prompt and accommodating response Taoiseach, and trust the position is clear.

Yours,

Stephen Manning (etc)

A Member of Integrity Ireland

LETTER OPENED, RESEALED & RETURNED TO SENDER

To the Taoiseach, Enda Kenny T.D.

Dear Taoiseach / Mr Enda Kenny,   November 2014

Previous correspondence refers. We note that we received no acknowledgement or response at all to our letter of June 16th last (the 16th in sequence since January 2012) which, amongst other things, highlighted the repeated failure or refusal of yourself to respond to other important letters addressed to you, which were also copied-in to Government Offices.

We write on this occasion in context of your recent heart-warming display of personal concern for Ms Maria Cahill, to ask you a direct and specific question regarding a series of criminal attacks committed against our family ongoing since 2009 – something which we have repeatedly brought to your personal attention without any due or proper response from you.

Given the utter failure of Gardaí to take proper action, and in the face of repeated deceptions, cover-ups and misdirection by various State agencies and agents, we took it upon ourselves to research and investigate the crimes being perpetrated against our family since 2009.

You will be pleased to hear that we have now identified the two persons chiefly responsible for those vicious, perverse and cowardly attacks, and we are preparing a file for submission directly to the DPP. However, it has also come to our attention that these individuals are it seems, related to you personally, and it has been suggested to us that the reason we encountered such widespread malfeasance and obstructionism in trying to have these criminals properly dealt with by the Gardaí and the Courts, is primarily because they are related to 'the Taoiseach'.

Naturally, we would not wish to cast *inaccurate* aspersions on anyone – most especially someone like yourself in an important political position; so we ask again Mr Kenny (reminding you that we live less than 3 miles from your private residence, and less than 5 miles from your local constituency office) that you meet with us without delay to clarify the situation – in the overall interests of justice. We are sure you will agree, that in light of your sterling public support of Ms Cahill in *her* personal ordeal, that for you NOT to respond to this pointed approach from a local constituent who voted for you, would suggest hypocrisy of the highest order, and would only serve to reinforce the assumption that something is seriously amiss here.

We await your prompt and accommodating response Mr Kenny, and trust the position is clear.

Yours,

Stephen Manning (etc)

A Member of Integrity Ireland

NO RESPONSE

To the Taoiseach, Enda Kenny T.D.

Dear Taoiseach / Mr Enda Kenny,   December 2014

Previous correspondence refers. We note that we received no acknowledgement or response at all to our letters of June 16th and November 6th last (the 17th in sequence since January 2012) which, amongst other things, highlighted the repeated failure or refusal of yourself to respond to other important letters addressed to you, which were also copied-in to Government Offices.

Accordingly, we now copy our letter of November 6th to Government Offices asking <u>again</u> that you please respond without delay. We respectfully advice Mr Kenny, that if you continue to evade, avoid or ignore us – and if you persist in these apparently-pusillanimous attempts to avoid answering critical questions regarding your personal foreknowledge and involvement (if any) in the criminal attacks against our family by State agencies and other individuals personally related to you, then you will understand that in the interests of justice, transparency and accountability, that we must reserve the right to publicise these matters in defence of our Constitutional rights.

Accordingly Mr Kenny, please be advised that if we have not received contact from you regarding these matters within 7 days – and if said contact does not satisfy our outstanding questions – then we will immediately publish all 17 of the letters sent to you – plus the various disingenuous 'responses' with a view to informing the general public of the situation.

We also advise that in the event that you, your staff, your subordinates, your colleagues or your relatives are subpoenaed to give information in the High Court, that we will be relying on these correspondences in support of our position; that you have at best, utterly and repeatedly failed in your moral, statutory and Constitutional obligations.

Decent law-abiding citizens should NOT have to be put through ordeals such as this Mr Kenny – where ordinary people's lives are literally being destroyed through the inactivity and malfeasance of so-called 'elected representatives' who are either too apathetic, too morally compromised or too corrupt to simply do the right thing.

We ask again – on behalf of our family and for all those who trusted you and voted for you; please do the right thing Mr Kenny, while the opportunity still remains.

Yours,

Stephen Manning (etc)

A Member of Integrity Ireland

NO RESPONSE

To the Taoiseach, Enda Kenny T.D.

Dear Taoiseach / Mr Kenny,   April 2015

In light of the consternation of opposition TD's and the increasing public disquiet surrounding the Government's plans to appoint a seemingly-conflicted organisation to investigate the circumstances surrounding the sale of *Site Serve* to *Millington-GMC Sierra* (a Dennis O'Brien-owned company) via the IBRC; we would like to offer you the services of *Integrity Ireland* to conduct any such investigative enquiry on the primary basis that we are completely independent of any of the parties affiliated with said sale, and that we have an abundance of qualified individuals who are willing to undertake a thoroughly professional, objective and transparent enquiry at no direct cost to the Government or the taxpayer – asking only that our legitimate vouched expenses be covered during the process.

We believe this is the solution that best serves the *legitimate* interests of all parties concerned inasmuch as there would be no partisan conflict of interest, and therefore no questioning of the independence and professionalism of any such enquiry. In addition, the substantial savings to Government and citizens alike will surely meet with the approval of all parties concerned.

The only prerequisite would be an undertaking by the Government that our investigators, once assigned, will be afforded the *full* cooperation of any State agencies or affiliates involved, and that the expenses incurred by the *Integrity Ireland* investigative team be reimbursed in a timely manner so as to facilitate a speedy conclusion to the work.

We would envisage the prospective *Integrity Ireland* team to consist of seven key personnel plus administrative support staff. The key personnel would consist of two lawyers with expertise in the banking sector; one qualified private investigator; two retired members of An Garda Síochána; and two academics – one of whom specialises in investigative journalism and report-writing. We would of course be obliged if the State could provide us with a functioning office, but if it will help encourage a speedy decision on your part Taoiseach, we can operate from our own offices and make an immediate start.

We understand how important it is that the Government is seen to be 100% behind any genuine efforts to clear up any misunderstandings about the circumstances surrounding this matter, and that you are eager to put to rest any erroneous implications that there may have been anything untoward in a transaction which appears to have cost the taxpayers over €100m; so may we assure you personally Mr Kenny that any review of the *Site Serve* sale by the *Integrity Ireland* team will be conducted to the highest professional and moral standards in the overall interests of justice, transparency and accountability.

Trusting this generous offer will meet with your speedy approval.

Yours,

Stephen Manning (etc)

A Member of Integrity Ireland

WOWEE! A RESPONSE!

(Abridged) *"We have every confidence that the retired High Court Judge that WE have appointed to do the investigation will be independent, thorough and completely impartial... But thanks for the offer anyway."*

APPENDIX

I

ARTICLES OF

INTEREST

On Mahon and Irish Corruption

[Village Magazine Editorial, April, 2012]

As Mahon finally grinds to a somewhat disappointing report, it is time to recognise that corruption, even more than its cousin greed, did for Ireland in our time.

Enda Kenny got into trouble by over-generalising on the sensitive issue of just who went mad with greed and borrowing during our distant boom, but he might just as well have gone the whole way and questioned which of us dabbled in corruption too.

Corruption, illegal and legal, has been endemic in banking, in the awarding of public contracts, in planning, in the exploitation of resources and the environment, in the unblinking repayment of unsecured bondholders and ultimately in the obscene maldistribution of wealth.

Ireland is regarded as suffering particularly high levels of "legal corruption" – perhaps as many (not you dear reader or I, of course) need to look into their souls to see if they have been party to corruption as need to see if they are party to greed.

While no laws may be broken, "strokes" and "cute hoorism" such as nepotism, patronage, jobbery, parochialism, political favours and political donations influence political decisions and policy to the detriment of the common good, disproportionately in this country. Influence-selling has yet to be completely outlawed, while political funding remains open to abuse through loose thresholds on political donations and weak disclosure criteria for political parties. Though legislation is proposed, political lobbying is entirely unregulated and political parties are not required to publish audited accounts.

Disgrace bears little consequence in this society. Ben Dunne still has a weekly column in the Irish Sun, although Moriarty found him corrupt and his principal defence seems to be that he had psychiatric difficulties. Bertie Ahern batted for the Star from behind the contents of a refrigerator and Celia Larkin pontificates on the issues of the day in the Sunday Independent. No-one cares what Moriarty said about civil servants. Denis O'Brien still dominates our Global Economic Forums, the Clinton Diaspora Summit and the horrible Ireland Inc St Patrick"s Day NYSE bell-ringing.

Whatever about the benighted Fianna Fáil, our current main ruling party raised, with corrupt Minister Michael Lowry"s involvement, €1.3 million to clear its debts between 1991 and 1994 and, despite that and an army of dodgy rezoning councillors, most of whom were recognised in the Mahon Report, it rose to political ascendancy last year as if it were a paragon of virtue. There was, and is, no sign of criminal proceedings for corruption against Haughey, Burke, Lowry, O"Brien, the Bailey Brothers or Liam Lawlor. Michael Lowry, Ray Burke, Ivor Callely, George Redmond, Liam Cosgrave Jnr, Frank Dunlop – that galaxy of unworthiness – all retain their government pensions. Government promises to address Mahon recommendations and seek prosecutions are as tenuous as the forgotten pledges it gave after Moriarty.

Village likes to look at human progress in terms of four spheres that comprise human activity – economic, social, environmental and cultural. On probably all, certainly on three, we live in a corrupt society, morally and often legally.

Economically, Ireland Inc (that well-worn if emasculated phrase!) turns out to believe in bailing out people who were paid excessively for taking risks and then avoided responsibility when the risks went wrong. This reveals as insincere the very premise of the capitalism it purported to believe in. In this respect if you have to do capitalism, it is better to do it the US way with competition and swift criminal penalties for dishonesty.

In Ireland, we failed to regulate, even to maintain functioning capitalism, let alone to facilitate an equal and sustainable society. And from the Beef Tribunal to the Moriarty Tribunal to the Planning Tribunal and various insipid banking inquiries as well as in cases involving insider trading, public tendering and the whole planning process, it is clear that there is widespread red-toothed corruption tainting important sectors of our economy and reaching right to the top; as well as ubiquitous "trading in influence".

During the boom all the main parties promoted or went along with a tax-reducing, officiary-over-remunerating agenda and the now-ruling parties supported insane stamp-duty reductions. If not corrupt this was at least unfair and reckless. The biggest recent instances of economic corruption are repaying largely foreign plutocrats with their unsecured bonds and Nama,,s decision in most cases to retrieve not the original value of loans, but the haircut price it paid, so losing the potential upside benefit to the taxpayer; and revealing it as sustaining burnt-out speculators when we were expressly promised it would not. Predictably too, NAMA pays some of them up to €200,000 a year to run their troubled companies.

Socially, budgetary policy favours expenditure cuts which affect the poorest most and taxation policy favours the rich. Even during the boom we had very low public expenditure relative to income, leading to unnecessarily poor public services and quality of life. During the boom there were famously more Irish golf courses than playgrounds (the Great Recession will have taken care of more of the former than the latter) and there is a certain corruption in the structuring of society to suit the rich and make equality between people, who are equal moral agents, impossible. The CSO recently showed that the average income of those in the top 20 per cent of the population was 5½ times higher than the average of those in the poorest 20 per cent. A year earlier it had been just 4.3 times higher. The Gini coefficient which measures income inequality more comprehensively was .34 in 2010, a disimprovement from .299 in 2009 (when Sweden"s, for example, was .23). Much other corruption derives from this social inequality. And as for the left campaigning against the idea of property taxes, this magazine despairs.

Environmentally, during the boom we had the highest resource-use per capita in the EU and the second-highest green- house gas emissions in the EU after Luxembourg. Though emissions have dropped from 18 to 14 tonnes per capita this is due to the economic fiasco, not good administration. Ireland has played the fullest role in international climate crimes.

Our water quality should be excellent due to demography and geography. In fact e coli levels in Ireland are seven times those of Northern Ireland and 28 times those of England and Wales (and our chosen antidote of chlorination now offers carcinogenic Thms in the drinking water of an extraordinary – and unknowing – 600,000 citizens). Yet septic-tank inspections, mandated by the EU were recently described by protesters from Galway West, as "an injustice to rural people . . . an insult", and environment minister, Phil Hogan, recently boasted that the new septic tank inspection regime would cover only ten per cent of houses near rivers and lakes. The debate on septic tanks proceeds on the basis that there is no value to the public in clean water. It is left to the EU to see the policy point; and the public interest.

We never had the appetite for good planning. The National Spatial Strategy was deliberately made toothless. Local authorities ignore it – as well as their own local plans, allowing Dublin for example to sprawl into surrounding counties; while cities and towns outside Greater Dublin languish. Around 50% of the State"s housing output is built in the least sustainable form – one-off. Since 2001, 170,000 new one-off houses have been permitted in Ireland. Despite this there is a conspiracy to make out that the national spatial problem is the difficulty of obtaining permissions for one-off houses.

We have failed to learn the lessons of the planning Tribunal which have been evident for a decade and a half. While codes of conduct and legislation aimed at curbing corruption are in place for public representatives and officials, there appears to be little understanding and repeated transgression of the codes at national and local level.

Politicians have not learnt the clear lesson that Development and other plans need to be assessed quasi-judicially, at the time of creation, for compliance with the National Spatial Strategy. Mahon recommends this only for decisions that counter managements" advice. In local government, the risk of fraud and corruption is particularly acute, heightened by the lack of adequate safeguards not just against planning corruption, but against false accounting, misuse of resources, influence-selling and fraud also.

Culturally, our contemporary artists have not held a mirror to our corrupt society. Too few of them have made targets of our ruling elite, too many of them seek the company of the wealthy and the corrupt. Ireland is the capital of the boy band and eurotrash. Colm Tóibín"s celebration of Michael Fingleton, Bono"s exaltation of capitalism and cultivation of Blair, Bush and Ahern, Seamus Heaney"s attendance at a Denis O"Brien dinner find no parallels in the worlds of Joyce, Beckett or Yeats. Aosdána (Irish Association of Artists) is the smuggest colloquium in cultural history. Jedward.

Transparency International"s Corruption perceptions Index 2011 shows that Ireland"s ranking has fallen recently and it now compares poorly to other northern European nations. Ireland ranks 19 out of 183 countries with a score of 7.5 out of ten, down from 8 in 2010. The culture of this country facilitates influence-selling and is indulgent of corruption, even in high places. That the national edifice should have collapsed was inevitable.

It is this infection mixed with a largely unadulterated celebration of greed, rather than our mere, derivative, fiscal come-uppance and debt, that will keep this country down for a generation. Greed and Corruption are each rooted in base deference to money and self, rather than the public interest.

Without a change in culture we are doomed.

European Rights Body Warns of 'Corrupt Ireland'

(Irish Examiner, Nov 2014)

There is growing concern about corruption in Ireland especially about elected politicians, Europe's foremost human rights authority has warned. Various reforms recently introduced, such as the freedom of information and ethics acts are too complex and in some cases conflict with one another.

The report, from the Council of Europe in which Ireland and 46 other governments are represented, warns that there is too much political interference in the appointment and promotion of judges and has called for changes to maintain their independence.

They also want laws that threaten government ministers, elected politicians and others with six months jail for disclosing confidential information scrapped as it discourages whistleblowing.

It notes that Ireland's reputation has been slipping with Transparency International placing it at its lowest ever ranking among the business community two years ago at 25th, behind Uruguay, Chile and the Bahamas.

The report calls for more stringent rules for politicians on conflicts of interest and asset declarations to include liabilities and those of their closest connections. More streamlined rules and more independent way of assessing politicians' compliance was needed. They say all the rules that apply to government ministers should be extended to cover all elected politicians, and to their staff, and it should not be limited to just getting money, but should be extended to cover other advantages.

It raised a red flag over the fact that the clerk of the Dáil or Seanad can dismiss complaints against members without referring it to the relevant committee. They question why complaints are only made public if there is a negative finding. They are also concerned that a minister can face six months jail for disclosing confidential government information, irrespective of the reason for doing so. This could mean that people are discouraged from becoming whistleblowers. While the Government pointed to a range of protections, the report believes it is not sufficient and recommends that the whole issue be clarified to ensure whistleblowers are protected.

The report took on board the complaints of the judiciary that the public campaign and referendum on cutting their salaries damaged their standing. There is now a two-tier payment for judges depending when they take up their posts and the constitutional ban on changing their salaries has been scrapped. A judicial council should be established to deal with such issues in the future, to be involved in appointments of judges, establish an ethical code and judicial training practices. The report is very critical of politicians' role in selecting judges and says judges' promotion "is even more susceptible to political interference" and urges a judicial council to be involved.

The report, from the Council of Europe's Group of States against Corruption to which Ireland has signed up, monitors anti-corruption laws and practices and focuses on the measures in place nationally to prevent corruption among elected politicians, judges and prosecutors. It makes 11 recommendations to the Government and has asked it to report in 18 months on the steps it has taken to implement the recommendations.

By Ann Cahill, European Correspondent

The full European Council Report entitled: "Corruption prevention in respect of members of parliament, judges and prosecutors" can be found on the I-I website under the 'Irish Government' tactical review tab.

The Psychology of Institutionalised Exploitation and Abuse

The fundamental problem with a culture which was described recently by Pope Francis as 'savage capitalism' is that it attracts, and rewards, those who are most adept at the ruthless exploitation of others. Such a culture ensures that the most selfish, the most greedy, the most clever and ambitious individuals will eventually rise to the top - as long as they can disguise their anti-social characteristics with the mask of respectability; because obviously, being *overtly* selfish and greedy isn't going to endear oneself to others. This is how routine deception on both the individual and corporate level has become a cornerstone of 'savage capitalism' - because ultimately it is a massive scam, based on the equally massive lie - that unbridled capitalism is 'good for the economy' - and therefore good for all of us. But what we aren't being told is that money is only being 'made' by a very select few, and it is being made at the great collective expense of the rest of us. Those who are most adept at this form of mass daylight robbery have learned to put profit to the fore - at all costs. But to be capable of such heartless ambition, a person must first be able to ignore their moral conscience and reject their empathy for others. Or, they have to be born without the capacity for a conscience in the first place.

Welcome to the world of the psychopath and the sociopath.

The following quotes from various professional sources should help us reflect on the type of people who (according to several studies) are increasingly ascending to the top positions in international corporations; to national governments; and to other positions of power and authority. The formula is relatively simple. If the ultimate 'value' is money and power, and the most efficient way to secure that 'value' is to ruthlessly manipulate and exploit others; and if there are NO moral checks-and-balances to prevent amoral people ascending the ranks - and if there are NO effective ethical constraints or professional restrictions in place; then naturally, one would expect the most ambitious and capable exploiters and manipulators to rise to the top.

And therein lies the moral root of the problem. The values we teach our children have no real place in a world of 'savage capitalism'. What use to shareholders is kindness, love and compassion - if it doesn't make a buck? What real profit is there in honesty, integrity and generosity? We can make courageous and determined efforts at the local level to tackle the by-products of this voracious culture of exploitation by a privileged few, but the problem will continue to resurface until such time as there is sufficient and widespread understanding of what *really* is going on; about who and what is driving this corporate 'Machine' and what the ultimate aims and objectives are. For we can be absolutely assured of one thing; the energies that drive this 'savage capitalism' are in direct opposition to all of the humane values and principles that are enshrined in our Constitution - as well as in our established faith traditions. This is one of the key messages that is being delivered in this Guide; that whilst our Constitution solemnly declares that we must uphold the virtues of a fair and humane society - at the same time the establishment is surreptitiously engaged in the underhanded destruction of the same. Why? Because there is profit in it - and because, quite frankly, they really couldn't give a damn about the rest of us. When the next election comes around, it might be an idea to ask yourself - or better still, ask a campaigning politician - if it is a good idea to allow, or even encourage selfish, greedy and ambitious people to run for office? Because we can be assured of one thing; that these particular leopards will not be changing their spots any time soon!

Psychopaths and Sociopaths *(From an article in The Guardian, UK, Sept 2011)*
"Psychopaths use charm and manipulation to achieve success in the workplace, according to a US study. The study, conducted by the New York psychologist Paul Babiak, suggests that they disguise the condition by hiding behind their high status, playing up their charm and by manipulating others. Favourable environmental factors such as a happy childhood mean they can function in a workplace rather than channelling their energies in more violent or destructive

ways. We have identified individuals that might be labelled 'the successful psychopath'. Part of the problem is that the very things we're looking for in our leaders, the psychopath can easily mimic. Their natural tendency is to be charming. Take that charm and couch it in the right business language and it sounds like charismatic leadership. ..psychopaths are actually poor managerial performers but are adept at climbing the corporate ladder because they can cover up their weaknesses by subtly charming superiors and subordinates. This makes it almost impossible to distinguish between a genuinely talented team leader and a psychopath. The higher the psychopathy, the better they looked – lots of charisma and they talk a good line. You have to think of psychopaths as having at their disposal a very large repertoire of behaviours. So they can use charm, manipulation, intimidation, whatever is required. A psychopath can actually put themselves in your skin, intellectually not emotionally. They can tell what you're thinking, they can look at your body language, they can listen to what you're saying, but what they don't really do is feel what you feel. What this allows them to do is use words to manipulate and con and to interact with you without the baggage of feeling your pain. Psychopaths' brains are wired to seek rewards, no matter the consequences

Psychopaths are often thought of as cold-blooded criminals who take what they want without thinking about consequences. However, a normally functioning person can also have the traits, which include manipulativeness, egocentricity, aggression and risk taking."

* * *

The Top Ten Careers With The Most Psychopaths – Is Your Job On The List?
(From an August 2015 article on the Higher Perspective website)

What comes to mind when you picture a psychopath? A crazy ax-murderer? Psychopaths don't always fit that mould. The clinical diagnoses is a person who has shallow emotions or lacks empathy. Kevin Dutton, a research psychologist at the University of Oxford, has dedicated much of his life to studying the brains of psychopaths and he's been able to piece together a list of the most likely professions psychopaths end up in. Is your career on the list?

1. CEOs   **2. Lawyers**   **3. Media (Radio/TV)**   **4. Sales People**   5. Surgeons

6. Journalists   **7. Police officer**   8. Clergy   9. Chefs   **10. Civil Servants**

* * *

Interestingly, the article goes on to list a number of reasons why these particular professions tend to attract higher levels of psychopathy, but in context of the *Integrity Ireland* project, it is worth noting that some of the most devious and ambitious of our politicians in recent years have displayed many of the characteristics required to be a top-functioning performer in many of the above-listed professions. For example, what is a Government Minister if not a publicly-funded CEO who is adept at spin, double-speak, and manipulating the media? These politicians have 'worked' their image to suit their objectives, which basically, is to mislead and deceive the public into reelecting them. Promises made mean nothing in the climb to success, and every lie, every pretence, every broken promise is justified by the end result; that of fulfilling their own deep-rooted selfish ambitions. This is how and why certain party leaders can declare 'absolute confidence' in one of their struggling colleagues in the face of some scandal or other, but can callously turn on a sixpence if that publicly-declared 'confidence' might interfere in their own reelection prospects. And then we (the longsuffering public) are treated to the usual lies and convolutions and other attempts at damage control, while the various 'special consultants' (hired at our expense) ply their devious trades. This is why it is crucially important that we recognise these particular personality traits for what they are—described in the following article as indicating 'a *predatory* type of human'—and why we must become more discerning when it comes to trusting those who would assume so much control over our lives. Because as the old saying goes, "If it walks like a duck and it talks like a duck... (then it just might be a sociopath)?"

THE PSYCHOPATH - The Mask of Sanity - *(abridged)*

From the Special Research Project of the Quantum Future School

Imagine - if you can - not having a conscience, none at all, no feelings of guilt or remorse no matter what you do, no limiting sense of concern for the well-being of strangers, friends, or even family members. Imagine no struggles with shame, not a single one in your whole life, no matter what kind of selfish, lazy, harmful, or immoral action you had taken. And pretend that the concept of responsibility is unknown to you, except as a burden others seem to accept without question, like gullible fools. In other words, you are completely free of internal restraints, and your unhampered liberty to do just as you please, with no pangs of conscience, is conveniently invisible to the world. You can do anything at all, and still your strange advantage over the majority of people, who are kept in line by their consciences will most likely remain undiscovered.

How will you live your life? Provided you are not forcibly stopped, you can do anything at all. If you are born at the right time, with some access to family fortune, and you have a special talent for whipping up other people's hatred and sense of deprivation, you can arrange to kill large numbers of unsuspecting people. With enough money, you can accomplish this from far away, and you can sit back safely and watch in satisfaction.

Crazy and frightening - and real, in about 4 percent of the population....

The prevalence rate for anorexic eating disorders is estimated a 3.43 percent, deemed to be nearly epidemic, and yet this figure is a fraction lower than the rate for antisocial personality. The high-profile disorders classed as schizophrenia occur in only about 1 percent of [the population] - a mere quarter of the rate of antisocial personality - and the Centres for Disease Control and Prevention say that the rate of colon cancer in the United States, considered "alarmingly high," is about 40 per 100,000 - is one hundred times lower than the rate of antisocial personality.

The high incidence of sociopathy in human society has a profound effect on the rest of us who must live on this planet, too, even those of us who have not been clinically traumatized. The individuals who constitute this 4 percent drain our relationships, our bank accounts, our accomplishments, our self-esteem, our very peace on earth. Yet surprisingly, many people know nothing about this disorder, or if they do, they think only in terms of violent psychopathy - murderers, serial killers, mass murderers - people who have conspicuously broken the law many times over, and who, if caught, will be imprisoned, maybe even put to death by our legal system.

We are not commonly aware of, nor do we usually identify, the larger number of nonviolent sociopaths among us, people who often are not blatant lawbreakers, and against whom our formal legal system provides little defence. Most of us would not imagine any correspondence between conceiving an ethnic genocide and, say, guiltlessly lying to one's boss about a coworker. But the psychological correspondence is not only there; it is chilling. Simple and profound, the link is the absence of the inner mechanism that beats up on us, emotionally speaking, when we make a choice we view as immoral, unethical, neglectful, or selfish. Most of us feel mildly guilty if we eat the last piece of cake in the kitchen, let alone what we would feel if we intentionally and methodically set about to hurt another person.

Those who have no conscience at all are a group unto themselves, whether they be homicidal tyrants or merely ruthless social snipers. The presence or absence of conscience is a deep human division, arguably more significant than intelligence, race, or even gender. What differentiates a sociopath who lives off the labours of others from one who occasionally robs convenience stores, or from one who is a contemporary robber baron - or what makes the difference between an ordinary bully and a sociopathic murderer - is nothing more than social status, drive, intellect, blood lust, or simple opportunity.

There are grounds for the view that psychopathy is quite common in the community at large. For example, there are cases of psychopaths who generally function normally in the community as businessmen, doctors, and even psychiatrists. Some researchers see criminal psychopathy - often referred to as anti-social personality disorder - as an extreme of a "normal" personality dimension (or dimensions). We would characterize criminal psychopaths as "unsuccessful psychopaths." The implication, of course, is that many psychopaths may exist in society who cope better than do those who come to the attention of the judicial and welfare systems. Some researchers have begun to seriously consider the idea that it is important to study psychopathy not as an artificial clinical category but as a general personality trait in the community at large. In other words, psychopathy is being recognized as a more or less a different type of human. This lack of "soul quality" makes them very efficient "machines." They can be brilliant, write scholarly works, imitate the words of emotion, but over time, it becomes clear that their words do not match their actions. They are the type of person who can claim that they are devastated by grief who then attend a party "to forget." The problem is: they really DO forget.

Many psychopaths are able to reach very high positions in life. It is only over time that their associates become aware of the fact that their climb up the ladder of success is predicated on violating the rights of others."Even when they are indifferent to the rights of their associates, they are often able to inspire feelings of trust and confidence." Our world seems to have been invaded by individuals whose approach to life and love is so drastically different from what has been the established norm for a very long time that we are ill- prepared to deal with their tactics of what Robert Canup calls "plausible lie." As he demonstrates, this philosophy of the "plausible lie" has overtaken the legal and administrative domains of our world, turning them into machines in which human beings with real emotions are destroyed.

The recent movie, "The Matrix," touched a deep chord in society because it exemplified this mechanistic trap in which so many people find their lives enmeshed, and from which they are unable to extricate themselves because they believe that everyone around them who "looks human" is, in fact, just like them - emotionally, spiritually, and otherwise.

The truth - when twisted by good liars, can always make an innocent person look bad - especially if the innocent person is honest and admits his mistakes. The basic assumption that the truth lies between the testimony of the two sides always shifts the advantage to the lying side and away from the side telling the truth. Under most circumstances, this shift put together with the fact that the truth is going to also be twisted in such a way as to bring detriment to the innocent person, results in the advantage always resting in the hands of liars - psychopaths. Even the simple act of giving testimony under oath is useless. If a person is a liar, swearing an oath means nothing to that person. However, swearing an oath acts strongly on a serious, truthful witness. Again, the advantage is placed on the side of the liar. [Robert Canup]

Oh, indeed, the psychopath can imitate feelings, but the only real feelings they seem to have - the thing that drives them and causes them to act out different dramas for effect - is a sort of "predatorial hunger" for what they want. That is to say, they "feel" need/want as love, and not having their needs/wants met is described as "not being loved" by them. What is more, this "need/want" perspective posits that only the "hunger" of the psychopath is valid, and anything and everything "out there," outside of the psychopath, is not real except insofar as it has the capability of being assimilated to the psychopath as a sort of "food." "Can it be used or can it provide something?" is the only issue about which the psychopath seems to be concerned. All else - all activity - is subsumed to this drive.

In short, the psychopath - and the narcissist to a lesser extent - is a predator. If we think about the interactions of predators with their prey in the animal kingdom, we can come to some idea of what is behind the "mask of sanity" of the psychopath. Just as an animal predator will adopt all kinds of stealthy functions in order to stalk their prey, cut them out of the herd, get close to them and reduce their resistance, so does the psychopath construct all kinds of elaborate camouflage composed of words and appearances - lies and manipulations - in order to "assimilate" their prey.

This leads us to an important question: what does the psychopath REALLY get from their victims? It's easy to see what they are after when they lie and manipulate for money or material goods or power. But in many instances, such as love relationships or faked friendships, it is not so easy to see what the psychopath is after. Without wandering too far afield into spiritual speculations - a problem Cleckley also faced - we can only say that it seems to be that the psychopath ENJOYS making others suffer. Just as normal humans enjoy seeing other people happy, or doing things that make other people smile, the psychopath enjoys the exact opposite.

Anyone who has ever observed a cat playing with a mouse before killing and eating it has probably explained to themselves that the cat is just "entertained" by the antics of the mouse and is unable to conceive of the terror and pain being experienced by the mouse, and the cat, therefore, is innocent of any evil intent. The mouse dies, the cat is fed, and that is nature. Psychopaths don't generally eat their victims. Yes, in extreme cases the entire cat and mouse dynamic is carried out and cannibalism has a long history wherein it was assumed that certain powers of the victim could be assimilated by eating some particular part of them. But in ordinary life, psychopaths and narcissists don't go all the way, so to say. This causes us to look at the cat and mouse scenarios again with different eyes. Now we ask: is it too simplistic to think that the innocent cat is merely entertained by the mouse running about and frantically trying to escape? Is there something more to this dynamic than meets the eye? Is there something more than being "entertained" by the antics of the mouse trying to flee? After all, in terms of evolution, why would such behaviour be hard-wired into the cat? Is the mouse tastier because of the chemicals of fear that flood his little body? Is a mouse frozen with terror more of a "gourmet" meal?

One thing we do know is this: many people who experience interactions with psychopaths and narcissists report feeling "drained" and confused and often subsequently experience deteriorating health. Many psychopaths.. ..can be found in white collar professions where they are aided in their evil by the fact that most people expect certain classes of people to be trustworthy because of their social or professional credentials. Lawyers, doctors, teachers, politicians, psychiatrists and psychologists, generally do not have to earn our trust because they have it by virtue of their positions. But the fact is: psychopaths are found in such lofty spheres also!

Psychopaths just have what it takes to defraud and bilk others: they can be fast talkers, they can be charming, they can be self-assured and at ease in social situations; they are cool under pressure, unfazed by the possibility of being found out, and totally ruthless. And even when they are exposed, they can carry on as if nothing has happened, often making their accusers the targets of accusations of being victimized by THEM. What makes psychopaths different from all others is the remarkable ease with which they lie, the pervasiveness of their deception, and the callousness with which they carry it out. Psychopaths are notorious for not answering the questions asked them. They will answer something else, or in such a way that the direct question is never addressed. They also phrase things so that some parts of their narratives are difficult to understand.

The callous use of the old, the lonely, the vulnerable, the disenfranchised, the marginaliszed, is a trademark of the psychopath. Psychopaths dominate and set the standard for behaviour in our society. We live in a world based on a psychopathic, energy stealing food chain, because that's just the way things are. Most people are so damaged they no longer have the capacity to even imagine a different system based on a symbiotic network. They are not only damaged by others, but also by the thousand little evils they have done to others to survive. For them to see the system for what it is, would require them to see the part they have played in perpetuating it. That is a lot to ask of a fragile ego.

Worth Considering...

Before the end of the last century, the power of corporate and financial giants had reached such a dizzying level that 51 of the world's 100 biggest 'economies' comprised transnational behemoths rather than sovereign countries. The aggregate sales of the world's 200 richest companies exceeded the combined gross domestic product of all but ten of the world's nations. The assets of the world's three richest people exceeded the GNP of the poorest 48 countries and their 600 million people. The assets of the 200 richest – who, with few exceptions, had corporate/financial ties – exceeded the combined income of over 40 per cent of mankind.

Today, 53 of the world's 100 biggest 'economies' comprise multinational corporate and financial giants rather than sovereign countries.

These are truly shameful statistics.

To an extraordinary degree, the world and its people are now dominated by the largest corporate and financial leviathans and by the mega-rich.

See Tom Hanahoe, *America Rules: US Foreign Policy, Globalization and Corporate USA*
(Dingle: Brandon, 2003), p. 17.

Greek historian Thucydides (c. 460 BC – c. 395 BC) observed that "large nations do what they wish, while small nations accept what they must." Today, one can, accurately, substitute 'large multinationals' for 'large nations'. Corporate giants – such as Shell – have more power than minnow nations, such as Ireland. Their economic clout is such that they can, and do, dictate to sovereign countries.

Democracy is dying.

Quoted in Noam Chomsky, *Hegemony or Survival: America's Quest for Global Dominance* (London: Penguin, 2003), p.16.

Words to the Wise

Those who have been once intoxicated with power, and have derived any kind of emolument from it, even though but for one year, never can willingly abandon it. They may be distressed in the midst of all their power; but they will never look to any thing but power for their relief.

It is the function of a judge not to make but to declare the law, according to the golden mete-wand of the law and not by the crooked cord of discretion.

Power gradually extirpates from the mind every humane and gentle virtue. Pity, benevolence, friendship, are things almost unknown in high stations.

When bad men combine, the good must associate; else they will fall one by one, an unpitied sacrifice in a contemptible struggle.

It is not, what a lawyer tells me I may do; but what humanity, reason, and justice, tell me I ought to do.

All who have ever written on government are unanimous, that among a people generally corrupt, liberty cannot long exist.

Corrupt influence, which is itself the perennial spring of all prodigality, and of all disorder; which loads us, more than millions of debt; which takes away vigour from our arms, wisdom from our councils, and every shadow of authority and credit from the most venerable parts of our constitution.

All persons possessing any portion of power ought to be strongly and awfully impressed with an idea that they act in trust and that they are to account for their conduct in that trust to the one great Master, Author, and Founder of society.

Hypocrisy, of course, delights in the most sublime speculations; for, never intending to go beyond speculation, it costs nothing to have it magnificent.

Justice is itself the great standing policy of civil society; and any eminent departure from it, under any circumstances, lies under the suspicion of being no policy at all.

Writers, especially when they act in a body and with one direction, have great influence on the public mind.

Whatever is supreme in a state, ought to have, as much as possible, its judicial authority so constituted as not only not to depend upon it, but in some sort to balance it. It ought to give a security to its justice against its power. It ought to make its judicature, as it were, something exterior to the state.

When the leaders choose to make themselves bidders at an auction of popularity, their talents, in the construction of the state, will be of no service. They will become flatterers instead of legislators; the instruments, not the guides, of the people.

All that is necessary for the triumph of evil is that good men do nothing.

APPENDIX II

FORMS & TEMPLATES

The various forms, chits and templates in this section have either been created or amended by *Integrity Ireland* and are designed to compliment the ideas, suggestions and 'direct action' tactics outlined in this Guide. They have been placed in the rear of this Guide for ease of photocopying and re-use. If you are not a signed up member or supporter of *Integrity Ireland* we would ask that you remove the logo before sending these forms to other parties, thank you.

If you have any suggestions for additional forms that would be useful to other members, please feel free to email those suggestions to: sos@integrityireland.ie. Thank you.

Index

- Form 15.3 Information for Common Informer procedure
- Form 15.1 Summons for Common Informer procedure
- Witness Summons for the District Court
- Notification of Submission of a Criminal Complaint
- Constitutional Grounds for Non-cooperation
- Letter of Authorisation
- Case Progress Record
- Constitutional Affirmation plus attachments etc.
- Legal Services Guarantee
- Court Hearing Report Form
- Compiling a Statement / Affidavit
- Statement of Delivery or Receipt
- Garda/Legal Interview Report
- Public Notification of a Criminal Complaint

I

AN CHÚIRT DÚICHE   THE DISTRICT COURT

No. 15.3

O.15, r.1 (2)
O.16, r.1 (1)

Information

District Court Area of...District No.................

.... Prosecutor

.... Accused

The information of ....

of...

who says on oath..

....

....

....

....

....

*(and the Informant binds himself/herself to attend when and where called on to give evidence against the said accused for the said offence, or otherwise to forfeit to the State the sum of...to the use of the Minister for Finance).

Signed...

Informant

Sworn before me this ....day of ....20.........

at...

Signed...
Judge of the District Court

* *Delete where applicable*

© Integrity Ireland 2015

AN CHÚIRT DÚICHE   THE DISTRICT COURT

No. 15.1

O.15, r.1 (3)

Summons

District Court Area of..District No................

....*Complainant *Prosecutor

of...

....*Defendant *Accused

*(in court area and district aforesaid)

WHERAS a complaint has been made to me that you, on the .... day of ....

20......., at .... *(in court area and district aforesaid)

did:..

....

....

....

....

THIS IS TO COMMAND YOU to appear on the hearing of the said complaint at a sitting of the
District Court for the court area and district aforesaid to be held at:

....on the ....day of ....20........

at....................*a.m. /p.m. to answer to the said complaint.

Dated this.......... day of ....20...........

Signed...
Judge of the District Court

To the above-named *defendant * accused..

of..

* Delete where applicable

Schedule B
O.21, r.1 (1)

No. 21.1
Witness Summons

District Court Area of...District No...........

Prosecutor...

Accused...

YOU ARE HEREBY REQUIRED to attend at the sitting of the District Court to be held at ....on the ....day of .... 20...., at.......
*am/pm and on any day to which the hearing of these proceedings shall be adjourned, to give evidence on behalf of .... on the hearing of a complaint that the above-named accused did:...................................
....
....
....

*AND YOU ARE REQUIRED TO BRING WITH YOU the following accounts, papers, documents (or things):...
....
....

Dated this...............day of................................. 20.......

Signed ....(Print name)...
* Judge of the District Court (or) Clerk of the District Court (or) Peace Commissioner

To...

Of..

NOTE: If, without lawful excuse, you do not obey this summons, a warrant for your arrest may be issued.

*Delete where inapplicable

(Optional – for official stamp)

NOTICE OF SUBMISSION OF A CRIMINAL COMPLAINT

This NOTICE is to advise you *(name of subject)*...

(of firm/institution/address)...

that as per the **Reporting Obligations of the Criminal Justice Act 2011** that you have been reported to the Statutory Authorities and named in a formal criminal complaint copied to An Garda Síochána HQ; to the Office of the DPP; to the Minister for Justice; and to the *Integrity Ireland HAFTA Database* in matters generally summarised as follows:

(Summary of allegations/offences)...

....

....

You are further advised that any attempts to interfere with or obstruct the lawful submission and advancement of the aforesaid complaint, or any attempts to suppress or otherwise improperly conceal said complaint in face of the supporting evidence and/or in context of the sworn affidavit of the complainant would constitute an offence against **Section 7 of the Criminal Procedure Act 2010** specifically; *"an offence against the administration of justice"* which is an arrestable offence. Accordingly, any parties so involved or who are implicated in affiliated unlawful or unconstitutional activities such as misfeasance, malfeasance or nonfeasance (especially by Statutory Authorities or their agents) may be subject to a criminal complaint and/or a citizen's arrest under **Section 4 of the Criminal Law Act 1997** whereupon said parties will be delivered to An Garda Síochána for the purposes of surrendering to due process as provided for in legislation.

(Print name of complainant)...

(Authorised signature)...

(Witness / I-I Reference)...

Any party named herein has the right to contest the contents of this NOTICE by writing to Integrity Ireland via the website 'www.integrityireland.ie'. Any such written submission, provided it meets the required criteria and is personally signed and accompanied by proof of I.D. will be duly logged on the I-I HAFTA Database in the interests of justice, transparency and accountability.

'One by one – together – we CAN make a difference!'

Constitutional Grounds for Non-Cooperation

"The highest law in the State is the Constitution of Ireland, from which all other law derives its authority. The Constitution is held to be the source of power exercised by the legislative, judicial and executive branches of government. The Irish Supreme Court and High Court exercise judicial review over all legislation and may strike down laws if they are inconsistent with the constitution."

1. The Constitution supersedes the law. The law is subject to the Constitution.
2. Judges swear a solemn Constitutional Oath to abide by the law and the Constitution.
3. If a judge – or any other agent of the State is engaged in unlawful or unconstitutional activity – then they are NOT operating under their Constitutional or Statutory remits.
4. No citizen (or person) is obliged to facilitate or comply with illicit directions, procedures or processes. In fact, we are constitutionally and legally obliged NOT to knowingly do so.
5. To knowingly comply with, facilitate, or cooperate with unconstitutional activity is therefore to be complicit in criminal activity.
6. No other citizen – regardless of position – has the Constitutional right, nor the legal power, nor the moral authority to coerce, direct or manipulate another person into wrongdoing.
7. We therefore assert our fundamental right to refuse to be made knowingly complicit in illicit, underhanded or criminal activity on the basis of the Irish Constitution and the law.

In the matter before the Court today, the following facts are beyond dispute and collectively demonstrate that improper, illicit and/or illegal acts are being committed by parties to this case, and that said acts, and the resultant response or lack thereof by those entrusted with the administration of justice, clearly constitutes a collective attempt to pervert, interfere with or obstruct the course of justice, which is a criminal offence, and in clear breach of Articles 34, 35, 40 & 45 of the Constitution:

(List the specific reasons here below – or – use the statement above as a stand-alone declaration)

- That to comply with such a process in these circumstances would be to sanction, or be complicit in unconstitutional or criminal activity, which the Respondent is NOT prepared to do.

Signed: Date:

Witnesses:

Constitutional Grounds for Non-Cooperation

"The highest law in the State is the Constitution of Ireland, from which all other law derives its authority. The Constitution is held to be the source of power exercised by the legislative, judicial and executive branches of government. The Irish Supreme Court and High Court exercise judicial review over all legislation and may strike down laws if they are inconsistent with the constitution."

1. The Constitution supersedes the law. The law is subject to the Constitution.

2. Judges swear a solemn Constitutional Oath to abide by the law and the Constitution.

3. If a judge – or any other agent of the State is engaged in unlawful or unconstitutional activity – then they are NOT operating under their Constitutional or Statutory remits.

4. No citizen (or person) is obliged to facilitate or comply with illicit directions, procedures or processes. In fact, we are constitutionally and legally obliged NOT to knowingly do so.

5. To knowingly comply with, facilitate, or cooperate with unconstitutional activity is therefore to be complicit in criminal activity.

6. No other citizen – regardless of position – has the Constitutional right, nor the legal power, nor the moral authority to coerce, direct or manipulate another person into wrongdoing.

7. We therefore assert our fundamental right to refuse to be made knowingly complicit in illicit, underhanded or criminal activity on the basis of the Irish Constitution and the law.

LETTER OF AUTHORISATION: Instructions

A 'letter of authorisation' is required by the authorities and the Courts before they are legally allowed to accept any submissions that are delivered by a third party on your behalf. In short, if you are asking someone else to submit paperwork, formal complaints or affidavits 'on your behalf' then you need to provide that person with a simple letter of authority such as is shown below.

You must include your full name and address and the 'witness' signature can be signed by anyone. It does not have to be a solicitor or commissioner of oaths.

It might be advisable to specify what exactly you are giving your authority for, and the duration of that authority, for example: *"To submit Court documents in case No. 1234567-P"* or *"To forward complaints to the Minister for Justice"* or *"To act on my behalf in this matter until further notice, and/or until my authority is withdrawn in writing"* etc..

There is no statutory fee or charge for creating a letter of authorisation.

Letter of Authorisation

To Whom It May Concern

I, (*your full name*), currently of (*your full postal address*), hereby authorise and appoint (*name and address of person you are appointing to act on your behalf*), to act as my agent regarding (*state reasons and limits of authority if appropriate*) from this date forwards.

Signed...

Witness...

Date...Time.................................

CASE PROGRESS RECORD

Page

CASE DETAILS/RECORD NUMBER

Date	Event	Notes/Comments

CONSTITUTIONAL AFFIRMATION

This affirmation is respectfully made with due deference to this honourable Court, in the sincere anticipation of a fair and just outcome.

As a citizen of this country, I respectfully assert my right to fair, equitable and expedient treatment, as per the respective Articles of the Irish Constitution; the Judicial Code of Conduct; and the Charter of Fundamental Rights of the European Union.

I respectfully request that any and all incidences of fraud, perjury or manifest deception that arise during this hearing result in the appropriate response by the Court; that those responsible will be referred for criminal prosecution; that any such tainted evidence will be dismissed; and that the Court rigorously applies whatever financial penalties are due, including the rule of costs.

This affirmation is respectfully made with due deference to this honourable Court, in the sincere anticipation of a fair and just outcome.

Articles in the Constitution that refer to Courts and Judges

Article 34.5. (i): Every person appointed a Judge under this Constitution shall make and subscribe the following declaration: *"In the presence of almighty God I (name) do solemnly and sincerely promise and declare that I will duly and faithfully and to the best of my knowledge and power execute the office of Justice without fear or favour, affection or ill-will towards any man, and that I will uphold the Constitution and the laws. May God direct and sustain me."*

Article 35.2: All Judges shall be independent in the exercise of their judicial functions and subject only to this Constitution and the law.

Article 40.1: All citizens shall, as human persons, be held equal before the law.

Article 40.3.(i): The State guarantees in its laws to respect , and, as far as practicable, by its laws to defend and vindicate the personal rights of the citizen.

Article 40. 2. The State shall, in particular, by its laws protect as best it may from unjust attack and, in the case of injustice done, vindicate the life, person, good name, and property rights of every citizen.

Article 40.6: The State guarantees liberty for the exercise of the following rights, subject to public order and morality:

(i)   The right of the citizens to express freely their convictions and opinions.

(ii)   The right of the citizens to assemble peaceably and without arms.

(iii)   The right of the citizens to form associations and unions.

Article 14 of the Judicial Code of Conduct: 'Ten Canons of Justice'

"It is to these truths and ideals that I shall hold my office and no other:"

1. That I (a judge) shall seek to perform the duties and responsibilities of office to the best of my abilities;

2. That I (a judge) pledge my allegiance to the constitution of United Ireland and shall do all within my power to protect its sovereignty and integrity;

3. That I (a judge) pledge my honor and duty to upholding the essential rights of every human being and the values of just society;

4. That I (a judge) shall always uphold the integrity and independence of the judiciary;

5. That I (a judge) shall executive the duties of my office without fear or favour;

6. That I (a judge) shall never allow my personal life, relationships or beliefs to be associated with, or influence in my judgment in any matter before me;

7. That I (a judge) shall seek to render judgment with care, precision and without delay;

8. That I (a judge) shall refrain from extra-judicial activities excepting those that seek to enhance the status of law and administration of justice;

9. That I (a judge) shall refrain from public and political comment whilst in office;

10. That I (a judge) shall avoid impropriety and the appearance of impropriety;

Constitution of the Association of Judges of Ireland*(Section 'B' – aims & objectives)*

B.1.a: To maintain and promote the highest standards in the administration of justice.
B. 1.d: To promote the highest standards of judicial conduct amongst members.

Committee on Court Practice & Procedure (Ireland)

(ix) Policy Objectives

The Committee is of the view that there is merit in enabling legislation setting out policy objectives for the Rules Committees. Issues which may be addressed include: simplicity of process, plain language, the cost of litigation, efficient and expeditious litigation, case management and e-courts.

Recommendation

Legislation may provide general policy objectives for the Courts Rules Committees. These may include policy objectives, such as:

(a) Rules should be drafted to enable a simple court process.

(b) Rules should be drafted using plain language.

(c) Rules should be drafted with a view to keeping the cost of litigation down.

(d) Rules should encourage expedition and discourage delay.

(e) Rules should enable the development of case management.

(f) The Rules Committees should, where practical, review regularly the Rules of Court.

(g) The Rules Committees should, where practical, introduce rules to enable the development of I.T. and e-courts.

CHARTER OF FUNDAMENTAL RIGHTS OF THE EUROPEAN UNION

TITLE VI: JUSTICE

Article 47: The right to an effective remedy and to a fair trial

Everyone whose rights and freedoms guaranteed by the law of the Union are violated has the right to an effective remedy before a tribunal in compliance with the conditions laid down in this Article.

Everyone is entitled to a fair and public hearing within a reasonable time by an independent and impartial tribunal previously established by law. Everyone shall have the possibility of being advised, defended and represented.

Legal aid shall be made available to those who lack sufficient resources in so far as such aid is necessary to ensure effective access to justice.

LEGAL SERVICE GUARANTEE / Terms of Reference

I, the undersigned, as an 'Officer of the Court' and in my role as lawyer/solicitor/attorney/barrister* to

(insert I-I Member name)...…....

hereby affirm that I will endeavour to fulfil my obligations to my client to the best of my ability according to the law and the Constitution; to the respective EU Codes of Conduct and Codes of Ethics; and according to international 'best practice' professional standards, specifically:

1. That I will advise the client of costs and fees *in advance* of any work undertaken.

2. That the client is not liable for costs and fees for work the client has not agreed to *in advance*.

3. That I will advance the client's case expediently and without undue delay.

4. That I will keep my client informed on a timely basis of developments in this case.

5. That I will adhere strictly to the respective rules and deadlines – or any similar time-related requirements when dealing with Courts, planning authorities, investigations or tribunals.

6. That any and all formal correspondence undertaken on behalf of the client will be approved by the client *before* dispatch to other parties.

7. That I will maintain a log of costs, fees and expenses in this case for inspection by the client.

8. That I acknowledge that the client is not responsible or liable for costs and expenses incurred due to *avoidable* delays on the part of myself, as the client's legal representative.

9. That I undertake not to engage in any deliberate acts of nonfeasance, misfeasance or malfeasance whilst representing my client or in dealing with the opposition in this case.

10. That in the event the client terminates our contract due to breaches of any of the above, that the client will not be held responsible for any *outstanding* costs or fees, and that I will surrender the case files to the client without further delays, costs or fees to the client.

I hereby accept these terms of reference:

Name:...Date..............…......................…..

Company:..……

Address...Tel...………

Signed...…......…..

Witness...…..…..

A copy of this document will be kept on record on the I-I Database. Legal professionals who refuse to agree to these terms of reference will be reported to the Integrity Ireland secure HAFTA Database.

I-I Court Hearing Report Form

(add extra detail overleaf or on extra blank pages)

Venue:..Date...............................

I-I Member name...Plaintiff / Defendant / Other etc

Member's legal team?..

Opposing party..

Opponent's legal team?..

Presiding...Registrar/Clerk.......................................

Type and purpose of hearing/tribunal (brief description)..

....

....Case/record No.................................

Other I-I Members / Supporters present	Opposition / Gardaí / Other parties present
....	....
....	....
....	....
....	....
....	....
....	....
....	....
....	.... Continue overleaf if needed
....	....
....	....

Report submitted by:...

Contact details: mobile:...email:...................................

Hearing Date: *I-I Member Name:*

Main Points: *(hearing dialogue or extra points should be noted on separate blank pages as necessary)*

1. Member's main argument / position...

....

....

Continue
overleaf
if needed

⇨

....

2. Opposition's main argument / position...

....

....

....

⇨

3. Judge's comments (especially anything unusual, odd or contradictory) ....

....

....

....

....

....

....

⇨

4. Observer comments...

....

....

....

....

....

⇨

5. Judge's Order / ruling / decision *(outcome of hearing)*..

....

....

⇨

(add extra detail overleaf or on extra blank pages)   *Make copies for yourself (if required) and send the originals to I-I, thank you.*

Instructions for Compiling a Valid Affidavit and/or Statement of Fact

These instructions are for <u>anyone</u> (including non-members) who wishes to submit a formal complaint / statement of fact / or affidavit in their own name. These statements may be forwarded to various authority figures or anti-corruption advocates for independent actioning, which means that they carry the same weight as legal documents. So please ensure that the details are accurate, and that you are willing to back up your statement in person, if needs be. If you are already a signed-up member of Integrity Ireland, or intend to become a member, you may submit this 'free-flowing statement' as an addendum to our standard complaint forms, but we will still need a valid application form and synopsis of your case if you wish to avail of the full benefits of I-I membership; such as support at court hearings, publication of your case, and access to our secure website and confidential databases.

Box 'A': Your statement must begin in a format that contains the following details:

Statement of Evidence / Affidavit of *(full name)*..D.O.B.............................

of *(full address)*...

I *(print your name)*...being eighteen years or older, hereby declare that this statement which contains *(no of pages)*........... pages, is true to the best of my knowledge and belief and I make this statement knowing that if it is tendered in evidence I will be liable for prosecution if I say anything in it which I know to be false or misleading or do not believe to be true.

(Your signature)...Date...

Ideally, the body of your statement should either be printed or typewritten, but <u>good</u> handwriting is also acceptable. It will be more helpful to the end-reader if you summarise the main issue(s) at the beginning, and then go into more detail using numbered paragraphs. Be careful not to leave large spaces between paragraphs so as to avoid any risk of subsequent alterations, and if there is any space between the end of your statement and the final signature(s), then you should draw a diagonal line through that space too. If you make any amendments yourself, you should initial each line where you have made changes – or better still, rewrite the statement from scratch. When you have finished your statement you should sign it again in the presence of an independent witness – preferably a solicitor or a commissioner for oaths (for which there may be a modest charge of around €10), and make sure the witness' name and contact details are clearly noted as shown in Box 'B' below:

Signed before me *(witness name)*..by *(your name)*...............................

Who is known to me, and I am a commissioner of oaths* / practising solicitor* *(delete as required)*

Location...Date...

Witness signature...Declarant...

Statement of Evidence / Affidavit of *(full name)*..D.O.B............................

of *(full address)*..

I *(print your name)*...being eighteen years or older, hereby declare that this statement which contains *(no of pages)*........... pages, is true to the best of my knowledge and belief and I make this statement knowing that if it is tendered in evidence I will be liable for prosecution if I say anything in it which I know to be false or misleading or do not believe to be true.

(Your signature)...Date...

Text of statement here..

Signed before me *(witness name)*...by *(your name)*.......................................

Who is known to me, and I am a commissioner of oaths* / practising solicitor**(delete as required)*

Location..Date...

Witness signature...Declarant...

STATEMENT OF DELIVERY OR RECEIPT

I ....a Member of *Integrity Ireland*, of *(address)*

....

hereby declare that I did deliver *by hand / by registered post / by recorded

post / by email; on *(date)*................................... the following documents:

(Description)...

Signed..Witnessed.....................................

Witness details:..

Receivers name and address:...

....Signed?...

Notes:...

....

STATEMENT OF DELIVERY OR RECEIPT

I ....a Member of *Integrity Ireland*, of *(address)*

....

hereby declare that I did deliver *by hand / by registered post / by recorded

post / by email; on *(date)*................................... the following documents:

(Description)...

Signed..Witnessed.....................................

Witness details:..

Receivers name and address:...

.... Signed?...

Notes:...

....

I-I Garda Interview / Legal Appointment Report

Venue:……………………………………………………………………Date………………………………

I-I Member name……………………………………………………………Client / Witness / Accused / Other etc

Accompanying?………………………………………………………………………………………………

Continue overleaf if needed ⇨

Interviewer(s)……………………………………………………………………………………………

Type and purpose of appointment (brief description)……………………………………………………

……

……………………………………………………………Case/record/pulse/ref No………………………………

Notes:………………………………………………………………………………………………………

……

……

……

……

……

……

………………………………………………………………………………Continue overleaf if needed ⇨

Was interview recorded?   YES   NO   By whom?…………………………………………………

I-I Disclaimer signed?   YES   NO   Comments……………………………………………

Copy of / signed Garda statement / legal contract / agreement / received?   YES   NO

Follow up………………………………………………………………………………………………

……

Report submitted by:………………………………………………………………………………………

Contact details: mobile…………………………………………email:………………………………………

PUBLIC NOTICE: Please be advised that..

of...

has been reported to the *Integrity Ireland HAFTA Database* for the following alleged acts of misconduct or alleged breaches of office.

....

....

I-I Disclaimer: The public naming-and-shaming of rogue authority figures is an initiative that is fully supported by I-I; however it remains the sole responsibility of the undersigned to ensure the accuracy of the information contained in this notice, for which the undersigned assumes full personal liability.

Full name (print)...

Signed...(A member of I-I)

'One by one – together – we CAN make a difference!'

www.integrityireland.ie

Citizens for Justice, Transparency & Accountability

PUBLIC NOTICE: Please be advised that..

of...

has been reported to the *Integrity Ireland HAFTA Database* for the following alleged acts of misconduct or alleged breaches of office.

....

....

I-I disclaimer: The public naming-and-shaming of rogue authority figures is an initiative that is fully supported by I-I; however, it remains the sole responsibility of the undersigned to ensure the accuracy of the information contained in this notice, for which the undersigned assumes full personal liability.

Full name (print)...

Signed...(A member of I-I)

'One by one – together – we CAN make a difference!'

www.integrityireland.ie

Citizens for Justice, Transparency & Accountability

APPENDIX
III

JOINING INTEGRITY IRELAND

- About Us
- General Rules & Guidelines for I-I Members
- J.U.S.T.I.C.E. Principles
- Application for Membership
- Seven-Minute Synopsis
- Short Complaint Form
  Breakdown of Complaint Categories
- Long Complaint Forms
- Format for Local I-I Meetings
- Attendance Record
- I-I Action Panel Setup
- Local Meeting Agenda
- Instructions for Facilitators - New Members
- Closing Comments - "Evil Succeeds Because.."
- About the Author

Note: Our sincere apologies to those who have been waiting for membership applications to be processed in recent weeks. We are working our way through those applications as quickly as we can. Thanks for your understanding.

ABOUT US

Here to support and encourage, and help pursue your complaints.

"At first, when you try to explain what's going on - people just don't believe it!"

In mid-2012, seven concerned citizens met to discuss their experiences. Each had, in one way or another, tried to bring a complaint to various Irish authorities - about the improper or illegal activities of other authority figures or, of certain 'well-connected persons' in Irish society. The responses they received were shocking - by any standards. Not only were the complaints not properly addressed, but each of these otherwise law-abiding citizens suddenly found themselves the target of unjust, prejudicial and intimidatory tactics by the very authorities they had approached for help and assistance. Some were ignored or obstructed. Others were harassed and threatened. Some were arrested without proper cause, and others, trying to seek assistance from their elected representatives or statutory oversight bodies were likewise treated with contempt. For some, this abuse spans many years. Finally, seeking redress through the Courts, they found themselves subject to unbelievably prejudicial and unjust decisions - despite overwhelming evidence in their favour. Shocked, appalled and disillusioned at the manner in which individual citizens could be targeted and abused in this way by highly-paid authority figures, a collective decision was made to take a stand.

You Are No Longer Alone
If you're reading this, then you are probably already aware that trying to take on 'the system' on your own is practically impossible; especially when that 'system' is so utterly compromised and dysfunctional. There are just too many ways that 'the system' can bend, break or change the rules at will, to achieve illegitimate ends, and the wronged citizen thus becomes repeatedly victimized, isolated and alienated. But by becoming a member of 'I-I' you place yourself at the heart of a community of dedicated and determined citizens who already know what you are going through, and are ready, willing and able to volunteer their support and assistance. You also gain access to the private members area where a range of 'special resources' await, including confidential complaints logs; special warnings and cautions; details of free member-to-member services; and direct access to panel members when you need immediate assistance.

What we do for Members

- Trust, confidentiality, action..

- Receive your complaints - confidentially

- Connect you to other helpful members

- Offer direct support, help and advice

- Attend your tribunals and Court cases

- Provide 'expert' witnesses and reports

- Offer publicity for your situation

..and lobby for justice for members at national and international levels by documenting and cataloguing members' complaints (in secure formats) for regular presentation to the media, the Courts, and Human Rights authorities.

Joining is Easy

Two membership levels..

(i) Support Members: Open to anyone who can offer any constructive help, support, advice or other service to members.

(ii) Active Members: Need to demonstrate that they have been ill-treated by the authorities, and lodge a standard confidential complaint form with us.

In addition, I-I Panel Members consist of active members who commit to extra responsibilities such as administration, website management, interviewing and assisting new members, hosting meetings, and documenting court hearings and tribunals.

But please remember that the most important principle of all is that you *get* help by *giving* help.

General Rules & Guidelines for Members

Dear Members and Prospective Members,

Because we are dealing chiefly with wrongdoing in the legal profession and in law enforcement, we need to do our best to protect all members—and the I-I group as a whole—from unwanted attentions by those who would prefer that law-abiding citizens like us would 'mind our own business' while the protected elite continue abusing our Constitution at will.

Accordingly, in order to join Integrity Ireland as a member—or remain as a member—you must agree to the following terms, conditions and guidelines, which may be updated or amended as required. We will do our best to keep the convoluted small-print to the minimum because we are a community of well- intentioned, decent citizens who operate on the basis of mutual trust and support - and NOT on contrived legalities or formal obligations.

The main reason for the establishment of these rules and guidelines is to guard and protect you as a member, and us as a group from further abuses. So please read this page carefully before committing to membership. Thank you.

We look forward to welcoming you to our proactive community.

1: Goals & Objectives

Integrity Ireland has two main goals; one short-term, and one long-term.

(a) Our short-term goals include assisting legitimate complainants to secure justice in their individual cases, through mutual support and advice between members, including attendance at scheduled meetings at venues throughout Ireland; by direct practical and moral support at interviews, tribunals or court hearings; through the documentation and reporting of cases; by lobbying on members' behalf; and through the deployment of a number of effective anti-corruption tactics, including 'direct action' as explained in the I-I SOS Guide.

(b) Our long-term goal is to bring about a radical change in the existing culture of cronyism, corruption and criminal cover-ups through the careful use of the combined facilities and resources of the membership. In short, to establish a citizens-driven 'support-and-oversight body' centred on the principles of justice, transparency and accountability, whereby public confidence in the integrity of the Irish legal system and the institutions of the State may be restored.

2: Rules

i. The *public* I-I website is open to all, and anyone can sign up to our email and webtext database.

ii. 'Support' membership is offered upon acceptance by I-I of a valid, signed application form.

iii. 'Active' membership is granted upon acceptance of a valid application form, *plus* a valid complaint form. From May 2015 new 'active' membership applications must also be approved by a majority of the I-I Action panel.

iv. Once accepted, 'active' members will be assigned a unique membership number, membership card and a username and password for access to the secure members-only area online.

v. Except in exceptional circumstances, membership cards must be collected in person by the applicant at a scheduled I-I meeting or, at another I-I event such as a Court hearing, protest or demonstration.

vi. Membership is unique to each individual, and is not to be transferred or shared.

vii. Membership is voluntary and may be denied, revoked or resigned at any time – by either party.

viii. Integrity Ireland and/or any directly-affiliated agency, association or individual thereof is not responsible for the actions of any other individual member, or group of members.

ix. With the exception of the registered owner(s), no member or group of members may claim to represent Integrity Ireland or speak on its behalf, but members (as stand-alone citizens) are encouraged to declare their membership and quote directly from the *public* area of the website.

x. The I-I logo is copyrighted and may only be used by I-I members (online) as a direct link back to the I-I public website or facebook page. In all other cases, approval must be sought beforehand.

xi. The I-I logo (on banners, stickers, badges, hi-visibility vests or business cards for example) may be used by I-I members when engaged in 'official' I-I events such as meetings, court hearings, demonstrations or protests that have been approved in advance by the I-I administrator or, which have been pre-advertised on the public I-I website.

xii. The secure 'Members Only' area online is to be accessed *only* by current, qualified members. Any third-party dissemination of *unpublished* data or materials from the members-only area is the sole responsibility of the member, who must ensure that any such data is qualified at source (by sworn statements / supporting documentation / evidence etc). (*See No's viii & xi above*)

xiii. Except by *unanimous* written I-I Panel decision, the materials in the secure area should <u>not</u> be shared with non-members, either directly or indirectly. However, members may refer to materials from the secure area, and may incorporate the same into official correspondence, and/or may quote the same in legal proceedings as evidence, provided they have *personally* qualified the data at source (as per rule xii above).

xiv. Members are bound to confidentiality concerning matters discussed at *private* I-I meetings, unless same is published on the public area of the website, or, as per rule 'xii' above.

xv. When engaged in any Integrity Ireland-related event, activity, meeting or demonstration, members undertake to behave in a respectful and law-abiding manner as outlined in the guidelines below.

xvi. Integrity Ireland does not sanction illegal or unlawful conduct. Members who engage in such do so under their own cognisance and may have their membership revoked as a consequence.

3: 'J.U.S.T.I.C.E.' Guidelines

- **J = JUSTICE vs INJUSTICE:** *Integrity Ireland* deals with issues, and with **individual incidences of injustice**. As such, anybody who has lodged a legitimate complaint against authority figures and who has the evidence to back it up can become an active member of *Integrity Ireland*.

- **U = UNITY & SOLIDARITY:** Some of the agencies and institutions whose activities we are challenging are headed by some of the most influential and powerful people in Ireland. To a greater-or-lesser extent these people control law enforcement, the justice system and the media - either directly, or through indirect influence. This is why it can be so terribly frustrating for the individual citizen to make any headway when faced with collusion, corruption and cronyism amongst the protected elite. It is therefore very important that we (as a group or as individuals) do NOT give unscrupulous persons any ammunition by which to attack or discredit us. **Our power lies in our unity as a cohesive, determined group of law-abiding citizens who are only seeking our legitimate Constitutional rights, and we have to behave as such.**

- **S = STEADFASTNESS & DETERMINATION:** We are in this for the long haul folks! We have to be, because the injustices we are confronting are deeply embedded in Irish State institutions, and those responsible are not simply going to roll over, apologise and go away just because we are challenging and exposing them. An absolute determination and a faith in our legitimate cause is therefore key to our long-term success, as well as a planned, systematic and unified approach.

- **T = TRUTH & OBJECTIVITY:** There are a range of outlets—including several online blogs— where wronged citizens can vent their anger and frustration, and name and shame the authority figures responsible for their travails. *(See the 'resources' page on the I-I website).* But if any given individual posts any inaccuracies, exaggerations or <u>unsubstantiated</u> allegations online, this opens the opportunity for counter-accusations of defamation - such as those recently used by ONE solicitor to shut down the whole of the 'www.rate-your-solicitor.com' website through the Irish Courts. As a result, a very informative website containing many valid reports of impropriety by various 'legal professionals' has been removed from public access.

- **I = INTEGRITY & PROFESSIONALISM:** The only way *Integrity Ireland* can function effectively on behalf of members whilst maintaining the respect of objective observers is to be absolutely scrupulous in presenting a fair, reasonable and fact-based platform that is beyond direct criticism by those who would prefer that the truth be suppressed. So, we ask members who wish to attend public functions (such as Court hearings, public meetings etc) to **show courtesy and respect for the authority figures**, institutions and agencies we are dealing with – at least until such time as they demonstrate *at an individual level* that they are undeserving of such respect. And even then, we must endeavour to maintain our dignity and the respect of objective observers, or else risk being denounced as cranks and complainers, and thereby lose our hard-won popular support.

- **C = COMPASSION & CONSIDERATION:** We also ask that members show respect and support for each other – most especially at public events, at meetings and at Court appearances. Our strength lies in our unified position against corruption, not in differing opinions about the particular merits of each other's positions, personalities or circumstances. We need to focus on the issues – and in particular, the terrible wrongs that have been done to fellow citizens. There is hardly a member of I-I who has not suffered considerably at the hands of unscrupulous authority figures. The wounds inflicted by those experiences, be they physical, emotional or psychological, often run very deep, so **it is important that we are compassionate, tolerant and supportive of each other, and keep our criticisms or any 'unhelpful' or divisive commentary to the minimum.**

- **E = EFFECTIVE TACTICS:** The panel members who guide the activities of I-I have invested a great deal of time and effort into developing tactics that will be of genuine assistance to citizens who find themselves subject to unjust, illegal or prejudicial activities by compromised authority figures. **But the key to success is that we all use these tactics in a unified and determined way, trusting in the support of the I-I Membership and the approval of all decent citizens.**

4: Public and Private Meetings

Public and private meetings will be scheduled regularly in various locations around Ireland. For practical reasons these meetings may be scheduled to coincide with a Court case or public event. The public meetings are of course open to everyone, but non-members may be asked to qualify their identity 'in confidence' before the meeting begins. In the event of a private meeting, only card-carrying I-I members or prospective I-I Members who are collecting membership cards may attend. These meetings—both public and private—are crucially important as an opportunity to network with other members, share your experiences, lodge your complaints, receive support and advice, and otherwise be actively involved. As always, care will be taken to accommodate members' confidentiality needs as-and-when necessary.

5: Logistics & Communications

Members are actively encouraged to network directly with each other especially when arranging for mutual support or assistance. This is why we are setting up Facilitators and local action groups, and you should communicate via your local group before contacting the Administrator directly. If you must contact the Administrator, please send an email to 'admin@integrityireland.ie' – but understand that it may be some time before you receive a reply. **Please, please, do not telephone the Administrator except in an emergency.** This is for practical and administrative reasons and to keep time, costs and confusion to a minimum. We also ask that I-I Central Panel Members are not contacted by members directly, other than by email, at meetings or via the secure website, except by private arrangement.

a. *Prospective members* should use email as the primary method of communication with us. Alternatively, you may simply turn up at a scheduled *public* meeting. If you are not computer- literate, then please find someone who can set up a free email account for you so you can receive all the benefits of membership.

b. *Existing members* should use the secure email facilities or the I-I forum in the private members-only area of the website, and/or turn up in person at meetings. When seeking support at interviews or Court hearings, please ensure you email the details well in advance to the designated email address, which is checked each Saturday before posting the details online and alerting the general membership.

c. (October 2015) If you need to contact us by post, please write to: ***Integrity Ireland c/o 1 Bridge Street, Cahir, Co. Tipperary*** with your full contact details (including your phone and email). Be advised however, that this is only a forwarding address, and that there is a high likelihood that mail is being intercepted and read before being forwarded to us. Thank you.

In all cases, please understand that due to an increasing volume of membership applications and other ongoing projects, that it could be some time before we can respond, so please be patient and allow us sufficient time to get back to you.

6: Official Forms

We use three main forms for membership, for complaints processing, and for publication of members' cases. These forms and processes are key to effective and efficient management of the I-I project, so **please be diligent and meticulous in filling them out – otherwise we then have to chase down the missing information – which takes time away from more pressing issues**.

a. *Confidential Membership Application Forms*
    For obvious reasons to do with transparency and accountability, every prospective member must fill out an application form. (From May 2015), each new member must also be vouched-for by an existing Active Member and/or have their personal details confirmed by an I-I Panel Member. This will usually be done by phone, or in person at an I-I scheduled meeting. Alternatively, you may

submit your application form by hand to an I-I Panel Member, or as a last option, by post to: ***Integrity Ireland c/o 1 Bridge Street, Cahir, Co. Tipperary, Ireland***. A recent passport-type photo or copy of photo I.D. will also need to be supplied (by email is okay) before we can issue your personal membership card and unique member number. Please be assured that we will NOT disclose any personal details to any other person or agency **outside of the I-I membership** without your express permission. However, by submitting an application form you agree to the conditional sharing of your contact details with other Members (using your chosen alias and mobile number as a first contact, by text message only). This is for the purposes of facilitating mutual help and support amongst members – especially locally.

b. *The 7-Minute Synopsis*
    This simple two-page form is a very important part of our cataloguing process, and helps compose your complaint(s) into easily-understood formats for presentation to third parties if required. These forms are used when collating information for the website and for sharing with other members at meetings, and are a very useful tool for you in composing your experiences into a condensed format that will be more easily accepted by media sources if you wish to publish. This is also the format we prefer if you choose to log your story on the I-I video database. **So please follow the instructions carefully, so you are well-prepared when the time arrives**.

c. *Official Complaint Forms*
    We now have two official complaint forms: The preliminary 'short-form' for prospective members is quick and easy to complete, and is available via the public I-I website, and in the new I-I SOS Guide. The more detailed 'long-forms' are also available in the SOS Guide and in the secure members' area, or, they can be collected in person at scheduled I-I meetings. Again, **it is important that you follow the instructions carefully** so that your complaint is properly filed and catalogued, and to ensure we assign the correct resources and contacts to you. **It is also important that the names of offending authority figures are catalogued on our HAFTA database**, and we now have a facility for this online. In some cases, we may ask for supporting documentation or evidence, and you may be asked to agree to publication of your complaint. If required, your identity will be protected throughout.

7: Security & Confidentiality

As a rule, and for the sake of privacy and confidentiality (if you wish), we will only refer to members in both the public and secure areas of the website by their chosen alias. Your membership card will NOT contain your name or your alias, and will only be used to identify you to other members at I-I meetings or at public events. You may of course choose not to use an alias, but that is your own personal decision. Other than qualified tip-offs or information from anonymous whistleblowers, persons who do not identify themselves fully and properly in the application process will not be engaged with by the I-I administrators.

8: Membership

There are absolutely no obligations on members other than to abide by these rules and guidelines, and all members will have access to I-I resources as appropriate to your membership type. However, the central purpose of membership is that you join a community of like-minded others who are willing to offer help and support as best they can. **In short, that you get help by giving help, and by networking with other Members at meetings, protests and Court hearings**. So please attend scheduled I-I meetings whenever you can.

9: Support Member

You can help in any number of ways from simply declaring your general support, to making a donation, or by offering direct help and assistance to other members. The main ways to help at present include turning up to support other members at public tribunals and Court hearings as observers, witnesses or note-takers; giving qualified legal advice; offering secretarial, I.T., or other services either free or attractively discounted (such as hotels or b & b's); facilitating scheduled meetings; and purchasing I-I marketing materials (available in the secure members' area and at scheduled meetings) which helps cover our administration costs.

10. Active Member

In addition to the above, you can help most of all by filing a formal complaint with us giving as much detail as possible, including your permission to publish. Our complaint forms are standardised to be short, succinct and easy to fill out, and your identity remains protected. Provided your complaint meets the required criteria we may showcase it on the website and will press for action from the respective authorities on your behalf. This will include coordinating formal representations to statutory authorities locally, nationally and internationally; making press releases to the media; forwarding case reports to human rights agencies; and publication of your case story in journal and e-book format, as well as online. Selected complaints will also be aired on social media networks such as Facebook, YouTube, Twitter, and Avazz.org, and may also qualify for inclusion in our video database and an upcoming TV documentary. You also have the opportunity of being a witness at other members' tribunals or Court cases (especially where members share similar complaints against the same agencies or individuals) and you may opt to join a group-initiated lawsuit, joining other members with similar stories and complaints. Likewise, other members may support you in your own case. New members will also be given the opportunity to summarise their cases at private I-I meetings, which is a great first opportunity to identify other I-I members who have experienced similar issues.

11: Volunteers

We welcome any sincere offers of help and assistance from any source. If you have a couple of hours to spare from time to time – or can offer a venue for meetings, or a special service or facility to I-I members in your area – we would greatly appreciate hearing from you. Most in demand at present are legal, secretarial or I.T. skills, as well as any insider information that will be of assistance to members. Please see the 'volunteers' and 'whistleblowers' pages under 'Join Us' on the I-I website for more details.

12: Whistleblowers

Being a whistleblower when there is so much corruption and illegality afoot is an act of genuine patriotism, courage and of moral conscience. You might work in the civil service, law enforcement or in the legal professions. You are being paid to do a specific job and you try daily to do your best, but you are unsettled by the lies, deception and fraud you see all around you. You want to do something about it, but you know your job is at stake if you step out of line. You want to do or say *something* that will make a difference, but you are worried about the repercussions. Well, now's your chance to make a difference. Please see the 'whistleblowers' page under 'Join Us' on the *Integrity Ireland* website for more details of how to contact us in complete confidence.

Last updated October 2015

One by one – together – we CAN make a difference!

www.integrityireland.ie

Information for Prospective Members

(i) Application Form, (ii) Case Synopsis, & (iii) Preliminary Complaint Form

Dear Prospective Member;

Thank you for your enquiry. Please find enclosed a confidential application form with attachments. (i) It is important that you furnish us with as much personal detail as possible so that we can communicate with you efficiently. We regret that Application Forms which are submitted *without* (a) full contact details, (b) an original signature and (c) photo I.D., cannot be processed.

(ii) The 2-page synopsis form is designed to help you tell your story clearly and succinctly, and provides us with a manageable document for our own administration purposes, as well as for prospective publication or video. So if your story is long or very complicated, you should break it into separate parts and submit a new synopsis form for each different part of your story. You can download more synopsis forms from the I-I website (see below). It is better that you send multiple synopses that *clearly* explain each event, rather than submit one complicated synopsis that may be difficult to understand or process. We are happy to receive multiple submissions.

(iii) Please also find attached a one-page 'preliminary complaints form' for our secure HAFTA Database. More detailed I-I complaint forms will be available to you via the secure website *after* you are confirmed as a member. In the meantime and to keep the administration process manageable we ask that members and prospective members contact us through the website, by email, or by post at the address at the foot of the Application Form. If you are not set up to receive emails and to use the facilities on our website, you will not be able to receive the full benefits of membership, so please consider this before applying. We also ask that members do not contact the administrators by phone except in an emergency, thank you. www.integrityireland.ie

Strictly Private & Confidential: the contents of this form will NOT be shared with outside individuals or agencies.

For 'I-I' use only

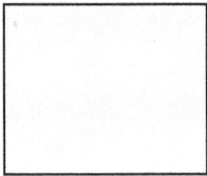

Form
M

Integrity Ireland Application for Membership

(Please see the 'resources' page at www.integrityireland.ie for full instructions)

1. Full Name/Title:*...

2. Full postal address:*..

3. Home Tel:*...4. Mobile(s):*...

5. Email* / fax / other:... Best day/time to call?..................

6. Occupation / Qualifications:...

_____

7. *(Optional)* What is your middle name / username / or chosen alias? *(one word only please)*...
This name may be used in place of your real name on publicly-viewable documents, on the secure 'members-only' forum, or, when contacting other members for the first time. If using a username or alias, please choose a 'normal' forename for ease of reference for website visitors.

_____

8. Membership is entirely voluntary and you can opt out at any time, but to help us with administration and to best assist you, please indicate below why you want to join Integrity Ireland. Thanks. *(Please circle as appropriate).*

As a support member: What type of support can you offer other members? *Please detail, for example; (a) attendance at meetings and local court hearings, (b) support services (secretarial, paralegal, printing, media etc), (c) professional advice (lawyers, I.T., police etc), (d) support facilities for members such as meeting venues / cut-rate hotels/b & b's/car-hire etc); (e) whistleblower / inside information?*

Other?..
...

As an active member: You should be willing to sign a formal statement that you have been ill-treated by the authorities or by the legal profession. In order to facilitate filing and support services, please indicate which of these agencies you intend complaining about, by marking an 'x' for each agency (in the brackets):

Garda Síochána ( )   *Attorney General* ( )   *Minister of Justice* ( )   *Chief State Solicitor* ( )   *DPP's Office* ( )

Garda Ombudsman ( )   *Law Society of Ireland* ( )   *Independent Adjudicator* ( )   *Courts Service* ( )

Solicitors ( )   *Barristers* ( )   *Judges* ( )   *TD's/Ministers* ( )   *Other?..*( )

_____

For 'I-I' use only

9. If your complaint qualifies, are you interested in being videoed / published / or be part of a 'class-action' (group) lawsuit? *Circle as appropriate:*   (a) Yes   (b) No   (c) Don't know/ tell me more.

I hereby agree to abide by the 'I-I' membership terms and conditions as described on the website.
I understand that my name and telephone number will be forwarded to other I-I Members *locally*.

Signed:*...Date:...

*Please return this form with a copy of your photo I.D. to **Integrity Ireland, c/o 1 Bridge Street, Cahir, Co. Tipperary**. Alternatively, you may scan this form and return it by email to admin@integrityireland.ie. You will be contacted shortly to confirm I-I membership and to discuss your circumstances. Please be prepared by filling out your 2-page synopsis, which may also be used (with your permission) to summarise your story online, for publication, or for the I-I video database.*

Note: This form and its contents are for the exclusive and confidential use of *Integrity Ireland*

Seven-Minute Synopsis*(please follow the instructions on the right <u>carefully</u> to assist our administration process)*

1. Background details:

2. Names and positions of the main authority figures or institutions with whom you have had problems:

3. How and why your problems started / the <u>beginning</u> of your story:

---

1. You <u>DO NOT</u>need to write your name any-where on this form. Introduce yourself in general termsstating your background, your occupation, where you live, and anything else that sets the backdrop to your case or will be of interest to other members.

2. These details should also go on the HAFTA database form (attached) so you can link up with members who have had difficul-ties with the same authority figures. If you need more space for names, it may be appropriate to start <u>another new synopsis</u> explaining the problems you had with these addi-tional persons <u>as a separate story</u>.

3. The circumst-ances that led to your story: were you the victim of an attack of some sort? Was a crime committed against you? Did you 'cross' some 'connected person'? Were you charged with an offence you didn't commit? When, where and how did your problem begin? (This part of your story may be merged with part 4 or continued overleaf if you wish).

4. Your main case synopsis / your story:

4. Try to keep your story succinct and to the point. Explai things in chrono logical sequence "this happened first, then that, and then that" for example. Focus o the <u>wrongs</u> that were done to yo and the effects these experience have had on you life. Remember that this form is designed for a <u>maximum</u> 7- minute synopsis that can be read out at meetings or summarised on the website o on video. Longer stories need to b broken into 7- minute chapters.

5. Complaint departments/ statutory authorities / oversight bodies you have approached to complain:

5. List the people departments or institutions you have brought your complaints to. This might include Gardaí, the Courts, TD's & Ministers, the GSOC, IHRC, the media etc..

For I-I use only

6. Conclusion: *(In your own words, what you feel needs to be done about the situation?)*

7. I attest to the truth of this synopsis by initialising this box.

Please return a copy of this synopsis via email to <u>admin@integrityireland.ie</u> or by post to: Integrity Ireland, c/o 1 Bridge Street, Cahir, Co. Tipperary

Integrity Ireland Condensed Complaint Summary

The confidential details you enter on this form will be logged on our secure members-only 'HAFTA' database (Holding Authority Figures To Account), so please type or PRINT THE DETAILS CLEARLY – especially the name of the individuals and agencies involved. Please use additional forms if necessary. You should summarise the offences committed (as shown in the example) – so that we can identify repeat offenders, document their wrongdoing, and arrange mutual support and advice for those who have suffered similar offences. Once you are a signed-up member, you will be supplied with more detailed complaint forms, so please do not attach extra information at this time. Thank you.

(This box for I-I use only)

Example:

Name	Agency / Firm / Rank-or-position / Location	General description of complaint(s)
John Smith	Garda Síochána, Sgt, Clontarf, Co. Dublin	Deception, collusion, conspiracy, false arrest, perverting course of justice
Mary Murphy	Secretary, Courts Service, Mallow, Co. Cork	Arrogant, obstructive, refusing to sign correspondence

Name	Agency / Firm / Rank-or-position / Location	General description of complaint(s)

*Your name/alias/I-I member number?.. I attest to the truth of this summary by checking (or initialising) this box:

**(For the purposes of transparency and accountability, we must have your personal contact details and your signature on file, before we can post these details on the secure website)*

Please return a copy of this summary via email to admin@integrityireland.ie or by post to: Integrity Ireland, 1 Bridge Street, Cahir, Co.

Breakdown of complaint categories by level of seriousness, with explanations.

For the avoidance of doubt, member complaints have been categorised under the <u>lowest</u> possible qualifiers in order to avoid any charges of overstatement or exaggeration. All complaints listed in this table have been validated by documentation, or by the sworn personal testimony of the complainant.

1-Incompetence: This lowest category of offence allows for the possibility that apparently obstructive, delaying or other unhelpful actions by persons in authority (or their staff) are simply due to occasional 'failures to communicate'; weaknesses in 'the system'; or due to an employee 'having an off day'. Routine superciliousness, apathy and contempt for the citizen are also included in level 1 offences. When these patterns become consistent or repeated however, this suggests deliberate obstructionism.

2-Obstructionism: This is when an individual *knowingly and willingly* decides to deny a citizen proper service, either for personal reasons or because they are acting on instructions from superiors. Examples include failing to respond to correspondence; deferring responsibility; deliberately sending out wrong paperwork; giving false information; running down the clock; and any other activity that is designed to deny due service and cause frustration, costs and anxiety to the citizen. Usually rooted in inappropriate attitudes of superiority and entitlement—or a warped sense of loyalty to one's colleagues—these cynical activities display a profound lack of understanding by the perpetrators of the concepts of public service, moral duty and common decency. When contributing to other unjust activities, those who carry out these acts of deliberate obstructionism are in effect, co-parties to those greater crimes.

3-Deception: One step beyond obstructionism – but often a co-party to it – this category includes individuals lying and making false statements both verbally and in writing – although most types of deception at this level are verbal. There is simply no excuse for employees of the State – and in particular law enforcement and legal professionals – to engage in routine deceptions unless they have an improper or illegal 'alternative agenda'. Lying is an obvious red flag for seriously wrong behaviour. It is inexcusable and abhorrent by persons trusted with public service, and needs to be eradicated.

4-Collusion: When two or more persons conspire together to deceive or obstruct the citizen in direct contravention of their terms of office; their respective duty to the citizen; to the Constitution and to the principles of truth and justice. This collusion is most alarming when it is openly facilitated in our Courts.

5-Cover-ups: When persons take active steps to knowingly cover up 'improper activities' by their subordinates, colleagues or superiors. Depending upon seriousness, these are often criminal offences.

6-Criminal (allegations): This category represents *serious* allegations against authority figures or their staff that have been documented in sworn statements by the offended parties, but where independent corroborating documentation or evidence has *not* yet been secured by Integrity Ireland.

7-Criminal activities (with proofs): The most serious category of all – where we have solid irrefutable proofs of criminal activities by authority figures, legal professionals or other 'connected persons'. These crimes include multiple instances of 'conspiracies to pervert the course of justice' but also range throughout the whole criminal spectrum, and are a disquieting reminder of the dreadful state of so many of our national institutions – and of the compromised authorities who oversee them.

The individual subjects of members' complaints are named and profiled in the secure members' area.

<table>
<tr><td>Form
D</td><td>'Integrity Ireland' Public Complaint Form 'D' Complaint ref no:</td><td></td></tr>
</table>

lease be advised: This form 'D' may be published online and sent to various agencies or media. It is important for our cataloguing rocess that you follow the instructions on the secure members area of the website carefully. In particular, you must ONLY use one et of forms for EACH agency, company or institution that you are complaining about – otherwise our catalogue system simply will ot work. If you have complaints against more than four individuals in one particular institution – or, if you have additional omplaints against other institutions, please use a completely new set of forms. Thank you. Do NOT write your real name or any ther identifying information on form 'D', and only write your confidential membership number and alias on form 'E'. Thank you.

Please identify the agency / institution / company that you are complaining about: *(circle or underline one only please)*

(A) Attorney General; (B) Barristers; (C) Chief State Solicitor's Office; (D) DPP's Office; (E) Courts Service; (G) An Garda Síochána;

(I) Independent Adjudicator; (J) Judges; (L) Law Society of Ireland; (M) Ministers/TD's; (O) Garda Ombudsman; (S) Solicitors;

Other (please specify)..

(For 'I-I' use only)

Offence No 1: Subject's name, rank/position:...

Department / Office / Division / Address:..

Type of Offence?	1	2	3	4	5	6	7
Approx Number?							

Offence No 2: Subject's name, rank/position:...

Department / Office / Division / Address:..

Type of Offence?	1	2	3	4	5	6	7
Approx Number?							

Offence No 3: Subject's name, rank/position:...

Department / Office / Division / Address:..

Type of Offence?	1	2	3	4	5	6	7
Approx Number?							

Offence No 4: Subject's name, rank/position:...

Department / Office / Division / Address:..

Type of Offence?	1	2	3	4	5	6	7
Approx Number?							

Please circle or underline the types of proofs you have to support these allegations: *Letters. Records or documents. Photos. Audio/ video. Legal papers. Digital recordings. Personal testimony .Independent eyewitness testimony. Other (detail below)*

....

....

Thank you for submitting your complaint. Please attach this to form 'B' and return to us by email or post.

Form 'E' accompanies form 'D' and is the confidential part of your complaint form. The details from form 'E' will be used to help profile those individuals responsible for crimes and other abuses against citizens, and the data will be recorded on charts and graphs on the Integrity Ireland website for the benefit of other members, and for the general public.

Form E	'Integrity Ireland' Confidential Complaint Form 'E'	Complaint ref no:	

(For 'I-I' use only)

1. Your 3 or 4-digit Membership Number:_____Alias/Username_____

2. In your own words, briefly describe the type(s) of offence(s) committed by the individuals named on form 'D':

....

....

....

3. Please list any other individuals/agencies who were complicit in these offences *(and submit separate complaint forms for each please)*

....

....

....

4. Your <u>approximate</u> financial costs to date:...............................Time spent on this to date: ....weeks / mths / yrs.

5. Emotional / psychological effects on you: (low)   1   2   3   4   5   6   7   8   9   10   (high)

6 .Describe *briefly* your overall experience *(we may return to you for a fuller summary for the website)*

....

....

....

....

7. Have you made any formal complaints, or taken legal action? *Yes / No*   To which person(s) / agencies / courts?

....

....

8. Was the outcome: *Acceptable / Unacceptable / Predictable / Unpredictable / Fair / Unfair / Ongoing / Other?*

....

9. What, in your opinion needs to be done?..

....

....

10. I would be willing to testify to these facts in a Court of law, and in support of other members. *(Check box)*

Declaration of truth: By submitting these forms to Integrity Ireland, you declare that the contents herein are accurate and true, and that you consent to the publication of these details as outlined in the rules and guidelines on the 'I-I' website.

Now please return these forms by email to admin@integrityireland.ie or by post to
Integrity Ireland, c/o 1 Bridge Street, Cahir, Co. Tipperary – or in person at the next I-I meeting. Thank you for taking action.

Event   Date   Venue

Existing I-I Members need not repeat their email and phone details

Full Name (print please)	Mobile (for text messages)	Email (write clearly please)	County

"One by one – together – we CAN make a difference!"

I-I Action Panel Setup

The *Integrity Ireland Community* has now grown sufficiently to allow for the setting up of regional branches with local Facilitators, for the purposes of consolidating our resources and making the overall I-I initiative more directly relevant and effective in each Members' own locality. The idea is to bring Members together on a regular basis so as to encourage closer ties and better mutual support as well as offer new prospects a local contact (the Facilitator) to answer their immediate questions.

1. These regional groups will be called *"I-I Action Panels"*
2. Groups will comprise a minimum of 3 members, and a maximum of 12.
3. Each Facilitator must be a signed-up 'Active Member' of Integrity Ireland, with full access to the secure website.
4. Other action panel members are required to be signed-up 'support' or 'active' members.
5. Facilitators' contact details will be made available to new prospects and existing I-I Members.
6. The identities of other panel members will remain confidential.
7. The panels will be named by location: i.e. *"I-I Action Mayo – 1"*
8. In Dublin, action panels will be named according to postal region: i.e. *"I-I Action Dublin 4 – 1"*
9. Meetings will be held weekly or fortnightly at a time and place nominated by the Facilitator.
10. If a group grows beyond 12 members – a new group should be set up – comprising no fewer than 3 members, and named accordingly: i.e. *"I-I Action Mayo – 2"*
11. Prospects may apply for membership via their local Facilitator or via the I-I Administrator.
12. Facilitators may recommend membership after vetting new prospects according to procedure.

Recommendations:

Facilitators should develop a structure for their weekly/fortnightly meetings which allows for Members to discuss strategy and mutual support. Specific targets should be set at each meeting in line with I-I objectives; for example, ensuring local Members are receiving direct support and assistance; that I-I formal complaint Notices are issued; that research continues for the HAFTA database; that new prospects are encouraged to join; that media opportunities are identified; that friendly professionals and experts are approached; that important messages and information are relayed to the I-I Administrator for the website on a timely basis, etc etc..

Action Panel Members are actively encouraged to engage in 'direct action' as they see fit, as long as any such actions are conducted in accordance with the I-I Rules & Guidelines. New initiatives and ideas which help to tackle corruption are also sought – and if proven successful – will be forwarded to the general Membership as suggestions – giving due credit to the initiating I-I Action Panel.

The use of social media is also encouraged – especially in light of the general reluctance of the mainstream media to properly cover corruption-related issues. Action Panel Facilitators should consider setting up Facebook / Twitter accounts in their own names *"as a Member of Integrity Ireland"* and should become proactive making regular posts on the I-I Facebook page.

A €2 collection should be taken up at each meeting from each of those present for use by the local Facilitator or appointed treasurer to cover immediate costs and expenses (such as postage, photocopies etc). A record should be kept of income and expenditure.

I-I merchandise will be made available to facilitators, at cost, for resale to assist in local funding.

I-I LOCAL MEETING AGENDA– *time allowed approximately 2 hours*

No	Item	Time	I-I Admin Notes
1	Welcome / apologies for absences / today's agenda / appoint timekeeper / collect €2 subs from members *(no charge to non-members on first visit)*	5 mins	
2	Introduction Statement */ who we are / what we do / invites for 7-min synopses to be read out later / display I-I merchandise and ask those present to please be generous* ☺	10 – 15 mins	
3	Registration of attendees / food & drink orders / application forms / issue member cards / check photos & I.D. / sell badges, stickers, t-shirts etc	5 – 10 mins	
4	*New member 7-min synopsis (i)*	7 mins	
5	*New member 7-min synopsis (ii)*	7 mins	
6	*New member 7-min synopsis (iii)*	7 mins	
7	BREAK *(followed by more 7-min synopses if time allows – to a maximum of seven)*	5 - 10 mins	
8	General Summary of 'the problem'. *What they do; their tactics: divide & conquer. Alienate. Eternal run-arounds. Refusing to address issues. Forwarding to other departments etc etc…*	5 mins	
9	Outline Main I-I **Support** Strategies: *Attendance at Court hearings etc / I-I report forms/secure website / 'legal' advice & phone number / information / education / templates*	5 mins	
10	Outline Main I-I **Defence** Strategies: *Database of evidence / use of caveat / membership of group / threat of publication and-or professional embarrassment*	5 mins	
11	Outline Main I-I **'Attack'** Strategies: *Rogues Gallery / HAFTA Database/ small claims / personal injuries claims / demonstrations / protests / publication of complaints / private prosecutions in District Court*	5 mins	
13	Speaker: presentation on some specialised area of the legal procedure	20 mins	
14	Upcoming Events	5 mins	
15	Questions from the floor? *Pass round the voluntary donations box and have treasurer sign off on the amount collected.*	10 mins	
16	Helpful suggestions? Improvements to the websites. Promotional ideas etc? *Ensure that any such ideas are workable. What is the plan? Who will take responsibility etc?*	5 mins	
17	Free association / members exchange contact details / admin takes photos, recordings, statements / more merchandising as time allows etc.		

I-I Admin notes / comments:

If you would like to be an I-I Facilitator, please contact Stephen at admin@integrityireland.ie for further details.

Instructions For Facilitators – Signing Up New Members

Process of becoming a member of Integrity Ireland

1. Prospective member fills out application form, and then email, posts or hands it back to us in person.
2. A copy of application form is filed in 'main office'.
3. Application form is delegated to a Facilitator for vetting and approval.
4. The Facilitator 'approves' the prospect on the basis that; (i) they know them personally, and/or (ii) have personally met with them and have seen photo I.D., and/or (iii) have otherwise confirmed that the details on the application form are accurate and correct.
5. 'Main office' assigns membership number and assigns membership card / alias / password etc.
6. Prospect is invited to next local meeting to share their '7-minute' story using the prepared I-I bullet-point list, and to collect their membership card and welcome pack.

Procedure with complaint forms

1. Only our own official complaint forms will be accepted.
2. Complaint forms are collated and filed according to the subject matter / the type and seriousness of complaint / and the agencies or individuals being complained about.
3. Two copies of every complaint will be kept on file: One in the secure digital master file that contains all complaints in order of receipt, and another paper copy in the respective category.
4. The details from the complaints (number and types of offences committed – by whom – which agencies etc) will be transferred onto a master table at the time they are filed.
5. The website charts and tables will be updated regularly with these figures and details.
6. The anonymous complaint forms will be collated into groups of ten according to offending agency, and (by Action Panel decision) copies will then be dispatched to government departments; to the media; and/or published online at regular intervals.

Management / administration of members and complaints

1. Membership numbers are coded in such a way so as to facilitate easy identification of members at meetings and public events.
2. A new password for the secure members-only area will be emailed to current members each month / or released at 6-weekly meetings (if deemed necessary).
3. The I-I website, the I-I Facebook page and scheduled meetings should be the primary source of sending information to members.
4. There will be a members-only forum / comments area in the secure website for members to chat to each other and get advice / support from other members.
5. Panel members should be cautious about giving out their phone numbers – use email instead.
6. If members want 'official' publicly-advertised support at their hearing or tribunal, they should approach their facilitator by email first. Otherwise, members can advertise the hearing in the secure area of the website – or notify administration by emailing 'support@integrityireland.ie'.
7. Attending Court hearings or committing to any official 'I-I' events should be decided in advance, at the specific request of a Facilitator, with the agreement of the Administrator.

Closing Comments

"Evil succeeds because 'good people' do nothing!"

It is clear to any right-thinking person that we have an increasingly serious problem with corruption in this Country. But it is also clear that this corruption could *not* continue without the passive compliance of the people. Understandably, this compliance is not so much a conscious decision being made by people who just don't care - rather, it is the by-product of a disillusioned populace so massively overburdened by the trials and tribulations of everyday life that they simply don't have the will - or the resources - to take on 'the system' - especially when that 'system' seems to be holding all of the proverbial cards. After all, we've seen what happens to whistleblowers in spite of the promised 'protection' afforded by the so-called whistleblowers charter. Those brave few who speak out soon find themselves the subject of official bullying and intimidation, of suspicion and ostracisation, and become the targets of sly accusations about their *real* motives and intentions - all of which adds up to an atmosphere of overt oppression that dissuades the well-intentioned from making a stand, and subtly, but clearly warns us <u>all</u> *not* to rock the boat! But what's the point in staying in a boat that is heading for the precipice - where we are, in effect, chained like galley slaves through political trickery, deception and unjust taxation? Why do we continue to take orders and instructions from those who have proven themselves to be so utterly unworthy? What is it about us that makes us so open to this craven exploitation? Where is the outrage and indignation at the fact that we have been paying this corrupted elite to rob us blind in the first place, and then, when all goes awry and we discover the unmitigated greed, the incompetence, the corruption, the lack of regulation, the shocking wastefulness of it all and the mind-boggling arrogance of those responsible - well, you'd expect any rational human being to wake up and smell the coffee - right? So why do we continue to vote these people back into office? What is it about us that allows ourselves to be deceived repeatedly, over-and-over again? Why is it that as we approach another general election that the Government is suddenly infected with benevolent impulses, and the compulsion to spend on a rash of public projects and financial give-aways? Are we really to be bought so easily? After all, we need to remember that it is in fact *our* money (which they stole from us in the first place in order to appease the banks and the bondholders) which they are now so generously 'giving back' to us. In fact, to make matters worse, we hear that the Government has actually borrowed *more* money from the bondholders (on our behalf of course) in order to fund these unnecessary and arguably reckless give-aways so as to bribe and manipulate us into ignoring their track record to date, and—we must presume—to numb us into foolishly voting for them again. It is easy to give away money when you don't have to foot the bill. Because we can be sure of one thing; that no matter how difficult it gets for us ordinary folk to make ends meet, to pay our bills, to feed our families - that there won't be any shortages in the various Ministerial households - nor for those who have made a career out of deceiving, exploiting and manipulating the public.

It is hard to see a solution to this problem - especially when the organs of the State are engaged in a massive deception designed to maintain an utterly unjust and certainly undemocratic status quo. But the solution is actually quite simple - if only we can get enough people to accept it, and then *act* upon it. You see, the articles on psychopathy (in Appendix 1) reveal a couple of very interesting facts about the make-up of our society today - where greed, avarice and rampant profiteering have become the means by which a 'savage capitalism' has ascended to the forefront of how 'daily business' is done worldwide. And make no mistake, this 'savage capitalism' also dominates the political world. The cardinal rule is that if there is a profit to be made, then any method or means is justified, and if human values or even lives get in the way - well, that's just hard luck! In'it? In this manner, deception, exploitation and manipulation of the masses becomes a necessary policy and political strategy, because no-one in their right mind is going to vote for psychopaths and sociopaths; that is, not for rogues and robbers, nor for tricksters, thugs, tyrants and thieves posing as caring politicians, pretending to have our best interests at heart.

Returning to our analogy of the baker and the bus driver for a moment, we might ask how they became qualified in the first place - and the answer is simple: the baker trained as a chef and the bus driver had the required professional licence to drive a bus. Technically therefore, they are both 'qualified' to be a baker and a bus driver respectively. But what if we discovered that the bus driver was a clinical psychopath who was constantly fantasising about running people over? Would that not be grounds to take away his licence? And what if we discovered that the baker had an infectious disease which contaminated all of his wares? Would that too not be sufficient reason to redirect him to a different occupation and seek medical treatment as well?

The point being made here is that there are certain conditions which obviously preclude certain people from doing certain jobs. It matters little how clever or capable you are in any other walk of life if you are physically or psychologically incapable of carrying out your job in a manner that does *not* put others at risk. And here we begin to approach the kernel of the problem. You see, many of our elected representatives and others in positions of power and authority over us are possessed of sociopathic impulses. Whether inherited at birth or learned over many years of conscience-numbing servitude to 'the system' these people are in effect, programmed to exploit, deceive and manipulate others. They do this frankly, because there is a profit in it, and making a profit (personal or otherwise) is their very *raison d'être* - their very reason to be. They have no real empathy with the suffering they cause; they feel little remorse at the injustices they visit on others; and they feel no genuine moral responsibility for the often inhumane policies and decisions they preside over. In short, they are devoid of the fundamental characteristics that would qualify any leader as a 'good' leader; the qualities of compassion and of genuine empathy.

To take this disturbing observation a step further we should ask ourselves what sort of person would we choose to look after our own families in the event we had to go away for some time? Would a moral dimension come into the question at all? Naturally, we would look for someone who was capable and competent - someone who could look after the family's practical needs. But obviously, we would also want to know that the person chosen was a decent, healthy, moral person - right? I mean, what loving parent would hand his children over to someone with an infectious disease - or perhaps even worse still - to a proven sociopath or a psychopath?

Why then do we trust these people with so much power and influence when it comes to running the country?

Sociopaths don't understand conscience, but they *do* understand consequences. In the short term therefore, the best way to deal with a sociopath is to firmly but politely alert them that there *will* be consequences if they attempt to abuse or exploit you - and that is one of the main reasons for compiling this 'SOS Guide'. In the long term, as more and more people come to realise that sociopathy and psychopathy are in fact serious aberrations that *should* (in an ideal world) preclude anyone so afflicted from holding a position of power or influence over others - we can but continue to remind these afflicted souls - with as much compassion and empathy as we can - that we, the majority, chose to live in a fair, moral and humane world. Accordingly, when questionable 'profit' comes at other people's expense - and especially at other's emotional and psychological expense - then in fact, it is no real profit at all.

In the meantime, as the political wheels and mechanisms begin to roll, and we are being primed again with electoral promises of a better future, we need to be asking ourselves some simple, but fundamental questions about the candidates being paraded before us, because the one thing we still have is a vote. Is this a decent moral person? Have they displayed a track record of openness, honesty and integrity? Is this the sort of person I would trust my children's future to? Can they be relied upon on tell the truth - no matter what? Is this a person of compassion, empathy and courage? Or are they something else? Why then would you possibly vote for them?

Remember… if it walks like a duck…   ☺

About the Author

Stephen Manning is a married father of three school-age children - one of whom has special needs. Stephen is well-travelled, having worked in many occupations in several different countries, including the military (NATO), the haulage and building industries, sports & fitness instruction, adventure tourism, retail management, and more recently as a book publisher and a teacher of English in schools, colleges and universities both here and abroad. He holds a number of academic qualifications and diplomas in fields as diverse as sports medicine to the study of psychology and world religions. Stephen has also worked in various volunteer capacities as a sports instructor and official with Special Olympics, with the Y.M.C.A in the USA, and (briefly) with the Mayo Mountain Rescue Team. He is currently a part-time FAI registered referee with the Irish Soccer Referees Society.

Having returned to Ireland in 2005, Stephen found himself embroiled in a situation where he was obliged to issue civil proceedings against a 'connected' individual. It was the resulting traumatic experiences—including multiple serious failures of duty by the statutory authorities—which eventually led to the setting up of the *Integrity Ireland* project in 2012.

Stephen is passionate about justice, and equally passionate about genuine democracy, which he believes is being lost to the unbridled ambitions of the connected elite.

Stephen is considering running as an independent candidate for Co. Mayo in the upcoming election. For more information, or to support the campaign, please go to his personal website *CheckPoint Ireland* at www.checkpoint.ie

STEPHEN MANNING
'the Ref'

www.integrityireland.ie
www.checkpointireland.ie

✅ *Derail the gravy train!*
✅ *Safeguard rural Ireland..*
✅ *Protect homes & families..*
✅ *Defend our Constitutional rights..*

@ STEPHEN T MANNING

Stephen is running as an active member of Integrity Ireland and will be basing his campaign solidly on the principles outlined on the Integrity Ireland website.

JUSTICE, TRANSPARENCY & ACCOUNTABILITY

www.integrityireland.ie

www.ingramcontent.com/pod-product-compliance
Lightning Source LLC
Chambersburg PA
CBHW080841270326
41927CB00013B/3057